ENTREPRENEURS

The Men and Women behind Famous Brand Names and How They Made It

ENTREPRENEURS

The Men and Women behind Famous Brand Names and How They Made It

Joseph J. Fucini and *Suzy Fucini*

G.K. Hall & Co., 70 Lincoln Street, Boston

We wish to acknowledge the following companies for permission to include the photographs used in this book: American Home Products (Chef Boy-ar-dee), p. 172; Anheuser-Busch Companies, pp. 19, 20; Borden Inc., p. 14; Brooks Brothers, p. 175; Calvin Klein Ltd., p. 88; Campbell Soup Company (Swanson), p. 246; Castle & Cooke, Inc. (Dole), p. 189; Chanel, Inc., pp. 139, 148; Coleman Co., p. 153; Deere & Co., p. 59; Famous Amos Chocolate Chip Cookie Co., p. 160; General Motors (Chevrolet), pp. 143, 144; Geo. A. Hormel & Co., p. 77; Gerber Products Company, p. 67; The Gillette Company, p. 56; H. J. Heinz Co., p. 104; Honda Motor Co., Ltd., p. 122; The Hoover Company, pp. 92, 94, 95; Howard Johnson's, pp. 135, 136; Ing. C. Olivetti & Co., S. p. A., p. 226; Jack Daniel Distillery, p. 1; Kinney Shoe Corporation, p. 80; Mary Kay Cosmetics, Inc., pp. 91, 97; Max Factor & Co., pp. 131, 132; The Maytag Company, p. 221; The Mennen Company, pp. 115, 117; Oscar Mayer Foods Corporation, pp. 127, 129; Otis Elevator Company, pp. 44, 45, 62; Pabst Brewing Company, p. 51; Rolls-Royce Limited, pp. 30, 31; Scott Paper Co., p. 85; Spalding Sports Worldwide, p. 141; Steinway & Sons, p. 49; Taylor Wine Co., Inc., p. 248; Thomas J. Lipton, Inc., pp. 108, 109; Toyota Motor Corp., p. 251; W. Atlee Burpee Company, pp. 5, 6; The Welch Company, pp. 70, 71; Wm. Wrigley, Jr., Company, p. 28; The Wurlitzer Co., p. 73. Permission to use "The Tupperware Party" by Joe Steinmetz (p. 252) was granted by The Photography Archive, Carpenter Center for the Visual Arts, Harvard University.

Fucini, Joseph J.
    Entrepreneurs, the men and women behind famous brand
names and how they made it.

    Bibliography: p. 261
    Includes index.
    1. Businessmen—Biography.   2. Entrepreneur—Biography.
3. Brand name products—History.   I. Fucini, Suzy.
II. Title.
HC29.F83   1985   338'.04'0922 [B]   84-15846
ISBN 0-8161-8708-8
ISBN 0-8161-8736-3 (pbk.)

Copyedited under the supervision of Michael Sims.
Designed and produced by Carole Rollins.
Set in 11/13 Century Old Style by Compset, Inc.

Contents

John Moses Browning
Browning Firearms
James E. Broyhill   *Broyhill Furniture*
John Brunswick
Brunswick Bowling Equipment
David Dunbar Buick   *Buick Cars*
Joseph Bulova   *Bulova Watches*
William Burroughs
Burroughs Information Systems
John Cadbury   *Cadbury Chocolates*
Joseph Campbell   *Campbell Soup*
James W. Cannon   *Cannon Towels*
Pierre Cardin   *Pierre Cardin Fashions*
William Carter   *Carter's Infant Wear*
Oleg Cassini   *Oleg Cassini Fashions*
Clyde Cessna   *Cessna Aircraft*
Walter Chrysler   *Chrysler Cars*
George W. Church
Church's Fried Chicken
David L. Clark   *Clark Bar*
Ruth Cleveland   *Baby Ruth Candy Bar*
William Colgate   *Colgate Toothpaste*
Samuel Colt   *Colt Revolver*
Marquis M. Converse
Converse Basketball Sneakers
Adolph Coors   *Coors Beer*
Oscar de la Renta
Oscar de la Renta Fashions
John Dewar   *Dewar's Scotch*
Christian Dior   *Christian Dior Fashions*
John Dodge and Horace Dodge
Dodge Cars
James Dole   *Dole Pineapples*
John B. Dunlop   *Dunlop Tires*
Eugene R. Durkee
Durkee Spices and Famous Sauce
Ole Evinrude   *Evinrude Outboard Motors*
Peter Carl Fabergé   *Faberge Cosmetics*
James Farah and William Farah
Farah Pants
Simon W. Farber
Farberware Kitchenware
Fannie Meritt Farmer
Fanny Farmer Candy
Enzo Ferrari   *Ferrari Cars*
Harvey Firestone   *Firestone Tires*
Herman G. Fisher and Irving L. Price
Fisher-Price Toys
Charles Fleischmann

Fleischmann's Yeast and Margarine
James A. Folger   *Folger's Coffee*
Henry Ford   *Ford Cars*
Robert T. French   *French's Mustard*
Roy Halston Frowick   *Halston Fashions*
Alfred C. Fuller   *Fuller Brushes*
Ernest Gallo and Julio Gallo   *Gallo Wine*
Hubert de Givenchy   *Givenchy Fashions*
Benjamin F. Goodrich
B. F. Goodrich Tires
Charles Goodyear   *Goodyear Tires*
Sylvester Graham   *Graham Cracker*
Guccio Gucci   *Gucci Loafers*
Arthur Guinness   *Guinness Beer*
Joseph M. Haggar   *Haggar Slacks*
Barbara Handler   *Barbie Doll*
Pleasant H. Hanes and John Wesley Hanes
Hanes Hosiery and Underwear
William Harley, Arthur Davidson,
William Davidson, and Walter Davidson
Harley-Davidson Motorcycles
John Harvey   *Harvey's Bristol Cream*
Howard Head   *Head Skiing Equipment*
Lawrence S. Heath   *Heath Bar*
Richard Hellmann
Hellmann's Mayonnaise
Richard Hennessy
Hennessy Cognac Brandy
Milton S. Hershey   *Hershey Chocolates*
William Hewlett and David Packard
Hewlett-Packard Information Systems
Austin H. Hills and Reuben W. Hills
Hills Brothers Coffee
Duncan Hines   *Duncan Hines Cake Mix*
Berta Hummel   *Hummel Figurines*
Carl Jantzen   *Jantzen Swimwear*
Mercedes Jellinek and Karl Benz
Mercedes-Benz Cars
Andrew Jergens   *Jergens Lotion*
Samuel C. Johnson   *Johnson's Wax*
Alexander H. Kerr   *Kerr Jars*
William Wallace Kimball
Kimball Pianos and Organs
John K. Labatt   *Labatt's Beer*
René Lacoste   *Lacoste Apparel*
René Lalique   *Lalique Glassware*
John Lane and Edward Lane
Lane Furniture
Ralph Lauren   *Ralph Lauren Apparel*

Herman W. Lay   *Lay's Potato Chips*

Henry D. Lee   *Lee Jeans*

Walter S. Lenox   *Lenox China*

Arthur Libby and Charles Libby
Libby Foods

Dr. Joseph Lister   *Listerine Mouthwash*

Sara Lee Lubin   *Sara Lee Cakes*

William H. Luden   *Luden's Cough Drops*

Maurice McDonald and Richard McDonald
McDonald's Hamburgers

John M. Mack   *Mack Trucks*

Rabbi Dov Ber Manischewitz
Manischewitz Matzo and Wine

Forrest Mars, Sr.   *Mars Bar*

Ernesto Maserati   *Maserati Cars*

Paul Masson   *Paul Masson Wine*

Prince Georges Matchabelli
Prince Matchabelli Perfume

Fred Maytag   *Maytag Washers*

Frederic Miller   *Miller Beer*

Howard Miller   *Howard Miller Clocks*

John Molson   *Molson Beer*

Joy Morton   *Morton Salt*

Christian F. Mueller   *Mueller Noodles*

Henri Nestlé   *Nestlé Chocolates*

Ransom E. Olds   *Oldsmobile Cars*

Camillo Olivetti   *Olivetti Typewriters*

George Safford Parker   *Parker Pens*

George Swinnerton Parker
Parker Brothers Games

Jeno Francisco Paulucci
Jeno's Frozen Pizza

Charles Phillips   *Phillips Milk of Magnesia*

Charles Pillsbury   *Pillsbury Cake Mixes*

William T. Piper   *Piper Aircraft*

Arthur Pitney and Walter Bowes
Pitney Bowes Postage Meters

Ferdinand Porsche   *Porsche Cars*

Dr. Albert Ralston
Ralston Purina Pet Foods and Cereal

Orville Redenbacher
*Orville Redenbacher's Gourmet Popping
Corn*

Harry B. Reese
Reese's Peanut Butter Cup

Adolph Rempp   *Adolph's Meat Tenderizer*

Louis Renault   *Renault Cars*

Richard S. Reynolds   *Reynolds Wrap*

Willard F. Rockwell
Rockwell Tools and Electronics

Helena Rubinstein
Helena Rubinstein Cosmetics

Yves St. Laurent
Yves St. Laurent Fashions

Jacob Schick   *Schick Razors*

Joseph Schlitz   *Schlitz Beer*

Jacob Schweppe   *Schweppes Soda Water*

Ignaz Schwinn   *Schwinn Bicycles*

Joseph Seagram   *Seagram Whiskey*

George Sealy   *Sealy Mattress*

Samuele Sebastiani   *Sebastiani Wines*

Walter A. Sheaffer   *Sheaffer Pens*

Henry Alden Sherwin and
Edward Porter Williams
Sherwin-Williams Paint

Zalmon G. Simmons
Simmons Bedding Products

Isaac Merritt Singer
Singer Sewing Machines

Amanda W. Smith   *Mrs. Smith's Pies*

Christopher Columbus Smith
Chris-Craft Boats

Lyman Smith and Wilbert Smith
Smith-Corona Typewriters

Jerome Smucker   *Smucker's Jelly*

Edward R. Squibb   *Squibb Vitamins*

John Batterson Stetson   *Stetson Hats*

Anna Stokely, James Stokely, and
John Stokely   *Stokely Foods*

Vernon B. Stouffer
Stouffer's Frozen Foods

Russell Stover   *Russell Stover Candies*

Levi Strauss   *Levi Jeans*

Bernhard Stroh   *Stroh's Beer*

Carl A. Swanson   *Swanson TV Dinners*

Gustavus F. Swift   *Swift Meat Products*

William J. Tappan
Tappan Microwave Oven

Walter Taylor   *Taylor Wine*

Melinda Lou "Wendy" Thomas
Wendy's Hamburgers

Samuel Bath Thomas
Thomas's English Muffins

Seth Thomas   *Seth Thomas Clocks*

Charles Lewis Tiffany   *Tiffany Jewelry*

Kiichiro Toyoda   *Toyota Cars*

Bibliography   261

Index   289

Acknowledgments

It would be impossible to list all of the people who so generously assisted us during the course of researching this book. We would like to single out a few individuals, however, whose help was especially invaluable. Our thanks to Jules Stiffel and Irvine Robbins for sharing their time, thoughts, and personal reminiscences. We would also like to thank Dr. Mary Louise Bopp of American Home Products for going well above and beyond the call of duty in tracking down important facts and figures. Last, and certainly not least, we would like to convey our deepest gratitude to Meghan Wander and Borgna Brunner of G.K. Hall & Co. Their faith in our idea, confidence in our ability, and thoughtful criticism of our efforts have meant more to this book and its authors than we can ever hope to express.

Introduction

Baskin-Robbins, Pabst, Max Factor, Bulova, Jacuzzi—the names are instantly recognizable, but most Americans know little about the men and women whose family names appear on our famous consumer brands. Although we encounter their namesake products every day on store shelves, billboards, and television, as well as in our homes, we are almost completely unaware of the people behind the ubiquitous logos—individuals like Frederick Pabst, a nineteenth-century Great Lakes steamship captain who originated the prize-winning Blue Ribbon Beer, or Max Factor, a Russian immigrant who attained fame and fortune as a Hollywood makeup artist during the early days of the silver screen, or Candido Jacuzzi, whose search for an effective physical therapy for his arthritis-stricken son led to the development of the Jacuzzi whirlpool.

With a handful of exceptions, the more than 225 men and women presented in this book are famous "in name only"; as a group they constitute what is paradoxically the best-known collection of unknowns in the world. Yet many of these product originators have made significant and lasting contributions to American life. By designing the first maternity apparel for street wear, New York seamstress Lane Bryant liberated twentieth-century expectant mothers from the practice of cloistering themselves during pregnancy; shaving might still be time-consuming and hazardous for millions of men were it not for the safety razor invented by King C. Gillette. Next to the wars, revolutions, and other milestones that mark our historical landscape, the accomplishments of Bryant, Gillette, and other enterprising individuals in this book may seem small, but they too have had a significant impact on our culture.

In this book we intend to give these largely forgotten product founders their due—to make them as widely known in fact as they are in name. Indeed, it is our hope that in an era dominated by big business, big government, and other impersonal Goliaths, this book will serve as a celebration of individual effort. The vast majority of famous products covered in this text were created not by committees or corporations, but by men and women working alone or with a small, loosely organized group of like-minded souls. Not surprisingly, most of the subjects in this book lived and worked in an earlier time, before Madison Avenue decreed that brands named after people lacked market appeal. Today, product-christening is a veritable science unto itself, with computer analyses and consumer surveys giving rise to such impersonal designations as "Bounce," "Bolt," and "Chewels." Products bearing the names of their creators have become a rarity, but refreshingly, they do appear every now and again, and we are pleased to be able to present a number of fascinating contemporary figures in this book—among them, cosmetics executive May Kay Ash, computer billionaire An Wang, and talent-scout-turned-cookie-manufacturer Wally Amos.

Looking at the subjects whose biographies follow, it becomes apparent that these are not predictable stories of entrepreneurial success. Among the individuals who have lent their names to famous products are a Bavarian nun, an American rabbi, a Russian prince, and a baseball player, as well as ministers, doctors, socialites, politicians, and homemakers. It was not always the lure of material success that led these individuals to become involved with the products that now bear their names—the motives of our subjects were as varied as their backgrounds. John Breck, a Massachusetts volunteer firefighter, simply wanted to find a cure for his own rapidly progressing baldness when he began experimenting with various hair and scalp preparations in the early 1900s. Schoolteacher George Safford Parker decided to design a better fountain pen after much frustration with the inferior writing instruments used in his classroom. That solution seekers like Breck and Parker went on to amass great fortunes was merely a by-product of their tenacious pursuits. Other men and women in this book cannot be held up as conventional models of entrepreneurial success because they did not personally reap the fruits of their inventive efforts. Such was the case of automobile maker David Buick, who was forced out of his namesake company in its early days, and, after involving himself in a series of unwise business ventures, died a poorly paid clerk.

In many instances the stories of people whose names became products serve to illuminate the development of business principles that have contributed to the structure of the marketplace as it exists today. As they creatively overcame the obstacles that stood in their way, these business pioneers laid the foundation for many of the production, sales, and marketing practices that have since become commonplace in the American business arena. When Massachusetts restaurateur Howard Johnson wanted to expand his business and open additional outlets in the 1930s, for example, he came up with what was then a novel scheme for raising the necessary capital. The gist of his plan was to sell the Howard Johnson's name and format to individuals who were willing to put up all or part of the capital required to build a new location. The investor then became part or sole owner of the new restaurant, agreeing, in turn, to buy all of his merchandise from Johnson and to adhere to certain operating specifications. The solution, arrived at independently by Johnson and other expansion-minded business founders, including shoe retailer George Kinney and the ice-cream-making team of Burt Baskin and Irv Robbins, paved the way for the present-day giant franchised retail chains.

As is the case with any anthology, this collection raises the question of why certain subjects were included and others omitted. Any commercial good or item widely known and used in the United States today, and named after an actual person or persons, was fair game for this book. We did not restrict ourselves to products developed in America, by Americans or during a specified era; hence the inclusion of such geographically and temporally disparate product founders as eighteenth-century English potter Josiah Wedgwood, Civil-War-era bourbon-maker Jack Daniel, and Japanese auto manufacturer Kiichiro Toyoda. Furthermore, our aim within this context was to provide as broad a sampling as possible of the different types of products that Americans come into contact with during the course of their daily lives—products such as coffee, denim jeans, and high-tech information systems.

Several additional criteria had to be met for a product to qualify as a candidate for this book. The item had to be national or nearly national in scope: thus, we omitted individuals like Tom Carvel and Frank Perdue whose namesake goods—ice cream and poultry, respectively—are distributed within a limited geographical region. Additionally, we restricted ourselves to concrete material products, thereby excluding Conrad Hilton, Richard Sears, and others whose names are attached to intangible services and institutions such as hotels and department store chains. Finally, all of the individuals appearing in this book are—or were—living people; we have left out Betty Crocker, Thom McAn, and similar fictitious personae who exist only on consumer trademarks.

During the course of our research, we came across a number of brands named after people who did in fact exist, but who played no role in the development of their namesake products. When Chicagoan Charles Lubin brought out a line of frozen pastries, for instance, he christened it in honor of his young daughter Sara Lee. Since our stated goal was to shed light on the individuals behind famous trademarks, whether or not they actually were involved in the creation of the item, we decided to include abbreviated entries on Sara Lee Lubin and other "honorary brand namers" from time to time, entitling such profiles "Borrowed Images."

This book is divided into two parts. The first part profiles the lives of 51 product originators; the second consists of 175 shorter biographical sketches. The individuals selected for lengthier treatment in the first part were not chosen because they were necessarily "more important," or their products more successful, than the other subjects of this book. We decided to spotlight these men and women because their stories, when taken together, provide a representative cross-section of the societal, personal, and circumstantial factors that have shaped the lives of all people whose names became products. We have grouped the fifty-one featured biographies into four chapters—Personality, Products, Marketing, and Fortune—based on what we believe are the four central, recurrent themes in the lives and careers of our subjects. The chapters are further divided into subchapters of three entries each, which illustrate a more narrowly defined common biographical theme.

At this point, it is important to state that this book is not intended to be a case history analysis of successful business strategies. Although success in business is the central theme of almost all of these biographies, this book is not meant to be a marketing text or a how-to manual for would-be entrepreneurs. We have not attempted to explain why the products included in this book have succeeded, but rather have narrated the stories of innovative men and women who, in response to needs or opportunities in their environments, created, adapted, or perfected products that have gone on to become an integral part of our lives and culture. Our goal is to illuminate the beginnings of now famous products, and to profile the spirited and fascinating individuals who initiated their ascent in the marketplace.

Thus, we must advise the reader that the subchapter headings in the first part—Teen Whizzes, Better Mousetraps Builders, and so forth—should not be viewed as summations of the "key success principle" behind each product. Rather, the headings allude to what we have found to be the central theme or salient characteristic of each individual's biography vis-a-vis the development of his or her namesake product. For example, by placing Henry Heinz in the Promotional Geniuses subchapter, we do not mean to imply that promotions were the sole, or even the overriding, ingredient in the ultimate success of the Heinz condiment line; efficient production techniques, quality products, and the excellent employee relations fostered by Heinz were all factors contributing to the growth of his business. The reason Henry Heinz appears in this subchapter, then, is because his story as the founder of his food company is most aptly characterized by his personal flair for imaginative promotions.

We would now like to discuss in greater detail the four chapters that make up the first part of this book. In the Personality chapter, we have included the stories of product originators whose temperamental, intellectual, or creative characteristics played especially significant roles in shaping their careers. Presented here is a wide cast of personality types, from the flamboyant podiatrist-salesman Dr. William Scholl, who carried around a skeleton of a human foot to use in his unorthodox sales presentations, to quiet, perfectionistic Willis Carrier, who applied his tenacious problem-solving skill to the task of developing the first workable air-conditioning system. One of the subchapters in the Personality chapter, entitled Partners, covers groups of two or more individuals who combined their divergent talents and personal styles to develop a successful product. In this chapter the reader will find the story of Charles Rolls and Henry Royce, a daredevil race car driver and a methodical engineer, respectively, who in the early twentieth century worked together to create one of the world's most prestigious automobiles.

The Products chapter looks at the ideas, needs, and motives that inspired individuals to develop their namesake products. Included in the subchapter Better Mousetrap Builders, for instance, is John Deere, a blacksmith from Vermont who settled in Illinois in the 1830s and designed his self-scouring steel plow after his fellow pioneers experienced difficulty tilling the rich Midwestern soil with the old-fashioned cast iron plows brought from New England. George Hormel (covered in the Budget Stretchers subchapter) was responding to a different kind of need when he and his son Jay introduced their namesake foods in the 1930s. Austin, Minnesota, meatpackers, the Hormels came out with a line of canned chili, beef stew, and other "poor man's dishes" to meet the demand for nutritious, low-cost meals created by the Depression. Also included in the Products chapter are the stories of people who developed their namesake products as a solution to a personal need or problem. These Personal Problem Solvers include Dan Gerber, a Fremont, Michigan, canner who created his line of strained baby food to spare his wife Dorothy from the time-consuming task of straining vegetables for their infant daughter's meals.

Presented in the Marketing chapter is a third major class of product originator, those whose genius lay in the area of divising innovative means of promoting, selling, or packaging their namesake goods. Japanese manufacturer Soichiro Honda is included in the Image Builders subchapter because of his role in changing the image of motorcycling in the United States. Prior to a massive ad campaign launched by Honda in 1962, built around the slogan "You Meet the Nicest People on a Honda," most Americans viewed motorcyles as strictly for black-leather-jacketed toughs. By showing homemakers, businessmen and other everyday citizens riding aboard his "Super Cub," Honda's ads conveyed the message that motorcycling could be enjoyed by "respectable" people too. The image-altering ads proved so successful that by 1968 Honda had sold one million motorcycles in America. Like Honda, the other product namers in this chapter demonstrated strength in a particular aspect of marketing; featured here are Sales Strategists, Promotional Geniuses, and Packaging Innovators. We have also included a Local Favorites subchapter in the marketing chapter containing the stories of individuals like Oscar Mayer who first secured a strong customer base for his meat products in his Chicago neighborhood then gradually expanded his market nationwide.

The fourth and final chapter, Fortune, was inserted as a vehicle for spotlighting individuals whose careers as product developers were buoyed by external circumstances or good fortune. The two subchapters in this chapter—The Talented and The Lucky—distinguish between two very different types of furtune that acted upon the lives of our subjects. In the first are stories of famous founders whose good fortune it was to be born with a particular talent, such as Albert Spalding, a Hall-of-Fame baseball great who got his start in the sporting goods business after he designed a ball for his own use as a player. The entries under the heading The Lucky concern individuals who inadvertently discovered a product and went on to manufacture it under their own names with great success. Among these resourceful businesspeople whose luck it was to be in "the right place at the right time" was pharmacist Charles Hires, who first tasted root beer during his honeymoon at a rural New Jersey inn, and was so impressed with the flavor that he obtained the recipe, began serving the drink at his Philadelphia soda fountain, and eventually developed a successful manufacturing business around the beverage he discovered by chance.

The second part of the book is comprised of 175 alphabetized short biographies of people who have created a wide range of notable products. Also featured are profiles of people who lent their names to products but played no actual entrepreneurial role in their evolution—the "Borrowed Images" described earlier. A bibliography of further readings on each of the individuals discussed appears at the end of the book.

As a final note, we would like to express our regrets about the product brand founders we have reluctantly omitted from this work. Spatial restrictions simply would not permit the inclusion of all the men and women who met our criteria as outlined above, and we have left out some worthy individuals and products. For this we can only apologize and hope that their stories might one day appear in a subsequent edition.

Jack Newton Daniel dressed in the planter's hat, frock coat, silk vest, and bow tie that became his personal trademark. The youngest of ten children, Daniel ran away from home at six and started his famous distillery at the tender age of thirteen.

Teen Whizzes

1877–1965

JOSHUA LIONEL COWEN

Lionel Trains

One day in 1884, seven-year-old Joshua Lionel Cowen attached a small steam engine to a wooden locomotive he had carved. Moments later, the precocious youngster watched in amazement as the world's first Lionel train exploded, taking most of the kitchen wallpaper with it and earning the boy a good paddling from his father, a New York City businessman. The locomotive incident was one of several ill-fated experiments conducted by Joshua Cowen (born Cohen), a small, dark-haired boy who was fascinated with mechanical devices of all kinds. Once, he impulsively cracked open the heads of his sisters' expensive porcelain dolls in an attempt to learn what made their eyes roll back and forth.

The boy's preoccupation with gadgets and gizmos was a thorn in the side of Hyman and Rebecca Cohen, who held more scholarly aspirations for Joshua, the eighth of their nine children. Eastern European Jews, the couple immigrated to the United States in the mid-1860s, arriving in New York where Hyman established what would become a prosperous hatmaker's shop. Like many immigrants who had made good, the Cohens expected their sons to excel in school and go on to college to learn a profession.

Joshua was enrolled in the prestigious Peter Cooper Institute, but he became increasingly bored and restless with his studies. The only part of the curriculum that held his interest was his technical shop class, where he was permitted to tinker to his heart's content. While at Peter Cooper, the teenager developed an early version of the electric door bell, using storage batteries for power. He dropped the idea, however, after a shortsighted teacher told him that it had no practical value.

Another of young Cowen's inventions, the "electric flowerpot," resulted in an even more ironic twist. The gadget consisted of a thin tube with a battery fitted into one end and a small light bulb in the other. When attached to a flowerpot, the tube illuminated the plant inside. Cowen sold the rights to his invention to a restaurateur named Conrad Hubert, who tried marketing it as a decorative object. After failing to generate much interest in the unusual flowerpot, Hubert decided to detach the tubes and sell them on their own illuminatory merit. Calling his revised product the Eveready Flashlight, he became a multimillionaire.

In 1899 Joshua Cowen realized his first significant profit from an invention, when he received $12,000 from the U.S. Navy for a mine detonator he had developed. With the capital from the sale, the twenty-three-year-old inventor and a friend named Harry C. Grant launched the Lionel Manufacturing Co. on September 5, 1900. The partners made a brief attempt at selling a portable electric fan, before Cowen came up with another idea. Reverting to his boyhood fascination with trains, he took the fan's small motor and attached it to a miniature wooden railroad car.

Initially, Cowen intended to sell the car, along with a circular strip of track, to retailers as a novel moving display to dress up store windows. "I sold my first railroad car not as a toy, mind you," he later recounted, "but as something to attract attention." The merchant who purchased that "first railroad car" was Robert Ingersoll, a Manhattan toy store owner. The following day, Ingersoll returned to Cowen's office and requested six more cars, explaining to the startled partners that customers had wanted to buy the display right out of his window.

Cowen promptly revised his marketing strategy and began promoting his electric railroad car as a toy for children. In 1902 he added a metal trolley car that sold for $6 and was equipped with thirty feet of track. Later that year, the train manufacturer initiated what would become a rite of passage for young American males by issuing the first Lionel catalog. The sixteen-page booklet featured two electrically powered cars, a metal suspension bridge, and a variety of track configurations. (By the 1950s, the Lionel catalog had become the third most widely distributed catalog in the nation, behind those of Sears and Montgomery Ward.)

Although Joshua Cowen's early mechanical genius had gotten his model train business started, it was his talent for marketing in his middle years that built the Lionel name into a national institution. In addition to issuing the elaborately illustrated Lionel catalogs, he promoted his trains in newspapers and magazines and later through a company-sponsored radio program. The underlying message in every ad was that Lionel trains were not just mere playthings, but a symbol of the perfect American childhood. Cowen repeatedly focused on the theme that a close father-son relationship could be fostered through a shared interest in model railroading. A particularly effective bit of psychology was demonstrated in a 1950s ad that showed a smiling father and son at a train layout and declared, "Lionel trains make a boy feel like a man, and a man feel like a boy."

After climbing to a post–World War II peak of $32.9 million in 1953, Lionel train sales fell sharply through the rest of the decade. The decline of railroads as a mode of transportation and changing American values were cited as factors. By 1958 sales had plummeted to $14.4 million. The following year, eighty-two-year-old Joshua Lionel Cowen disassociated himself from the company he had founded, selling his 55,000 shares of Lionel stock and retiring to Palm Springs, Florida.

Today, after undergoing a massive reorganization, the Lionel Corporation is a holding company that operates a diverse range of enterprises, including retail toy store chains. The company has not been in the model railroad business since 1969, when it leased the Lionel brand name to General Mills, which currently manufactures the trains through its Fundimensions subsidiary. Ironically, the Lionel Corporation is now a customer of Fundimensions, buying its namesake trains to sell at its toy stores.

Lively writing, colorful anecdotes, and homespun humor made the Burpee seed catalog popular reading material among rural Americans in the late nineteenth and early twentieth centuries.

W ——————————— 1858–1915
WASHINGTON ATLEE BURPEE

Burpee's Seeds

In 1872 an English pedigreed poultry fancier traveled to Philadelphia to meet a fellow breeder-exhibitor with whom he had been corresponding for several years. The two knew each other only through letters, and the Briton was eager for the opportunity to sit down over some brandy with his learned friend and exchange ideas on the care and mating of high-class fowl. When he arrived at the train station, however, there was no one to greet him but an ungainly fourteen-year-old boy. "Would you happen to be the son of W. Atlee Burpee, the poultry authority?" asked the fancier. "No sir, I am the son of Dr. David Burpee. *I* am W. Atlee Burpee, the poultryman," came the startling reply.

It was nothing unusual for poultry prodigy Atlee Burpee to astonish his elders in this manner. As a small boy, the Philadelphia youth had taken up the hobby of breeding fancy pigeons, chickens, geese, and turkeys, and by the time he entered high school he was sufficiently well versed on the subject to contribute articles to poultry trade journals. At seventeen the precocious Burpee launched a mail-order business out of his parents'

David Burpee, who succeeded his father as president of the W. Atlee Burpee Co. in 1915 at the age of twenty-two, is pictured here more than fifty years later with his favorite flower, the marigold. In 1959 Burpee led a campaign to have the American Marigold named the national flower. He even christened a marigold "Senator Dirksen" in honor of the Illinois legislator's efforts on the flower's behalf.

home, selling purebred fowl and two instructional manuals he had written to fanciers throughout the Northeast.

Dr. David Burpee, nevertheless, remained singularly unimpressed with his son's poultry accomplishments, insisting that the boy uphold family tradition and become a physician. Reluctantly, Atlee enrolled in premedical classes at the University of Pennsylvania in 1875. He disliked his studies intensely and dropped out after just one year when a wealthy Philadelphian named August S. Benson, Jr., offered to back him with $5,000 in a purebred poultry and livestock enterprise.

Atlee soon had cause to wish he were back in school. Almost from the very beginning, the eighteen-year-old breeder and his benefactor clashed over a wide range of issues. Burpee once complained that his older partner opposed "every plan I had to increase trade." The business lost $3,500 its first year, and a third partner was added to help meet expenses. The following year the company broke even, but dissent among the associates worsened and Burpee finally withdrew. At that point, his father, resigned to the fact that Atlee would never become a doctor, lent the youth money to go into business for himself.

W. Atlee Burpee & Co. was formed in Philadelphia in 1878 as a catalog mail-order house selling purebred livestock and fowl. To provide his customers with the proper feed for their pedigreed animals, the twenty-year-old company founder also included several varieties of farm seed in his catalog. Much to Burpee's surprise, the majority of early orders received by the firm were for seeds rather than livestock.

Once it became apparent that his sideline would eclipse his principal product in sales, Burpee decided to pursue the seed end of his business aggressively. In his 1880 catalog, he featured a collection of tomato, cucumber, turnip, and other vegetable seeds, normally valued at $1, at a special introductory price of 25¢. As a further promotional step, a sewing machine (valued at $22) was offered to anybody who acted as a Burpee agent and sold three hundred of the quarter packages to their friends and neighbors. The tandem promotions worked so well that, during one stretch, each of the several daily mailings arriving at Burpee headquarters brought more than four hundred orders.

As the demand for them increased, seeds began to take up proportionately more space in the Burpee catalog. (A limited selection of livestock was listed until 1917, two years after W. Atlee Burpee's death.) Every summer, Burpee traveled to Europe to search for superior varieties of vegetables, fruits, and flowers that could be added to his catalog offerings. Seeds from the candidate plants would then be brought back to Burpee's Fordhook Farm at Doylestown, Pennsylvania, for further testing. When Burpee became convinced he had indeed found a plant that produced a plumper tomato or a sweeter berry, it would be introduced with great fanfare in the Burpee catalog. Among the seedsman's more widely known produce discoveries are Burpee's Iceberg lettuce (1894), Golden Bantam corn (1902), and Bush Lima beans (1907).

In addition to the high quality of its seeds, a major factor behind W. Atlee Burpee & Co.'s early success was the popularity of its catalog as a source of entertainment among farm families. Written by Burpee himself in a witty, anecdotal style, it offered a wealth of suggestions for using the various plants and flowers. Spanish peanuts, wrote Burpee, were "excellent for fattening hogs and children." A vine that produced a yellow flower resembling a curled-up caterpillar could be enjoyed as "a harmless practical joke . . . put into salads for the purpose of startling those who are unfamiliar with it." The catalog (which at one time ran to two hundred pages) also contained tales about its adventurous author's search for new plant varieties, and it invited subscribers to enter their produce in company-sponsored contests.

As a result of reading the catalog, thousands of individuals throughout the nation began to identify with W. Atlee Burpee. Many customers named their sons after the seedsman, an honor he acknowledged by presenting the children with silver mugs. On his frequent cross-country seed-hunting trips, Burpee would often stop off and visit his young namesakes.

The company founder had two sons of his own who, from their boyhood, were encouraged to enter the seed business. Every year, at the family's Christmas dinner, a copy of the new Burpee catalog would be put beside each of the boys' places, with dollar bills scattered throughout its pages. Burpee reasoned that his sons would become familiar with the company's product line while searching for the money. The seedsman's efforts paid off. In 1915, after a year of failing health, W. Atlee Burpee died of a liver ailment. His twenty-two-year-old son David, who apparently inherited his father's precociousness, stepped in and successfully took over the reins of the world's largest seed company.

J̲ACK NEWTON DANIEL
1846–1911

Jack Daniel's Whiskey

The youngest of ten children, and small for his age to boot, Jack Newton Daniel hated being known as the runt of the litter. At age six, the gritty Tennessee tyke ran away from his rural Lincoln County home and convinced a neighboring family to take him in—a brilliant move, considering that he managed to elevate his status overnight to the privileged position of oldest boy in his new household. Such cunning and spunk did not go unnoticed by those who met him, and just one year later young Jack was offered a paying job as a houseboy by Dan Call, a local farmer, merchant, Lutheran minister, and whiskey distiller. Like any high-spirited kid, Jack found his new employer's moonshine still much more intriguing than either his dairy cows or his general store. Resolving that he too would become a distiller, the seven-year-old badgered Call to teach him the secrets of sour mash making.

Jack's opportunity to get into the whiskey business came sooner than he expected. In 1860 Call, who was under pressure from his congregation to choose once and for all between the pulpit and the still, offered his ambitious protégé a chance to buy the distillery on credit. Although only thirteen years old, Jack had been squirreling away his $5 a month salary; he possessed the necessary start-up capital, plus plenty of mash-making experience, and so the deal was struck.

The teenage distiller's first goal for his new business was to move his whiskey still closer to Lynchburg, Tennessee, where a recently built railroad could be utilized to transport his product to distant cities. With characteristic wisdom beyond his years, Jack reasoned that the move would boost the distillery's profits by allowing him to expand his market beyond the confines of sparsely populated Lincoln County. The Civil War, however, threw a wrench into his plan, forcing him to remain at his original site on the Call farm and devise some other means of getting his whiskey to prospective customers.

Huntsville, Alabama, was the nearest big city (located fifty miles away), and throughout the war Jack and a friend named Button Waggoner made weekly sales trips there. Button, who was just a year older than Jack, would help his friend load a wagon with jugs of sour mash, and then the two boys would cover the whiskey with hay to hide it from would-be marauders. Their journeys to Huntsville were perilous; they ran the risk of being mistaken for Yankees or Confederate deserters and in either event probably would have been shot. Upon reaching Huntsville, Jack and Button had to wait at the outskirts of town until midnight, when the local sheriff and his deputies went off duty. The teenagers had been forbidden by authorities to sell whiskey in the city, and thus they had to peddle their wares clandestinely to saloons, restaurants, and grocery stores between midnight and dawn. For a long stretch during the war, Huntsville was occupied by Union troops, and the young whiskey sellers found northerners just as receptive to good mash as "good ole boys." The Yankees, it was said, did not harm Jack Daniel or his friend because they did not wish to cut off their source of liquor.

After the war, Jack, now in his late teens, was able to achieve his long-deferred goal of setting up a production facility near Lynchburg. He leased property at a site known as Cave Spring, where conditions were ideal for whiskey making; a spring on the property turned out almost sterile water at a perfect temperature of fifty-six degrees devoid of any iron content. Jack further ensured the quality of his product by using a technique known as the Lincoln County process in which the whiskey was "leached," or run through a filter of sugar maple charcoal, to remove impurities.

As one of a dwindling number of whiskey manufacturers to continue using this laborious technique in the years following the Civil War, Jack Daniel developed a word-of-mouth reputation as a maker of top-quality spirits. Although his distillery employed no road salesmen, demand for its products spread, and its two brands of bottled whiskey—Belle of Lincoln and Jack Daniel's Old No. 7—became a common sight in retail establishments throughout the South. By 1890 the Jack Daniel Distillery had attained the status of the largest sour mash maker in Tennessee. National fame came in 1904, when the Old No. 7 brand took first place in a taste competition held at the Louisiana Purchase Exposition in St. Louis.

As Jack Daniel prospered, he donated much of his time and wealth to civic and religious causes. The distiller became known for his sponsorship of an annual spring dinner, in which the entire congregation of a Lynchburg Baptist church was invited to his home for a lavish spread that took a week to prepare and included dozens of hams, turkeys, and roasts. Each year, more than three hundred people attended the feast.

With a large bankroll, a genial personality, and a dashing black mustache, Jack Daniel came to be regarded as one of the most eligible bachelors in the South. However, despite being linked romantically with many attractive women—some young enough to be his daughter or, in later years, his granddaughter—the Tennessee mash maker never married. He lived for most of his adult life with a sister and brother-in-law, Elizabeth and James Conner. When he died heirless at the age of sixty-five (as a result of gangrene), his namesake company passed on to a favorite nephew, Lemuel Motlow, who had been involved in the Jack Daniel Distillery for many decades.

To the end, Jack Daniel remained fastidious about one thing above all else—his personal appearance. From the time he turned twenty-one, he never appeared in public unless formally attired in a knee-length frock coat, planter's hat, silk vest, broad bow tie, and fine linen shirt. When his hair and mustache began to gray, he dyed them their former jet black. Some speculated that his obsession with his appearance stemmed from feelings of inadequacy about his size, for Jack Daniel never grew beyond five-foot-five and one-hundred-and-twenty pounds; among whiskey lovers, however, his name will always stand tall.

Inveterate Tinkerers

W———— 1902–1978
ILLIAM P. LEAR

Lear Jet

An eighth-grade dropout from Hannibal, Missouri, the man who designed the Lear Jet became a multimillionaire from his inventive efforts long before his namesake aircraft made its debut in the early 1960s. Although he is typically associated with aviation, Bill Lear spawned a host of other major inventions—ranging from the first practical automobile radio to the eight-track stereo cartridge—and acquired some 150 patents in all.

As a boy growing up in Chicago, where he and his mother moved following his parents' 1908 divorce, Lear was inspired by the books of Horatio Alger. A mechanically gifted youth, he dreamed of becoming an inventor. However, his tinkering efforts were constantly frustrated by the poor economic circumstances of the household, which was headed by his stepfather Otto Kirmse, a German-born plasterer. At the age of twelve, the boy worked out a blueprint for his future: "I resolved first to make enough money so I'd never be stopped from finishing anything," he later recalled to an interviewer.

School did not fit into this plan, and at sixteen Bill left home to join the navy, lying about his age. While in the service he studied radio technology, and after his discharge he went to work for several Illinois electronics firms.

In the late 1920s Lear took a job as a design engineer at Galvin Manufacturing Co., a Chicago-based maker of radio chassis. It was while at Galvin that the mechanical genius startled the industry by designing the first workable radio for automobiles. Prior to this time, the prevailing wisdom was that the government would never permit radios in cars, out of the concern that they would be a distraction to drivers. Such opposition never materialized, however, and the invention made a wealthy man out of Lear's boss, Paul Galvin, who changed the company name to Motorola (a combination of *motor* and *victrola*). Lear didn't fare too badly either. In 1931, when most of America was feeling the effects of the depression, his salary from Motorola and royalties from various radio-related patents totaled $35,000, and the twenty-nine-year-old engineer could afford to buy his own biplane.

Aviation, then in its primitive stages, presented Lear with a whole new set of challenges for his inventive genius. During his early cross-country flights the inventor, like all aviators of his day, experienced great difficulty finding his way from city to city; navigation back then consisted simply of training one's eyes on the ground and following railroad tracks, rivers, and similar landmarks. Realizing that this was not the most reliable method of keeping an airplane on course, Lear began to experiment with devices that could navigate automatically by use of radio signals. His invention, the Learoscope, became the industry standard; by the late 1930s more than half of the private aircraft in the United States were using Lear's direction finders.

Another of Lear's big aviation breakthroughs was a miniature automatic pilot that weighed only twenty five pounds and was compact enough to be installed in small fighter planes. In 1939 the inventor formed Lear, Inc., a Grand Rapids, Michigan, manufacturer of aircraft instruments. During World War II, the company filled more than $100 million worth of defense contracts and employed close to two thousand technicians, scientists, and engineers. The firm continued to grow through the 1950s, adding new plants in California and Pennsylvania and branching out into stereo systems and miniature communications satellites.

As chairman of the board of his namesake company, Bill Lear amassed a vast personal fortune. Never one to sit back and simply watch the dollars roll in, however, he soon had his eye on another dream—to build a small, low-priced general aviation jet aimed at the business executive. No such plane existed, and when the board of directors of Lear, Inc. were presented with their chairman's radical new idea, they voted it down. It was argued from an engineering standpoint that the craft Lear proposed could never be built and that, in the unlikely event it were, it would never be accepted among corporate executives.

Lear's response was to sell his 23 percent interest in the company he had founded for $14.3 million and use the money to finance a new enterprise, Lear Jet Inc. in Wichita, Kansas. Holding true to his childhood resolution, the self-made millionaire had accumulated enough money to "never be stopped from finishing anything"—not even a project as capital-intensive as the creation of a visionary "baby jet."

By the time the first gleaming white Lear Jet took to the sky in 1963, more than $8 million had been spent on its development (the craft was actually a redesigned Swiss military fighter), and aviation industry "experts" were forced to agree that sixty-one-year-old Bill Lear had achieved the impossible. He had built a high-performance eight-passenger jet that could travel at six hundred miles an hour and climb to an altitude of forty thousand feet in less than 6½ minutes, about half as long as it took any other craft. Furthermore, Lear's jet sold for an affordable (by general aviation standards) $649,000 fully equipped. This relatively low price was made possible by economies Lear had incorporated into the plane's design, such as standardized interiors and low headroom.

Having disproven the skeptics who said it couldn't be built, Bill Lear's next stunning upset was scored in the marketplace. His trim little jet was an immediate commercial success, selling to corporations that wanted an efficient means of flying their executives around the globe. Sales the first year reached $52 million, making Lear the world's largest manufacturer of private jet aircraft.

In 1967, the sixty-five-year-old aviation pioneer sold his business to Gates Rubber Co. Intending to retire, he moved to Los Angeles with Moya, his wife of twenty-five years, and Tina, the youngest of their four children. (Lear was married three times previously and had seven children in all.) But the life of an idle Beverly Hills millionaire didn't square well with the pudgy-faced midwesterner, who was partial to hamburgers and Permanent Press Farah slacks and whose pockets were usually filled with tools. Bored, depressed, and in declining health, Lear could no longer stay away from the engineering laboratory. He moved to Reno, Nevada, and established a facility to design an experimental steam-powered automobile engine. Lear failed to develop an efficient steam engine, but he remained undiscouraged and immediately turned his attention to creating improved business jet aircraft, a project he worked on until his death in 1978. Although he knew he was dying of leukemia, the tireless inventor remained at his workbench. His last words to an associate concerning the jet project were "Finish it, you bet we'll finish it." In the end, Bill Lear had run out of neither energy nor ideas—just time.

G ⸺ 1801–1874
GAIL BORDEN

Borden's Milk and Ice Cream

Some years after he made his fortune in the dairy business, Gail Borden purchased a grave site at Woodlawn Cemetery in the Bronx and, over it, erected a large stone monument in the shape of a milk can. The tall, rail-thin dairyman passed the cemetery every morning on his way to the office and, for reasons known only to himself, took comfort in gazing out the train window at his unusual marker. When Borden died in 1874, his family replaced the milk can with a more conventional tombstone. On that second stone is an inscription that reads: "I tried and failed, I tried again and again and succeeded."

The original monument and the final epitaph provide equally revealing insights into the personality of the man who ushered in the modern dairy

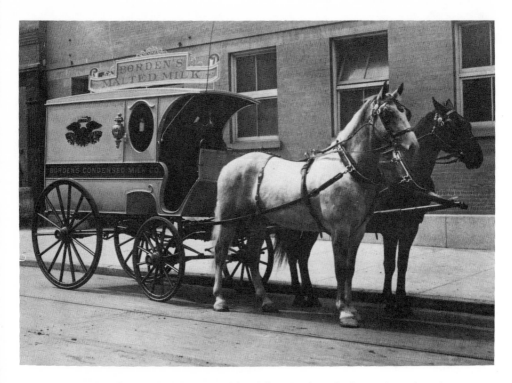

Horse-drawn wagons were used to deliver Borden's fresh, condensed, and evaporated milk to residents of big cities. The wagon pictured dates from after 1899, when Borden's son and successor, Henry Lee Borden, and other stockholders changed the name of the business from the New York Condensed Milk Co. to the Borden Condensed Milk Co.

industry. Gail Borden can be described accurately both as an eccentric dreamer and a tenacious fighter. Born on a farm in upstate New York, Borden did not start his first successful dairy business until he was fifty-six years old and on what he called "the downhill side of life." Most of his early and middle years were spent in various parts of the South, where he busied himself as a schoolteacher, newspaper editor, real estate salesman, customs collector, and surveyor (he prepared the first topographical map of Texas). Despite his frequent career changes, there was one activity that consistently held Borden's interest—inventing. From 1835 until his death, he unleashed a mind-boggling assortment of inventions, most of which ranged from the slightly questionable to the completely absurd.

One of Borden's more memorable creations was the "Terraqueous Wagon," a four-wheeled contraption with sails and a rudder designed to travel equally well on land or sea. He had to drop his plans for the vehicle rather suddenly, however, after a group of town elders from Galveston, Texas, nearly drowned in the Gulf of Mexico during a demonstration ride. The death of Borden's wife during a yellow fever epidemic in 1844 provided another springboard for his fertile mind. Reasoning that hot weather aided the spread of yellow fever and other contagious diseases, he proposed that Galvestonians spend the summer months in a giant refrigerated building. Borden even went so far as to construct a prototype of his brainchild, but no one in Galveston was willing to move into the ether-cooled structure.

Unable to interest his fellow townspeople in his plan to "freeze out disease," Borden turned the refrigerated building into a food plant and used it to manufacture another invention—the flat meat biscuit. Like everything else that Gail Borden had invented up to that point, the dehydrated beef product was a commercial failure. The meat biscuit, however, did represent the struggling inventor's first glimmer of success, earning him a gold medal at the London Crystal Palace Exposition in 1851.

While he was on his way back to America after receiving the award, Borden turned his attention to the subject of milk. During the ocean voyage from London to New York, he saw four children die as a result of drinking the contaminated milk of the ship's two sickly cows. Tragic as they were, such deaths were not unusual in the mid-nineteenth century, when the ever-present threat of spoilage and contamination made parents justifiably leery of serving their youngsters milk. Still, Borden remained deeply disturbed by the deaths of the young passengers, and he vowed to find a way to make milk safer for human consumption.

Through his experience with the dehydrated beef biscuit, Borden knew that food could be kept fresh and pure over a longer period of time if its moisture content were reduced, and he began to experiment with different methods of removing the water from milk. At first, Borden simply boiled the milk in open pans, which worked to evaporate water but gave the beverage an objectionable burnt taste. Then, during a visit to friends at a Shaker colony in New Lebanon, New York, he discovered a way to remove water from milk without sacrificing its flavor. The Shakers were using vacuum pans to condense maple sugar; and after watching them work Borden realized that by placing milk in vacuum-sealed pans before boiling it he could achieve evaporation with less heat and thus eliminate the unpleasant burnt taste. Another advantage was that vacuum condensation would be more effective than Borden's previous open-pan method in retarding spoilage, because the milk would not be exposed to air during evaporation.

In 1856 Borden received a patent for a vacuum-condensation process that removed 75 percent of the water from milk and added sugar to the residue as a preservative. With the backing of a lawyer friend, he opened a small condensation plant in Wolcottville (now Torrington), Connecticut, but a lack of capital and the refusal of local dairy farmers to sell milk on credit drove the partners out of business within a year.

No stranger to failure, Borden came back with a second condensation plant in 1857. This time, the business was on a more solid financial footing, thanks to the substantial backing of a wealthy New York banker named

Jeremiah Milbank, whose investment in the company eventually totaled $100,000. The young company's first big break occurred shortly after the start of the Civil War, when the U.S. Army placed an order for five-hundred pounds of condensed milk. From that point on, Borden's problem became one of turning out enough milk to keep up with the army's seemingly insatiable demand. By 1863 Borden had opened two additional facilities, including his "perfect plant" in Brewster, New York, which was capable of producing twenty-thousand quarts of condensed milk a day.

The success of his condensed milk did not diminish Gail Borden's enthusiasm for tinkering with novel ideas. He experimented with several new methods of condensing fruit juices and making jellies, and he set up an Elgin, Illinois, factory to make an instant coffee he had invented. During his later years the famous dairyman spent much of his time in Texas, where he educated farmers in dairy techniques, organized schools for blacks, built six churches, and supported poorly paid ministers, teachers, and students.

G̲̅E̲O̲R̲G̲E̲ ̲W̲E̲S̲T̲I̲N̲G̲H̲O̲U̲S̲E̲ — 1846–1914

Westinghouse Appliances

Nobody could have blamed experienced railroad men for being skeptical when George Westinghouse came to them with plans for a compressed-air brake that, according to the twenty-two-year-old inventor, would make it possible to bring a moving train to a quick halt. Stopping a train was a lengthy process in 1868, requiring a mile's advance notice and a large crew of brakemen to apply heavy brake shoes to every car. So when Westinghouse, an unknown upstate New Yorker, claimed to have developed a revolutionary device that would allow a single engineer to brake an entire train at the twist of a valve, most industry veterans did not take him seriously.

After two frustrating years of trying to interest railroad officials in his invention, Westinghouse finally got a chance to demonstrate his air brake, when executives of the Panhandle Railroad agreed to install the apparatus in one of their passenger trains for a test run between Pittsburgh and Steubenville, Ohio. On the April afternoon of the trial, the young inventor nervously climbed aboard the train's observation car, hoping that his braking device wouldn't let him down now that the big opportunity was at hand.

What started out as a mere test, however, turned into a matter of life and death when, just outside of Pittsburgh, a man was thrown from his frightened horse directly into the path of the oncoming locomotive. Frantically, the train's engineer, Dan Tate, reached for the Westinghouse brake valve, and moments later the vehicle came to a screeching halt just four feet away from the sprawled horseman. When the confusion cleared, it became apparent that George Westinghouse's invention, in its first application, had been directly responsible for saving the man's life.

The dramatic proof of the air brake's ability to stop a train quickly and efficiently convinced even the most die-hard skeptics that Westinghouse had indeed developed a mechanism that was far superior to conventional manual braking systems. Within a few weeks, the tall Schenectady native had taken out a patent on his air brake, and in July 1869 he and a group of six investors went into business to manufacture it, forming the Westinghouse Air Brake Co. in Pittsburgh.

Although Westinghouse was only in his early twenties when he designed the brake that dramatically improved the safety of rail travel, the air-powered device was not the first invention he had patented. Since boyhood, the mechanically gifted youth had enjoyed experimenting in his father's farm machinery shop, and by the time he was nineteen he had received a patent for a rotary steam engine. A year later, Westinghouse built an innovative apparatus for putting derailed freight cars back on track. Nevertheless, this invention, like the rotary engine, was not financially rewarding.

Things would be quite different with the air brake, however. Five years after the life-saving Panhandle Railroad demonstration, the brake was being used in nearly ten-thousand locomotives and cars throughout the United States. Westinghouse continually perfected his compressed-air-powered braking system (receiving more than one-hundred patents on it in all), and he became a millionaire from the invention before his thirtieth birthday.

With the vast fortune he acquired, the inventor was able to move into a lavish estate in Pittsburgh's most opulent neighborhood, Point Breeze. His property covered an entire city block bordering along the tracks of the Pennsylvania Railroad, where he maintained his own private railroad car, complete with sleeping quarters, a kitchen, and an office. Described by Edith Wharton as one of the five "Lords of Pittsburgh" (the others were Heinz, Carnegie, Frick, and Mellon), Westinghouse became a prominent figure in the city's cultural life. He and his wife, Marguerite, a sculptor who became famous in her own right, were active supporters of various art museums, botanical societies, and other institutions.

Despite the trappings of wealth that surrounded his life, Westinghouse's favorite activity remained tinkering. The air-brake millionaire often spent up to seventeen hours a day, six days a week, in his Pittsburgh workshop. During the course of his prolific career, his tenacity and inventive genius combined to produce more than four-hundred patents, ranging from a gas meter for measuring the amount of fuel used by consumers to an air spring for taking the shock out of automobile riding.

In 1885 Westinghouse turned his attention to the field he would become most remembered for—alternating electric current. He laid the foundation for the modern electric industry by developing a system of generators and transformers that made it possible for the first time to utilize alternating current (AC) as an everyday power source. Previously, the only type of electricity that had been put to practical use was the less-powerful direct current, which, because of its low voltage, could be transmitted a maximum distance of only one mile. Alternating current, on the other hand, could travel over longer distances, but prior to Westinghouse's innovation, engineers had not been able to control its extremely high voltage.

Westinghouse formed the Westinghouse Electric Company in 1886 to build alternating-current equipment. But despite his success in overcoming the technological obstacles involved in developing a practical AC system, he soon found himself up against another, far more stubborn, problem. Many scientists and power company engineers (including Thomas Edison) were opposed to the idea of switching from direct current to the higher voltage form of electricity, which they regarded as unsafe. Opponents vilified "Westinghouse current" as an "electric murderer" and warned of its horrifying dangers in newspaper stories with headlines like "Electric Wire Slaughter" and "Another Lineman Roasted to Death."

Undaunted by these attacks, the engineer continued to push for the acceptance of AC power. In 1892 he was given the opportunity to demonstrate the safety and efficiency of the unfairly maligned electricity to the world when he won a contract to provide lighting for the Columbian Exposition in Chicago. During the six-month event, a quarter of a million lamps powered by AC electricity burned brightly without a single accident, thus convincing the public that alternating current was not a hazard to life and property. Other contracts soon followed, and by the early 1900s, the AC electricity pioneered by Westinghouse was enjoying widespread use as a source of power for homes and businesses.

George Westinghouse stepped down as president of the Westinghouse Electric Co. in 1910 before it began to manufacture the refrigerators, toasters, and other electrical appliances that have made his name a household word. Retiring to his estate in Lenox, Massachusetts, he continued to tinker with new mechnical ideas even though failing health eventually confined him to a wheelchair. It was typical of the man's indefatigable spirit that he was working on designs for an electrically powered wheelchair at the time of his death.

Super Salesmen

1839–1913
ADOLPHUS BUSCH

Busch Beer

As the principal creditor of the bankrupt Bavarian Brewery, Eberhard Anheuser suddenly found himself in the beer business after he acquired the St. Louis firm's assets in 1857. Fully aware that the Missouri city was saturated with beer producers (the result of an influx of German immigrants some years earlier), Anheuser wasn't overly thrilled at the prospect of owning the small brewery. To make matters worse for the middle-aged businessman, the Bavarian Brewery's product was not distinctive in taste and thus it was lost among the dozens of beers in the crowded St. Louis market.

The company limped along under Anheuser's halfhearted management for nearly a decade before his son-in-law of four years, Adolphus Busch, joined the firm as a junior partner and salesman in 1865. No stranger to the beer industry, Busch, who was twenty-six, had worked for a brewers' supply company owned by his father back home in Germany. The enterprise had made the Busch family very wealthy, and Adolphus was educated at some of Europe's most prestigious schools, but as the youngest of twenty-one children he felt he would be better off seeking his fortune in America. Arriving in St. Louis the same year that Eberhard Anheuser acquired the Bavarian Brewery, the teenage immigrant took a job as a clerk with a wholesaling firm. Two years later, upon learning that his father had died and left him an inheritance, Busch went into business for himself selling brewers' supplies.

It was through his business dealings that Busch met Anheuser and began courting the brewer's daughter, Lilly. After the couple's 1861 marriage, Busch turned his eye toward his father-in-law's marginal brewery,

BUDWEISER GIRL

Realizing the importance of keeping his name in front of the public, Adolphus Busch was an early user of advertising novelties. The St. Louis brewer distributed tens of thousands of corkscrews, matchboxes, and other gifts, all emblazoned with the name of his product, to bar owners and their customers in the later nineteenth century. Two of the most noteworthy giveaways were the Budweiser Girl items (such as the poster pictured here) and the pocket-knife calling card (previous page). Just in case someone forgot who gave him the knife, a look into the peephole would reveal a portrait of Adolphus Busch himself.

making suggestions to the skeptical Anheuser for improving its sales and, eventually, buying an interest in the struggling firm.

Much to Eberhard Anheuser's surprise, his son-in-law proved to be a spectacular salesman who was able to upgrade the brewery's fortunes almost immediately. From the start, the personable Adolphus adopted the strategy of selling himself as aggressively as he sold his product. A robust young man with a flowing mustache and commanding voice, Busch took to the road, cultivating friendships with beverage merchants and tavern owners. To make himself stand out from the scores of other beer salesmen in the city, he devised a unique "calling card," a jackknife emblazoned with the E. Anheuser & Co. logo. At one end of the knife was a peephole that, when peered through, revealed a picture of Adolphus Busch himself.

Not limiting his efforts to the retailers who sold his product, Busch also concentrated on enhancing his brewery's image with the consumers who bought beer. Having purchased a new fleet of gleaming delivery wagons, he drove through the streets of St. Louis with teams of high-stepping show horses. He also remodeled the brewing facility and began offering guided tours to the general public—something that none of the city's other beer producers did at the time.

As a result of these promotional steps, E. Anheuser & Co. rose to become one of the leading St. Louis breweries. The company's sales volume, which had been hovering at the 8,000-barrel-a-year level when the young German joined the firm, increased to 25,000 barrels by 1873.

The talented salesman, however, had got about as much mileage as he could out of an indifferent beer. In 1876 Busch finally was able to bring out a premium product that could be sold on its own superior merits. The new beer had been "discovered" by a St. Louis businessman named Carl Conrad while lunching in the German village of Budweis. So impressed was the American with its smooth, light taste that he brought the recipe back to his friend Adolphus Busch. (The two men remained partners in the beer's production until Busch bought out Conrad in 1891.) What made Budweiser—as it came to be called—unusual was its natural carbonation, brought about by an ancient European brewing process known as Kraeusening, in which fermentation is induced a second time just as the beer is beginning to age.

Besides producing a beer of extraordinary smoothness and taste, the brewing formula offered another significant advantage; Budweiser, if pasteurized and bottled, would retain its flavor for long periods of time and thus could be shipped to distant cities. As far as super-salesman Adolphus Busch was concerned, the easily preservable beer provided an ideal opportunity to extend his market well beyond St. Louis and establish one of America's first national brands of beer.

In his campaign to win nationwide acceptance for Budweiser, Busch used the same approach that had served him so well locally—selling his personality. A gregarious man, he visited cities across America to introduce his premium beer, hosting lavish banquets for potential customers at each stop along the way. After he had moved on to the next town, a team of Anheuser-Busch salesmen remained behind for several days to take orders.

Wanting to keep the Budweiser name in front of tavern owners and customers even when he and his sales reps were gone, Busch handed out an array of decorative novelty items promoting his beer. Trays and posters featuring the comely "Budweiser Girls" became a common sight on taproom walls across the country. Equally familiar to bar patrons was a panoramic reproduction of the Little Big Horn massacre, entitled "Custer's

Last Fight," which Busch commissioned artist F. Otto Becker to paint and subsequently distributed to more than a million saloon keepers.

Following the success of Budweiser, Busch decided to market a draft beer aimed at the very top of the American market. In 1896 he brought out a heavily hopped, super-premium beer called Michelob, which was sold only in draft (the beer wasn't available in bottles and cans until 1961). National distribution of Michelob was achieved through an innovative railroad system created by Busch, who designed specially equipped refrigerated cars and built a string of icehouses along major rail routes.

By the time Budweiser's twenty-fifth anniversary was celebrated in 1901, the Anheuser-Busch brewery had become the largest beer company in the world, selling 1 million barrels annually and overtaking the previous leader, Pabst. Adolphus Busch, who had become one of the nation's richest men, left behind a personal fortune of $60 million when he died a dozen years later. The Missouri beer baron's namesake Busch label did not appear until 1955 when the premium-oriented brewery, under the stewardship of his grandson August A. Busch, Jr., finally decided that it needed an entry in the popularly priced segment of the market.

D———— 1882–1968
R. WILLIAM SCHOLL

Dr. Scholl's
Foot Care Products

Even as a boy growing up on his parents' LaPorte County, Indiana, dairy farm, William "Billy" Scholl demonstrated the interest in shoes and foot care that would play a prominent role in his adult life. After designing and sewing a leather harness set for the farm's horses, the youth became his family's unofficial cobbler, making and repairing shoes for his father, mother, and twelve brothers and sisters.

Recognizing his skill as a shoemaker, Billy's parents apprenticed him to a local cobbler when he was sixteen. The boy learned his new trade quickly, and one year later he left his small farming community for Chicago, where he found work at a shoe store as a cobbler-salesman.

The Indiana teenager hadn't been at the store long before he grew alarmed by the appalling condition of his big-city customers' feet, most of which were marred by bunions, corns, and fallen arches. Wanting to do something about the problem, Billy Scholl embarked on a self-appointed mission to become "foot doctor to the world." His first step toward realizing this goal was to have his hours at the store switched to evenings so that he could enroll in day classes at the Illinois Medical College (now part of Loyola University).

Although he put in a full schedule at school and at his shoe store job, Scholl still managed to find the energy to work on his ideas for new foot care products. By the time he graduated in 1904, the twenty-two-year-old foot specialist had patented his first invention, an arch support that he called the Foot-Eazer.

Scholl rented a small shop and, with the help of one employee, began to manufacture his arch supports for sale to shoe stores in the Chicago area. To interest store owners in his new product, the young doctor devised a memorable sales demonstration. Walking into a store, Scholl would casually produce the skeleton of a human foot from his pocket and toss it on the counter in front of the startled proprietor. Having thus captured the prospective customer's attention, he would proceed to discuss the anatomy of the human foot and the causes of different foot ailments. At the conclusion of this talk, Scholl would explain the merits of the Foot-Eazer to the mesmerized store owner, who almost invariably placed on order for the product.

Unorthodox as it might have been, the practice of tossing a skeletal foot before a prospect was more than a mere attention-getting stunt. On a deeper level, it marked the beginning of Billy Scholl's sales strategy of using showmanship to promote not only his own products but foot care awareness in general. He would follow this sales plan consistently during the course of a career that would span more than sixty years, becoming almost as well known for his podiatric views as for his namesake products.

Believing that a knowledge of foot care was essential to selling his products, Scholl established a podiatric correspondence course for shoe store clerks. He also hired a staff of educational consultants who crisscrossed the country giving lectures on proper foot care procedures.

However, the most persuasive spokesman for the podiatric cause was Dr. Billy Scholl himself. A colorful, outspoken individual, he wrote several books on the subject, including *The Human Foot: Anatomy, Deformities, and Treatment* (1915) and *Dictionary of the Foot* (1916). Scholl promoted foot care in his frequent interviews with the press. He once told a reporter that "bad feet" were so common because only one person in fifty walked properly. To remedy this problem, he advised walking at least two miles a day "head up, chest out, toes straight forward." The foot doctor also recommended that people wear two pairs of shoes a day, changing at noon and letting the worn shoes "dry out" for two or three days before being put on again.

In 1916 Dr. Scholl created a national upsurge in foot consciousness by sponsoring a Cinderella foot contest. Women throughout the country visited their local Dr. Scholl's stores to leave their footprints on a "Pedo-Graph," a device invented by the doctor to measure and graphically illustrate the balance and weight distribution of a foot. A panel of qualified judges evaluated the prints to select the woman with the "best pair of feet" in America.

Following the success of the Cinderella contest, Dr. Scholl sponsored a series of walking marathons in 1918, awarding generous prizes to the walkers who logged the most miles on their pedometers (purchased at Scholl's stores) over a designated period of time. Public interest in the marathons was so keen that crowds would often form outside the stores when the latest results were due to be posted. One determined individual, who took an ocean cruise while he was entered in a marathon, spent the better part of his vacation walking around the promenade deck.

As a result of his salesmanship and promotional genius, Billy Scholl achieved success quickly compared to most self-made businessmen. Three years after he started making the Foot-Eazer, he was able to leave his small shop for a five-story building on the Chicago Loop. In 1908 his company became international with the opening of a Canadian factory, followed two years later by the formation of the Scholl Manufacturing Co. of London, England. When he celebrated his company's golden anniversary in 1954, the former farm boy's namesake products were enjoying annual sales of more than $25 million.

His great fortune notwithstanding, Billy Scholl remained a hardworking man of unpretentious tastes, often putting in seven-day weeks at his office and continuing to serve as the active president of his company until a month before his death at eighty-five. A lifelong bachelor, he lived for part of each year in a single room (with a bath down the hall) at the Illinois Athletic Club in Chicago.

One of the millionaire's favorite forms of recreation was travel. He covered virtually the entire globe on his numerous journeys and was a passenger on the maiden voyages of the *Graf Zeppelin* and the *Hindenburg*. Years later, he was on board the first international flight of a Pan American Boeing 707 jet.

The main interest in Billy Scholl's life, however, remained the human foot. He claimed never to have forgotten a foot the way others never forget a face. Among his most prized possessions was the world's largest collection of ancient shoes.

WILLIAM WRIGLEY, JR.

Wrigley's Gum

When eleven-year-old Bill Wrigley ran away from home in the summer of 1873, his parents probably weren't too surprised. The oldest of William and Mary Wrigley's eight children, Bill had already acquired a well-deserved reputation as the "class bad boy" at his Philadelphia grammar school. On several occasions, the curly-haired youngster's disruptive pranks had gotten him expelled from the classroom, and in each instance the senior Wrigley was obliged to take time off from his busy soap factory to accompany young Bill to the principal's office.

This time, Bill hopped a train to New York City. Arriving in Manhattan with just a few pennies in his pocket, the boy earned some money selling newspapers along Park Row and later worked as a cook's helper on ships docked in New York harbor. At night, he joined other street urchins sleeping in doorways and under delivery wagons.

The vagabond life was great fun for a few months, but the onset of autumn's cold weather dampened Bill's spirits, and he returned to Philadelphia. Upon his arrival home, his angry parents promptly carted him back to school. A short time later, though, he was expelled for good after he hurled a pie at the nameplate over the school entrance.

Hoping that some hard manual labor might yet straighten out his troubled son, William Wrigley, Sr., sent the boy to work at the family soap factory. Bill was given the job of stirring pots of boiling soap with a wooden paddle, the most physically demanding task at the plant. (During the period he performed this job, Bill Wrigley developed a powerful, muscular physique which he kept for most of his life through regular exercise.)

At thirteen, Bill left home again—this time with the grudging acquiescence of his father—to sell soap in the "tall-grass towns" of rural Pennsylvania, New York, and New England. Much to the surprise of his parents, the teenage troublemaker proved to be remarkably adept as a salesman.

Right from the start, Bill demonstrated the tenacity needed to make it on the selling circuit. On his very first call, he followed a reluctant West Chester, Pennsylvania, dealer around for two hours before the man finally relented, saying, "Well, sonny, I can see that I will have to buy some of your soap if I expect to do any business today." Sometime later, the boy salesman caught up with a large, and particularly elusive, country wholesaler by camping out overnight on the man's doorstep in the middle of the winter.

Bill Wrigley possessed more than a bulldog sense of determination; he also had the successful salesman's knack for getting along with all types of

Operating under the credo "tell them quick and tell them often," William Wrigley, Jr., poured some $100 million into advertising his namesake chewing gum between 1892 and 1931, making him the largest advertiser of any single product during that period. This ad, which touted Wrigley's gum as a tasty, economical refreshment, appeared in the August 10, 1918, edition of the Saturday Evening Post.

people. One of the keys to selling, he later said, was to be "always polite, always patient and never to argue." Whenever the young salesman failed to get a soap order, he made it a point to thank the dealer warmly for having listened to him. This politeness often caused unsold merchants to change their minds and take a couple of boxes of soap just to "help out" the courteous boy.

Wrigley continued to work for his father off and on until 1891, when he moved to Chicago to start his own business as a manufacturer's representative. The first product he handled was his father's soap, and later, as his volume grew, he added a line of baking powder.

To encourage business, the shrewd salesman offered premiums, such as free toiletries and cookbooks, with all his products. In 1892 Wrigley made a deal with the Zeno Manufacturing Co. to supply him with chewing gum. He enclosed two free sticks of gum as a premium with every package of baking powder, and within a few months he noticed an unusual pattern developing—more and more customers were writing to his office asking if they could buy the gum without the baking powder.

By the end of the year, Wrigley had dropped all his other products to concentrate exclusively on selling gum. During the early days of his gum venture, he relied on his own considerable power of persuasion to get his product on grocery shelves. A tireless worker, he crisscrossed the country, calling on candy jobbers and large merchants and spending a total of 187 nights in railroad sleeping cars his first year in the gum business.

Bill Wrigley promoted his new product by giving a free counter scale to every dealer who purchased at least $15 worth of gum. Scales were soon followed by other premiums aimed at the store owner, including cash registers, coffee makers, cheese cutters, and display cases. Although the cost of awarding premiums cut deeply into his profits, Wrigley believed that by giving grocers the chance to earn free merchandise he would be encouraging them to push his gum over competing brands. The astute salesman scored another marketing coup when he arranged to have his gum displayed on the cash register counters of restaurants all over the country, where it quickly became a popular impulse item among diners. By 1910 Wrigley's Spearmint (introduced in 1893) was the number one selling brand in the United States, and Juicy Fruit (also dating back to 1893) wasn't too far behind.

As his business grew, Bill Wrigley began to devote more attention to consumer advertising. In 1915 he collected every telephone directory in the country and mailed four free sticks of gum to the 1.5 million listed subscribers. Four years later, the gum maker repeated this feat, even though the number of phone subscribers had climbed to 7 million. By the time of his death in 1932, Wrigley had invested more than $100 million in advertising gum, making him the largest single-product advertiser of his day.

Despite the fact that his gum sold for a modest 5¢ a pack, Bill Wrigley's profits were enormous, growing from $8.5 million in 1921 to $12.2 million in 1930. By shrewdly investing the money he made from gum, Wrigley expanded his financial empire to include holdings in real estate, mining, hotels, railroads, and other ventures. In 1919 he purchased the entire island of Santa Catalina (except the town of Avalon) for $3 million and developed it into a major resort. Five years later, he built the thirty-two-story Wrigley Building, now a Chicago landmark.

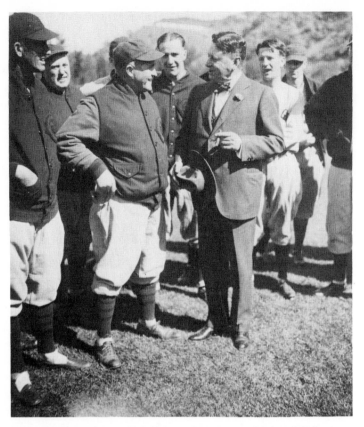

William Wrigley chats with Cubs' manager Joe McCarthy, coaches, and players circa 1929–30. Despite an investment of more than $6 million in strengthening the Chicago team, Wrigley never realized his long-held dream of a World Series championship.

His impressive list of business accomplishments notwithstanding, Bill Wrigley remained frustrated in his quest to achieve one, more personal, goal. The gregarious gum manufacturer spent more than $6 million in an attempt to strengthen the Chicago Cubs after he purchased a majority interest in the team in 1919. Yet, despite this generous financial backing, Wrigley's beloved "Cubbies" never realized his dream of winning a World Series.

Partners

C ———— 1877–1910
CHARLES ROLLS

H ———— 1863–1933
(FREDERICK) HENRY ROYCE

Rolls-Royce Automobiles

The men whose initials would become linked over the grill of the world's most prestigious automobile were as different from each other as their namesake car is from a subcompact. Rolls, the dashingly handsome son of an English baron, was a devil-may-care race car driver in search of a more powerful vehicle. Royce, a no-nonsense engineer, wanted nothing more than a dependable means of transportation. Together, this incongruous pair created something that was more than a mere automobile; rather it was a dream on wheels.

One of Britain's pioneer auto racers, Rolls was driving cars as early as 1895. In addition to being a competitive driver for Panhard, Mors, and other leading automakers, the Cambridge-educated aristocrat sold French and Belgian cars to his wealthy English friends.

Unlike Rolls, Royce possessed neither the connections nor the education of a gentleman. The son of a miller, he was turned out to fend for himself at the age of ten, following the failure of his father's business. As a youth, he supported himself by selling newspapers on the streets of London and later became a telegraph boy and a railroad workshop apprentice, before landing a job with the Electric Light and Power Company of London in 1881.

A year after being hired by the electric company, Royce was transferred to a higher position at its Liverpool subsidiary. Things were progressing nicely for the former newspaper boy, until he suddenly found himself out of work in 1884, when the Liverpool company went out of business.

Undaunted, Royce, now twenty-one, borrowed a small sum of money (70 pounds) and established his own firm, F. H. Royce, Ltd., to manufacture lamps, cranes, and other electrical devices. The youth's strict insistence on quality and his near-fanatical attention to even the most minute detail resulted in products that were far superior to the competition's. Not

Charles S. Rolls at the wheel of the "Light 20" Rolls-Royce shortly after winning the 1906 Tourist Trophy race. The Cambridge-educated Rolls was an accomplished race car driver when he met Henry Royce, an automaker and electrical engineer, in 1904. Under Rolls's influence, the cautious, methodical Royce made his finely engineered cars bigger and faster.

surprisingly, F. H. Royce, Ltd., grew into a prosperous business, and by 1902 its founder felt confident enough in the future to treat himself to one of the new motorcars that were being made in France.

Like virtually every motorcar of its day, the 10-HP Decauville that Royce purchased was unreliable, uncomfortable, and very noisy—all of which offended its owner's sense of precision. Vowing that he could design a better car, the self-made engineer set aside a small area of his electrical shop and built a sturdy two-cylinder vehicle with a meticulously balanced crankshaft that minimized noise and vibrations. Royce made three of his cars: one for himself; a second for A. R. Claremont, his partner in the electrical business; and third for Henry Edwards, a recently named director of Royce, Ltd., and a friend of the Honorable C. S. Rolls.

It was through Edwards that Charles Rolls got his first look at the "Royce car," and the experienced auto racer was immediately impressed with the precision engineering that had obviously gone into the vehicle's construction. With an eye toward what might be accomplished if that same engineering skill were applied to a larger, more powerful car, Rolls had his friend arrange a meeting with Henry Royce.

Although the middle-aged engineer was at first leery of the younger man, Rolls's charm and enthusiasm eventually won Royce over. In 1904 the two men formed an automotive partnership, with Royce producing cars at his Manchester shop and Rolls selling them from a London showroom. The name of the company, it was later agreed, would be Rolls-Royce, Ltd.

Sir (Frederick) Henry Royce driving a prototype of the "New Phantom" Rolls-Royce in front of his Sussex home. In contrast to Charles Rolls, who was the son of a baron, Royce was of humble origins. Born to a miller, he left home as a child and worked at a number of menial jobs before eventually starting his own electrical equipment business when he was twenty-one years old.

The daring vigor of Charles Rolls proved to be an ideal balance to Royce's thorough, mechanical nature. Under Rolls's influence, the company's cars became progressively bigger, faster, and more stylish, while still retaining the almost obsessive attention to detail that was characteristic of Henry Royce. In 1907 Rolls-Royce, Ltd., unveiled a car that was a perfect blend of the partners' divergent, but complementary, talents. Officially, the car was called the 40/50, but it soon became known, and revered, as the Silver Ghost—a name chosen because of the vehicle's silver-gray color and because it was so free of engine noise that it ran as quietly as a ghost.

With a six-cylinder 48-HP engine, the Silver Ghost offered speed to satisfy the sportsman; yet its smooth, quiet ride was unmatched by any other vehicle. This unheard of combination of power and comfort was possible because every part of the car was meticulously designed and made with only the best materials. Crankshaft bearings were ground to a quarter of a thousandth part of an inch, and the nickel steel timing wheels were polished with jeweler's rouge. The vehicle was so solidly built that it was said that a penny placed on the edge of its radiator cap would remain perfectly still while the engine idled.

The success of the Silver Ghost forced Royce to move his car-making operation out of the electrical shop and into larger facilities in Derby, England. It was here that the engineer often put in twenty-hour days perfecting the car that was already universally regarded as one of the best in the world. On some occasions, Royce would become so involved in a project that he would have to be coaxed into stopping for meals by his concerned colleagues.

Rolls, on the other hand, remained an alter ego to his compulsive partner. He was a familiar sight at fashionable parties and prestigious auto racing events. Still a "daring sport" who loved a challenge, Rolls took up flying, crossing the English Channel by balloon in 1906 and by airplane a few years later.

Perhaps the difference between the two men is best illustrated by the way each left this world. Charles Rolls died in 1910 when a plane he was piloting crashed; Royce's death in 1934 was said to be brought on by overwork. Following the passing of Henry Royce, his successors at the company changed the color of the famous "RR" nameplate that appears over the car's grill from red to black as a sign of mourning. The letters have remained black ever since.

B——— 1913–1967 I——— 1917–
BURTON BASKIN IRVINE ROBBINS

Baskin-Robbins Ice Cream

The name "Baskin" without "Robbins" is like ice cream without the cone, but when the two southern California brothers-in-law first entered the ice-cream business in late 1945 and early 1946, each went his separate way. Chicago-born Burt Baskin (who was married to Irvine Robbins's sister Shirley) opened Burton's Ice Cream in Pasadena, while the twenty-eight-year-old Robbins launched the Snowbird Ice Cream Store in nearby Glendale.

It wasn't that the two aspiring ice-cream makers were opposed to the idea of joining forces. They had simply heeded the advice of Irv Robbins's father, Aaron, who warned, "If you become partners right away, you'll compromise too many of your ideas in an effort to get along." The senior Robbins was no stranger to the pitfalls involved in the ice-cream business, having run a wholesale and retail dairy farm in Tacoma, Washington, for almost twenty years.

As a teenager, Irv Robbins worked at his father's downtown dairy, where he learned all about ice-cream making, experimenting with unusual flavor combinations after closing hours. In contrast, Burt Baskin acquired his ice-cream expertise as a navy PX operator in the New Hebrides during World War II. Obtaining an ice-cream freezer from an aircraft carrier supply officer, the young Chicagoan churned out creamy treats flavored with local tropical fruits for his fellow servicemen.

After trying out their own ideas for about a year, the brothers-in-law were ready to become partners in 1947. Their union was a harmonious one from the start, since both shared the same basic marketing philosophy—to sell nothing but ice cream and to offer a multitude of flavors.

Burt and Irv also shared the same career objective, which, in light of their ultimate success, seems incredibly modest. "We just wanted to make $75 a week. And we wanted to enjoy ourselves doing it," recalled Irv, adding, "Of course, when we reached that goal we upped it to $100, then $125, and so on."

By 1948 the partners had set their sights on a much higher goal. They already owned eight busy ice-cream stores, and their plan was to launch new ones throughout southern California. Further expansion was hampered, however, by a lack of capital to invest in the opening of additional units. At this point, Baskin and Robbins came up with a franchising plan; instead of operating stores themselves, they would "sell" preselected locations to individual investors. Under the terms of the agreement, the company furnished ice cream, merchandising aids, and advertising, while the investor-operator was responsible for the day-to-day management of his or her store.

With its franchising plan providing the needed influx of capital, the ice-cream chain expanded rapidly, growing to forty-three stores (all franchised) by the end of 1949. A decade later, Baskin-Robbins made its first appearance outside California, when it contracted the Lilly Ice Cream Co. to operate a Phoenix, Arizona, franchise. In 1960 the number of stores in the chain passed the one-hundred mark, and new locations were being opened every few weeks.

Fueling the phenomenal growth of the company was the popularity of its multiflavored ice-cream lineup. In addition to selling ice cream in the standard vanilla, chocolate, and strawberry varieties, Baskin and Robbins marketed thirty-one "exotic flavors"—one for each day of the month. The partners attracted attention to their bountiful selection by giving their flavors offbeat names such as ChaChaCha (cherry chocolate chip), Plum Nuts (plums, vanilla, and walnuts) and Tanganilla (a tangerine-vanilla combination).

Each month Baskin and Robbins rotated the mix of exotic flavors sold at the stores so that their selection would remain interesting to regular customers. By 1983 their namesake firm could boast that it had marketed more than five-hundred flavors during its thirty-seven-year history, many of which—Tanganilla, Fudge Brownie, and Jamoca Almond Fudge, to name but a few—have become minor American classics.

Not all of Baskin-Robbins ice-cream creations have enjoyed the sweet taste of success. One flavor devised by Irv Robbins himself, called Goody Goody Gumdrops, was pulled off the market because the company feared that someone would break a tooth on one of the tiny gumdrops, which became rock hard when frozen in the ice cream. Then there were dubious offerings like "Ketchup" ice cream, "Lox and Bagels," and "Grape Britain," which were turned down in the testing laboratory, long before they reached the top of a single sugar cone.

In 1967 Baskin and Robbins sold their thriving ice-cream empire, which by then consisted of five-hundred stores, to United Fruit (now United Brands) for an estimated $12 million. Six months after the deal was consummated, fifty-four-year-old Burt Baskin died suddenly at his California home.

Irv Robbins, meanwhile, remained with the company following the death of his brother-in-law. The gregarious University of Washington graduate (class of '39) served as president and later chairman of the board of the firm, which is now a wholly owned subsidiary of Allied–Lyons North America Corporation. Robbins retired in 1978, a year in which some 20 million gallons of his ice cream was sold through more than two thousand Baskin-Robbins stores in the United States, Canada, Japan, and Europe.

Hailed by his successors as "the Walt Disney of the ice-cream business," Robbins now lives in a Rancho Mirage, California, home that is equipped with its own six-flavor ice-cream counter. A trim and vigorous retiree, he starts many days with a bowl of breakfast cereal topped by a scoop of banana ice cream.

R———— 1845–1910
ROBERT JOHNSON

J———— 1856–1932   E———— 1852–1934
JAMES JOHNSON   EDWARD JOHNSON

Johnson & Johnson
Health Care Products

When famed English surgeon Joseph Lister addressed a Philadelphia medical congress in 1876, his speech received only a lukewarm reception. Sir Joseph's esteemed reputation inspired the respect of the medical gathering, but his plea for more sanitary operating-room procedures fell largely on deaf ears. The science of bacteriology was still in its infancy at the time, and most surgeons (who usually operated in their "civilian clothes" and used sweepings from mill floors as surgical dressing) scoffed at Dr. Lister's theory that invisible airborne germs caused serious, and often fatal, infections in postoperative patients.

One member of the audience who did not greet the speaker's message with skepticism was Robert Johnson, the thirty-one-year-old co-owner of the Brooklyn pharmaceutical firm Seabury & Johnson. A tall, ruddy-complexioned businessman, Johnson had been dealing with the medical profession since he was a teenage apprentice at a Poughkeepsie, New York, apothecary shop. Having seen firsthand the unsanitary conditions then prevalent in American operating rooms, the practical pharmacist found it easy to believe in the English physician's description of "invisible assassins." A strong-willed man who was not afraid to go against the opinion of established medical experts, Johnson became an outspoken advocate of Lister's views on the need for a more sterile surgical environment.

Among the converts Robert Johnson won over to Listerism were his younger brothers James and Edward Mead Johnson. Although James was trained as a civil engineer and Mead an attorney, both had previously given up their careers after Robert convinced them to join Seabury & Johnson as plant manager and salesman, respectively. The younger Johnsons were accustomed to following the lead of their domineering sibling, and when Robert declared his intention to develop a Lister-inspired antiseptic surgical dressing, they quickly agreed to assist him in his effort.

For the next several years, the Johnsons experimented with different methods of mass producing cotton and gauze dressing, while continuing to devote most of their time to their positions at Seabury & Johnson. By 1885, however, it had become apparent to the brothers that they would be better able to develop new surgical dressings if they left the pharmaceutical firm and formed their own company.

James and Mead resigned from the drug company and, with $1,000 in capital, they founded Johnson & Johnson on the fourth floor of a former wallpaper factory in New Brunswick, New Jersey. Meanwhile, Robert Johnson worked out an arrangement with George Seabury to sell his interest in the Seabury & Johnson company, and in 1886 he was able to join his brothers in their new firm.

The small company prospered quickly, thanks largely to the efficient meshing of the brothers' divergent talents. James, the studious engineer, designed state-of-the-art production equipment, while the gregarious Mead was a successful salesman of the company's products. Robert, who was named president of the firm, maintained strict control over the administrative end of the business.

Soon after the founding of their company, the brothers saw a long-held dream come to fruition when they introduced a ready-made antiseptic surgical dressing. The new cotton and gauze dressing, which came sealed in individual germ-resistant packages, could be shipped to hospitals in even the most remote areas of the country without involving undue risk of infection.

To promote their product to the medical profession, the Johnsons published a series of highly regarded books and magazines, including *Modern*

Methods of Antiseptic Wound Treatment (1888), which became a standard text among doctors for many years. A major contributor to many Johnson & Johnson publications was Fred Kilmer (the father of poet Joyce Kilmer), who joined the company in 1888 and remained with the firm for forty-five years.

As the medical community became more aware of the threat posed by airborne bacteria, the demand for Johnson & Johnson's antiseptic surgical dressings increased. The company expanded its facilities steadily during the late nineteenth and early twentieth centuries, and by 1910 it occupied a sprawling forty-building complex in New Brunswick.

Despite the impressive growth of the family business, Mead Johnson began to resent his older brother's autocratic rule. Unlike the quiet, mechanically minded James who, a company history recounts, "was far more comfortable with his complicated machinery than with complicated people," Mead's aggressive personality often put him at odds with the forceful Robert. This conflict was aggravated by Robert's reluctance to go along with his younger brother's plans to add pharmaceuticals to the company's product line. (At Mead's instigation, however, Johnson & Johnson formed subsidiary companies to produce and sell pharmaceuticals.)

In 1897 Mead decided to strike out on his own and, in a friendly arrangement with his brothers, he sold them his interest in Johnson & Johnson. Following the sale, Mead began making papain digestants in a rented Jersey City factory. He eventually built this business into the highly successful Mead Johnson & Co., a pioneer baby formula manufacturer.

Robert and James Johnson also continued to prosper after the breakup of the original partnership. In 1897 they achieved a major medical breakthrough by developing an effective sterilizing technique for catgut sutures. This was followed two years later by the introduction of a quick-sticking zinc oxide type of adhesive plaster that gained widespread acceptance among surgeons.

Ironically, it was James Johnson, the most reserved of the three brothers, who was responsible for introducing the product that would make the Johnson & Johnson name a household word. In 1920 James, who was then president of the firm, was shown an unusual self-stick bandage developed by Earl Dickson, a cotton buyer in the purchasing department. The recently married Dickson had come up with the idea of putting a small gauze pad in the middle of a thin strip of surgical tape to provide his accident-prone wife with a convenient at-home dressing for minor cuts and bruises. After seeing the new bandage, James Johnson decided to market it under a name that would soon become one of the most recognized trademarks in America—BAND-AID.

Perfectionists

1858–1913

R UDOLPH DIESEL

Diesel Engine

Born in France to Bavarian parents, Rudolph Diesel distinguished himself early by winning scholarship awards at his Parisian grammar school. The handsome boy also demonstrated artistic talent and a strong mechanical aptitude. When Rudolph was twelve years old, he and his family, considered German by their fellow Parisians, were forced to flee France following the outbreak of the Franco-Prussian War. The Diesels traveled by refugee train to London, where they settled into a shabby apartment. The move depleted the family's already meager resources, and they sank deeper into poverty. To ease their financial burden, the Diesels sent their son to live with relatives in Augsburg, Bavaria. It was while attending a technical junior high school in Augsburg, the Königlichen Kreis-Gewerbsschule, that Rudolph developed an ambition to become an engineer.

In 1876 Diesel became the youngest student in history to graduate from Augsburg's industrial high school, and he was awarded a four-year scholarship to the München Polytechnikum. He continued to rack up academic honors in college, where his studies centered around the mechanics of steam engines. One thing in particular captured Diesel's interest and inventive fancy—the fact that the best steam engines of the day were only 6 to 10 percent efficient. At least nine-tenths of the fuel fed into an engine was burned to no purpose. Such wastefulness was anathema to the perfectionist Diesel, and finding a way to improve the efficiency of engines became almost an obsession.

In the years following his graduation from college, Diesel worked as an engineer for several manufacturing firms in Switzerland and France, all the while experimenting with designs for a more efficient engine. In 1892 he achieved his goal, when he was issued a patent for an internal combustion engine in which ignition is brought about by heat resulting from air compression, rather than by an electric spark as in a gasoline engine. The new power plant offered about triple the efficiency of any designed heretofore, and it brought Diesel considerable income and notoriety. (His name has since evolved into a generic term describing engines of this type.)

Unfortunately, Diesel's business acumen and common sense didn't come close to matching his inventive genius. The early royalties from his engine were substantial; he received 50,000 marks annually from two German firms alone, and in America beer baron Adolphus Busch gave him a million gold marks for exclusive U.S. manufacturing rights. Perhaps to compensate for his impoverished childhood, Diesel spent the money as quickly as it came in on luxuries for himself, his wife Martha, and their three children. He constructed a great mansion overlooking the Isar River in Munich (the price of the lot alone was 50,000 marks). Inside the villa were hand-carved and painted ceilings, marble fireplaces in every room, five state-of-the-art bathrooms, and a basement bicycle corridor where the children could ride their two-wheelers on rainy days. Furniture was upholstered in silk, and many of the salons featured ivory walls and Oriental tapestries. In keeping with their new position of wealth, the Diesels cultivated an active social life, hosting lavish dinner parties for their upper-class friends and often attending the theater and the opera. Rudolph became a frequent spectator at automobile races, and after viewing the 1904 Gordon Bennett contest in Germany, treated himself to a bright red NAG touring car.

As his personal spending accelerated, Diesel's bank accounts were also being depleted by a series of unsound business ventures. In 1899 he lost 300,000 marks on a Balkan petroleum investment, and several years later a prominent real estate firm sued him for payment on some land speculations he had made. The lawsuit, which Diesel lost, cost him 600,000 marks in cash. The inventor's financial problems were compounded when demand for the diesel engine began to slacken because of technical difficulties involved in applying it commercially.

To satisfy his creditors, Diesel was forced to mortgage his opulent Munich estate and sell his prized automobile. As his money problems grew worse, he began to suffer from insomnia and severe migraine headaches. Doctors diagnosed his affliction as nervous exhaustion, and twice the inventor was sent to take extended rest cures, first at a sanitarium in Neuwittelsbach, northwest of Munich, and later at a hospital in the Tyrolean Alps. Although he stayed at each institution for several months, the treatments apparently were of little help; his headaches continued to rage.

The life of Rudolph Diesel came to an abrupt and mysterious end on September 29, 1913, on board a steamship bound from Antwerp, Belgium, to England. After dining with some traveling companions and going for a leisurely stroll around the deck, Diesel said good night and retired to his stateroom. He was never seen again. Speculation was rife after the inventor's disappearance. Some said that Diesel had been murdered by business competitors, and others that he had been killed by the kaiser's agents to prevent him from passing technical secrets to Germany's British adversaries. Because Diesel was some $400,000 in debt and on the verge of bankruptcy when he vanished, however, his family and others who knew him well believed that the engineer had taken his own life by jumping into the sea.

J———— 1730–1795
JOSIAH WEDGWOOD

Wedgwood China

Pottery making was not a very exact science before the mid-eighteenth century. A craftsman might produce an exquisite vase of remarkable delicacy and color clarity, but if he later attempted to duplicate his creation, more often than not the subsequent piece would be different in body character, luster, or hue. This lack of consistency was due to the fact that early potters simply did not bother to measure or record the ingredients used in their clay mixtures, glazes, and colorings; nor did they attempt to regulate the temperatures at which their pieces were fired or the length of time the objects remained in the kiln. For centuries, the making of pottery was an undisciplined cottage craft, practiced by artisans who clung to the techniques handed down by their fathers and grandfathers.

It was to one such family of potters in Staffordshire, England, that Josiah Wedgwood was born in 1730. The youngest of twelve children, he received some early schooling before being sent to the family pottery works at the age of nine after his father's death. Serving as an apprentice under his brother Thomas, Josiah quickly demonstrated a love of experimentation. He took it upon himself to explore new ways of coloring clay by treating it with various oxides. His inventiveness and suggestions for change were a constant source of irritation to Thomas Wedgwood, who wanted the business to continue operating as it had under their father. The rift between the brothers widened, and at twenty-two Josiah struck out on his own. After working for several other area potters, he went into business for himself in 1759, leasing a small shop in the town of Burslem.

As his own master, Wedgwood was free to try out new glazes, materials, and firing techniques to his heart's content. This in itself was nothing new, as other potters had experimented before. What was different about Wedgwood was that he was the first in his field to take a scientific approach toward his experiments, keeping meticulous records of the ingredients and processes used in each trial. His findings were logged in a series of notebooks; thus, when a procedure resulted in a new or improved color or clay, Wedgwood had the formula on hand to repeat the technique.

The potter's systematic tenacity paid off. In the early 1760s he perfected a method for making creamware, a substance consisting of an earthenware body covered with a thin white glaze. Creamware had been around for several decades. Before Wedgwood, however, there was no known way of ensuring that its color would be consistent every time; the pieces in the same set of dinnerware often varied from a yellowish cream tone to a stark white. Wedgwood's scientifically developed process made it possible to turn out creamware in a standardized pearly white hue—and the potter's work was heralded as a major breakthrough.

The simple elegance of creamware was right on target with the changing taste of European aristocrats who were moving away from the ornate excesses of the baroque and rococo periods to the uncluttered neoclassical look. Wedgwood's creamware came to the attention of England's royal court, and in 1765 the potter was called on to make a tea service for Queen Charlotte. Every bit the promoter, Wedgwood was well aware of the publicity value of such royal patronage, and he proceeded to play it for all it was worth. He sought and received permission from Queen Charlotte to rechristen his creamware "Queen's ware."

In 1768 Wedgwood formed a partnership with Thomas Bentley, a wealthy Liverpool merchant, who took responsibility for the selling end of the business. A well-informed gentleman in matters of taste, Bentley also helped determine the artistic course of Wedgwood's work, steering his talented partner in directions that were likely to find commercial acceptance. The two made an excellent business team, and their association lasted until Bentley's death in 1780. Together, they designed and built a large pottery works outside of Burslem, called Etruria, which included a Georgian mansion for Wedgwood's family and bachelor quarters for Bentley (a widower who later remarried).

At Etruria Wedgwood continued his experiments, eventually perfecting two wares that achieved even greater fame than his creamware. One of these, basalt ware, was a hard black stoneware used primarily for neoclassical vases. The other, a fine stoneware called jasper, was the pottery that would become most closely associated with the Wedgwood name. It consisted of a solid color body (usually blue or green) with a raised white design often adapted from a Greek vase or other classical source. Jasperware was used to make decorative cameos, as well as functional objects such as vases, bowls, and teapots.

The success of both wares earned vast fortunes for Wedgwood and Bentley. Continuing a tradition begun with the creamware order from Queen Charlotte, the partners' Etruria works serviced a long list of monarchs and aristocrats, including Empress Catherine of Russia, who commissioned a 952-piece set of dinnerware in 1773.

Despite his personal wealth and association with European nobility, Josiah Wedgwood remained a man of strong democratic views. He was an early supporter of the American Revolution, although he confined the expression of his beliefs to a small circle of family and friends. Later, he was more outspoken in his opposition to slavery, joining an abolitionist group called the Society for the Suppression of the Slave Trade. Among the potter's contributions to the group was an "antislavery cameo," which showed a slave in chains and bore the inscription "Am I not a man and a brother?"

Wedgwood's most jarring personal tragedy came in 1768 when, after suffering chronic pains in his right leg (the result of a childhood bout with smallpox), his doctors advised amputation. The operation was a success, and Wedgwood was fitted with a wooden leg that served him adequately for the rest of his life.

Upon his death at sixty-five, Wedgwood's business was taken over by two sons, Josiah, Jr., and Tom, who guided the pottery works through a period of further growth. But talent in the Wedgwood family did not end with pottery making. Tom Wedgwood (who died at the age of thirty-four) was one of the first individuals to produce a discernible photographic image, and he is credited with making many contributions to the development of photography. Josiah Wedgwood's most famous descendant, however, was the son of his daughter Susannah Darwin—a boy named Charles who in 1859 would set forth his theory of evolution in *On the Origin of Species*.

W—— 1876–1950
WILLIS CARRIER

Carrier Air Conditioners

In 3000 B.C., a wealthy Assyrian merchant created what was probably the world's first air-conditioning system, when he had his servants spray water on the walls and floor of the room below his courtyard in the hope that the resultant evaporation would provide some relief from the heat. Our attempts to keep cool in the face of hot, humid weather improved very little over the next several thousand years. Roman emperors brought snow down from the mountains to cool their gardens in the summer. In the eighth century, the Caliph Mahdi of Baghdad built a summer palace that had a layer of imported snow packed between its double walls.

More than a thousand years later, after the telephone and electric light had become realities, an effective means of keeping comfortable on a muggy summer's day still remained beyond the grasp of nineteenth-century technology. By the 1880s, a few large restaurants and other public places were embedding air pipes in a mixture of ice and salt and circulating the cooled air by means of fans. The Madison Square Theatre in New York was equipped to consume four tons of ice a night using this type of system.

The problem confronting nineteenth-century engineers was not how to lower air temperature (the first American ice-making machine was patented by Dr. John Gorrie of Florida in 1851) but how to remove the humidity from air. It was not until July 1902, when an unassuming twenty-five-year-old perfectionist named Willis Carrier developed a system that both cooled and dehumidified air, that the world was finally able to breathe a sigh of relief during the dog days of summer.

Even in childhood, Carrier demonstrated the problem-solving ability that would one day earn him the title "Father of Air Conditioning." Born on an upstate New York farm to parents of old New England stock—one of his ancestors was hanged as a witch at Salem in 1692–the boy acquired a reputation as an accomplished fixer of agricultural implements while still in his teens.

The biggest influence on the development of Willis's early mechanical skill was exerted by the women in his life. When he was nine, his mother taught him fractions by having him cut apples into halves, quarters, and eighths and then add and subtract the parts. On another occasion, when the pump was removed from the farm's well for cleaning, the boy's Aunt Abbey took him aside and showed him exactly how an air pump worked, explaining that "the atmosphere exerts a pressure of about fifteen pounds per square inch." This was the first time that the inventor of air conditioning heard of atmospheric pressure—and it left an indelible impression on him. "That fifteen pounds pressure is a number I'd never forget, even if I'd not made air my main interest through the years," Carrier later recalled.

With such help and encouragement from home, it's not surprising that Willis won a scholarship to Cornell, where he earned a degree in engineering in 1901. A month after graduation, he took a job with Buffalo Forge Co., a maker of heating and ventilation systems. Less than a year later, the young engineer was given an assignment that led him to develop the first practical air conditioner.

One of Buffalo Forge's customers was Sackett-Wilhelms Lithographing and Publishing Co. of Brooklyn, New York. Like all printers of the day, Sackett-Wilhelms was hampered by the disruptive effects of atmospheric conditions on the printing process. Paper expanded or contracted depending on the amount of heat and humidity in the print shop. Ink flowed and dried at a different rate of speed on humid days than it did on dry days, making it difficult to obtain consistent colors from one printing run to the next. Obviously, the situation was not conducive to meeting deadlines, and the Brooklyn firm wanted an effective means of controlling the temperature and humidity in its plant.

Willis Carrier tackled the Sackett-Wilhelms problem with the methodical approach he had been taught as a child. After experimenting with different devices, he succeeded in modifying a conventional heater so that, instead of steam, cold water could be run through its heating coils. Moving air over the coils by fan would produce a cold draft that would lower the temperature in the print shop—a process that in itself was not entirely new.

Unlike previous fan-coiling systems that simply made incoming air as cold as possible, however, Carrier's followed a meticulously developed formula that balanced the temperature of the air against the rate at which it flowed into the print shop. By operating at the correct balance between air temperature and air flow, the system caused moisture in the air to condense—and, in so doing, it not only cooled the Sackett-Wilhelms plant but dehumidified it as well.

Following the Sackett-Wilhelms project, Carrier continued to design and install air-conditioning systems for Buffalo Forge. Then, in a 1914 effort to reduce operating costs, the company's owners eliminated their new "refrigeration department" to concentrate on their more proven heating and ventilating products. At this point, Carrier and six associates raised $32,600 to form their own air-conditioning company. Carrier's new venture got off to an auspicious start; he signed more than forty contracts to install air-conditioning systems within one year.

In 1925 Carrier entered a profitable new market when he installed a 133-ton air-conditioning unit at New York's Rivoli Theatre. Air conditioning proved to be such a crowd pleaser at the Rivoli that by 1930 Carrier had installed units in more than three-hundred theaters across the country.

The growth of his namesake air conditioner made Willis Carrier a multimillionaire. Despite his wealth, he remained the prototype of the hardworking engineer who would forget all else when involved in a project. Once, he was so absorbed in solving a mathematical problem that he reportedly boarded a train and then forgot where he was going. Not surprisingly, Carrier remained involved in his work until shortly before his death, even though a heart ailment forced him to remain in bed up to twenty hours a day during the last three years of his life.

Notoriously unsafe in the mid-nineteenth century, elevators were trusted only to hoist freight and machinery. It was many years before Elisha Otis convinced a sceptical public that he had invented an elevator entirely safe for passengers.

Purveyors of Quality

Henry Steinway

Steinway Pianos

With some twelve thousand moving parts, each meticulously measured and shaped and then painstakingly fitted together by expert craftsmen, the Steinway grand piano is as intricate as the most esoteric sonata. Once the construction of a grand is completed, a process that generally requires an entire year, an inspector spends days tuning and voicing the piano, carefully adjusting hammer felts to produce the "Steinway sound." Indeed, it is Steinway's supple sound, free of even the faintest click or clatter, that has made the piano the undisputed king of the concert grands.

The man whose name appears over this prestigious keyboard was a short-statured German (five feet four inches tall), who developed an interest in music after serving as a bugler in the Prussian army that defeated Napoleon in the Battle of Waterloo. Born Heinrich Steinweg in the small Hartz Mountain hamlet of Wolfshagen, the future piano maker joined the army at eighteen, after two twists of fate had virtually wiped out his family.

Young Heinrich experienced his first tragedy in 1806 during the Franco-Prussian War, when his mother and most of his siblings died from cold and hunger as they fled from advancing French troops. Some years later, the boy was helping his father and three surviving brothers clear a road through the forest when a sudden thunderstorm materialized. The Steinwegs took shelter in a small collier's hut, which was struck by lightning, killing them all except Heinrich.

In 1815 the orphaned Steinweg joined the army of the duke of Brunswick. In the army Heinrich displayed a remarkable musical ability, despite the fact that he had received no formal training in his remote mountain village. He not only served as a bugler during the last Napoleonic war but also entertained his fellow soldiers with the zither and pianoforte. The young man from Wolfshagen consistently amazed his friends by playing songs after hearing them only once. By the time Heinrich's four-year tour of duty was completed, he was making as well as playing instruments, fashioning mouth organs out of whatever materials he could obtain.

Not surprisingly, Steinweg decided to pursue a career as a musical instrument maker after leaving the army. Realizing that a solid background in woodworking would be essential to his success, the practical veteran took a job with a cabinetmaker for one year. This was followed by work at several organ factories in various German cities.

By 1825 Steinweg was employed by an organ maker in the village of Seesen, where he also served as an organist in the local church. At night he worked in the kitchen of his small home to build square pianos that combined many of the best features of the English and German instruments then on the market. Initially, the young craftsman sold his handsome pianos as a sideline, while still keeping his job at the organ factory; but as word of his superior workmanship spread, he soon had enough orders to devote his full attention to piano making.

As Steinweg's sons, Theodore, Charles, Henry Jr., William, and Albert, grew, they joined his expanding piano business. The family venture continued to prosper until a redrawing of national borders in 1844 put a new—and very high—tariff barrier between their Seesen factory and its major Hanover markets. Steinweg's sales plummeted even further as a result of the turmoil following the 1848 revolution, and the family decided to start a new life for themselves and their piano business in the more promising land of America.

Arriving in the United States in 1850, the Steinwegs hoped to hasten their adjustment to their newly adopted country by changing the family name to the more Anglicized Steinway. They also decided that it would be necessary to familiarize themselves with the American piano industry before they launched their own business in the new land. To do this, every man in the family—including fifty-three-year-old Heinrich—took a job at a different New York piano factory.

After three years of working for others, the Steinways felt that they were ready to enter the American market. Using capital they had saved in Germany, they founded the House of Steinway & Sons in Manhattan on March 5, 1853. The venture began on a modest scale, with fewer than half a dozen employees and an output of one square piano a week. The Steinway family's quality product soon was attracting considerable attention, however. A little over a year after starting their business, the Steinways earned national notoriety when one of their square pianos with an innovative design that featured cross strings and a full cast-iron frame won a first-prize medal at the American Institute Fair in New York. This was followed by other impressive awards at the 1867 Paris Exposition and the 1876 Philadelphia Centennial Exposition.

Quality was undoubtedly the key to the House of Steinway's growing reputation, but the firm also benefited from the shrewd promotional savvy of Henry Steinway and his sons. Early in their U.S. history, the Steinways embarked on an aggressive advertising campaign that featured paid endorsements from noted pianists like Hector Berlioz and Gustav Doré. The testimonial ads protected the German immigrant family from unscrupulous competitors who invaded the market with instruments labeled "Steinmay," "Stannay," and "Shumway" in the hope of capitalizing on the success of the Steinway piano. To keep up with the increasing demand for their pianos, the Steinways purchased an entire city block for the construction of a new factory in 1858. Eight years later, they built Steinway Hall, a four-story structure on East Fourteenth Street, which was then one of New York's most fashionable neighborhoods. In addition to housing retail showrooms, the new building had a two-thousand seat concert hall. The expanding piano firm achieved a major milestone in 1872 with the completion on Long Island of Steinway Village, a state-of-the-art plant and employee village that included model homes, a school, a library, and a free bathhouse.

Through the years, the name *Steinway* has remained associated only with quality pianos. Even during the darkest days of the depression, when it was hard-pressed for cash, the company spurned offers totaling $2 million from promoters who wanted to make "Steinway radios" and "Steinway refrigerators." Instead, the proud piano maker preferred to shut down for two years until the economy began to bounce back.

Located on Manhattan's East 14th Street between Union Square and the Academy of Music, this handsome marble structure was built by the Steinway family as a piano showroom in 1863. Four years later, a 9225 sq. ft. concert hall was added to the rear of the building. Known as "Steinway Hall," the 2000-seat auditorium was the site of many of the nation's most celebrated musical events, including Anton Rubinstein's first American concert. The Steinway family closed the hall in 1890, turning it into a warehouse.

Although it was purchased by CBS Inc. in 1972, Steinway is still a family business. John Steinway, a great-grandson of the founder, is currently chairman of the board, and William T. Steinway, a great-great-grandson, heads the research and development department.

C———————————— 1836–1904
APTAIN FREDERICK PABST

Pabst Beer

In the mid-1850s, Phillip Best, the owner of the Empire Brewery in Milwaukee, opened a Chicago sales office and warehouse. A farsighted businessman, Best realized that the day of the strictly local brewery was drawing to a close; and the expansion into Chicago, only ninety miles to the south, seemed like an ideal way to increase the size of his market.

As things turned out, the opening of the out-of-town branch office had a far greater impact on the future of Best's little brewery than even he could have imagined. It was during his frequent travels between his Milwaukee plant and Chicago location that the brewer met Frederick Pabst, a Great Lakes steamship captain who would soon become Best's son-in-law and who would, in the course of the next two decades, mold the Empire Brewery into an industry giant.

Captain Pabst piloted the *Comet,* a passenger steamer that Phillip Best used on his regular Milwaukee-Chicago commutes. When the genial brewer started bringing along his daughter Maria on business trips, the girl's natural beauty caught the appreciative eye of the bachelor captain. Young Pabst courted the brewer's daughter, and Maria, attracted by the dashing manner, neatly trimmed beard, and smart uniform of her suitor, returned his interest. The two were married in 1862 with the blessings of Phillip Best, who later prevailed upon his son-in-law to join the family brewery.

Giving up the seafaring life was not easy for Frederick Pabst, who had virtually grown up on board the ships of the Great Lakes. The son of impoverished German immigrants, Pabst left home early, becoming a cabin boy on the steamer *Sam Ward* and working his way up to the rank of captain before his twenty-first birthday.

Despite his lack of experience or formal training in brewing beer, Pabst showed a genuine talent for the business after joining the brewery in 1864. He put in long hours at the Milwaukee plant to learn the Best family's brewing secrets, and before long he was making suggestions for improving the overall efficiency of the operation.

Phillip Best retired in 1866, and control of the business passed into the hands of Pabst and another of the old brewer's sons-in-law, Emil Schan-

Workers pose in front of the Pabst Milwaukee brewery circa 1900. At the time this photograph was taken, Pabst was vying with its St. Louis rival, Anheuser-Busch, for leadership of the U.S. beer market.

dein. The former sea captain quickly became the dominant member of the partnership, embarking on an ambitious plan to transform the five-thousand-barrel-a-year brewery into a major national beer company.

Pabst's first significant step in achieving this goal was to raise more working capital by turning the family business into a corporation in 1873. As president of the newly formed Best Brewing Co., Pabst persuaded shareholders to sacrifice dividends temporarily so that the brewery's profits could be used to buy better equipment, including an advanced refrigeration unit.

To further improve the quality of his beer, Pabst traveled to Germany and convinced several Old-World brewmasters to return with him to America and lend their skills to the Best brewery. He also hired a team of chemists and other scientists to work at the brewing laboratory he had established at his Milwaukee plant. The idea of creating a laboratory to study the effects of different brewing and storage techniques on beer was almost unheard of in the nineteenth century, when virtually every brewer relied on inexact rule-of-thumb methods that were handed down from one generation to the next. By combining the traditional secrets of German brewmasters with a modern, scientific approach toward brewing, Pabst was able to turn out a superior beer that was consistent in color, clarity, and taste.

The superlative quality of the beer produced by the ex-skipper was recognized with gold medals at major fairs in Philadelphia (1876) and

Atlanta (1881). Pabst, however, undoubtedly received the greatest personal satisfaction from an award won at the Columbian Exposition in Chicago, which declared his beer to be "America's best."

Looking for a means of conveying an appropriate image for his "select" beer, Pabst began tying blue silk ribbons around the necks of his bottles in 1882. A few years later, the brewery was going through twenty-five thousand yards of silk a month, and to hold operating costs down Pabst had to stop using real ribbons. The brewer continued to feature a large, illustrated ribbon on his label, however, because by this time the beer had become nationally known as "Pabst Blue Ribbon."

With its quality product, scientific production techniques, and aggressive marketing, the captain's brewery racked up an ever-increasing sales volume. When its output passed the half-million-barrel-a-year milestone in 1889, a grateful group of stockholders voted to rename the firm (which was still officially called the Best Brewing Co.) in Frederick Pabst's honor. The business continued to flourish after the rechristening, and in 1892 Pabst became the first American brewery to achieve an annual output of more than 1 million barrels.

A charismatic individual, Captain Pabst became a prominent figure in Milwaukee's large German community. He and Maria Best Pabst spent a great deal of their leisure time traveling and raising prize-winning Percheron horses and cattle at their Wauwatosa farm in Wisconsin.

Following Pabst's death on New Year's Day 1904, his sons Gustave and Frederick, Jr., were named president and vice-president of the brewing company. Both young men shared their father's managerial ability (they built the brewery into a $12-million-a-year firm), but it was Fred, Jr., who most resembled his famous parent. A likable man, the younger Pabst shared his father's interest in animal breeding and was honored by the International Livestock Exposition as the "architect of the Holstein-Friesian breed of cattle." Fred Pabst, Jr., even emulated the captain by falling in love with the pretty daughter of a brewer from Milwaukee. He married Ida Uihlein, whose father, August Uihlein, was head of the crosstown rival Schlitz brewery.

1899–1971

THEODOPHOLOUS A. STIFFEL

Stiffel Lamps

As a boy, Theodopholous Stiffel had two favorite pastimes: playing the violin and tinkering with machines. The son of a middle-class shirt manufacturer, young Ted satisfied his mechanical curiosity by taking apart and reassembling the wall and mantel clocks that decorated his family's Memphis, Tennessee, home. His ability to master the workings of even the more elaborate timepieces in the house was a constant source of amazement to his parents and their friends.

When it came time to choose a career, however, the gifted youth decided to pursue his other boyhood interest and become a violinist. He had inherited his love of classical music from his mother, Sarah Rosenthal Stiffel, a former concert pianist from Vicksburg, Mississippi. With his mother's encouragement, Ted Stiffel left Memphis after high school to study the violin in Chicago.

Stiffel wasn't in his new city long before the United States entered World War I in 1917. With his country at war, the teenage violinist put his musical aspirations aside and joined the Marines. Serving as a bombardier in France, Stiffel intended to resume his studies after completing his tour of duty. By the end of the conflict, however, he had lost his desire to become a concert performer, and following his honorable discharge, he took a job at the Western Electric Company's Chicago office.

The young veteran's inquisitive temperament was not well suited to the confining routine of a desk job, and Stiffel soon began to seek more challenging career opportunities. His search eventually took him to the Nellie Kaplan Co., a Chicago manufacturer of residential lamps. At the lighting firm, Stiffel got the chance to apply his mechanical talents by designing new lamps and electrical components.

After several years with the Kaplan company, the thirty-three-year-old lamp maker decided to strike out on his own in 1932. Stiffel used his modest military pension of less than $1,000 as start-up capital to establish the T. A. Stiffel Company in a small commercial basement on Chicago's near North Side. Working without the help of any employees during his first year in business, he concentrated on making simply designed functional floor lamps aimed at the moderately priced segment of the market.

In 1933 the new company's fortunes took a decided turn upward after it received a large floor lamp order from the May Co. department store in Cleveland. This was soon followed by other big orders from several Chicago-area utility companies, which, at the time, sold lamps door to door to their residential customers to increase electricity consumption during off-peak hours.

As the demand for his products grew, Stiffel was able to move his company to a 60,000-square-foot factory at 615 North Aberdeen Street in the early 1940s. By the end of World War II, the firm had built up a profitable business, selling 90 percent of its lamps through the nationwide chain of Montgomery Ward stores. (Sales to utility companies accounted for most of the remaining volume.)

The T. A. Stiffel Co. might have remained a successful but obscure manufacturer of medium-priced lamps had not its founder decided to make a dramatic change in the firm's direction in 1947. Believing that a market existed for a premium-priced lamp of superior construction and aesthetic design, Stiffel embarked on a program to create a product that would be "not only a source of light but an object of taste and elegance."

To achieve this ambitious goal, the Chicago lamp maker engaged the services of Edwin Cole, a noted furniture designer. Late in 1947, Stiffel and Cole unveiled a collection of thirteen artfully fashioned table lamps, ranging from traditional late Georgian styles to free-form modern pieces. The collection featured lamps made of some of the finest crystal, cast metals, and porcelain available, including Rosenthal china. With price tags as high as $300, the lamps were intended for the upper echelon of the home decorating market. (By contrast, the most expensive lamp made by Stiffel prior to this point sold for $75.)

Introduced as the Stiffel Collection, the prestigious lighting products were promoted with appropriately understated advertisements in upscale publications like the *New Yorker* and *Town and Country*. The magazine ads succeeded in conveying a quietly sophisticated image for the Stiffel line by showing photographs of the lamps in elegant room settings, with only a minimal amount of copy.

Encountering virtually no competition at the upper end of the home lighting market, the Stiffel Collection quickly became a commercial success. By early 1949, the lamps were being sold in major department stores across the country, including Wanamakers in Philadelphia, B. Altman in New York, and J. L. Hudson in Detroit. Marshall Field, the premier store in the lamp maker's own city, even went so far as to create an entire "Stiffel room."

A decade after the introduction of its Stiffel Collection, the company was selling an estimated 100,000 lamps a year. To meet its ever-increasing production needs, the firm moved to a 120,000-square-foot factory and tripled its number of employees in the 1950s. Among the new employees to join the company was Ted's son, Jules Stiffel, who began working in the customer service department after returning home from the navy in 1957.

Ted Stiffel sold his company to Beatrice Foods in 1965, but continued to serve as president of the firm until his death seven years later. Although the former music student attended concerts throughout his life, he never resumed his active interest in playing the violin, apparently finding that lamp making offered a more harmonious outlet for his particular blend of artistic and mechanical talents.

Better Mousetrap Builders

KING CAMP GILLETTE

Gillette Razors

Tall, broad-shouldered, aristocratically handsome, and the possessor of an oversized ego, King Gillette was convinced that future generations would remember him as the man who brought the world a new social order—not a closer shave. In 1894 the successful thirty-nine-year-old bottle cap sales-man from Boston published a rambling, discordant blueprint for social re-form entitled *The Human Drift*. Immodestly dedicated to "All Mankind," the book proposed that the entire world be run as a single corporation with everyone an equal shareholder. Under the Gillette plan, all citizens would be required to spend five years working for the common good before being free to devote their remaining days to the pursuit of cultural and artistic enrichment. The North American center of this utopia was to be a mega-lopolis of glass-domed, circular apartment towers located near Niagara Falls, where ample water power would be available to generate electricity for the roughly 60 million residents of the city.

Gillette was sorely disappointed when the masses did not rise up to embrace his new social order. *The Human Drift* was a critical and commer-cial failure; but the world had yet to hear the last of its author. Less than a year after publishing his manifesto, the frustrated social architect was busy pursuing the far less ambitious goal of building a workable model of the shaving razor he had just invented.

Few of King Gillette's contemporaries would have disputed the claim that vast improvements were needed in shaving technology. The traditional straightedge razor that was universally in use at the time was an extremely inconvenient device, primarily because it had to be sharpened before each shave. This was accomplished by stroking the blade against a heavy leather strap for five or ten minutes, a process known as stropping. Unlike the straightedge, which was one integral unit, the razor that Gillette envisioned would consist of two parts—a double-edged blade made of paper-thin sheet metal and a sturdy handle to hold the blade. The waferlike blade would be so inexpensive to make, reasoned its inventor, that when one became dull the shaver could simply throw it away and replace it with another instead of having to go through the trouble of stropping.

Dissect My Razor

The "GILLETTE"

Observe its convenience—its perfection in every detail. Figure out how much time and money you can save by adopting the "Gillette" habit.

You will then know why over two million men are proclaiming the superiority of the "Gillette."

BECAUSE it gives you a clean, comfortable, safe shave in three to five minutes—no matter how inexperienced you are.

BECAUSE the harshest beard, though on the tenderest skin, willingly yields to the soft, easy action of the keen "Gillette" blade.

No Stropping, No Honing.

BECAUSE the holder lasts a lifetime.

BECAUSE its blades are so inexpensive that when dull you throw them away as you would an old pen.

King C. Gillette

The Gillette Safety Razor Set consists of a triple silver-plated holder, 12 double-edged flexible blades—24 keen edges, packed in a velvet lined leather case, and the price is $5.00.

Combination Sets from $6.50 to $50.00

Ask your dealer for the "Gillette" to-day. If substitutes are offered, refuse them, and write us at once for our booklet and free trial offer.

GILLETTE SALES COMPANY

206 Times Building   206 Kimball Building   206 Stock Exchange Building
New York   Boston   Chicago

Gillette Safety Razor

NO STROPPING NO HONING

King C. Gillette served as a spokesman for his namesake product in this 1908 advertisement, which promised to free men from the time-consuming task of stropping and honing straight-edge razors. Two years after this ad ran, Gillette withdrew from the management of his company under pressure from its principal investor and moved to California, where he rediscovered his earlier interest in Utopian philosophy and wrote a book (his second) with the help of Upton Sinclair.

Throughout the last half of the 1890s, the visionary bottle cap salesman devoted almost all his free time to perfecting models of his new razor. Finally, in the fall of 1901, Gillette was ready to begin manufacturing his invention. Backed by a handful of investors, he started the American Safety Razor Company in a small loft over a fish store at 424 Atlantic Avenue in Boston.

Public response to the Gillette razor was encouraging, but the company had difficulty turning out its product in sufficient volume, because it lacked the capital needed to buy mass-production equipment. This problem was soon solved, however, when a millionaire Boston brewer named John Joyce agreed to back the company with $60,000 in return for a controlling interest in the business. The influx of much-needed capital, coupled with the shrewd brewery owner's marketing and management wisdom, proved to be a boon to the young razor company's fortunes. By 1904 (two years after Joyce's arrival on the scene), the company had moved to a larger, more efficient production shop and had run its first national magazine ad. In December of that year, it sold nearly twenty thousand $5 razor sets, which consisted of the handle and twenty disposable blades.

Despite the growing success of the company, a bitter personal rift developed between its founder and its principal stockholder. The daring, egotistical Gillette and the cautious, methodical Joyce were constantly at odds over everything from the hiring of new employees to the opening of branch plants. Not surprisingly, the professional disagreements eventually spilled over into the personal realm, with each man regarding the other as dishonest and arrogant. The antagonists finally decided to put an end to their bickering in 1910 by agreeing to have Joyce buy out most of Gillette's interest in the company for close to $1 million.

Following the stock sale, Gillette moved to California, where he purchased an orange farm and resumed his activities as a political philosopher. Fame and fortune had not wrought any ideological changes in the author of *The Human Drift*. He still hoped to build a utopia; only now he proposed to relocate the entire world population (then estimated at 1.5 billion) into Texas, rather than Niagara Falls, to create a harmonious—albeit crowded—Garden of Eden.

Years after he moved to the West, Gillette wrote another book that elaborately detailed his plans for restructuring society. To ensure that this work would be more readable than his earlier effort, he paid an unannounced visit to the home of Upton Sinclair to seek help in editing his manuscript. Although the muckraking novelist agreed to help, he later had cause to regret his decision, recalling in his autobiography: "Mr. Gillette was coming over two mornings a week to tell me his ideas—the same ideas over and over again." In 1924 the book was published as *The People's Corporation*. Yet, even with the assistance of Sinclair, it was still too ponderous to gain any widespread acceptance.

Undaunted by his literary reversals, King Gillette continued to pursue his utopian dreams until his death on July 9, 1932. Despite the success of his namesake Gillette razor, he remained disappointed over not being granted what he regarded as his rightful place in history as one of the world's great thinkers.

J—— 1804–1886
JOHN DEERE

John Deere Farm Equipment

Anyone who has ever been to farm country knows the name John Deere. Tractors and other implements bearing the company's famous running-deer logo are as familiar a sight down on the farm as towheaded youngsters and whitewashed picket fences.

The man behind this all-American enterprise was a rugged blacksmith from the town of Middlebury, Vermont. Born to an English father and

American mother, John Deere was educated in Middlebury's common schools before being apprenticed to a local blacksmith at the age of seventeen. Four years later, the young New Englander had become skilled enough with a hammer and anvil to set out on his own as a journeyman blacksmith, traveling from village to village in rural Vermont.

Deere built up an excellent reputation among the state's farmers over the next decade as a result of his quality craftsmanship and his highly polished hayforks and shovels. The friendly, broad-shouldered blacksmith might have continued to earn his livelihood turning out implements for Vermont farmers had not a depressed state economy cut into his market in the mid-1830s. Anxious over local economic conditions, Deere traveled west in 1836, joining a group of fellow Vermonters who had established a small settlement in Grand Detour, Illinois.

Within two days of his arrival in Grand Detour, the thirty-two-year-old pioneer had built a forge and was busy shoeing horses and repairing equipment for local farmers. As the village blacksmith, John Deere soon became aware of a problem his new neighbors were having tilling the heavy midwestern soil with their wood-and-iron "eastern plows." Unlike the sandy soil of New England, which fell away cleanly from a plow, the rich, black soil of the Illinois prairie would stick to the plow's bottom. This made it necessary for a farmer to stop every few yards and scrape off the soil, almost doubling the time required to plow a field. The situation had so frustrated some of the settlers that they were talking of packing up and heading farther west in search of more manageable land.

The plight of his fellow settlers prompted Deere to see if he could fashion a better plow. After studying the problem, he determined that two changes would be needed in the design of the eastern plow to make it more suited to the sticky Illinois soil. First, the plow's bottom would have to be given a curved shape, and then, instead of iron, highly polished steel would have to be used in the construction of the plow blade.

Working with a discarded sawmill blade and other materials, Deere built a prototype of his invention and took it to the farm of a neighbor, Lewis Crandall, for a test run. As a crowd of Grand Detour farmers looked on with interest, the new plow cut a clean furrow slice in Crandall's field without collecting sticky soil on its bottom. Furthermore, not only did the local blacksmith's implement remain "clean," it also turned soil at a faster speed than other plows because of its lighter draft.

Deere and a partner, Leonard Andrus, began to manufacture self-scouring plows out of his Grand Detour blacksmith shop in 1837. The plow's labor-saving features made it extremely popular with farmers, who bought all that the partners could produce. Early plow sales were limited only by the difficulty in obtaining sheet steel, which was either taken from saw blades or imported—at considerable expense from England. Then in

Vermonter John Deere had the powerful shoulders commonly associated with his blacksmithing trade. He also possessed a resourceful mind, which he put to use to design a self-scouring steel plow in 1837, after he moved to Grand Detour, Illinois. Deere's invention represented a significant improvement over the older cast iron plows and helped to make widespread cultivation of the rich midwestern soil possible. By the time the 1840s drew to a close, the former village blacksmith was producing some 1600 plows a year.

1846 Deere signed a contract with the Jones & Quigg steelworks of Pittsburgh to roll a supply of steel to his specifications. This marked the first time that the product that has since become known as plow steel was ever made in the United States.

By 1847 it had become apparent to Deere that Grand Detour's limited transportation facilities and power supply could no longer meet the needs of his growing plow-making operation. The former blacksmith relocated his business to Moline, Illinois, where the Mississippi River provided an accessible means of transporting plows to distant markets as well as an abundant source of water power. In Moline, the business flourished; sales rose from 1,000 plows in 1846 to 1,600 in 1850 and 10,000 in 1857.

Throughout this time, John Deere continued to make improvements in the construction of his plow. The blacksmith refined his plow design no fewer than ten times during one twelve-month period. Each technological advance brought Deere more notoriety and more plow orders, helping to make him an early leader of the agricultural implement industry.

Just as important to the growth of Deere's business as his mechanical genius was his ability to develop an effective marketing strategy. During the early years of his business, Deere would simply load up a wagon with plows and ride from one farm to the next until all were sold. Later, this method was replaced by a more sophisticated plan that called for selling plows through a network of local dealers.

One of the more unusual methods of procuring dealers was tried by a Deere representative in Iowa, who dropped in on a session of the state legislature and asked each lawmaker for the names of the leading merchants among his constituents. The merchants were then contacted by the representative to see if they were interested in becoming John Deere dealers. Those who agreed were given a selection of plows to sell on commission. Leaving valuable plows with distant dealers involved considerable financial risk in the days before credit agencies, and John Deere tried to protect himself by keeping a book on different merchants in which each one was rated as either "honest" or "appears to be honest."

Even dealers of the highest integrity often had to pay Deere in hams, skins, wood, and other bartered goods, because cold cash was sometimes scarce in nineteenth-century rural America. Deere stored this merchandise in a warehouse near his factory and made periodic trips to St. Louis to sell the goods or trade them for raw materials needed in the plow-making operation.

In 1858 Deere's son, Charles Deere, joined the company, followed five years later by a son-in-law, Stephen H. Velie. The business was incorporated as Deere & Company in 1868, and it gradually diversified into the manufacture of other farm implements. John Deere was still the active head of the company in 1874 when it achieved another milestone by introducing the Gilpin sulky, the first practical plow that a farmer could actually get on and ride. Using the two-wheeled sulky, a skilled farmer could plow three acres in twelve hours, not a very efficient output compared to the modern John Deere eleven-bottom plow that can turn ten acres per hour.

E———— 1811–1861
ELISHA G. OTIS

Otis Elevators

Few people were willing to risk riding in an elevator back in the mid-nineteenth century, when a break in the lifting cable would send the machine plummeting to the bottom of the shaft. This safety hazard made the elevator virtually worthless as a passenger carrier and relegated it to factories and warehouses, where it was used to hoist freight and machinery.

It wasn't until Elisha Otis, an inveterate tinkerer from Yonkers, New York, invented the world's first "safety hoist" in 1852 that people had a reliable means of vertical transportation. The master mechanic at the Yonkers Bedstead Company, Otis was responsible for supervising the firm's relocation into a new factory on the east bank of the Hudson River. One of the forty-one-year-old mechanic's duties was to move the company's heavy woodworking equipment into the building's second-floor production area, a task he accomplished by constructing a platform hoist.

Unlike other elevators of its day, the hoist designed by Otis included a unique feature that prevented it from falling in the event of a cable break. A model of engineering simplicity, the safety device consisted of a used wagon spring that was attached to both the top of the hoist platform and the overhead lifting cable. Under ordinary circumstances, the spring was kept in place by the pull of the platform's weight on the lifting cable. If the cable broke, however, this pressure was suddenly released, causing the big spring to snap open in a jawlike motion. When this occurred, both ends of the spring would engage the saw-toothed ratchet-bar beams that Otis had installed on either side of the elevator shaft, thereby bringing the falling hoist platform to a complete stop.

Although his elevator would one day play a major role in ushering in the era of the modern skyscraper, Elisha Otis was apparently unaware of the vast opportunities presented by his invention. After his work at the new bedstead factory was finished, the burly six-foot mechanic planned to go to California, where he hoped to strike it rich as a gold miner.

Shortly before he was to leave New York, the aspiring prospector was contacted by Benjamin Newhouse, a minor partner in the bedstead company and the owner of a Manhattan furniture business. A serious elevator accident, caused by a broken lift cable, had occurred recently at the Newhouse plant. Not wanting a repeat of the tragedy, the furniture maker asked Otis to postpone his trip west and build two safety hoists at the Hudson Street factory. The mechanic consented, and while he was working at the furniture plant he received a request for another of his hoists from the owner of a neighboring picture frame company.

Encouraged by this unsolicited interest in his invention, Otis abandoned the idea of prospecting and formed the E. G. Otis Company on September 20, 1853, to manufacture elevators. As things turned out, the early flurry of orders proved to be the exception rather than the rule. Most building owners refused to believe that the new elevator was any less hazardous than the unreliable lifting devices already on the market. Otis sold a small number of machines to factories as freight hoists, but there wasn't a single landlord in New York, or any other city, willing to risk installing the device as a passenger elevator in an office building, hotel, or apartment.

After six frustrating months in business, Otis became convinced that the future success of his company depended on overcoming the resistance of landlords and gaining acceptance for the elevator as a safe, dependable means of transporting people to the upper floors of buildings. To do this, the inventor gave a dramatic demonstration of the effectiveness of his safety hoist at the American Institute Fair then going on at New York's Crystal Palace.

A dapper Elisha Otis acknowledges the cheers of spectators after he dramatically proved the effectiveness of his new "safety hoist" at the 1854 American Institute Fair in New York. Few people believed that the overhead safety spring designed by Otis could really prevent a runaway elevator from crashing to the ground in the event of a broken cable, so the frustrated inventor decided to stage his spectacular demonstration. Riding an open hoist far above the Crystal Palace pavilion, Otis had an assistant cut the elevator's cable. Moments later, as a large crowd looked on in disbelief, the safety device brought the machine to an uneventful halt. Despite the publicity created by the stunt, it would be another decade before the Otis elevator finally gained acceptance among building owners.

Installing a large model of his elevator in the main exhibition hall, Otis climbed on board the open hoist platform and had himself lifted far above the crowd. Then, as thousands of people looked on with mild curiosity, he gave the signal for the lift cable to be cut. The big crowd reportedly let out a horrified gasp as man and machine began their harrowing descent, before being brought to a quick and uneventful stop by the activated safety spring. With the audience below shouting its appreciation, the frock-coated inventor removed his top hat and made a deft bow, proclaiming, "All safe, gentlemen, all safe."

Otis repeated the demonstration several times during the course of the exposition, earning reams of free publicity for his invention. Yet, despite this notoriety, the expected flood of orders never materialized. He sold only fifteen elevators in 1855 and twenty-seven the following year, all of them freight hoists for factories and warehouses. It wasn't until 1857 that Otis finally sold his first (and the world's first) passenger elevator, an enclosed platform hoist installed at the five-story E. V. Haughwout fine china store at Broadway and Broome street in Manhattan. (That elevator was still in use at the Haughwout building in 1984.)

Elevator sales continued to grow at a glacial pace over the next four years, and when Elisha Otis died of diphtheria in 1861, his company was still an undistinguished middle-sized enterprise, with a plant valued at only $5,000 and fewer than a dozen employees. Following his death, control of the firm passed into the hands of his young sons, twenty-five-year-old Charles and twenty-one-year-old Norton. It was under the brothers' leadership that the Yonkers company became famous as the world's largest elevator manufacturer.

Charles and Norton Otis inherited their father's inventive genius, receiving patents on a total of fifty-three improvements in elevator design during their long careers. Among their many technical innovations were the development of elevator brakes (1864) and the first practical electrical elevator, which was installed in 1869 at the Demarest Building in New York. The brothers also installed several historic elevators, including ones at the Washington Monument (1888) and the Eiffel Tower (1899).

One of the most significant contributions to the growth of the Otis company was not made by the two brothers, however, but by a Chicago architect named William LeBaron Jenney. In 1885 Jenney revolutionized construction technology by perfecting a method that made it possible to support a building's weight on an iron frame. The new load-bearing technique allowed architects to design structures of a height that went far beyond the ten-to-twelve-story limit of all-brick buildings. By the turn of the century, the iron-frame method had been employed to erect towering edifices of twenty stories and more, creating a tremendous demand for foolproof elevators and sending Otis sales soaring along with city skylines.

Personal Problem Solvers

C ANDIDO JACUZZI

Jacuzzi Spas

Although it has become one of the most conspicuous symbols of the laid-back California life-style, the Jacuzzi spa had surprisingly unglamorous beginnings. The famous whirlpool was developed in the early 1950s by a Berkeley, California, father who wanted to provide a measure of relief for his arthritic son.

Ever since childhood, Kenny Jacuzzi suffered from rheumatoid arthritis. To ease his pain, the boy's parents took him for hydrotherapy treatments at a Bay-area hospital, where the gently swirling tepid water of the institution's whirlpool bath worked wonders on his afflicted muscles and joints. One day Kenny's father, Candido Jacuzzi, noticed that the jets used to propel water in the medical tub worked on a principle very similar to the large industrial water pumps made by his own company. Hoping to find a means of giving his son hydrotherapy treatments at home, Jacuzzi ordered his engineers to design a small pump that could effectively circulate water through an ordinary bathtub.

The result of this undertaking was the world's first Jacuzzi, a portable aerating jet pump that, when placed in a filled tub, would set the water pulsating in a circular motion. Although it bore little resemblance to today's sleek Jacuzzi spas with their designer shapes and colors, the strictly functional device was ideal for Kenny Jacuzzi, who was now able to receive frequent therapy in the comfort of his own home. Several years later, when the pump was made available to the general public, it would be aptly billed as the whirlpool that "grew out of a father's love."

The company that developed the revolutionary home hydrotherapy unit was no stranger to the bonds of familial devotion. Dating back to 1915, it was founded by Candido Jacuzzi's six older brothers, who immigrated to California from their native village of Casarsa de Delicia, Italy. Starting out as manufacturers of wooden aircraft propellers, the Jacuzzis received a lucrative government contract during World War I, enabling them to send for the rest of their large family in Italy, which included their parents, six sisters, and youngest brother Candido. After the war, the brothers moved into the area of aircraft design, developing the first closed-cabin monoplane;

but when twenty-six-year-old Giocondo Jacuzzi was killed in the crash of a test plane in 1921, his family was so grief-stricken that they got out of the aviation business altogether.

For the next several years, the Jacuzzis tried manufacturing a number of products, eventually achieving success with a water-injection pump invented in 1926 by the oldest brother, Rachele, which found ready acceptance among drilling companies. From there, the family concern branched into pumps, filters, and water systems for a variety of industrial uses. As California became more populous and affluent following World War II, Jacuzzi Brothers, Inc., foresaw the demand for swimming pool equipment and added a line of pumps and filters for residential and institutional pools. Thus, when Candido Jucuzzi needed a hydrotherapy whirlpool pump for his ailing son, it was only natural that he turn to the research and development department at his own company.

After seeing the medical benefits that the water-propelling unit provided to Kenny, the Jacuzzi family became convinced that the pump would find favor among other arthritis sufferers, and they began manufacturing it at their Berkeley plant. Far from being promoted as the glamorous leisure product it is today, however, the first Jacuzzi whirlpools were marketed as therapeutic aids for sufferers of bursitis, rheumatism, and other chronic muscle and joint disorders. Sold primarily on a doctor's recommendation, the units were available only at medical supply stores.

It wasn't long, however, before the portable Jacuzzi pump began to catch on with athletes and other healthy individuals who simply enjoyed the soothing effects of a leisurely soak in a tub of hot, swirling water. Realizing for the first time that the market for their unit could be extended beyond medical patients, the Jacuzzi family hired Ray Schwartz, a former Oakland sportswriter, to act as publicist for the whirlpool in the mid-1950s. To convey the idea that the muscle-relaxing device could be used by the beauteous and the healthy, Schwartz commissioned Jayne Mansfield and Randolph Scott to endorse the product. A major publicity coup was scored when Schwartz managed to get the whirlpool offered as a prize on television's lachrymose "Queen for a Day," providing exposure to millions of late-afternoon viewers. Consumer interest was further sparked by the 1966 Jack Lemmon/Walter Matthau comedy *The Fortune Cookie*, which featured a Jacuzzi unit.

Another big step toward reaching the home leisure market was taken in 1968, when third-generation Roy Jacuzzi (his grandfather, Joseph, was one of the original seven brothers) designed the first self-contained Jacuzzi whirlpool bath, which incorporated all the water-propelling pumps and jets into one integral tub unit. With the electronic gadgetry completely concealed inside the walls of the tub, the Jacuzzi spa could now be an aesthetically pleasing addition to a room's decor.

The whirlpool did not reach its full sales potential until the Me Generation dawned in the mid-1970s, however, turning sneakers into running shoes, sweatsuits into jogging apparel, and hot tubs into the near-generic Jacuzzi. With its connotations of fitness and physical well-being, the Jacuzzi whirlpool spa was suddenly a very trendy item. *The Sensuous Woman* recommended it to readers as a "heavenly" means of self-gratification. Even Richard Nixon availed himself of its tension-easing benefits, installing one in his bathroom in the Executive Mansion at the onset of Watergate. His successor, Gerald Ford, liked it so much that he added Jacuzzi inlets to the shallow end of the White House pool.

As for the boy whose arthritic condition led to the development of the home whirlpool, Kenny Jacuzzi grew up sound enough of limb to head the family firm's European division in Italy. His father Candido served as president of Jacuzzi Brothers, Inc., until 1969, when he resigned his position and left the country after being indicted by a federal grand jury in San Francisco on five counts of income tax evasion. The business harmony of the onetime closely knit Jacuzzi clan, however, was strained long before Candido's tax troubles surfaced. Through the years, as the number of descendents of the thirteen original siblings multiplied, disagreements and power struggles began to erupt. "When there was just us brothers, we'd put a bottle of wine on the table and solve our problems," Candido remarked in a 1975 interview. "Today there are too many of us to do that." The company is no longer owned by the Jacuzzi family, having been sold in 1979 to Kidde, Inc., for $70 million.

D__ 1898–1974
DAN GERBER

Gerber Baby Food

When it comes to feeding baby, mother knows best. At least that was what Dan Gerber discovered one Sunday evening in the summer of 1927. Dressed and ready to leave for a social engagement, the Fremont, Michigan, businessman grew fidgety waiting for his wife to finish straining vegetables for seven-month-old daughter Sally's dinner. His impatience increasing by the minute, Dan walked into the kitchen to hurry his pretty spouse along. That was when Dorothy Gerber decided to teach her husband of four years a lesson in the messy job of straining baby food. "To press the point," Mrs. Gerber later recalled, "I dumped a whole container of peas into a strainer and bowl, placed them in Dan's lap and asked him to see how he'd like to do that three times a day, seven days a week."

Dan soon saw his wife's point. The tedious experience of straining peas left him convinced that there had to be a better way to prepare food for a baby. When he arrived for work the next morning at the small but successful cannery he and his father, Frank Gerber (1873–1952), owned, Dan decided to look into the feasibility of making strained baby food commercially.

At the time, most infants were kept on liquid diets their entire first year, even though leading women's magazines advocated serving strained foods to babies. The mother who wanted to feed her child strained food had only two options: she could go through the time-consuming process of preparing it herself or (in some parts of the country) she could buy it at a drugstore with a doctor's prescription. However, even when available, "drugstore strained food" cost 35¢ a can, putting it beyond the means of most young families of the 1920s.

Dan's initial canvassing of mothers in Fremont convinced him that Dorothy Gerber was not alone in her dislike of straining baby food. Still,

Magazine ads run by the Gerbers in 1928 offered mothers the chance to get six cans of baby food for a dollar. All they had to do was put the names of their favorite grocers on the coupon at the bottom of the ad and mail it to the Gerber factory along with their orders. Armed with this list of "local" grocery shoppers, Dan and Frank Gerber were able to convince food store owners and wholesalers that a demand existed for their new and unproven product. The Gerber company continued to invest heavily in advertising as the demand for its baby food grew. It became one of the earliest TV advertisers in the 1950s, sponsoring such kiddie classics as "Captain Kangaroo."

A Gerber salesman with one of the little Austin cars that the company used to promote its baby food in the eastern U.S. during the early 1930s. The car's horn played "Rock-a-Bye-Baby," and the famous "Gerber Baby" looked out at motorists from the rear windows. Years later, when Gerber purchased its first corporate airplane, the company christened the craft "Sky Baby" and had a likeness of the Gerber Baby painted on the fuselage.

more tangible proof of a widepsread demand for canned baby food was needed before the money could be invested in the necessary straining equipment, so Dan commissioned a market survey. The results were very encouraging, indicating that the typical American mother would buy baby food if it cost 15¢ a can instead of 35¢ and were sold in grocery stores instead of the less convenient pharmacies.

While the market researchers were gauging consumers' attitudes toward the proposed product, Dan and Frank Gerber were busy testing different recipes for strained baby food. Father and son worked long hours in a special section of the cannery to prepare a variety of strained fruits and vegetables. Unbiased appraisals of their efforts were obtained by serving the dishes to Sally and other Fremont babies. If the infants gurgled appreciatively, the food was considered a candidate for commercial production.

By the end of 1928, the Gerbers were ready to market a line of strained baby foods that included vegetable soup, carrots, peas, prunes, and spinach. In November, Dan Gerber ran an ad in *Good Housekeeping*, offering readers a chance to buy six 4.5-ounce cans of baby food for a dollar through the mail. To take advantage of the offer, readers were required to send in the name and address of their regular grocery store.

Armed with long lists of "local" baby food customers obtained from this and subsequent advertisements, the Gerbers were able to persuade food wholesalers located in cities throughout the country to take a chance on the new, unproven product. Within three months of the original *Good Housekeeping* ad, Gerber Strained Foods had achieved national distribution. By the end of its first year on the market, 590,000 cans of baby food had been sold, a figure that exceeded even Dan Gerber's most optimistic expectations.

Predictably, the Gerbers' early success encouraged an influx of competitors, most of them large food companies that added baby food as a sideline. There were more than sixty manufacturers of baby food by 1935, and yet Gerber remained the undisputed leader. One reason for this, Dan Gerber always maintained, was that the small Michigan company became known as a "baby expert." Gerber published a series of booklets on child rearing and mealtime psychology in the early 1930s, and thousands of questions from mothers around the country arrived at the company's offices. Many of these questions were answered by Dorothy Gerber, who also wrote a newspaper column, "Bringing up Baby."

Another key factor in the success of the company was Dan and Frank Gerber's ability as promoters. They purchased a fleet of pint-sized Austin cars for their sales force equipped with horns that sounded out the tune "Rock-a-Bye Baby." Years later, the company became the first baby food manufacturer to advertise on television, sponsoring Kate Smith in 1952.

The Gerbers' biggest advertising coup occurred in 1928, when in an effort to find a suitable graphic for their upcoming magazine ads, they invited artists from around the country to submit illustrations of happy, healthy babies. One of the submissions they received was a unfinished charcoal sketch of a baby's head. Dorothy Hope Smith, the artist, enclosed a note offering to complete it if the baby was about the age and size that the company had in mind. The sketch was never completed; Dan and Frank Gerber felt that additional work would only spoil its fresh innocence. They purchased the sketch "as is," and it has been reproduced billions of times since as the "Gerber baby."

Gerber's fortunes were given a big boost by the post–World War II baby boom. In 1941 the company sold 1 million cans of baby food a week. Seven years later, volume had shot up to 2 million cans a day. This made a multimillionaire out of Dan Gerber, who purchased a posh 140-acre estate in Fremont Lake, Michigan. A winner of France's Croix de Guerre during World War I, Dan devoted much of his time in his later years to civic work, serving on the boards of the Nutrition Foundation of New York and the United Negro College Fund. At the time of his death in 1974, the venture inspired by his wife's aversion to straining peas was the world's biggest baby food empire, claiming 60 percent of the U.S. market.

D———— 1825–1903
DR. THOMAS B. WELCH

Welch's Grape Juice

A devout Methodist and ardent prohibitionist, Dr. Thomas B. Welch cringed at the thought that an intoxicant like wine was being used in his church's communion service. Somebody should come up with a nonalcoholic substitute, the dentist often thought, and in 1869 he decided to give it a try. Dr. Welch happened to have an ample supply of grapes on hand. He lived in the town of Vineland, New Jersey (named for its many vineyards) and it was common for him to receive bushels of the fruit as payment for dental services. Experimenting at night in his kitchen, Welch tried to create a grape beverage that would not ferment and become alcoholic. Fermentation, the dentist knew, occurred when the natural sugar in grape juice was converted to alcohol by tiny yeast particles that collected in the fruit. To prevent this, the yeast would have to be destroyed, a feat that Welch accomplished by placing bottles of grape juice in pots of boiling water and allowing the heat to kill the yeast.

With his long white hair and flowing beard, Thomas Welch looks as if he would have been right at home in the 1960s. But the teetotalling New Jersey dentist no doubt would have frowned on the era's drug culture. Adamantly opposed to intoxicating beverages, Welch "invented" grape juice in 1869 because he wished to find a nonalcoholic replacement for the wine used in his church's communion services.

Calling his creation "Dr. Welch's Unfermented Wine," the dentist tried to persuade his fellow Methodists to adopt it as a sacramental beverage. The weight of tradition was solidly against him, however. Wine, the church elders politely informed Welch, was a staple of the communion ceremony and replacing it with anything else would be nothing short of heretical.

The rejection was a disappointment to Welch, who had been temperance-minded since childhood. His father Abraham, a Watertown, New York, merchant, was a hardworking family man who occasionally liked to take a few sips of whiskey from a jug he kept in the cellar. This led to terrible fights with Mrs. Welch, who viewed alcohol as the work of the devil. In all probability, his parents' arguments played a major role in shaping young Tom's belief in the evil nature of alcohol. This conviction was

The Welch Company spent an average of $575,000 a year between 1912 and 1926 to promote its product. A good portion of this money went into magazine ads that touted grape juice as a blood-building elixir and a wholesome, nonalcoholic alternative to wine. This 1914 advertisement strikes a temperance theme, suggesting that the attractive young woman will never kiss a man who drinks anything harder than Welch's grape juice.

further strengthened as he grew more active in the Methodist church. (At nineteen Welch became a minister, but he left the pulpit three years later because the preaching requirements were too taxing for his weak vocal cords.)

Although the prohibitionist dentist was unhappy when the church spurned his beverage, he put the rejection behind him and soon was busy serving the cause of temperance in other ways. He became a self-appointed guardian of Vineland's dry law, seeing to it that anybody who sold intoxicants within the city limits was prosecuted. During 1870–71 he led crusades to the neighboring communities of Millville and Bridgeton, attempting to convert the towns to Vineland's prohibitionist ways. Both cities eventually became dry, although in Bridgeton there were three days of bloody riots before all the saloonkeepers were arrested and their establishments closed down.

For the next twenty years, Dr. Welch's Unfermented Wine remained in the background as a family refreshment, enjoyed by the Welches at home and sold to a few isolated churches for communion purposes. Then in 1892 Thomas Welch's youngest son, Dr. Charles Welch (he too was a dentist), decided to test out his long-held belief that the pleasant-tasting grape drink could be successful as a commercial product. Borrowing $5,000 from his father, forty-year-old Charles set up a juice production facility in a barn behind the family home. With the idea of making his product more appealing to the general public, he changed its name to Welch's Grape Juice. The following year, Charles introduced his rechristened beverage at the Columbian Exposition in Chicago, giving out free samples of Welch's Grape Juice to millions of fairgoers. As a result of this national exposure, demand for the drink grew to the point where Charles was able to give up his dental practice and devote full time to juice making.

Following his success at the Chicago fair, the former dentist launched a massive advertising campaign in national magazines such as the *Epicure, Carter's Monthly,* and *McClure's.* To attract the attention of readers, the manufacturer inserted word puzzles and contests in his ads, once offering $10 to the individual who could form the largest number of words from the phrase "Welch's Grape Juice." (The winner came up with 1,366 words.) Not one to overlook any market for his product, Charles also promoted the juice as a temperance beverage and healing tonic. A famous company ad featured a comely maiden with a glass of grape juice and the caption, "The lips that touch Welch's are all that touch mine." As a medical aid, Welch's was touted as an elixir for "typhoid fever, pneumonia, pluritus . . . and all forms of chronic disease except diabetes melitus."

By 1897 Welch's Grape Juice had become a familiar sight at soda fountains alongside root beer and sarsaparilla, and Charles Welch found it necessary to relocate the company to Westfield, New York, to be near a larger source of grapes. Elderly Thomas Welch, who had started it all with his unfermented wine, remained behind in New Jersey, but he continued to be a silent partner in the business until he sold out to Charles shortly before his death in 1903.

The inventor of Welch's Grape Juice did not live to see the realization of his lifelong temperance dream with the passage of the Eighteenth Amendment in 1919. Appropriately, the growing national Prohibition movement provided a tremendous boost to the fortunes of the Welch company by spurring the demand for grape juice as a social beverage in place of wine.

Budget Stretchers

Wurlitzer jukeboxes, like the "Model 1050" pictured here, became a symbol of the 1930s and 1940s swing era. Ironically, the man who lent his name to the famous music-making machine died long before the earliest big band struck its first note. A German immigrant, Rudolph Wurlitzer began his business in 1856, selling inexpensive musical instruments in the Midwest. From retailing, Wurlitzer branched out into manufacturing, building instruments and later coin-operated pianos and organs, thereby paving the way for the 1934 introduction of his legendary namesake jukebox.

R———— 1831–1914 ————
RUDOLPH WURLITZER

Wurlitzer Instruments

Arriving in America in 1853 with no money, no friends, and only a marginal grasp of English, twenty-two-year-old Rudolph Wurlitzer made himself a promise—a quarter of whatever he earned in his new land would be put aside so that he could one day start a business. The small, brown-haired German wasn't certain what type of business he wanted to own, but his lack of an exact plan did not diminish his determination.

Wurlitzer soon landed a $4-a-week job as a porter at a Cincinnati dry-goods store. Despite his modest earnings, he managed to squirrel away a dollar each week by sleeping in a packing box in the store's warehouse to save on rent. The following year, he found a more rewarding position as a cashier at the Heidelback and Seasongood bank. Although his salary was doubled to $8 a week, the frugal immigrant remained as determined as ever to avoid paying rent, and with the approval of his employer, he slept in a small loft above the bank's office.

His austere life-style enabled Wurlitzer to amass $700 in savings by 1856. The question of what business to invest this money in was answered suddenly one day, after he visited a Cincinnati music store. Browsing through the shop's selection of instruments, he was dismayed by the high prices. When Wurlitzer spoke of this to the store's owner, the man explained that before an instrument reached his shop from Europe (where almost all musical instruments were then made), it had to pass through the hands of a European sale agent, an exporter, an American importer, and a local jobber. It was the excessive number of middlemen that kept prices so high, said the store owner.

By the time he left the music store, Wurlitzer was convinced that there was money to be made by anyone who could eliminate the network of middlemen and import European instruments directly to dealers in the Midwest. He sent his entire savings home to relatives in Saxony with detailed instructions to buy as many clarinets, oboes, bassoons, flutes, English horns, and flageolets as possible. A short time later, the Wurlitzer family—which counted several prominent instrument makers among its ranks—furnished its American relative with every item on his list, and by the end of 1856, Rudolph was ready to launch his business.

Operating out of a small fourth-floor office in downtown Cincinnati's Masonic Building, Wurlitzer wholesaled instruments to music shops throughout the city in his spare time, while still keeping his job at the bank. His handcrafted German instruments sold for well below the prices charged by local jobbers. Before long, his entire stock had been depleted, and he had to order more instruments from his Saxon relatives. By the end of the decade, Wurlitzer was able to leave his bank position to devote his full attention to the music business, which now occupied a new, larger facility at 123 Main Street.

As the demand for his products continued to grow, Wurlitzer reasoned that he could lower the cost of his instruments even further by manufacturing them himself. In 1861 he established a Cincinnati plant and began producing a variety of band and orchestra instruments. The new factory's first big order came from the U.S. government, which requested drums and trumpets for the Union Army during the Civil War.

Following the conflict, Wurlitzer continued to prosper by marketing quality instruments at popular prices. The importer-turned-manufacturer often sold directly to the consumer through company-owned stores and his mail-order catalogs. Many people who had previously considered a musical instrument to be beyond their means were attracted by Wurlitzer's advertised offers of "rock bottom manufacturer's prices," and by 1890 the business that had started as a part-time venture had mushroomed into a national corporation with $200,000 capitalization.

In addition to being a pioneer in the mass marketing of instruments, Rudolph Wurlitzer was a leader in the development of music-making machines. His early catalogs featured items such as a hand-cranked reed organ with pin cylinders that could play six or eight tunes and a crank-operated pipe organ capable of reproducing twenty-seven tunes.

With the advent of electrical power, the instrument maker became interested in automatic music machines. He sold the world's first coin-operated electric organ in 1892, followed in rapid succession by an automatic harp picked by tiny mechanical "fingers" and a pianino—an electrically powered piano with a mandolin attachment. At the turn of the century, he introduced the Wurlitzer Tonophone, an electric piano that played one of ten classical or ragtime pieces when a nickel was deposited in its coin slot.

Upon Rudolph Wurlitzer's retirement as company president in July 1912, he was succeeded by his oldest son, Howard Wurlitzer. Two other sons, Rudolph H. (vice-president) and Farny (treasurer), also were active in the management of the company, and together the Wurlitzer brothers carried on their father's policy of making a wide range of instruments available to consumers at moderate prices. One of the brothers' most significant marketing innovations was the "pay-as-you-play" plan begun in 1914. Promoted in national magazine ads with headlines like "10¢ a Day," the plan offered customers easy installment terms (plus a free one-week trial) on any of the more than two thousand instruments included in the company's catalog.

The Wurlitzer brothers also inherited their father's interest in electrically powered instruments and music-making machines. During the second decade of this century, Farny Wurlitzer (1883–1972) worked with noted organ maker Robert Hope-Jones to develop the legendary "Mighty Wurlitzer." A pipe organ capable of producing a rich orchestral sound, the Mighty Wurlitzer has been manufactured in sizes ranging from the two and three manual consoles that were familiar sights in old movie theaters to massive multikeyboard machines designed for major auditoriums and cathedrals.

It was Farny Wurlitzer who was behind the development of another notable Wurlitzer product. In 1934, when the depression cut deeply into instrument sales, the youngest of Rudolph Wurlitzer's sons revived the company's sagging fortunes by introducing the Wurlitzer Simplex—the first in the firm's famous line of jukeboxes.

GEORGE A. HORMEL

Hormel Foods

In 1931 George A. Hormel submitted a paper to President Herbert Hoover that advocated, among other things, the adoption of an unemployment relief program and the payment of a $100-a-month federal pension to all retired workers over the age of sixty. The implementation of such measures, asserted the millionaire meat packer, would be the surest way of pulling the country out of the depression and getting people back to work.

Herbert Hoover spurned this advice, but the following year he was defeated by Franklin Roosevelt, whose New Deal would include both unemployment relief and a federal pension for retirees. Encouraged by the actions of the new administration, Hormel continued to speak out on economic issues, expressing his views in a 1935 booklet, "The Golden Rule Way to Unemployment Relief."

No armchair reformer, the Austin, Minnesota, businessman put his liberal beliefs into practice at the meat-packing house he founded in 1891. He became an early practitioner of the profit-sharing plan, paying his employees bonuses equal to as much as eight weeks' pay when times were good. In 1931, when conditions were far from good, Hormel's company protected its employees from the seasonal fluctuations of the packing industry by adopting a "straight-time plan" that offered fifty-two equal paychecks throughout the year.

Hormel contributed to the welfare of America's working class in a different sort of way in 1935, when his company began selling 1.5-pound cans of beef stew for only 15¢. The hearty canned food provided an affordable, but filling and nutritious, meal for the unemployed and their families. Following the quick acceptance of its stew, Hormel & Co. introduced other budget-stretching canned products such as corned beef and cabbage, spaghetti and meatballs, and chili con carne, all of which became valued throughout the nation's industrial heartland as "poor man's dishes."

This time, however, George Hormel's motives were not purely altruistic. As board chairman of his namesake firm (his son, Jay, was president), he was interested in developing a line of products that would allow the meat-packing company to expand into the canned food market.

Several years earlier, the company had introduced a full line of soups, but with the exception of onion soup (which was popular in New York, San Francisco, and Los Angeles), the new line was unable to make much headway against its established competitors Campbell and Heinz. Hormel & Co. suffered a similar fate after it introduced America's first successfully produced canned ham in 1927. Although the product sold well enough for a

George Burns, Gracie Allen, and a friend doing a radio spot for Spam. Introduced by Hormel in 1937, the pink blend of chopped ham and pork shoulder was promoted with an ambitious advertising campaign that featured what is often regarded as the first singing radio commercial, a jingle set to the tune of Bring Back My Bonnie to Me. Spam acquired an international following during World War II, when large quantities of it were shipped to our allies, including the Soviet Union, where it was facetiously referred to as "the second front" and "Roosevelt sausage."

time, it was soon overcome by the more aggressively promoted canned hams brought out by corporate giants Armour and Swift.

George and Jay Hormel hoped that their new low-priced line of canned food would be able to establish the strong brand identity needed to discourage an influx of big competitors. To create such an identity, the Hormels invested heavily in an advertising and publicity campaign. They promoted their chili con carne (the first canned chili ever marketed in the United States) by sponsoring the "Hormel Chili Beaners," a twenty-member Mexican song-and-dance troupe that performed at fairs and festivals throughout the Midwest. As a result of its marketing efforts, Hormel & Co. was able to create a recognizable consumer image for its "poor man's dishes," and the company's canned food output reached almost 30 million pounds in 1936, compared to roughly half that amount three years earlier.

Encouraged by the success of its poor man's dishes, Hormel & Co. introduced an economical pork loaf in 1937. The canned meat ran into a major problem before it even got to market, however, when the U.S. government would not allow the company to call it a ham, because it was made from pork shoulder instead of the hindquarters.

In an effort to come up with a substitute name for the humble luncheon meat, Princeton-educated Jay Hormel turned to his country-club circle of friends. The younger Hormel threw a party at his 170-acre Austin estate and asked guests to "pay" for cocktails by suggesting a name for the new product every time they ordered a drink. "Along about the third or fourth drink they began showing some imagination," the executive later recalled. It was Kenneth Daigneau, a visiting New York radio actor who suggested the name that was eventually chosen—Spam.

Like its predecessors, inexpensive Spam found a ready market in depression America. Sales of the proletarian pork dish were greatly aided by an advertising campaign featuring George Burns and Gracie Allen, which urged people to try a "Spamwich" or "Spambled eggs" for an economical lunch.

There is a measure of poetic justice in the fact that George Hormel's namesake company finally found a place for itself in the canned food market by developing a line of products for those on limited budgets. The third of twelve children of German immigrant parents, Hormel knew poverty first-hand. His father's struggling Toledo, Ohio, tanning business failed in 1873, forcing the not-yet-thirteen-year-old boy to take a job to help support the family.

Hormel left Toledo when he was fourteen to go to work at a Chicago meat market. By 1891 he had risen above his childhood poverty and was able to start his own packinghouse in an abandoned creamery on the banks of Austin's Cedar River. Although the business got off to a slow start (only 610 hogs were killed the first year), it grew steadily, as Hormel began to sell his hams and sausages in the big Minneapolis–St. Paul market. Sales at the packinghouse neared the $1 million milestone in 1900, and Hormel had become one of Austin's leading citizens.

When George Hormel died in 1946, he was succeeded as chairman of the board of the $126-million-a-year company by his son, Jay. Every bit his father's son, Jay Hormel took a liberal (for a company head) view of labor-management relations. In a 1936 speech to a Minnesota Rotary Club gathering, he said, "It is my belief that labor troubles would not occur if business could understand labor." Such statements often put Jay Hormel at odds with fellow businessmen, who according to the March 11, 1946, issue of *Life* magazine—labeled the Minnesotan "everything from pale pink to red." On one occasion, the free-spirited Hormel ended up regretting his involvement in an ill-advised cause. An ardent isolationist, he and a group of friends conceived of the America First Committee in the living room of the Hormel home prior to World War II.

GEORGE ROMANTA KINNEY

Kinney Shoes

The manager of the Lester Shoe Company's Waverly, New York, store, George Kinney suddenly found himself unemployed when the Binghamton-based firm went bankrupt in 1894. For twenty-eight-year-old Kinney, a widower with a young son to raise, the loss of his livelihood created a severe hardship. The out-of-work manager was used to coping with adversity, however, because he had been followed by a cloud of bad luck since childhood.

When Kinney was still a boy, his father's Candor, New York, general store failed, causing painful financial difficulties for the family. A few years later, when he was only nine, his father died, leaving a hard-pressed widow and two children nearly destitute. At seventeen Kinney left home to seek better opportunities in the nearby city of Binghamton, where he landed a job as a stock clerk with the Lester company. The tall, intelligent youth rapidly worked his way up to head shipping clerk and then manager of the firm's Waverly retail outlet. By 1888 he was earning enough money to marry his sweetheart Phoebe Wadsworth, and one year later a son was born to the young couple; but tragedy struck in 1890, when Phoebe died giving birth to a daughter (the infant girl also died shortly thereafter), and Kinney was left to raise his son Charles alone.

All of these misfortunes had combined to produce a strong survivor's instinct in George Kinney, and when the young store manager lost his job with the Lester firm, he was able to bounce back quickly. Scraping together $1,500, he bought a portion of his former employer's inventory and opened his own retail shoe store in Waverly. The business started out modestly with only one employee, Milner Kemp, an English cobbler who made shoe repairs and helped out with sales.

Soon after its opening, the shop showed definite signs of becoming a success, thanks mainly to its proprietor's novel concept of marketing shoes for the entire family at discount prices. Few retailers of the day sold footwear for men, women, and children under the same roof, and as one of the first to do so, Kinney was able to attract a greater number of customers to his shop. It was because of this high volume that the store owner could afford to take a smaller mark-up on each pair of shoes, thereby keeping his prices well below those charged by competitors.

Kinney drew attention to his footwear bargains with simple-but-effective outdoor advertising displays. Samples of the shoes, marked with their prices, were posted on wallboards in front of the store to give passers-by an idea of the money-saving deals offered inside. The discount message

George R. Kinney (left) poses in front of his first store in Waverly, New York, with the shop's cobbler, Englishman Milner Kemp. When this photo was taken in 1894, as the store's window display indicates, Kinney had already embarked on a plan to attract customers with low shoe prices. Within the next fifteen years, Kinney would see his number of stores grow to twenty-four, thanks to his discount prices and a pioneering franchise plan.

was reiterated in blunt fashion by an overhead sign: "Our Prices Beat the World."

As a result of its low prices, the Kinney store became popular with budget-minded families in Waverly, and within a year its ambitious owner was able to open a second location in Corning, New York. Sales and profits climbed steadily at both stores, and by 1899 Kinney had eight retail outlets that yielded an annual volume of $140,000.

One year later, the widower's personal life also took a decided turn upward when he married Ella Cook, a secretary at his company. The new Mrs. Kinney remained an active participant in her husband's business, playing a role in the firm's development as a major retail chain and later serving on its board of directors.

With help from his second wife and Edwin Krom, an old boyhood friend turned business partner, Kinney embarked on an ambitious expansion program at the beginning of the century that boosted the number of stores in his chain to twenty-four by 1909 (total sales in that year were

$586,524). To finance the opening of new outlets, the innovative retailer devised a "partnership" plan with his store managers that, in essence, amounted to one of the earliest applications of the modern franchising concept.

Under Kinney's plan, each manager was required to invest a specified sum of money as start-up capital for a new store. In return, the manager-investor became a part owner of his store and shared in its profits. All day-to-day operations, including the hiring and firing of employees, the placement of local newspaper ads, and the arrangement of window displays, were the responsibility of the individual managers. The only task handled by the central office—which in 1913 was moved into the Woolworth Building in Manhattan—was the purchasing of shoes.

Because his company was able to order shoes in large quantities for its many stores, Kinney received generous discounts from his suppliers. This volume buying, coupled with the firm's policy of taking only a bare-bones mark-up on its products, resulted in some of the lowest retail prices in the shoe industry. In 1913 Kinney was offering customers such bargains as women's lace dress shoes for 98¢ and men's welt shoes for $1.98 (low prices even by early twentieth-century standards).

Growth of the discount footwear firm continued to accelerate during the second decade of this century, and by 1917 the G. R. Kinney Co. was operating forty-nine stores in thirteen states throughout the East, Midwest, and South. With its inventory demands increasing rapidly, the company acquired four shoe factories between 1917 and 1920 to begin manufacturing its own products.

The phenomenal expansion of his retail chain made George Kinney a very wealthy man, but ill fortune plagued him for most of his adult life. He was stricken with a circulatory problem in 1907 that caused temporary paralysis in his legs and confined him to bed for six months. Kinney continued to suffer from poor circulation until his premature death in 1919 at the age of fifty-three.

Trend Setters

M—— 1914–
MARCEL BICH

Bic Pens

Even his most bitter business rivals have been forced to acknowledge Marcel Bich's genius for anticipating consumer trends. An early prophet of the "throwaway culture," the astute Frenchman has built a $700 million company since 1953 by catering to the worldwide demand for inexpensive—but reliable—disposable products, first with ball-point pens and then with cigarette lighters and razors.

Born in Turin, Italy, to French parents (his father was a civil engineer), Bich began his career at eighteen selling flashlights door to door in Paris. A few years later he went to work for a large ink manufacturer and eventually was made production manager, before he was called up by the French air force at the outbreak of World War II.

Following the war, Bich and a friend, Edouard Buffard, raised $1,000 and bought a leaky shed in the rundown Paris suburb of Clichy, where they manufactured ink refills for the ball-point pens that were just beginning to appear in France.

At the time, the French pen market was dominated by the traditional "inkwell" models. Ball-point pens (mostly American imports) were regarded as novelties, their popularity limited by their relatively high price tags and unreliable performance. Marcel Bich was very familiar with the ball-point's shortcomings through his ink business, but he became convinced that the new pen could claim a bigger share of the market if its price were brought down and its quality improved.

Working in his small factory-shed, the ink maker began to experiment with different ball-point designs in 1949. Unlike the ball-points then on the market, virtually all of which were refillable, the prototypes that Bich developed were intended to be used only until their ink ran out and then thrown away. The farsighted businessman believed that this disposable feature would increase his pen's appeal to the convenience-oriented consumer of the post–World War II era.

After four years of research and development, Bich finally came up with a pen that met all his requirements. The simple stick-shaped writing instrument was rugged and dependable; and because it consisted only of a thin plastic ink tube, a tiny metal ball-point, and a rigid plastic outer tube, it could be made and sold very inexpensively. Bich christened his new disposable pen by slashing a letter off his name to create the catchy "Bic."

As its inventor had expected, the Bic pen was an immediate hit with the French public. Three years after introducing the pen in 1953, Marcel Bich was selling a quarter of a million disposable ball-points a day in his native land and was beginning to market his product in other European countries. The spectacular success of the unpretentious Bic (it sometimes sold for less than 5¢) startled the entire pen industry, which had traditionally been controlled by high-priced, high-status products.

In December 1958 the stocky, balding pen maker entered the U.S. market by acquiring the Waterman Pen Company. Disposable ball-points were all but unheard of here at the time, but the handy Bic fit comfortably into the American life-style, and within a decade of its introduction the French product was accounting for half of all retail pen sales in the nation. To measure this achievement another way, Bich was selling 330 million ball-points a year, more than one and a half pens for every American.

Encouraged by the success of his pen, Bich test-marketed a disposable cigarette lighter in Sweden in 1972. A year later, he introduced the lighter to America, where it challenged the already established leader, the Cricket Lighter, made by Gillette. The two companies had done battle once before when the surprising Bic ball-point had catapulted past Gillette's line of Papermate pens to become the king of the U.S. retail pen market.

This time, however, Gillette was determined to put up a better fight. Both companies invested heavily in television advertising, Gillette depending on its singing Cricket cartoon character to counter Bic's "Flick My Bic" slogan. They also engaged in some fierce price competition, shaving 60¢ or more off lighters that originally were supposed to retail for $1.49. When the dust finally settled, Bic emerged the winner once again. Its lighter passed Cricket in 1977 and has remained well ahead of the Gillette entry in sales ever since.

History seemed about to repeat itself in 1976, when Bich brought yet another of his throwaways to America—the Bic razor. Gillette responded to this assault on the very product the company had started with by introducing its own disposable razor, Good News. Backed by Gillette's reputation and expertise in shavers, Good News outsold its French competitor from the beginning, relegating Bic to a less than 20 percent share of the U.S. disposable razor market by 1981.

Bich's failure to top Gillette in the razor market was one of the rare setbacks that he has experienced in his success-studded career of more than three decades. The competitive Frenchman (who once was described by *Time* magazine as a "stubborn, opinionated entrepreneur") hasn't been as lucky in his favorite avocation, however. A dedicated yachtsman, Bich has tried and failed on several occasions to win the America's Cup race. In 1970 he spent $3 million and worked fourteen hours a day preparing for the event, only to lose ignominiously when his sloop *France* got lost in the fog off Newport.

Bich's yachting activities have provided the public with its few chances to see the pen millionaire. A very private person, he shuns interviews and forbids photographs in a manner reminiscent of the late Howard Hughes. When not on his yacht, Bich's leisure time is usually spent with his family, which includes his wife and ten children. Outside counsel is very seldom sought or appreciated by the wealthy businessman, who once attributed his impressive success to his refusal to listen to anyone's advice but his own.

C———— 1848–1912 E———— 1846–1931 LARENCE SCOTT DWARD IRVIN SCOTT

Scott Paper Products

With their sharp, prominent features, high foreheads, and neatly cropped beards, Edward Irvin and Clarence Scott were easy to recognize as brothers. The upstate New York siblings were born within three years of each other in rural Saratoga County, and in addition to their striking physical resemblance, they shared a common ambition—to become partners in a successful business.

The Scotts realized this dream in typical Horatio Alger fashion, turning $2,300 in capital (most of it borrowed) into a million-dollar paper products enterprise. In the process, the brothers helped to change the way domestic paper goods would be packaged and marketed during the twentieth century.

It all began in 1879, when the Scotts, who were then living in Philadelphia, started a paper jobbing business at 25 North Sixth Street. Using their $300 savings, plus $2,000 borrowed from Irvin's father-in-law, they purchased a supply of bags, wrapping paper, scratch pads, and other products, which they then peddled through the streets of the city by pushcart. Two years later, Irvin and Clarence were able to replace the pushcart with a horse-drawn wagon. Yet, despite their modest early growth, the brothers realized that they would have to become more efficient and specialize in a single product if they hoped to create a truly profitable business.

Indoor plumbing was becoming more commonplace at the time, and the Scotts capitalized on this trend by concentrating their sales efforts on bathroom tissue. Although the country's first commercially packaged bathroom tissue had been introduced by Joseph Gayetty back in 1857, the product sold only on a very limited scale. The majority of Americans preferred

Women sense it immediately

—that atmosphere of elegance and refinement—those necessary little appointments, noticed but not discussed, which contribute so much to the comfort and well-being of guests and family.

Scot Tissue has made a place for itself in well-conducted homes. It is the choice of discriminating women everywhere, because of its hygienic purity and safety.

A highly-absorbent, snow-white, soothing tissue, marvelously soft as fine old linen. Kind to the most sensitive skin. Peculiarly adapted to the needs of women of intuitive daintiness. Ask your doctor.

No conversation. Just say "ScotTissue" to your storekeeper and receive a big, economical, dustproof roll.

SCOTT PAPER COMPANY, Chester, Pa.

Waldorf
Another Tissue
Fibre Product
5 rolls 25c

ScotTissue
Soft as old Linen
The absorbent and white Toilet paper
SCOTT PAPER COMPANY

15 cents
a roll

Philadelphia brothers Clarence and Irvin Scott became the first toilet tissue manufacturers to advertise their product nationally when they ran a small ad in the Atlantic Monthly *in 1890. Early ads were low-key because the Scotts feared offending the sensibilities of nineteenth-century readers. But the company's advertising grew bolder in the new century with ads like this one, which relied on snob appeal to promote Scott toilet tissue over less expensive competing brands.*

to equip their outdoor privies with old catalogs and newspapers or sheets of scrap paper. However, Irvin and Clarence Scott correctly predicted that the advent of the modern bathroom would create a new market for a superior paper product.

Unlike Gayetty's tissues, which were available only in five-hundred-sheet packages, the Scotts' product was marketed in convenient rolls. Buying large "parent rolls" of tissue paper from distant mills, Irvin and Clarence would cut them to a length and width suitable for a late-nineteenth-century bathroom. At first, the brothers sold bathroom tissue either in a plain brown wrapper or under a particular retailer's private label. (At one time, the Scotts were handling more than two-thousand different "store brands" of tissue.) Then in 1896 Irvin's son, Arthur H. Scott, joined the firm and quickly persuaded his father and uncle to phase out their private-label business and concentrate on marketing their own brands of bathroom issue.

In 1902 the brothers scored their first national success with a company-branded product, when they introduced Waldorf tissue (the oldest continuously marketed toilet paper in the United States). By the end of the decade, the Scotts' six house brands accounted for 80 percent of their $726,264 sales volume. As a result of the growing popularity of its brands, the company was able to move to a larger production facility in a converted soap factory in Chester, Pennsylvania.

With its own line of tissues accounting for an ever-increasing share of sales, the Scott Paper Co. discontinued its private-label business completely in 1913. That same year, Irvin and Arthur Scott (Clarence died in 1912) introduced the distinctively packaged ScotTissue. Unlike most other brands of bathroom tissue, which were only partially wrapped in packaging paper, Scott's new product was completely encased in a protective dust-proof wrapper. Every ScotTissue package bore the slogan "soft as old linen" to convey a quality image for the premium tissue.

Since 1890, when it became the first bathroom tissue company ever to run a national magazine ad (a small piece in the *Atlantic Monthly*), Scott relied on advertising to gain public acceptance for its products. Although its early ads were low-keyed in deference to the public's sensibilities concerning bathroom tissue, the company became much bolder after World War I and attempted to create a "snob appeal" around its ScotTissue brand. An example of one such ad headline: "They have a pretty house, Mother, but their bathroom paper hurts."

It was through their growing tissue business that the Scotts chanced on a second product that would later become a mainstay of the domestic paper industry. One day in 1907, they received an order of parent roll tissue that was too heavy and wrinkled to be converted into bathroom tissue. No one in the company knew what to do with the defective shipment until Arthur Scott suggested perforating the thick tissue so that it could be torn off into hand-towel-sized sheets and sold as paper towels. This was America's first commercially packaged paper towel, according to the Scott company. Initially, Scott called the product Sani-Towels and sold it primarily to hotels, restaurants, and railroad stations for use in public washrooms. In 1931 the name was changed to ScotTowels and the product was marketed to consumers in twenty-five cent rolls of 200 sheets for household use.

Irvin Scott retired from the paper firm in 1921 and was succeeded as president by Arthur Scott. When Arthur died six years later, control of the company passed into the hands of his Swarthmore College fraternity brother, Thomas McCabe. A shrewd businessman, McCabe guided Scott Paper through an impressive period of growth over the next four decades as its chief executive officer. He was still with the firm as a director in 1979 when it celebrated its one hundredth anniversary.

CALVIN KLEIN

Calvin Klein Jeans

When Barry Schwartz's mother took him shopping for clothes back in the early 1950s, she would make it a point to ask her son's best friend to come along. Mrs. Schwartz was not just extending a cordial invitation; she truly valued young Calvin Klein's presence on apparel-buying trips. The slender, sandy-haired boy seemed to have a knack for putting together outfits that looked just right on Barry.

Like Barry, Calvin was the son of a Bronx grocer, and the two boys remained close friends throughout high school, even though their personalities developed in very different directions. Barry grew into a forceful and conventional young man who planned to enter his family's food business. Meanwhile, the artistically inclined Calvin enrolled in Manhattan's Fashion Institute of Technology, hoping one day to turn his flair for fashion into a career as a designer.

Yet, despite the young New Yorker's early show of talent, his career in the fashion industry did not get off to a fast start. Six years after his graduation from FIT, Klein was still an obscure, low-paid "rank-and-rack" designer for a large Seventh Avenue coat manufacturer. With a wife and daughter to support, the aspiring couturier was seriously considering dropping out of the fashion industry and entering into a partnership with his old chum Barry in the Harlem grocery store that Schwartz owned. After some discussion, however, the boyhood friends decided that instead of Calvin joining the grocery business, Barry would enter the fashion field by investing $10,000 capital to start Calvin Klein Ltd.

In 1968, the partners launched their new firm in a Seventh Avenue hotel suite which served as both workshop and office. Barry handled the sales and administrative end of the business, leaving Calvin free to devote his energy to designing and sewing women's coats (the only product then sold by the company). Given the chance to express his own ideas, the twenty-six-year-old designer exhibited an almost uncanny ability to anticipate changes in the fashion market. His first coat collection was characterized by quietly elegant, classical designs that were in sharp contrast to the hippie style of the era. Although his low-keyed outerwear went against the prevailing miniskirt-and-see-through-blouse look, Klein was confident that female flower children would grow tired of psychedelic costumes and seek more traditional clothing once they matured.

As it turned out, the young couturier's confidence was well founded. Within a year after launching his studio, he sold $50,000 worth of trench coats to Bonwit Teller. Mildred Custin, then president of the fashionable

Calvin Klein, the Bronx-born couturier who began his career in 1962 as a $75-a-week apprentice designer for Dan Millstein in New York. Klein and boyhood friend Barry Schwartz used their combined savings of $12,000 to launch Calvin Klein Ltd. in 1968. Within a decade, the partners had built the business into a $100,000,000 fashion empire.

Fifth Avenue store, later recalled that what impressed her most about Klein's coat collection was "the purity of his line and the simplicity of his designs."

With his reputation enhanced by the Bonwit Teller sale, Klein began to receive coat orders from other New York department stores. In 1970 he expanded his collection to include suits, skirts, blouses, and slacks, which, like his outerwear, featured a clean, uncluttered look. The new Calvin Klein sportswear was an immediate commercial success, finding favor among young women who, with their college counterculture days behind them, were taking their places in the job market and wanted clothing that was fashionable, yet easy to wear. Klein's youthful, versatile designs fit comfortably into the active life-style that was emerging in the 1970s, and as the decade progressed, the couturier became a major figure in the fashion world.

Industry experts praised Klein for his efforts in pioneering many of the most notable fashion developments of the era, including the transition from the miniskirt to longer skirt lengths. In 1975 Klein received an unprecedented third consecutive Coty Award (the fashion industry's version of the Oscar). The same year, he became the youngest ready-to-wear designer ever to be inducted into the Coty Hall of Fame.

Klein's prowess as a molder and forecaster of fashion trends was convincingly demonstrated in the mid-1970s when he played a leading role in elevating the lowly blue jean into a haute couture item. Following a suggestion from Bloomingdale's buyer Connie Dowling in 1975 that he try to refashion the familiar denims into a shapelier garment, Klein began working on his own blue jean designs. One year later, he introduced Calvin Klein jeans, which, despite their high price ($50), succeeded beyond all expectations, selling at the rate of 250,000 pairs a week by the end of the decade.

The statusy denims were more than just a success story in their own right, however; they were a driving force behind the wave of interest in designer apparel that swept the country in the late 1970s. For many Americans, Calvin Klein jeans were the first designer garment they had ever owned, and having thus been introduced to couture, they became more name conscious when shopping for clothes. This growing fashion awareness led to several significant changes in the way apparel is merchandised—including the appearance of labels on the outside of garments and the proliferation of designer boutiques in department stores.

America's obsession with designer labels netted a vast fortune for Schwartz and Klein, who earned a reported $8 million profit on their line of ready-to-wear apparel in 1980. This was in addition to the $1 million royalty the partners received every six weeks that year from Puritan Fashions, the firm that was licensed to manufacture Calvin Klein jeans at the time.

Throughout their meteoric rise from their Bronx neighborhood, Barry and Calvin have remained the best of friends, even though their life-styles continue to be worlds apart. The prototype suburban commuter, Barry lives in Westchester with his wife and children and devotes much of his free time to his favorite hobby, stamp collecting. Calvin, who has been divorced since 1974, lives the life of a Manhattan bachelor, frequenting Studio 54 and other discothèques. A trim six-foot-one, he maintains his youthful good looks with regular visits to health clubs and biweekly trips to his dermatologist's office, where he receives silicone injections to smooth out wrinkles.

Mary Kay Ash greets beauty consultants at the company's annual seminar in Dallas. The highlight of the event is "Awards Night," when the skin-care company's top sales performers are called on stage to receive diamond jewelry, fur coats, pink Cadillacs, and other "dream prizes."

Demonstrating a Hoover Senior vacuum cleaner, circa 1920.

W———— 1849–1932
ILLIAM H. HOOVER

Hoover Vacuum Cleaners

Necessity has been called the mother of invention, and such was certainly the case with the Hoover vacuum cleaner. The world's first commercially successful portable vacuum cleaner came into being as a result of an aging tinkerer's attempt to hold on to his janitorial job. James Murray Spangler, a would-be inventor who had fallen on hard times, was reduced to cleaning floors at a Canton, Ohio, department store in 1907. As his "temporary position" dragged on, the luckless janitor was confronted by a new problem; the dust kicked up by his employer's clumsy, inefficient carpet cleaner aggravated a chronic respiratory condition and gave him a debilitating cough. His woes were further compounded by the great bulk and weight of the carpet cleaner, which made it extremely difficult for him to wheel the machine around the large store. If something weren't done to remedy the situation quickly, Spangler would be forced to quit his job, a move that he could ill afford to make in light of his financial situation.

Desperate to save his position, the inventive janitor set to work designing a cleaner, lighter-weight carpet sweeper. He took a discarded soapbox, sealed the cracks with adhesive tape, and put it on a small set of wheels. Then he attached a roller brush and a small fan motor to one end of the box and a broom handle and pillowcase to the other. The fan motor furnished power to rotate the brush, and the pillowcase served as a bag to hold dirt and dust. Spangler was so pleased with his new "electric suction sweeper" that he patented it on June 2, 1908. Soon, the hopeful inventor was making a limited number of sweepers in his small workshop and selling them door to door in the Canton area.

One of the first sales that Spangler made was to his cousin, Susan Hoover, the wife of a prosperous New Berlin (now North Canton), Ohio, saddlemaker. When Susan's husband, William "Boss" Hoover, saw her new sweeper, he was immediately impressed. A former railroad president and the first elected mayor of New Berlin, Hoover had a well-deserved reputation for being an astute businessman. He was keenly aware that the growing shadow of the automobile would soon eclipse the saddle and harness industry, and he was on the lookout for new investment opportunities.

William "Boss" Hoover was every bit the somber, patriarchal business leader portrayed in this photograph. A well-to-do saddlemaker, and a leading citizen of what is now North Canton, Ohio, Hoover did not become involved with his namesake vacuum cleaner until he was in his late fifties.

Although the compact cleaner invented by his wife's cousin was still in its earliest stage of development, Hoover recognized its commercial possibilities. He correctly foresaw that the demand for Spangler's suction sweeper would increase as the machine was perfected and more and more people came to accept electric household appliances.

In August 1908 Hoover solved Spangler's financial problems for good by purchasing the rights to manufacture the suction sweeper. The original Hoover vacuum operation employed three men who worked in a corner of the saddle shop and turned out five or six machines a day. Like many new ventures, the first question the vacuum business faced was how to market its product. The best way to sell vacuum cleaners, decided "Boss," was to develop a strong national network of hardware store owners who would act as Hoover dealers. This was no small order for an unknown company operating in a little Ohio town, but William Hoover achieved this goal almost overnight through the use of a simple, but brilliant, marketing gambit that began with an ad in the December 5, 1908, issue of the *Saturday Evening Post*.

In the two-column advertisement (which cost roughly $207), Hoover offered readers the chance to use an electric suction sweeper for a free ten-day in-home trial. Hundreds of homemakers responded to the ad, and the Ohio saddlemaker sent a letter to each one, informing her that the trial sweeper would be delivered through a store in her area. Hoover then wrote to a selected store owner in the homemaker's town and advised him that a sweeper was being shipped to him express prepaid for delivery to the woman's home. If the customer purchased the cleaner, the merchant received a full commission on the sale. If she returned it, he was invited to keep the cleaner as a free sample. In either event, the store owner was usually so pleased that he agreed to become a Hoover dealer.

Within one year, Hoover had established a large network of dealers, yet sales did not develop as expected. The problem, he quickly realized, was that most store owners had neither the time nor the expertise required to sell something as new and different as a portable electric vacuum cleaner. Many women were still leery of the newfangled machine, and the only sure way to overcome their doubts would be to take the vacuum into their homes and demonstrate its effectiveness on their living room carpets. Years later, William Hoover explained how he came to this realization: "My great good luck consisted in finding out the right way to sell vacuum cleaners. . . . I would stock up a hardware store with cleaners, go out two months later and find none of them moved. I would get busy and demon-

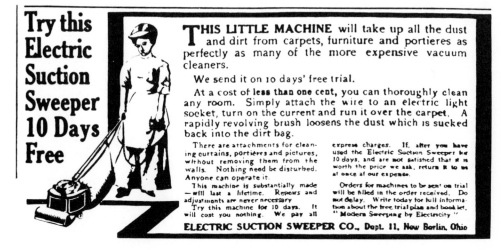

Try this Electric Suction Sweeper 10 Days Free

THIS LITTLE MACHINE will take up all the dust and dirt from carpets, furniture and portieres as perfectly as many of the more expensive vacuum cleaners.

We send it on 10 days' free trial.

At a cost of less than one cent, you can thoroughly clean any room. Simply attach the wire to an electric light socket, turn on the current and run it over the carpet. A rapidly revolving brush loosens the dust which is sucked back into the dirt bag.

There are attachments for cleaning curtains, portieres and pictures, without removing them from the walls. Nothing need be disturbed. Anyone can operate it.

This machine is substantially made — will last a lifetime. Repairs and adjustments are never necessary.

Try this machine for 10 days. It will cost you nothing. We pay all express charges. If, after you have used the Electric Suction Sweeper for 10 days, and are not satisfied that it is worth the price we ask, return it to us at once at our expense.

Orders for machines to be sent on trial will be filled in the order received. Do not delay. Write today for full information about the free trial plan and booklet, "Modern Sweeping by Electricity"

ELECTRIC SUCTION SWEEPER CO., Dept. 11, New Berlin, Ohio

With its free ten-day trial offer, this ad (which first appeared in the December 5, 1908, issue of the Saturday Evening Post) helped William Hoover establish a national network of dealers for his newly formed vacuum cleaner company. When it became apparent that the dealers had neither the time nor the inclination to explain the features of the new-fangled electric machine to shoppers, Hoover recruited an army of door-to-door salesmen to give in-home demonstrations.

strate them to housewives and move the stock. Quite unwittingly, I stumbled on to the fact that specialty demonstrations were the correct way to sell vacuum cleaners."

Thus enlightened, Hoover shifted his emphasis from dealers to door-to-door salesmen. He recruited an army of eager young men to demonstrate his suction sweeper in homes from Maine to California. Believing that a good salesman should know his product inside out, Hoover had all new recruits disassemble and reassemble vacuum cleaners repeatedly as part of their training. He also saw to it that every salesman received continuing training in sales psychology. An ordained minister in the Church of Christ, William Hoover inspired his sales force by publishing an impressive series of motivational newsletters and house organs. To provide an added boost to morale, the company had its own theme song ("All the Dirt, All the Grit"), its own band (the Hoover Suction Sweeper Band), and its own semiprofessional baseball team.

The door-to-door salesman remained an important factor in the Hoover company's marketing strategy until long after its founder's death in 1932. Rising traveling costs and the changing buying habits of American women, however, made door-to-door selling less effective after World War II, and coming full circle, the company returned to William Hoover's original idea of selling vacuums through a strong network of dealers.

M————?–
ARY KAY ASH

Mary Kay Cosmetics

It is a sight that usually commands a great deal of attention on the highway: an ordinary-looking, middle-aged woman driving along in a flashy pink Cadillac. Why, other motorists wonder, is this seemingly average homemaker behind the wheel of such an uncommon luxury automobile?

More often than not, the answer to this question will involve Mary Kay Cosmetics, Inc., a skin-care products company that motivates its sales force of more than 120,000 "beauty consultants" (recruited from the ranks of suburban housewives) by offering them the chance to compete for an assortment of storybook prizes. In addition to the pink Cadillacs, the Dallas-based firm awards mink coats, diamond jewelry, posh vacations, and similar luxuries to the beauty consultants with the best sales records. Mary Kay Cosmetics has been using this mix of friendly competition and glamorous prizes to rally it sales people since shortly after the company was founded in 1963 by Mary Kay Ash, a retired woman from Hot Wells, Texas.

A straight-A student in high school, Mary Kay entertained thoughts of becoming a doctor, but was forced to drop this idea because her parents

Pink Cadillacs have become an unofficial trademark of Mary Kay, who is shown here with her own automobile.

could not afford to send her to college on the meager earnings of the family's small restaurant. With her plans for a higher education thwarted, the attractive girl married a guitar player named Ben Rogers, whom she once described as "the Elvis Presley of Houston." The marriage lasted eleven years and produced three children, before Rogers sought a divorce.

Left on her own, Mary Kay supported her young family by selling cleaning supplies at in-home demonstrations for Stanley Home Products. In 1953 she left Stanley and joined another direct sales organization, rising to the $25,000-a-year job of national training director. She resigned this position, however, after an outside efficiency expert advised the company to curtail her growing power.

Following her less-than-amicable resignation, Mary Kay planned to retire and write a "how-to-sell" book for businesswomen. But she soon became restless with retirement living and decided that, instead of putting her business ideas down on paper, she would put them into practice by launching her own company. On Friday, September 13, 1963, the unsuperstitious Texan opened Beauty by Mary Kay, a retail cosmetics shop, in a five-hundred-square-foot downtown Dallas storefront. A short time later, Mary Kay was joined in the business by her youngest son, Richard Rogers, a twenty-year-old ex-Marine who had been earning $480 a month as a Prudential Life Insurance salesman. Working together, mother and son devised a brilliant marketing strategy that allowed them to transform their small store into an $800,000-a-year direct sales company within three years.

The new company's entry into the direct sales cosmetics field was made easier by the fact that Mary Kay and her son positioned themselves at the skin care end of the market, where their established—and very powerful—competitor, Avon, was weakest. More important to the firm's early success than the absence of major competition, however, was the herculean effort of its small, but highly motivated, sales force. Instead of simply going from door to door to drop off catalogs and take orders, Mary Kay's salespeople conducted two-hour "beauty shows" in the homes of women who agreed to act as hostesses. Participants at each show were treated to a talk on skin care and a personalized makeup lesson. The beauty shows required greater effort on the part of the sales force, but they helped interest more women in trying the firm's skin care products.

To ensure that her beauty consultants had the necessary degree of motivation, Mary Kay returned the highest commissions in the direct sales field. She also began awarding prizes to her top producers. An added incentive for beauty consultants was the opportunity to earn more money in commissions and prizes by advancing up the managerial ladder to the positions of sales director, senior sales director, and ultimately, national sales director. Mary Kay's success in motivating her sales force helped the company achieve an impressive growth record in its early years. By 1972 the firm's annual sales volume reached $18 million.

The company's fortunes took a decided turn for the worse a few years later. Sales growth failed to keep up with inflation between 1974 and 1978, and Mary Kay Cosmetics might have continued its financial slide had not its founders revamped their marketing strategy.

After analyzing the company's problem, Mary Kay and Richard Rogers came to the conclusion that the quality of their sales organization had suffered because the cash bonuses and prizes awarded to their saleswomen did not keep pace with inflation. In the late 1970s the average Mary Kay sales director was still earning $12,000 a year—the same amount she made at the beginning of the decade. Consequently, the company was no longer attracting as many high-caliber saleswomen as it had in the early years. "We lost our competitive edge in the job market," lamented Rogers. To regain that edge, Mary Kay and her son improved their compensation program. In addition to Cadillacs, they began to award pink Buick Regals so that a greater number of saleswomen would have a chance to win a car. They also introduced a $300-a-month volume bonus to augment the existing commission schedule. As a result of the company's efforts, the average sales director was earning close to $25,000 a year in the early 1980s, and that, said Rogers, caused a "real explosion of growth in the sales organization."

Today, Mary Kay Cosmetics is continuing to grow, with Mary Kay Ash as its chairman of the board and Richard Rogers as president. Now a great-grandmother, the peaches-and-cream-complexioned executive is a living advertisement for her skin care products. Everyone who meets her is impressed with how young she looks for her age—although exactly what her age is remains a matter of conjecture, since Mary Kay keeps her date of birth a closely guarded secret. "A woman who will tell you her age will tell anything" is her stock reply to questions on the subject.

E———— 1893–1970
EMMETT J. CULLIGAN

Culligan Water Softeners

Soon after he arrived in southern California on his honeymoon in December 1919, Emmett Culligan decided to take his bride, Anna, on an automobile tour of the state. So the twenty-six-year-old Minnesotan shopped the used-car market, engaged in some careful bargaining, and drove off with a secondhand Ford for $310. Two months later, after the newlyweds had completed a long, meandering motor trip from the Redlands to San Francisco, Culligan sold the car for a $25 profit.

It was this kind of shrewd horse-trading ability that earned Emmett Culligan the nickname "Gold Dust" back home in Porter, Minnesota, where he was already firmly established as a farmer and land developer. The pleasant, round-faced young man had amassed a small fortune since leaving college in his sophomore year, buying unwanted prairie land, sowing it to flax, and selling it at a hefty profit.

By the time he celebrated his twenty-eighth birthday, Culligan's total landholdings were worth more than $200,000. Then a farm recession hit in 1921, driving the price of some agricultural products down 50 percent and more and causing a rash of farm failures. As prices tumbled, the value of Culligan's property fell to almost nothing, and he was unable to repay his bank loans. Wiped out by the economic calamity, Culligan moved with his wife and baby to his mother's house in St. Paul.

One day, after their relocation, the young entrepreneur came across an old friend who was selling a conditioning machine which used the natural greensand, zeolite, to filter the hard minerals (magnesium and calcium) from water. Intrigued by the unusual device, Culligan obtained a small bag of zeolite from his friend. When he returned home, he emptied the bag into a perforated coffee can and ran some tap water through it. After using the filtered water to wash his baby's diapers, Culligan was so impressed with its softness that he decided to stake his chances for a business comeback on the future of the water conditioning industry.

Following a brief tenure as a salesman for his friend's company, Culligan launched his own St. Paul–based water softener firm in 1924. Early sales were encouraging, but the business soon became embroiled in a patent suit that dragged on for seven years and cost Culligan $41,000. (He eventually won the case.) Weakened by its prolonged legal battle, the fledgling firm was in no position to withstand the shock waves of the stock market crash. Few Americans were able or willing to pay $195 to $395 for something as nonessential as a water softener, and in 1932 Gold Dust Culligan went broke for the second time in a little over a decade.

Approaching forty, the discouraged entrepreneur moved to La Grange, Illinois, to take a job with the National Aluminate Corporation. He wasn't at his new position long, however, before the dream of starting his own business took hold once again. Despite his earlier setback, Culligan remained convinced that the water softening industry held great promise, provided he could overcome the public's resistance to the high price of conditioning equipment.

Culligan was still working for National Aluminate when he came up with a solution to the price resistance problem: instead of trying to sell the conditioning equipment directly to the customer, he would market a water softening service. Modeling his strategy on the telephone company's practice of "using equipment to sell service," he drew up plans to install water softening machines at no charge in the homes of customers who agreed to pay a $2-a-month user's fee.

In 1936 Culligan was ready to put his new marketing plan to the test. Using his $50 savings, plus a small bank loan, he rented space in Jock McLachlan's Northbrook, Illinois, blacksmith shop. Short on capital, the ingenious businessman cut corners where he could, making his conditioning machines from discarded hot water tanks picked up from local junkyards and powering his manufacturing equipment with a modified Willy-Knight automobile engine to lower electricity costs.

Despite the early hardships, the business grew quickly, thanks in part to Culligan's "no deposit, no obligation" offer, which allowed customers to cancel the water softening service at any time without penalty. The rejuvenated businessman began franchising dealers in other cities to sell his service in 1938. A little over a decade later, Culligan's national dealer network was servicing 600,000 subscribers, who paid an average monthly fee of $2.75 to $3.00.

The company continued to prosper until the 1950s, when a change in consumer attitudes threatened to render its dealer sales force obsolete. For years, Culligan dealers had relied on in-home presentations to sell the firm's water softening service to customers. Public acceptance of this type of selling declined after World War II, however, when most homeowners began to regard the "door-to-door salesman" as a slightly untrustworthy nuisance.

Hoping to overcome the negative connotations surrounding in-home sales (at least as far as their own sales force was concerned), Culligan and his top executives developed an upbeat advertising campaign in 1959. Designed by Dallas Williams Productions of Los Angeles, the ads featured a shrill female voice calling "Hey Culligan Man!" In addition to their obvious effectiveness as attention getters, the commercials made it possible for Culligan dealers to overcome the general antipathy toward in-home sales by giving the water softener salesmen a humorous, good-natured public image.

As a result of this improved image, Culligan, Inc., was able to boost its annual sales volume from $11.2 million in 1961 to $22.5 million in 1965, when Emmett Culligan retired from active participation in his company. At the time of his retirement, there were some 1,100 Culligan dealers in the United States and Canada. Not surprisingly, all of them were trained to begin their sales presentations by saying, "Hello, I'm your Culligan Man."

Promotional Geniuses

H—— 1844–1919
HENRY J. HEINZ

Heinz Ketchup

While riding in a New York elevated train in the early 1890s, Pittsburgh food condiment manufacturer Henry Heinz saw a placard for a local store advertising "21 Styles of Shoes." In a moment of inspiration, he reworked the phrase to suit his own purposes, creating what would become one of the standout numerical slogans of all time: "57 Varieties." That his company was already producing well over sixty different kinds of pickles, relishes, and vinegar didn't bother marketer Heinz, who simply liked the way the number 57 looked.

He proceeded to display the 57 Varieties monogram in thousands of streetcars across America, on four-hundred canary-yellow rail-freight cars owned by his firm, and in ten-foot-high concrete figures on two dozen of the nation's most prominent hillsides. Garish as such exhibitions of self-aggrandizement might have been, they unarguably were a key factor in the success of the H. J. Heinz Co., which by 1896 had made its founder a multimillionaire and earned him national repute as the "Pickle King."

Getting to the top wasn't easy for Heinz, the son of a German immigrant brickmaker. As a teenager, the Sharpsburg, Pennsylvania, youth demonstrated a talent for business, bottling his own horseradish and selling it to local grocers. By twenty-one he had saved enough money to buy a half interest in the brickyard owned by his father, John Heinz. Several years later when the elder Heinz returned from a visit to Germany, he was shocked to discover that Henry had built the family a new, larger home. Construction of the Victorian-style house was financed entirely by money that Henry collected from recalcitrant accounts whom John Heinz had previously written off as bad debts.

Nevertheless, when Henry Heinz first ventured into business on his own at twenty-five, forming a horseradish and pickle company with L. C. Nobel, the results were disastrous. The partners overextended themselves, and in 1875 their Pittsburgh firm was forced to declare bankruptcy. Angry creditors had Heinz arrested twice for fraud, and although he was subsequently cleared of both charges, his reputation suffered considerable damage.

Undaunted by the calamity, Heinz returned for a second try in the food business a year later. Backed by $3,000 obtained from relatives, he was paradoxically both more cautious and more flamboyant this time around. He was slower to extend himself on borrowed capital, but much bolder in masterminding promotional gimmicks to create publicity for his products. His success in building up strong consumer recognition for the Heinz label, at a time when bottled and canned foods were just beginning to be marketed under brand names, is generally regarded as a major factor behind his company's phenomenal growth.

One of Heinz's most brilliant and innovative promotional schemes came during the Columbian Exposition held in Chicago in 1892–93. The Heinz Co. had set up an elaborate exhibit at the fair; because of its out-of-the-way location on a second-floor gallery, however, it did not draw the anticipated crowds. Once the problem became apparent, Henry Heinz decided that it would be necessary to give fairgoers an added incentive to visit his display. Dashing off to a local printer, he had small white cards made up that offered the recipient a free pickle charm souvenir if redeemed at the Heinz Co. booth. Thousands of the cards were distributed at the fair, and the resultant flood of people to the Heinz booth made it necessary for exposition officials to strengthen the supports of the gallery floor to keep it from buckling. More than 1 million pickle charms were given away during the fair, and Henry Heinz's promotional ingenuity was praised in numerous magazine and newspaper articles. The Heinz pickle, which was later distributed in lapel pin form, became a fad object among late-nineteenth-century schoolchildren.

In 1889 Heinz built a state-of-the-art industrial complex on the north bank of the Allegheny River, which won many awards for its utility and architectural beauty. Ornately Romanesque in style, the facility not only succeeded in meeting the company's production needs but also served as a public relations tool, when Heinz became one of the earliest industrialists to offer guided plant tours. Visitors, numbering twenty-thousand a year, marveled at the then-unheard-of employee amenities, which included an indoor gym and swimming pool, a restaurant, and a fully equipped hospital. Even more impressive was the company's turreted, three-story stable, where the Heinz delivery horses were fed, watered, and brushed by electrically operated machinery. The animals were provided with such luxuries as a foot bath, a Turkish sauna, and a landscaped roof garden, all of which served to make the Heinz stable a subject of national attention.

Always in the vanguard of new promotional ideas, Heinz became one of the first advertisers to use an outdoor electric sign when he erected a six-story billboard at New York's 5th Avenue and 23d Street in 1900. The sign, which featured a forty-foot pickle, contained 1,200 light bulbs and cost $90 a night to illuminate.

Promoter nonpareil Henry Heinz erected New York's first large electric sign in 1900. Located at the corner of Fifth Avenue and 23d Street, the sign used 1200 Mazda bulbs which cost $90 a night to illuminate. In July 1901 Heinz was forced to dismantle the impressive billboard to make room for another technological marvel, the twenty-two-story Flatiron Building, one of Manhattan's earliest skyscrapers, which was constructed on that site.

Although he spared no expense in his promotional activities, Henry Heinz held to one steadfast rule—no ads could be run in Sunday newspapers. A religious man, Heinz was a member of several Protestant churches and was active in the World Sunday School Association throughout most of his life.

The most notable personal luxury the condiment millionaire treated himself to was travel. As his business prospered, Heinz embarked on a series of journeys throughout the Orient, Europe, and the Mideast, often accompanied by his wife Sallie and their four children. His travels eventually took him to most parts of the world, and wherever he went he unfailingly brought back trunkloads of art objects and other assorted curios—paintings, tapestries, pottery, ancient weapons, and even an Egyptian mummy. He returned from one Florida trip with an eight-hundred-pound live alligator, which he installed in a glass tank in his factory for the enjoyment of his employees.

Recognizing the publicity value of his massive artifact collection, Heinz displayed some of the more interesting pieces in the Heinz Ocean Pier, an Atlantic City pavilion he acquired in 1899. The most ambitious promotional venture ever undertaken by the Pickle King, the pavilion featured a large green pickle on either side of its entrance and was crowned with a giant "57" sign. Inside the pavilion were, among other things, a gallery of paintings, marble busts of historical figures, a Buddhist household shrine, a pair of nine-foot elephant tusks, a chair belonging to General Grant, and a display of Heinz pickles and relishes revolving around exotic plants. The exhibit, which drew fifteen-thousand visitors each season, was kept in operation for several decades following Henry Heinz's death—until a 1944 hurricane damaged it severely, causing the "5" from its gargantuan "57" to fall into the sea.

C——— 1854–1914
CHARLES W. POST

Postum, Post Cereals

An itinerant cowboy, inventor, artist, and real estate developer, Charles Post found both his health and his finances in poor straits when he traveled from Fort Worth, Texas, to Battle Creek, Michigan, in February 1891. The tall, soft-spoken, thirty-seven-year-old had lost almost all his money a year earlier when a land development scheme and textile mill he had started with several family members failed. To make matters worse, the stomach ailments and nervous disorders that had plagued Post since early adulthood were aggravated by his business problems, driving him into a deep depression.

At the urging of relatives, Post, his wife, Ella, and their three-year-old daughter, Marjorie, journeyed to Battle Creek, where it was hoped that the restorative treatments offered by Dr. John Harvey Kellogg at the city's Seventh-Day Adventist Sanitarium might return C. W. to his former state of health. Dr. Kellogg, an outspoken vegetarian and apostle of "biologic living," had attracted considerable national attention with his unorthodox treatments, which included inspirational talks, a regular exercise regime, frequent hot tub baths, and—most important—a strict health food diet. The doctor and his younger brother, Will K. Kellogg, made many of the cereal products featured on the vegetarian menu in the sanitarium dining room, including "Carmel Coffee," a caffeine-free beverage that consisted of burnt bread crusts, bran, and molasses.

Trading in a supply of blankets (leftovers from the bankrupt mill) to defray the cost of medical treatments, Post was admitted as a patient at the sanitarium. He remained there for more than ten months, his condition growing steadily worse as he became more withdrawn and emaciated. He refused to take solid foods, and his weight dropped from 170 to less than 130 pounds. Finally, Ella Post withdrew her husband from the Kellogg institution and took him to the home of a local Christian Science practitioner. C. W. remained at the Christian Scientist's home for several weeks, listening attentively to lectures and following a new program of diet (this one included meat) and exercise, until his health was restored in the winter of 1892.

Post's recovery, after he had been withdrawn, still sick, from the prestigious Seventh Day Adventist sanitarium, made him something of a celebrity in Battle Creek. Ever the entrepreneur, C. W. capitalized on this notoriety by borrowing money to start his own health sanitarium, La Vita Inn.

On March 23, 1892, he signed a contract for a farmhouse with ten acres on the outskirts of town, and La Vita Inn, Inc., was born. The next year, Post followed the Kelloggs' lead and cooked up cereal products in a small barn on the farm's grounds for his sanitarium patients. One of the more popular products among La Vita Inn patients was a coffee substitute that Post made out of New Orleans molasses, bran, and wheat berries.

Despite Charley Post's best efforts, the upstart La Vita Inn was unable to make much headway against the more established Kellogg institution. In an effort to support his struggling sanitarium, Post began to diversify into new ventures. He started a small mail-order suspender business on his sanitarium grounds, and then in 1895 he decided to market his coffee substitute to the retail grocery trade under the name Postum.

Sales of the new product were pitiably slow at first (Post lost $800 on Postum the first year), because few consumers were willing to give up the pleasures of real coffee for an unknown cereal drink. Postum's fortunes changed quickly, however, when Post convinced a Chicago advertising agency to lend him the money needed to buy ads in *Scribner's, Harpers Weekly,* and other national publications.

Unleashing his formidable talent as a copywriter, Post wrote his own advertisements and literally scared thousands of coffee drinkers into switching to Postum with outlandish broadsides that blamed the caffeinated beverage for everything from rheumatism, heart disease, and blindness to cowardliness, laziness, and diminished mental capacity. An examples of Postian advertising prose: "Is your yellow streak the coffee habit? Does it reduce your working force, kill your energy, push you into the big crowd of mongrels, deaden what thoroughbred blood you may have and neutralize all of your efforts to make money and fame?"

By the end of 1896, Postum sales had reached $3,000 a month. Following the success of Postum, Post introduced a precooked cereal in 1898 that was made of yeast, whole wheat, and malted barley flour. The cereal was called Grape Nuts, because its baking process reduced starches to dextrose or "grape sugar," and because it had a distinctive nutty texture.

The commercial success of Grape Nuts was also helped along by its creator's flamboyant advertising practices. In magazine and newspaper ads for his cereal, C. W. touted Grape Nuts as a builder of red blood cells, brain cells, and "steady nerves" and a preventer of malaria, consumption, and appendicitis. Post's reckless advertising evoked the wrath of some publishers and the medical community, but it nevertheless sold cereal. His combined profits on Postum and Grape Nuts were almost $1.1 million in 1903.

T——— 1850–1931
HOMAS J. LIPTON

Lipton Tea

Americans liked their coffee, plain and simple. It was all downhill for tea in this country following the Boston Tea Party. That is, until a wealthy Scottish businessman named Thomas Lipton ordered a cup of tea at a Chicago restaurant and was told, "Sorry, mister, we don't carry that stuff." Lipton decided on the spot to wage an all-out campaign to promote his favorite beverage on this side of the Atlantic. He was, at the time, the owner of several Ceylon tea plantations and a major supplier of the beverage in Europe.

Born to a poor Glasgow couple, Tom was the only one of six children to survive into adulthood. His parents operated a small provisions store which barely earned enough to meet the family's living expenses. Not seeing much opportunity for advancement, the youth decided to seek his fortune in America, and he set sail for New York in the steerage compartment of a cargo steamer shortly before his fifteenth birthday.

In Manhattan Lipton found work as the assistant manager of a large grocery store. It was at the bustling big-city market that he got his first glimpse of modern retailing methods, witnessing how shoppers could be persuaded to buy more merchandise through slick product displays and clever advertisements. When the homesick Scottish teenager returned to Glasgow in 1869, he was ready to apply the merchandising principles he had learned in New York to his parents' struggling grocery.

One of Lipton's first promotional steps was to engage a nationally known cartoonist, Willie Lockhart, to create a weekly poster for the shop's window. The act produced the desired results; each week throngs would

Yachtsman Thomas Lipton came up short in his five attempts to win the America's Cup races around the turn of the century. The Scottish-born businessman was far more successful at promoting his namesake tea in this country through the skillful use of newspaper ads and sales demonstrations.

gather outside Lipton's store to see Lockhart's new cartoon. One poster that attracted considerable attention showed a pig slung over the shoulder of an Irishman. Tears were coming out of the animal's eyes, and its owner was explaining to a bystander that the poor pig was an orphan because all its relatives had been taken to Lipton's and converted into ham and Irish bacon. Tom Lipton capitalized on the popularity of the cartoon by purchasing two of the largest pigs he could find, adorning them with pink and blue ribbons and parading them through the streets under the banner "Lipton's Orphans." The words soon became a neighborhood catch phrase; anybody wearing tattered clothing or having a ragged appearance was referred to as a "Lipton Orphan."

The store benefited hugely from its new household-word status. Sales of ham, bacon, and eggs multiplied, and as his capital increased, Tom Lipton's promotional stunts became more elaborate. He dropped leaflets from hot-air balloons advertising his products, created gigantic sculptures from sausage and butter and displayed them in his window, and distributed imitation one-pound notes that could be redeemed for discounts at the store.

One of Thomas Lipton's early food stores in his native Glasgow. The son of a struggling grocer, Lipton had already built the family business into one of Britain's leading retail chains by 1888, when he began packaging his namesake tea.

His profits snowballed further, and by the mid-1870s Lipton had opened three other Glasgow locations.

Using capital generated by his growing chain, the young entrepreneur continued to promote and expand his business. One of his most famous stunts came during Christmas 1881, when he imported the "world's largest cheese" from America. Gold coins were inserted into the cheese, and when it was finally cut up on Christmas Eve, the crowd of eager buyers was so large that a special police force had to be dispatched to the scene. By this time, Lipton owned more than twenty stores.

The number of units in the chain eventually reached three-hundred, making Thomas Lipton a millionaire long before he became associated with his namesake tea. His involvement with the beverage began in 1888, when the grocery genius realized that he could save his customers 20¢ a pound (in American currency) by eliminating the middleman and blending his own tea. He also conceived of the idea of selling tea in prepackaged pound, half-pound, and quarter-pound bags. (Prior to this, tea was stored in bulk and measured out individually for each customer.) With more convenient packaging and a significantly lower price, Lipton's tea trade took off. Soon the demand for his product had spread beyond his stores, and he was selling tea to groceries and restaurants throughout Europe.

The Chicago restaurant incident occurred in 1890, when Lipton traveled to the United States to check out the tea market here. Tea had scarcely been drunk in America following the introduction of coffee to the nation by German and Austrian immigrants in the mid-nineteenth century. In the few places tea was available, Lipton found it to be overpriced, lacking in freshness owing to improper storage, and inferior in quality. Nevertheless, the Scottish merchant was convinced that Americans could be persuaded to like tea, once they were exposed to a top-quality blend and were taught how to store and serve it properly.

Lipton invested heavily in his "American project," running newspaper ads to educate the public about tea and commissioning an army of agents to sell his product to hotels and restaurants, where it could be sampled by people who never before tasted the beverage. Widespread publicity for tea was achieved in 1893, when Lipton convinced the nation of Ceylon, a major tea leaf producer, to take out a booth at the heavily attended Chicago Exposition. In 1909 Lipton set up a blending and packaging plant on the south end of Manhattan, thereby lowering the cost of his product even further. A decade later, the growing demand for his tea necessitated a move across the Hudson River to larger quarters in Hoboken, New Jersey.

Perhaps the biggest factor in promoting tea to Americans was the public's fascination with Thomas Lipton himself. Tall, blue-eyed, and ruddy-cheeked, the tea millionaire had achieved notoriety on both sides of the Atlantic for his association with European royalty and his yacht-racing activities. Five times in the late 1890s and early 1900s he entered his *Shamrock* yachts in the prestigious America's Cup races, and although he went down to defeat each time, his gentlemanly sportsmanship continued to charm turn-of-the-century Americans.

Today, more than fifty years after his death, the millionaire Scotsman is still "promoting" his namesake beverage—the distinguished yachtsman on every package of Lipton Tea is Thomas Lipton.

Packaging Innovators

J AMES LEWIS KRAFT
Kraft Cheese

Cheese hardly seemed like a promising product to build a new business around when James Kraft began wholesaling it to Chicago grocery stores in 1904. The average American of the era consumed less than a pound of cheese a year (compared to more than nineteen pounds today), and the dairy food's prospects of winning a more prominent place on the national menu appeared slim.

The biggest obstacle standing in the way of increased cheese sales was spoilage. Cheese had a notoriously short shelf life, and because of this, it was regarded suspiciously by consumers and shopkeepers alike. Stores that carried cheese usually kept a sixty-pound wheel of American cheddar on the sales counter, covered by a protective glass bell jar. When a customer wanted cheese, the grocer would cut a wedge from the wheel. Once this was done, the wheel's exposed edges would invariably dry out, making it necessary for the store owner to trim off the spoiled sections. More often than not, a large chunk of the store's cheese profits would be thrown away along with the dried-out trimmings.

Spoilage became an even bigger concern in the summer, when high temperatures caused the cheese to separate quickly into butterfats and solids, creating an identifiable odor that effectively kept customers a safe distance away. Understandably, many store owners, particularly those in the southern states, refused to carry cheese between June and September.

A former grocery clerk himself, James Kraft was familiar with all the problems involved in handling cheese, but he was confident that the dairy product could reach a far bigger market if it were packaged in a more convenient, less perishable form. The Chicago wholesaler put this theory into practice soon after he launched his business, when he sold small individual portions of cheese in glass jars and tinfoil packages.

Kraft's prepacked product represented a major improvement over wheel cheese. Grocers no longer had to worry about dried-out wheel edges, and consumers were able to buy cheese in a convenient container. Despite the advantages it offered over its predecessor, however, Kraft's cheese was plagued by the familiar shelf life problem. Like all cheeses, it spoiled too quickly (especially during warmer months) to realize its full market potential.

In 1916 Kraft solved his spoilage problem by patenting a method of blending, pasteurizing, and packaging American cheddar that dramatically increased the cheese's shelf life. Packed in four-ounce tins, the new "processed cheese" retained its freshness and flavor over long periods of time in any climate. This allowed Kraft to achieve a level of sales and distribution that was previously unknown in the cheese industry. Sales at the one-time Chicago wholesale house hit $2 million in 1917, aided in part by the U.S. Army, which purchased 6 million pounds of Kraft's canned cheese during World War I.

Following the war, refinements in Kraft's cheese-processing methods made it possible for him to substitute foil-wrap packaging for the heavier and less efficient tins without compromising the shelf life of his product. This paved the way for the arrival of the company's famous cheese loaf. Wrapped in foil and set inside a rectangular wooden case, the five-pound loaf was the perfect shape for cutting sandwich-sized slices of cheese. Consumer response to this handy new package was swift and enthusiastic. Less than one month after Kraft introduced the foil-wrapped product, his plant was turning out fifteen-thousand cheese loaves a day.

Powered by the popularity of its cheese loaf, the Kraft company's sales soared to $22 million in 1923. Five years later, James Kraft merged his firm with the rival Phenix Cheese Co. As a result of this union, the Kraft cheese line acquired what would become one of its best-selling products— Philadelphia Cream Cheese. (The cream cheese was never made in the City of Brotherly Love; the New York State–based Phenix company named the product after Philadelphia because the city enjoyed a reputation throughout the East for its fine food.)

The new Kraft-Phenix company accounted for 40 percent of the nation's cheese consumption in 1930, when it was acquired by National Dairy Products Corporation, a large holding company. James Kraft stayed on as president of his subsidiary firm, following the acquisition.

Once settled in his new executive position, Kraft displayed a talent for advertising that rivaled his genius as a production and packaging innovator. Under his leadership, the Kraft company became an early radio advertiser, sponsoring the Kraft Music Hall, a popular one-hour show that featured such luminaries as Al Jolson, George Gershwin, and Bing Crosby. Kraft's radio advertising helped the firm launch a host of products that have since become supermarket mainstays, including Miracle Whip salad dressing (1933), Parkay maragarine (1973), and Kraft French salad dressing (1938).

Ironically, there was little in James Kraft's early life to suggest that he would one day enjoy such outstanding success. One of eleven children born to a Stevensville, Ontario, farm family, Kraft was a short, pudgy boy with an undiagnosed eye problem that caused blurry vision and almost daily headaches. He was raised in a strict Mennonite environment, where hard work and harsh discipline were the rule. His mother, Minerva, wore a thimble on the stump of a finger that had been severed in a farm machinery accident. When one of her youngsters misbehaved, Mrs. Kraft would rap her thimble sharply on the child's head.

Kraft graduated from the local high school and took a job at a grocery store. For a time it seemed as if he would live out his life as an obscure retail clerk, but in 1903 the twenty-nine-year-old Kraft moved to Buffalo, New York, to go to business college. Kraft attended college for one year before he moved to Chicago, where he rented a wagon and a horse named Paddy and started delivering cheese to local grocers.

After he had achieved success in the cheese business, Kraft became an avid amateur lapidarist. Described by *Popular Mechanics* as "America's No. 1 rockhound," the package cheese pioneer is credited with discovering American jade.

Throughout his life, James Kraft remained deeply rooted to his Mennonite background, becoming an deacon of Chicago's North Shore Baptist Church and a trustee of the Northern Baptist Theological Seminary. A modest man, he refused to take full credit for building his multimillion dollar business, often saying it was the work of God, and giving Paddy recognition as a cofounder of Kraft cheese.

W——— 1830–1913   A——— 1836?–1894
WILLIAM SMITH   ANDREW SMITH

Smith Brothers Cough Drops

Imitation may be the highest form of flattery, but this was small consolation to William and Andrew Smith in the late 1860s, when unscrupulous competitors tried to capitalize on the popularity of Smith Brothers Cough Drops by bringing out similar confections with names like "Schmitt Brothers," "Smyth Brothers," and "Smythe Sisters."

Clearly, something had to be done to distinguish the brothers' black aromatic product from its many imitators. With this thought in mind, the Smiths registered their portraits as a trademark and had their likenesses fixed to the large glass bowls that were used to display their drops at general stores and apothecary shops.

Despite this protective step, the problem of counterfeit drops continued to plague the brothers. Any merchant who wished to pad his profits could do so simply by filling the "Smith Brothers jar" with a cheaper brand of cough drops and then passing the bogus lozenges off as the real thing.

William and Andrew finally came up with a foolproof way to safeguard the integrity of their product in 1872, when they began selling Smith Brothers Cough Drops in prepacked boxes. This was the first time that cough drops were marketed in "factory-filled" packages. In fact, the brothers were among the earliest confection makers of any kind to box their product. Most other manufacturers of the day sold their candies loose from large counter jars.

Not only did the Smiths' farsighted packaging thwart their imitative competitors, it also spawned a thriving cottage industry in the brothers' hometown of Poughkeepsie, New York. Early every evening, a wagon loaded with five-gallon cans of cough drops left the Smith Brothers factory and traveled down a nearby street, depositing a can of drops and a supply of boxes at some thirty houses along the way. After dinner, the families who lived on what became known as "Cough Drop Street" would sit at their kitchen tables and package the cough drops, sixteen pieces to the box.

Like the glass bowl displays it had replaced, the new cough drop box featured the distinctive trademark-portraits of the two brothers. By pure chance, the word *Trade* was printed under William's likeness, and *Mark* appeared under Andrew's. This arrangement prompted local wits to refer to the pair as "Trade and Mark Smith." The popularity of the joke spread, and eventually it got to the point where a bearded man in any part of the country might be called either Trade or Mark, depending on the length of his whiskers.

Although they probably grew tired of hearing Trade and Mark jokes, the brothers voiced no objections, especially since the ensuing notoriety was good for business. Aided by their unintentionally humorous trademark and novel prefilled package, William and Andrew sold cough drops at a prodigious rate. During the course of the brothers' lifetimes, output at their factory increased from five pounds to roughly four tons of drops a day.

The Smith brothers' cough drop empire began long before they came up with their famous trademark. It was their father, Poughkeepsie restaurant owner James Smith, who got the family into the cough drop business back in the decade before the Civil War. Legend has it that the senior Smith bought the formula for the drops for $5 from an itinerant notions peddler named Sly Hawkins. However he obtained his formula, James quickly established a profitable cough drop sideline to his restaurant business. By 1852 he was touting his product in local newspaper ads as being "highly recommended for coughs, colds, hoarseness, sore throats, whooping coughs, asthma etc., etc."

When James Smith died in 1866, his sons took over the restaurant and cough drop enterprises. Although they were able to blend their divergent talents into a harmonious and successful partnership, "Trade" and "Mark" Smith were worlds apart in temperament and style.

It was William (Trade) who was clearly the dominant brother. He controlled the company's finances and had the biggest voice in major policy decisions. The depth of Trade's frugality was legendary; to save paper, he kept the firm's bookkeeping records on the backs of old envelopes. An ardent prohibitionist (he forbade the serving of ginger ale at the family restaurant because its name was suggestive of an alcoholic beverage), William believed that money led workers to drink and other evils, and so he dutifully kept wages at rock-bottom levels.

William did, however, give generously to charity. Among his benefactions to Poughkeepsie were the YMCA and YWCA buildings, the Old Ladies Home, College Hill Park (called Cough Drop Park by townsfolk), and the headquarters of the local chapter of the Women's Christian Temperance Union. Encouraged by his dry supporters, William Smith entered politics, making unsuccessful bids for the state senate, governorship, and mayor's office. The temperance-minded cough drop maker was resoundingly beaten in the mayoralty race by William Frank, a Poughkeepsie brewer.

Andrew (Mark) Smith did not share his brother's prohibitionist views. A good-natured bachelor, he was not averse to lifting an occasional glass at the local tavern. He differed from William in matters of money as well. Generous to a fault, the younger Smith brother was such a soft touch for any friend in need of a fast loan, that he became known in Poughkeepsie as "Easy Mark."

1856–1902
GERHARD MENNEN

Mennen Toiletries

At twenty-three, Gerhard Mennen already was earning a comfortable livelihood from his busy Central Avenue drugstore in downtown Newark, New Jersey. Although many other young men would have been content to rest on this achievement, Mennen had his sights set on a higher ambition. The

German-born pharmacist's plan was to move from retailing into manufacturing, where the opportunities for outstanding success were greater.

In 1879 the aspiring manufacturer brought out his first product, Mennen's Sure Corn Killer, a foot remedy he had invented. Despite the hard work and driving ambition of its creator, the corn killer was only a marginal seller, and the young drugstore owner soon was looking for a more promising product to make in his back-room laboratory.

Mennen's inspiration for the product that would eventually establish him as a successful manufacturer came from his customers. Many of the new mothers who frequented his shop complained that the chalk-type powders then on the market were ineffective in relieving diaper rash. When considering alternative products that might prove more helpful, Mennen's mind went back to a gentle carbolated talc (powdered soapstone) that was occasionally sold at a former employer's store. One day, it occurred to him that in addition to providing a measure of relief to his customers' babies, a talc-based powder might be an ideal product for his fledgling manufacturing enterprise.

Obtaining a sample of carbolated talc from his old employer, Mennen began experimenting with ways to improve the product. After several years of research, he devised a powder formula that consisted of costly (but extra soft) Italian talc, boracic acid (a mild antiseptic), and—to impart a pleasant fragrance—oil of roses. In July 1889 he gave free samples of the "Borated Infant Talcum Powder" to his drugstore customers and then waited anxiously to learn of their babies' reactions. A short time later, happy mothers were returning to the pharmacy with the news that the powder had worked wonders in soothing diaper rash.

At last Gerhard Mennen had found a product that could be sold to a broad, appreciative market. Before he could begin large-scale production, however, it would be necessary to find a suitable package. In the late 1880s most powders were sold in small cardboard boxes, but Mennen disapproved of this material because it allowed impurities and moisture to penetrate the package and reduce the talcum's effectiveness. Wanting a sturdier container that would better protect the integrity of his product, Mennen departed from the standard practice and packaged his powder in tin cans. As an added innovation, the pharmacist-turned-manufacturer made it easier for customers to apply the borated talcum by perforating the tops of his cylindrical containers, thus allowing the powder to be sprinkled like salt, once the can's outer cap was removed.

The new Mennen talcum was the first product of its kind to be sold in sifter-topped tin cans, and the revolutionary package—with its attractive security and convenience features—contributed greatly to the powder's early success in the marketplace. Soon talcum had become more than a sideline for Mennen, and the powder business was incorporated in 1892 as

"Have you any Talcum Powder?"
"Do you wish MENNEN'S?" asked the clerk, politely.
"No, vimmen's," was the ignorant reply.

The Mennen Company, Morristown, New Jersey.

As sales of his borated talcum powder increased, pharmacist-turned-manufacturer Gerhard Mennen invested more money in magazine advertising. Some of the ads touted the powder's effectiveness in soothing skin irritations; others, such as this one, relied on a more humorous selling message. The company's unique sifter-top tin can package was included in this and many other Mennen ads. The evolution of the packaging is illustrated on page 115.

the Gerhard Mennen Chemical Company with $50,000 in capital stock. Five years later, Mennen was forced to build a new three-story factory on Newark's Orange Street to keep up with the demand for his uniquely packaged powder.

As his sales increased, Mennen invested heavily in advertising, becoming one of the first in the pharmaceutical industry to run a national ad campaign. He sponsored cross-country tours of circus and theater groups, purchased billboard space on major thoroughfares, and ran ads in publications like the *Saturday Evening Post*. A primary goal of the Mennen ads was to expand the powder's appeal beyond the baby market by touting it as a relief for sunburn, collar rash, and other adult skin irritations.

Gerhard Mennen viewed his product's package as yet another form of advertising. Reasoning that his powder would have greater appeal to women if it came in a container that could be used to decorate a vanity table, he enlivened his cans with an attractive design of tiny orange sunbursts against a dark blue background. A smiling baby appeared on the label of every container, and a likeness of the powder maker himself was imprinted on the removable outer cap.

Not all the changes that Mennen made in his powder container were cosmetic. Almost obsessed with protecting the purity of his product, the fastidious manufacturer supervised the development of a more airtight double-seam can (later known as the "Mennen seam"). He also devised a revolving sifter cover that "opened" the can when its perforations were aligned with those of the inner cap.

Following Gerhard Mennen's death from pneumonia in 1902, his widow Elma succeeded him as company president. Ten years later, the couple's son William G. Mennen (1884–1968) took over the reins of the New Jersey–based business. A bright, articulate Cornell graduate, the younger Mennen inherited his father's genius for devising packaging innovations. Soon after assuming the presidency of the firm, he brought out Mennen Lather Shave Cream, America's first successfully marketed shaving cream packed in a tube. William Mennen was the firm's chief executive in 1931 when it introduced one of its most famous products—Mennen Skin Bracer.

Image Makers

L——— 1879–1951
LANE BRYANT

Lane Bryant Apparel

With its ornate grandeur and straitlaced officials, the Oriental Bank in Manhattan must have seemed an imposing structure to Lithuanian-born seamstress Lena Bryant when she ventured there one afternoon in 1906. A young widow who supported herself and her son sewing lingerie and bridal gowns, Lena had put away $300 and now was ready to open her first savings account. As she filled out her deposit slip, however, the shy immigrant was so awed by her gilded surroundings that she nervously scrawled her first name "Lane" instead of "Lena." Being too timid to correct the mistake, she thereafter accepted Lane Bryant as the title of her garment-making business, eventually adopting it for personal use.

Thus was born a name that would become synonymous with maternity wear and stout apparel for millions of women across America. Before the end of her career, the eastern European dressmaker would see her modest shop balloon into a $50-million-a-year ready-to-wear empire, with twenty-five Lane Bryant outlets around the country selling specialty garments for pregnant, plump, and otherwise hard-to-fit females.

Back in 1906, Lena Himmelstein Bryant was happy just to be earning enough money to put food on the table. Life had not been easy for the petite immigrant girl, who had come to New York as a steerage passenger at the age of sixteen. After working in a lingerie factory for one dollar a week, Lena married Brooklyn jeweler David Bryant in 1899. Six months after their first child was born, David died of tuberculosis, leaving his young bride with little except a pair of diamond earrings that he had given her as a wedding gift. Pawning the earrings to buy a sewing machine, the twenty-one-year-old widow fell back on the only trade she knew and began making lingerie in her West 112th Street apartment.

Lena's delicate lace-and-silk negligees were well received by neighborhood women, and soon she was producing bridal and hostess gowns as well. The young dressmaker developed a reputation for her skill at designing clothes that flattered the wearer's figure. Her clientele grew steadily, and within six years she was able to move into a loft at 19 West 38th Street and establish her first bank account at the Oriental institution.

The big turning point for the business came when one of Lane Bryant's customers, upon learning she was pregnant, begged the seamstress to make her "something pretty and practical" so that she could continue her active social life. Maternity clothes for street wear were unheard of at the time, since expectant women were supposed to stay at home out of public view. Disregarding this Victorian precept, Bryant took the then revolutionary step of fashioning a comfortable and concealing maternity gown by attaching a bodice to an accordion-pleated skirt with an elastic band that would expand with the wearer's waist. The pregnant socialite was so pleased with the $18 dress that she praised it to all her friends, and soon Lane Bryant was receiving orders from mothers-to-be all over the city.

In 1909 the thirty-year-old widow married Albert Malsin, a Lithuanian-born engineer, who adopted her son Raphael. (The Malsins later had two boys and a girl of their own.) With sales of his wife's lingerie, gowns, and maternity wear approaching $50,000 a year, Malsin assumed control of the financial end of the business.

One day while walking past Crocker's, a store that specialized in funeral apparel, Malsin was struck by an idea; if a shop could be successful catering to the special clothing needs created by a death, why not have one devoted exclusively to those needs created by a birth? Thus, in 1910 Lane Bryant dropped all other garment categories to specialize in ready-to-wear maternity fashions.

Malsin and Bryant ran up against a formidable obstacle when they attempted to publicize their stylish collection of dresses for mothers-to-be. Guided by nineteenth-century standards, most newspapers refused to accept advertising for something as suggestive as maternity wear. Finally, in 1911, the *New York Herald* relented, and Malsin placed an ad that claimed, among other things: "It is no longer the fashion nor the practice for expectant mothers to stay in seclusion. Doctors, nurses and psychologists agree that at this time a woman should think and live as normally as possible. To do this, she must go about among other people, she must look like other people."

Response to the ad was sensational. The day it ran, the store's entire inventory of maternity wear was sold out for a total of $2,800. Within a year, Lane Bryant's business doubled, and soon afterward the Manhattan shop was outfitting expectant mothers across the country through a mail-order catalog featuring thirty-two pages of maternity street dresses. By 1917 the company's sales reached $1 million, helped by a sharp rise in the birthrate.

Wanting to capitalize on their nationally known label, partners Malsin and Bryant next turned their attention to another category of hard-to-fit females who had been ignored by traditional clothiers—overweight and large-proportioned women. Usuing her talent at camouflaging ample dimensions, Lane Bryant created a collection of fashionable dresses in colors and lines designed to flatter fuller figures. Like maternity wear, the revolutionary apparel was promoted in hard-hitting magazine ads that advised overweight women that "Appearing Stout Is Merely a Matter of Clothes." Overjoyed at the prospect of being able to outfit themselves in stylish, slenderizing costumes, large-size women flocked to Lane Bryant. The shop gradually added a full array of wardrobe accessories for stout customers, including hosiery, shoes in widths to EEE, and even king-size umbrellas.

Albert Malsin died in 1923, and by the time of his death, the company (which was now selling more stout apparel than maternity wear) had branch stores in Chicago, Detroit, and Brooklyn and was doing an annual volume of $5 million. With twice-widowed Lane Bryant remaining at its helm, the firm continued to expand, opening branches in Philadelphia, Baltimore, Pittsburgh, Cleveland, and St. Louis. New special-size categories also were added, including a department for tall women (complete with extra-long necklaces and earrings) and a section of youthful fashions for chubby teenage girls.

In 1947, during a special ceremony held to mark the modernization of the company's Fifth Avenue headquarters, gray-haired Lane Bryant was a featured speaker. Gazing up at the ten-story building, the slightly built designer, who would have been "swimming" in any of her own creations, whispered, "It's like a dream." Upon her death four years later, control of the $50 million business passed on to her son Raphael Malsin—the "baby" whom, half a century earlier, she pawned her diamond earrings to support.

S———— 1906–
OICHIRO HONDA

Honda Motorcyles

There was a time when only police officers and Hells Angels types were seen on motorcycles. Like pool halls and pinball arcades, the loud, overgrown two-wheeled machines were universally avoided by nice, respectable people. Marlon Brando rode around on a motorcycle; Pat Boone did not. It was all that simple until the little Honda Super Cub wheeled its way into the life of middle-class America in the early 1960s.

The man responsible for bringing about the first socially acceptable motorcycle was a short, bespectacled executive from the village of Iwata-gun (now part of Hamamatsu), Japan. A blacksmith's son, Soichiro Honda began making motorcyles in 1948, when he formed the Honda Motor Company on $3,300 capital in a small workshop near his home. His earliest machines were made largely out of discarded military parts and were designed

One of the most successful advertising campaigns, "You Meet the Nicest People on a Honda," transformed the public's attitude toward motorcycling almost overnight. Prior to 1962, when this ad began to appear in national magazines like Time and Life, the typical American viewed motorcycling as something strictly for black-leather-jacket toughs. By showing a variety of ordinary middle-class people astride the two-wheel machine, Honda created a new, more respectable image for motorcycles. The impact of the ad on Honda's business was awesome—within six years of launching the "Nicest People" campaign, Honda tallied its one-millionth motorcycle sale in the United States.

to run on pine resin as well as gasoline. Although the little vehicles were barely more than motorized bicycles, they sold extremely well in war-devastated Japan, where people were desperate for any reliable means of transportation.

As his business grew, the manufacturer added bigger and more sophisticated motorcycles to his line. By 1950 he was distributing his product to some five-thousand dealers throughout Japan and had to shift his expanding operation to larger facilities in Tokyo.

Despite his continued growth, Honda remained relatively indistinguishable from the fifty or so other motorcycle makers crowding the Japanese market. Then, in August 1958, he unveiled a new lightweight vehicle called the Super Cub. Combining the durability of a bigger motorcycle with the economy and handling of a motor scooter, the little 50 cc Super Cub took Japan by storm. Sales at Honda's Tokyo showroom totaled $140,000 on the day the motorcycle was introduced. Two years later the Japanese manufacturer was able to build the biggest motorcycle factory in the world at Suzuka on the strength of his Super Cub sales.

By the beginning of the 1960s, the Super Cub was a familiar sight in cities and villages throughout much of Asia, and the motorcycle's maker was ready to introduce the vehicle to the United States. Honda was confident that the American motorcycle market could be expanded well beyond what he called "the black leather jacket set" to include a wide cross section of consumers. He based his optimism on the belief that Americans would buy the Super Cub not as a primary means of transportation like the automobile but as a little recreational vehicle.

Before this could happen, however, it would be necessary to change the tough-guy label that was attached to motorcycles in the United States. Thus, Honda's first step in selling the Super Cub here was to upgrade the general image of motorcycling, rather than to tout the specific merits of his product. He achieved this goal in stunning fashion with a 1962 national magazine ad built around the slogan "You Meet the Nicest People on a Honda."

Designed by Grey Advertising of Los Angeles, the ad coordinated this slogan with bright, upbeat illustrations of respectable Americans from various walks of life—students, homemakers, businessmen, retirees, young parents—all happily riding a Honda Super Cub. Honda ran the ad in *Time, Life, Look,* and other prominent general-interest publications, where it could be seen by millions of readers who had never before ridden a motorcycle. The underlying message of the ad was one that Honda would repeat many times over in the years to come—motorcycling could be clean, wholesome fun when it involved a quiet little machine like the Super Cub.

Honda's magazine ads gave motorcycling a new image, and his company sold Super Cubs to thousands of Americans who never would have dreamed of climbing on a motorcycle just a few months earlier. Encouraged by this success, the company expanded its advertising campaign to include television in 1963. The following year, it purchased a one-quarter sponsorship of the Academy Awards telecast. Customer traffic at Honda showrooms reached an all-time high on the day following the broadcast of the Oscar ceremonies.

In 1968 (only six years after the inauguration of its "You Meet the Nicest People on a Honda" campaign), the Japanese manufacturer could celebrate the sale of its one-millionth motorcycle in the United States. When Soichiro Honda retired as president of his firm to become "supreme advisor" in 1973, the company claimed an amazing 46 percent share of the American motorcycle market.

Motorcycles were, of course, only the tip of the Honda iceberg. In 1963 the company entered the automobile industry when it introduced the S 500, a sports car. It wasn't until the next decade, however, when it came out with the Civic (1975), the Accord (1976) and the Prelude (1978), that Honda established itself as one of the world's major automobile makers.

The road to international business success was not an easy one for

Soichiro Honda. Born into rural poverty, he saw five of his eight siblings die for lack of proper medical care before they reached maturity. At fifteen he left his small village to work at a Tokyo auto repair shop, returning home six years later to open a garage of his own. Honda prospered as his own boss, thanks to his skill as a mechanic and the royalties received from a metal-spoked automobile wheel he patented in 1928.

Later, Honda turned his attention to designing and driving race cars, and became one of Japan's most competitive drivers. Then in July 1936, he suffered a near-fatal accident when his modified Ford crashed into another car at 100 miles per hour, leaving the left half of his face crushed, his shoulder dislocated, and his wrist broken.

Honda's recovery took eighteen months, and during that time his family prevailed upon him to give up racing. It was at that point that he went into manufacturing, at first producing piston rings and then—following World War II—motorcycles. The first motorcycle model made at his factory was called the Honda Dream, a name Soichiro Honda chose to reflect his belief in a brighter future, not only for his own fledgling company, but for his war-wrecked nation as well.

J —— 1891–1982
OYCE C. HALL

Hallmark Greeting Cards

More than a few of the townspeople who paused to survey the burned-out ruins of the Hall brothers' Kansas City greeting card warehouse on January 12, 1915, must have commented on the poor luck of the business's young owners. The fire that swept through the building the night before had destroyed thousands of cases of Valentine's Day cards that were waiting to be delivered to drugstores in Kansas, Missouri, and Oklahoma. In just a few weeks, the large Valentine stock would have been shipped and paid for, bringing in money that twenty-three-year-old wholesaler Joyce Hall and his brother, Rollie, were counting on to pay off their ceditors. Now, with their entire inventory lost in the blaze, the brothers would be unable to meet their $17,000 debt.

Coming when it did, the loss was particularly heartbreaking for Joyce Hall, who was just beginning to establish himself as a successful businessman after years of struggle and poverty. The Norfolk, Nebraska, native had been working since the age of nine, when his father, an itinerant preacher, abandoned the family, leaving Joyce and his two older brothers to provide for their semiinvalid mother. Young J. C. (as he preferred to be called) peddled perfume door to door and later went into business with his brothers selling picture postcards imported from Europe. At eighteen, seeking brighter opportunities, he took a supply of cards to Kansas City, where he began wholesaling them to local druggists. Soon he added a line of imported Christmas and Valentine's Day cards, and within a year he was joined by his brother Rollie. Gradually, they expanded their sales territory into nearby cities and states, before the fire wiped them out.

"If you want to quit, that's a good time to quit. But if you are not a quitter, you begin to think fast," J. C. said later of the calamity. Rising to the challenge, the young businessman borrowed more money and purchased a local engraving firm so that he and Rollie could replenish their stock quickly and cheaply by printing their own greeting cards. The first two original designs made by the company that would later become Hallmark were ready in time for Christmas 1915. Sold in midwestern drugstores, the tiny (2½″ × 4″) hand-painted Yuletide greetings were a success with holiday shoppers, providing a badly needed inflow of cash to the Halls' devastated firm.

Now that he had his own printing press and some capital behind him, Joyce Hall began to experiment with different card concepts. Within a few years, his efforts would produce an entirely new image for greeting cards in America.

At the time, most of the greeting cards sold in the United States were elaborately engraved imports from England and Germany, which were made for only two occasions, Christmas and Valentine's Day. Hall believed, however, that Americans, who were more informal than Europeans, would respond favorably to the idea of inexpensive "everyday" greeting cards that could be sent to friends and family members not only on holidays but throughout the entire year. He envisioned colorfully illustrated cards containing upbeat verses expressing sentiments like friendship, congratulations, and even sympathy.

Convinced that the sending of casual, me-to-you messages would eventually catch on as a social custom in America, Hall came out with his first everyday-card design in 1916. Carrying a friendship theme, the card featured a line from Edgar Guest: "I'd like to be the kind of friend you've been to me." The succinct verse captured a feeling that many people wanted to express, and the card quickly became a commercial success. Encouraged by its reception, J. C. and Rollie soon expanded their card themes to include birthday and anniversary tidings and inspirational get-well messages. World War I was a boon to the brothers' business, creating a demand for "missing you" cards that could be sent to soldiers stationed overseas.

By the early 1920s, the Halls' all-occasion greeting cards were being sold in stores throughout the East and Midwest, and their Kansas City plant employed 120 people. To expand further and attain national recognition, Joyce Hall created an identifiable brand name for his product in 1923 by extending his last name into a word suggestive of the highest quality—Hallmark.

In the decades that followed, the greeting card pioneer, who was once described by the *Wall Street Journal* as having a "near-obsession with promoting an image of quality," found many other ways to associate Hallmark Cards with the trait of excellence. It was Hall who coined the now-famous advertising slogan, "When you care enough to send the very best." The cards were made to live up to this claim through their widely touted use of illustrations and verses from popular artists and writers of the day—among them, Norman Rockwell, Grandma Moses, Ogden Nash, and Pearl Buck. (Hallmark has even sold Christmas cards designed by Winston Churchill and Jacqueline Kennedy Onassis.)

Hall's most effective means of building a reputation for his company as a purveyor of quality was his sponsorship of the "Hallmark Hall of Fame" in the 1950s and 1960s. A critically acclaimed series of television productions, the "Hall of Fame" featured such classics as *Hamlet, Macbeth*, and George Bernard Shaw's *Man and Superman*. Although the shows won many awards for their artistic merit, most earned only fair Nielsen ratings, bringing a spate of criticism from marketing "experts" who questioned the wisdom of spending so much money ($500,000 a show) to reach a relatively small audience. "Good taste is good business," countered the greeting card manufacturer, who was able to impose his personal style of advertising on the company because it was privately owned and he was not accountable to public stockholders.

In every other aspect of Hallmark's operations as well, Joyce Hall was a die-hard autocrat. Until his retirement in 1966 (when his son, Donald, took over as president), the company founder had to give his stamp of approval to every single greeting card illustration and verse before it could be added to the product line. Even the artists and writers who were often at odds with him agreed that the unpretentious midwesterner displayed an uncanny knack for knowing what the public would buy. Under Hall's guidance, Hallmark defined and developed messages for three-thousand different "sending situations"—ranging from "So You Have a New Apartment?" and "Sorry You're Sick on St. Patrick's Day" to "Congratulations on Your Ordination." Hundreds of other themes have been considered and rejected, including "Sorry You're Divorced" and "Sympathy on the Death of Your Dog." At the time of Hall's death in 1982, his namesake firm was turning out 8 million greeting cards a day—among them the one that started it all, the Edgar Guest friendship verse, which, after more than half a century, remains one of Hallmark's strongest sellers.

Local Favorites

The original Oscar Mayer shakes hands with "Little Oscar," a diminutive goodwill ambassador who attended store openings, visited children's hospitals, and made other appearances in a sausage-shaped vehicle called the "Wienermobile." Introduced to the public in 1936, Little Oscar appeared in many of the meatpacker's ads and played a big role in making Oscar Mayer's name a household word.

1859–1955
OSCAR F. MAYER

Oscar Mayer Wieners

The little Kolling Meat Market was in sorry shape when it was leased by Bavarian immigrant Oscar Mayer in 1883. After a prolonged period of mismanagement, the near North Side Chicago store had lost most of its customers to other neighborhood butcher shops, and its discouraged owner was only too glad to unload his failing business on the twenty-four-year-old Mayer.

However, despite the store's poor reputation, its new operator's skill as a *Wurstmacher* quickly turned the business around. Mayer's artfully prepared house specialties like bockwurst, liverwurst, and weiswurst (a mixture of pork, veal, eggs, and spices) became immediate favorites of the neighborhood's German-born residents. Within a few years, the store's fortunes had been so dramatically reversed that its original owner began to cast a covetous glance at Mayer's business. Hoping to capitalize on the shop's revitalized trade, the man refused to renew Mayer's lease when it expired in 1888, announcing that he would resume control of the business himself.

This avaricious scheme soon backfired on the original Kolling proprietor, primarily because he did not account for the tenacious spirit of Oscar Mayer. A strapping young man who had immigrated to America at fourteen, Mayer acquired his powerful physique and gritty determination working at different meat markets and stockyards in the Midwest. Now that he had finally established a place for himself as a respected neighborhood merchant, he was not about to allow anyone to take it away without a fight. Borrowing $10,000 from a bank and some friends, he built a new store only two blocks south of his former location, where he would be close enough to continue serving his original customers.

At the close of his first day in the new store, the twenty-nine-year-old sausage maker had tallied $59 in sales, an impressive figure considering that most of his pork products sold for under 12¢ a pound. Soon it became apparent that the shop was not only holding on to its old customers, but attracting new ones from well beyond its immediate area. By the early 1890s, Mayer was able to buy a glass-paneled wagon and a handsome horse named Strawberry to deliver sausages to retail shoppers and grocery stores in Chicago's other German neighborhoods.

Ever mindful of how his landlord had tried to pirate his former shop's reputation, Mayer prevented imitators from capitalizing on the growing fame of his products by developing recognizable brand names for his sausages, bacon, and hams. The idea of branding meats was very progressive for a local pork packer at the turn of the century, when even some of the biggest packinghouses were selling their products anonymously.

With shoppers now able to ask for his products by name, Mayer began to expand into new markets. In 1904 he had eight wagon salesmen selling sausages to some 280 grocery stores in northern Illinois and parts of Wisconsin. The Chicago sausage maker built up goodwill for his products by running advertisements in community newspapers and sponsoring German oompah-pah bands, which acted as roving ambassadors for the company, playing at picnics and holiday parades.

Despite the increasing growth of his business, Oscar Mayer might never have seen his name become a household word throughout America had not his son, Oscar G. Mayer, joined the firm in 1909. A forward-looking Harvard graduate, the younger Mayer recognized that the trend toward

Although he had long been a major meat packer, Oscar Mayer did not forget his old neighborhood during the depression. He ordered his Chicago plant to produce special "free sausages" for the needy, which he is shown distributing in this photo.

bigness in the meat-packing industry would eventually jeopardize the company's survival unless the firm expanded beyond the Great Lakes region. Thus, he developed a plan for selling Oscar Mayer products to an ever-widening geographical market, with the ultimate goal of national distribution.

The company took its first major step toward achieving this objective in 1919, when it acquired a farmer's cooperative meat-packing plant in Madison, Wisconsin. (This facility later became Oscar Mayer's corporate headquarters.) With the added production capacity afforded by their Madison plant, the Mayers were able to open new markets, first in the Midwest and East and later in the South and West.

As the size and scope of their business increased, the Mayers devoted a greater percentage of their budget to advertising, phasing out the folksy oompah-pah bands for more sophisticated marketing tools. In 1929 they began to promote the product that would become most closely associated with the company, when they put a bright yellow Oscar Mayer band around every fourth wiener that came off their production line.

Seven years after they started banding wieners, the Mayers introduced "Little Oscar," a pint-sized chef who attended store openings, visited children's hospitals, and made other goodwill appearances in a sausage-shaped vehicle called the "Wienermobile." At every stop, the diminutive spokesman would sign autographs, give away "wiener whistles" and other toys, and pass out samples of the wiener that Oscar Mayer advertising promoted as "the wiener with a conscience." (The purpose of this slogan was to reassure consumers that only the finest ingredients went into an Oscar Mayer wiener.)

Under Oscar G. Mayer's leadership, the company also developed many technological breakthroughs that have since become industry standards, including a tube machine that encased liverwurst in "chub-sized" plastic tubes (1949), the Slice-Pak, which vacuum packed sliced meat in plastic (1950), and a stripping machine that removed the cooking cases of sausages and made possible the advent of the skinless sausage (1953). All these innovations were leased by Oscar Mayer to competing meat packers, which is one reason the company has consistently been among the most profitable firms in the industry.

Oscar Mayer retired as company president in 1928 to be succeeded by his son, but he continued to serve as chairman of the board until his death at ninety-five in 1955. The former stockyard worker remained vigorous and active until six weeks before his death and was at his office on his last birthday receiving congratulatory phone calls.

Although his namesake company was doing a $225-million-a-year business when he died, Oscar Mayer remained very much the friendly neighborhood merchant. This was demonstrated during the depths of the depression, when he distributed free sausages to the crowd that lined up every day outside his office at the corner of Sedgwick Street and Beethoven Place in Chicago—the same corner where the young sausage maker had defiantly built his own store more than forty years earlier.

M—— 1877–1938
MAX FACTOR

Max Factor Makeup

Henry B. Walthall will never be counted among the Barrymores and Oliviers, but the silent screen actor, who appeared in many of D. W. Griffith's films, made cinema history in 1914 when he became the first in his trade to wear motion picture makeup. The man responsible for creating that notable greasepaint was Max Factor, a Russian cosmetician who amassed a great personal fortune applying his artful preparations to the faces of Hollywood's earliest stars.

Born to a poor family in the city of Lodz (now part of Poland), Factor began his career in cosmetics at the age of thirteen, when he dropped out of his synagogue school to become a makeup boy with a traveling opera troupe. During his apprenticeship, the youth learned the secrets of mixing powders, shadows, and rouges, as well as the art of wigmaking. Factor exhibited a remarkable talent for his new craft, and his skill eventually earned him an appointment as a makeup man with the prestigious Royal Ballet.

Despite his early advancement, Factor desired more freedom than could be found in Czarist Russia. In 1904 the twenty-seven-year-old cosmetician, his wife, and their three children immigrated to the United States, where he set up a wig and makeup concession stand at the St. Louis World's Fair. Later the family moved to California, and Factor established a small cosmetics shop in downtown Los Angeles. The Royal-Ballet-trained makeup artist put in long hours at his one-man studio, selling and manufacturing his own beauty products, aided only by his young sons, Davis and Max, Jr., who ground face powder and other preparations in hand-cranked machines.

When the budding motion picture industry began to shift its center of operations from New York to California, the little makeup shop's fortunes took a decided leap upward. Newly arrived filmmakers came to the store with their makeup problems, and the personable Factor was always ready to help. If a director needed his services in a pinch, the cosmetician would drop what he was doing, run out to a movie set with a stick of greasepaint, and assist actors and actresses in its application. Word of the Russian

Max Factor, beauty consultant to the stars, applies makeup to Joan Crawford. Factor's well-publicized "Hollywood connection" helped him establish an international following for his namesake line of cosmetics.

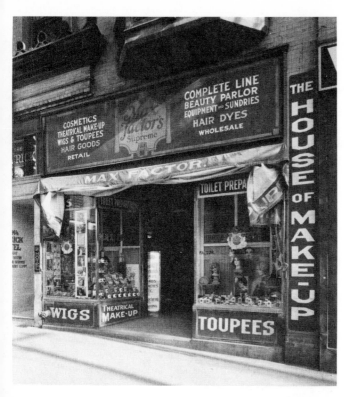

This early Max Factor cosmetics store in downtown Los Angeles was a far cry from "the world's greatest cosmetics factory" that he built in 1935, after his work as a movie makeup man had made him a celebrity in his own right.

makeup man's attentiveness spread quickly through Hollywood's growing movie colony, and soon Max Factor was in demand by virtually every studio in town.

Through his early work with moviemakers, Factor came to realize that the new medium, with its harsh lighting and revealing close-up shots, called for an entirely different kind of makeup than the stick greasepaint then used by stage players. The very thick, traditional stage makeup went on unevenly, causing actors' faces to have an unnatural, caked appearance on film.

After experimenting with different formulas in his Los Angeles shop, Factor developed the first greasepaint in cream (rather than stick) form. His new makeup could be applied in a thin, even layer to give performers a smooth, more realistic look on the screen.

When the cream greasepaint was worn by Walthall in 1914, it created a sensation, and a short time later it became the standard for the motion picture industry. Factor followed this innovation with several other pioneering breakthroughs, including the development of Panchromatic film makeup (1928) and Pan-Cake makeup for use in technicolor films (1937).

Actresses who were first exposed to Max Factor makeup on the movie set were so impressed with its natural-looking effects that they began wearing it outside the studio as well. As the popularity of Factor's cosmetics spread, many of Hollywood's leading ladies came to regard him as the final authority on everything from hair coloring to skin and nail care. For three decades, reigning screen stars like Gloria Swanson, Mary Pickford, and Joan Crawford flocked to the gregarious cosmetician for personal consultations. As part of the Factor beauty regime, the movie queens had their facial contours analyzed by a specially designed machine, and they received "color harmony guidance" (aided by a spectroscopic device) to achieve the most flattering combination of eye shadow, lipstick, and rouge for their particular complexion and coloring.

By 1935 Factor's Hollywood following had grown so large that he was able to erect "the world's greatest cosmetics factory" in the movie center. Built at a cost of $600,000, the neoclassical structure featured a fluted white facade with a gigantic marble portal. A crowd of over nine-thousand turned out for the studio's grand opening in early December, creating one of the biggest traffic jams the city had ever seen. The assembled throng was treated to a spectacle that had all the glitter of a major movie premier. Chartreuse and raspberry floodlights bathed the building's entrance, and most of filmdom's major celebrities were on hand to participate in the inaugural ceremonies. Jean Harlow dedicated the powder blue "Blonde Room," while another Factor friend, Claudette Colbert, opened the "Brunette Room," done in dusty pink.

Factor capitalized on his well-publicized association with beautiful Hollywood actresses by making his glosses, creams, and powders available to women throughout America. Promoted with personal endorsements from celebrated Factor clients like Mabel Normand, the cosmetics were readily accepted by housewives and working women who hoped to add a dash of theatrical glamour to their looks—if not their lives. The California cosmetics maker was selling his products nationally by 1927, and just three years later his rapidly growing company began international distribution by opening markets in eighty-one foreign countries.

When Max Factor died of a liver and kidney ailment in 1938, management of the company passed into the hands of his sons. The family-run business was America's third largest cosmetics firm in 1973, when it was acquired by Norton Simon for a reported $480 million.

H————— 1896–1972
HOWARD D. JOHNSON

Howard Johnson's Ice Cream

To his friends in Wollaston, Massachusetts, it must have seemed as if Howard Johnson were jumping from the frying pan into the fire when he purchased a run-down drugstore-newsstand near the town's railroad station in 1924. The twenty-seven-year-old World War I veteran already owed creditors some $10,000 following the liquidation of the cigar store he had operated with his late father. Now, by agreeing to assume the financial obligations of the troubled pharmacy, Johnson was putting himself $28,000 deeper into debt.

Johnson's friends needn't have worried, however, because the young entrepreneur had a plan for turning the business into a money-maker. His first goal was to increase the volume of the newsstand by developing a home delivery service. Recruiting a crew of seventy-five eager "paper-boys," Johnson promoted his service to home owners in Wollaston and surrounding communities. Within a few years his annual newspaper volume was an impressive $30,000.

After getting the newspaper delivery service underway, Johnson turned his attention to the store's soda fountain. Like most drugstore fountains of 1924, the one at the Wollaston establishment dispensed a variety of sodas, ice-cream dishes, and other snacks—but it was ice cream that most interested the store's new owner.

The most popular ice cream in Wollaston at the time was the rich, flavorful product sold by an elderly German pushcart vendor. Realizing that such a quality product would be an invaluable traffic builder for the store's soda fountain, Johnson persuaded the peddler to sell his "secret recipe" for $300. What made the ice cream so delicious, Johnson then discovered, was that the German used almost twice as much butterfat as was typically found in commercial ice cream.

Howard Johnson followed the old German's formula to turn out batches of ice cream in the basement of his shop. Not content to confine himself to the standard vanilla-chocolate-strawberry mix, the drugstore owner began to experiment with different ice-cream flavors. When he came up with a new flavor that he liked, he would add it to his soda fountain menu. Johnson's selection grew to include twenty-eight flavors, and he used this number as the basis of an advertising slogan that eventually became his trademark.

With its quality ice cream and wide assortment of flavors, the drugstore's soda fountain soon was attracting customers from well beyond the confines of Wollaston. Johnson took advantage of his principal product's

Howard Johnson's original location was this modest pharmacy/newsstand in the Boston suburb of Wollaston, Massachusetts. As the window signs show, ice cream was only one of many products sold at the store in the mid-1920s. Less than a decade later, Johnson had a chain of orange-roofed restaurants such as the Mineola, New York, location pictured below. By then, the franchise pioneer had dropped patent medicine, stationery, and most other "drugstore items," but ice cream remained, having become Johnson's best-known product.

A crowd gathers for the grand opening of this Howard Johnson's restaurant in Mineola, New York, in the 1930s. The bright orange roof and weathervane were intended to attract the attention of passing motorists.

growing popularity by opening small ice-cream stands at beaches in Boston's south suburbs. Aided tremendously by word-of-mouth advertising, the stands caught on quickly with sun-baked beachgoers. On one particularly hot August day, a Howard Johnson's stand on a Wollaston beach sold fourteen-thousand ice-cream cones.

In 1928 the total volume of Howard Johnson's ice-cream sales at his store and beach stands was $240,000, and he was able to pay off his original debt in full. Encouraged by this success, the ambitious ice-cream maker branched out, opening a family-style restaurant in downtown Quincy, Massachusetts. Johnson's new restaurant received an early break when Eugene O'Neill's *Strange Interlude* was staged across the street at the Quincy Theatre after being banned in Boston. Theatergoers crowded into the restaurant during the exceptionally long play's ninety-minute intermission. The unexpected windfall was short-lived, however; once the O'Neill play closed, most of the restaurant's customers disappeared.

Johnson was forced to close his Quincy restaurant at a $45,000 loss in 1929. Despite this reversal, he was back in the restaurant business later that year after signing what, at the time, was a very unusual agreement with a man named Reginald Sprauge. A family friend, Sprauge wanted to capitalize on the excellent reputation Johnson's ice cream enjoyed in the Boston area by putting the name Howard Johnson on a highway restaurant he planned to open south of the city. In exchange, Sprauge agreed to three conditions; to pay Johnson a cash fee, to buy all his ice cream and (when possible) other food products from Johnson, and to allow Johnson to set the standard for all foods served at the restaurant.

Later, Johnson signed similar agreements with other restaurateurs, beginning what is generally acknowledged to be America's first franchise restaurant chain. By 1935 there were seven Howard Johnson's restaurants in Massachusetts. Five years later, the former Wollaston drugstore proprietor had his name on 135 company-owned and franchised restaurants that stretched along the East Coast. Most of the restaurants were located on major highways, and to make them unmistakably visible to motorists, their roofs were painted a bright orange.

One factor behind the chain's phenomenal early growth was its founder's steadfast insistence on maintaining high standards. An unorthodox executive who—even when his company reached the $100-million-a-year level—had neither a secretary nor a regular office, Johnson devoted two days a week to conducting unnanounced inspection tours of his restaurants. On one occasion, he walked into the kitchen of a Howard Johnson's in Cleveland and, without a word to anyone, began rummaging through the refrigerator. The alarmed manager called the police. When a local officer arrived a short time later, the indignant restaurateur protested, "I'm Howard Johnson." Amused, the officer retorted, "And I'm Christopher Columbus."

By the time Johnson retired in 1964, the company he had started in a small Wollaston drugstore had mushroomed into the nation's third largest distributor of food, trailing only the army and navy. In addition to its restaurants, the company operated motels (since 1954), an institutional catering service, and food processing plants. Yet, throughout this period of growth and diversification, the name Howard Johnson remained most closely associated with ice cream—which is exactly the way the man behind the name wanted it. An avowed ice-cream fanatic, Johnson ate at least one cone a day throughout his life and kept ten flavors stored in his home freezer at all times. Looking back on his career, the famous food executive observed the ironic side of the public's attitude toward ice cream: "I've spent my life developing scores of flavors, and yet most people still say, 'I'll take vanilla.' "

Gabrielle "Coco" Chanel revolutionized fashion in the early decades of this century by stressing comfort and simple elegance over the elaborate and restrictive costumes of the Victorian era. Rarely seen in later years without a hat—the wide brim with small crown pictured here is typical of her style—Chanel began her phenomenally successful fashion dynasty by opening a small hat boutique in 1913. Critical of the fussy millinery styles that were then the rage, Chanel remarked, "How can the brain function under those things?"

The Talented

1850–1915

Albert Goodwill Spalding

Spalding Sporting Goods

By the time he was seventeen years old, Albert Spalding's pitching arm had brought him offers of up to $2,500 to sign with baseball teams in cities like Washington, New York, and Cleveland. To a small-town youth of the 1860s who had been "discovered" playing amateur ball for the Forest City Club of Rockford, Illinois, the money seemed like a fortune—especially when compared to his $5-a-week salary as a grocery clerk.

The Forest City pitcher surprised everyone, however, and turned the ball clubs down. Instead, he heeded the wishes of his widowed mother, Harriet Spalding, who was afraid that the life of a sports hero would make her tall, muscular son too conceited. She instructed Albert to use the training he had received in school as a bookkeeper and find work with a reputable Chicago firm.

Before long, it became apparent that the young man's prowess in the corporate world did not match his skill on the playing field. Over a five-year period, Spalding was employed by seven different companies in industries ranging from insurance to publishing. Every firm he worked for went bankrupt shortly after he arrived—a coincidence that understandably left the Rockford youth wondering if he was jinxed in business. Finally, in 1871, the desperate athlete disobeyed his mother and signed on as a pitcher-outfielder with the Boston Red Stockings.

Spalding's stellar performance on the mound over the next five seasons was enough to convince even Harriet Spalding that baseball was where he belonged. Using a unique underhand pitching delivery, the right-hander amassed an incredible record of 207 wins against only 56 losses, achieving the distinction of becoming baseball's first 200-game winner. A relentless competitor who also served as the captain of the Boston team, Spalding pitched in almost every game (he collected all but 20 of the team's 227 victories during this period). At the plate, the strapping six-footer maintained a lofty .320 batting average. Led by Spalding's pitching and hitting, the Boston Red Stockings won four successive pennants in 1872–75, and the former sandlot player from Rockford, Illinois, was propelled into the limelight as a national hero.

Hall of Fame pitcher Albert Spalding, a stellar performer for the Boston and Chicago clubs in the 1870s, became the first major league hurler to rack up more than 200 career victories. Although only twenty-eight years old, Spalding retired in 1878 to devote more time to the baseball supply company he and his brother James Spalding had founded two years earlier. From baseball, the company branched out into tennis, football, golf, and other sports, eventually becoming one of the world's largest athletic supply houses.

In 1876 Spalding's successful career with Boston came to an end, when, after helping John A. Hulbert establish the National League of Professional Baseball Clubs, he switched his allegiance to the Chicago NL team. Hulbert, who owned the Chicago club, had persuaded the pitching ace to join his team in the capacity of player-manager. During Spalding's first season at the post, he guided Chicago to an NL pennant victory. He also continued his pitching heroics, leading the new league in both wins (46) and earned-run average (1.78).

Despite the fact that his pitching arm was still in excellent shape, Spalding's next two years on the baseball diamond were spent primarily as a first baseman. He subsequently retired from active play at age twenty-eight following the 1878 season. One reason for the superstar's early retirement was that he wanted to devote more attention to a baseball supply business he had established with his brother, James Walter Spalding, during his first season in Chicago. In just over two years, the company had grown by leaps and bounds, largely as a result of its premier product—a baseball that Albert Spalding had first designed for his own pitching use. Later, when he made his "Spalding ball" available to the public through his downtown Chicago store, it won immediate acceptance from ballplayers and was adopted as the official baseball of the National League.

Spalding then decided to capitalize on the popularity of his baseball by branching into the manufacture of other sporting goods. He relocated his company to Chicopee, Massachusetts, where he began turning out tennis balls, footballs, golf clubs, baseball gloves, and tennis rackets. To promote his sporting goods, Spalding came up with the then novel idea of using personal endorsements from well-known athletes who, in exchange for a fee, allowed their signature to be imprinted on a particular equipment model. By associating the Spalding brand with superstars, the former sports hero was able to build up a strong following for his products among athletes of all levels of ability.

In 1891 Albert Spalding was approached by an instructor at the Springfield, Massachusetts, YMCA college, Dr. James Naismith, who wanted help in designing a ball for a new game he had just invented. The contest was to be played in a gymnasium by two opposing teams, with players racking up points by tossing a ball through goals raised high off the floor. Spalding designed a ball of suitable size and texture, and in December a trial run of the gymnasium sport was scheduled. Prior to the game, Dr. Naismith sent the school janitor to obtain two boxes that could be used as goals. Not finding any boxes, the janitor returned with two half-bushel peach baskets—and thereafter the new sport was known as basketball.

His role in the development of basketball notwithstanding, baseball remained Albert Spalding's favorite sport. He maintained his connection with the Chicago club, serving as its president from 1882 to 1891, and he even found time to edit a number of baseball publications, including an annual handbook entitled *Spalding's Official Baseball Guide*. In 1888 the former pitcher introduced America's national pastime to the world, taking two teams on a six-month tour of Europe, Asia, Africa, and Australia, where they gave baseball exhibitions in nearly fifty cities.

During his later years, the ex-athlete's interests broadened to include religion and politics. After moving from Chicago to southern California in 1900, he became involved with the Raja Yoga Theosophical colony. In 1910 Spalding attempted to cash in on his fame as a sports hero by entering the California primary for U.S. senator. When he was defeated in his bid for the nomination, he retired to his Point Loma, California, home, where he died of heart failure five years later. Although he lost the senatorial contest, Spalding "won" another election in 1939, when he was posthumously voted into the National Baseball Hall of Fame in Cooperstown, New York.

L ———— 1878–1941
LOUIS CHEVROLET

Chevrolet Cars

Few of the spectators who turned out at New York's Morris Park on May 20, 1905, had any doubt that the automobile race they were about to witness would boil down to a contest between two men—Barney Oldfield and Walter Christie. Plenty of other good drivers were entered in the race, but Oldfield, who had won a long string of races in Henry Ford's famous 999 car, and Christie, the inventor of a challenging new front-wheel-drive vehicle, were clearly the class of the field. As the three-mile race unfolded, however, there emerged a third car whose driver was obviously intent on setting the pace for the event. Scarcely slowing down at the curves, the 90-hp Fiat screeched around the track at a death-defying speed, putting an ever-increasing distance between itself and the rest of the pack. The Italian-made car maintained a record-setting 68 miles per hour average throughout the course, finishing well ahead of the competition and making a celebrity out of its handsome twenty-seven-year-old driver, Louis Chevrolet.

Described by one newspaper as "the most audacious driver in the world," fearless Louis Chevrolet was signed to the Buick racing team by GM founder Will C. Durant in 1907. Three years later, Chevrolet left GM to join a new company started by Durant in Flint, Michigan. There, the former race car driver designed a stylish six-cylinder car that was christened the "Chevrolet."

Louis Chevrolet (circled on the left) and others admire the first production model Chevrolet car. Introduced in 1912, the stylish six-cylinder vehicle was an immediate commercial success for its manufacturer, Will C. Durant (front row, furthest right). Using his substantial Chevrolet profits, Durant was able to wrest control of General Motors away from rivals who had forced him out of the company in 1910.

The son of a Swiss clockmaker, Chevrolet had been racing cars for less than a year when he won the Morris Park event. His stunning upset made him one of the favorites in the prestigious 1906 Vanderbilt Cup on Long Island, but he crashed his Fiat into a fence and failed to complete the race. Although he escaped injury on that occasion, Chevrolet would not always be so lucky; between 1905 and 1920, the time he spent recovering from serious accidents amounted to almost three years.

Many of Chevrolet's accidents were the consequence of his fearless racing style. The large, mustached driver had a reputation for being an intense competitor who had very little concern for his personal safety when the outcome of a race was at stake. One newspaper report of the day described him as "the most audacious driver in the world."

Chevrolet's intrepid behavior on the race course soon attracted the attention of William Crapo Durant, an entrepreneur who applied a similar daredevil approach toward the running of his business, which happened to be a recently formed company called General Motors. In 1907 Durant invited Louis and his younger brother, Arthur Chevrolet, to "audition" for a job as a chauffeur by staging a match race behind General Motors's Buick plant in Flint, Michigan. (Auto racing was not very lucrative in its early years, and many drivers took auto-related jobs to augment their winnings.) Louis won the race easily, but Arthur got the job as Durant's chauffeur because he drove more carefully. There was, however, a nice consolation prize for Louis; Durant made him a member of the Buick racing team.

During the next three years, Louis Chevrolet racked up an impressive string of victories for the Buick team, including one in 1909 at the 158-mile Yorick Trophy race in Lowell, Massachusetts, where he finished a full twenty minutes ahead of his closest competitor. Then in 1910, Durant was forced out of GM in a colossal stockholders' dispute. Loyal to the man who had hired him, Chevrolet left General Motors and joined a new automobile company the entrepreneur had formed. As part of his contribution to the new venture, the champion driver offered to design a small, but luxurious touring car for Durant to manufacture.

The result of this effort was the Chevrolet, a stylish six-cylinder vehicle that revealed Louis's skill as a designer to be at least equal to his talent as a race car driver. Despite its high price tag ($2,150), the Chevrolet was an immediate success. Almost three thousand of the cars were sold in 1912, the first year of production. During the next two years, the newly formed Chevrolet Motor Company made a profit of $1.3 million on the sale of sixteen thousand vehicles.

By this time, however, Chevrolet and Durant were at odds over the latter's plan to expand the Chevrolet line by adding an inexpensive runabout model. Offended by the idea of his name being attached to a cheap car, the famous driver disassociated himself from his namesake company in 1914 and sold his stock to Durant. Chevrolet received only a small fraction of what the stock would be worth six years later, when Durant used the profits made from Chevrolet Motor Company to reacquire General Motors.

Following his split with Durant, Louis Chevrolet became a prolific and successful designer of race cars. His 1920 Frontenac car finished first at Indianapolis, driven by another brother, Gaston Chevrolet (who died in a racing accident several months later). The next year, a Chevrolet-designed automobile won the Indianapolis 500 again.

Despite his impressive accomplishments on the racing circuit, Chevrolet still came up a loser in the business world. He lost a substantial sum of money in 1922, when his attempt to produce a line of Frontenac passenger cars failed. Four years later, he and Arthur manufactured an efficient aircraft engine called the Chevrolair 333, but, marred by bad management, the business soon was dissolved, causing a bitter personal split between the brothers. Louis then joined Baltimore Ford dealer Glenn L. Martin in a new aircraft company. After the stock market crashed in October 1929, however, a hard-pressed Chevrolet was forced to turn over his shares in the company to Martin, who eventually built an aircraft empire around the "Martin 4-333 (née Chevrolair)."

In 1934 Chevrolet received two crushing personal blows; his eldest son died, and his sister's New Jersey home burned, destroying most of the memorabilia and engineering drawings he had acquired during his career. The dejected former auto racer and designer then took a consultant job with the Chevrolet division of GM and remained there until a cerebral hemorrhage forced his retirement in 1938. He died three years later while on a visit to Detroit from his retirement home in Florida.

The final tragic chapter in the saga of the Chevrolet brothers was written in 1946 when Arthur Chevrolet, then working as a master mechanic for a boatmaker, hanged himself in New Orleans. He was sixty-one years old.

G ——————————— 1883–1971
GABRIELLE [COCO] CHANEL

Chanel Perfume

Like the formula for her namesake perfume, the details surrounding Gabrielle (Coco) Chanel's early life are cloaked in secrecy. Ever since the petite, dark-eyed Frenchwoman became the queen of Parisian haute couture following World War I, those who have tried to delve into her past have run into a tangle of conflicting dates, names, and places. The cause of this confusion was Chanel herself; an elusive, secretive woman, the famous designer kept would-be biographers off balance by giving them differing and often contradictory accounts of her youth.

Some early—and obviously untrue—stories had Chanel leading a sheltered girlhood as the daughter of a prosperous wine merchant, while others told of her growing up on a horse farm owned by two strict aunts. Far more likely is the bleak account of Gabrielle's childhood given in Edmonde Charles-Roux's landmark biography *Chanel*, which describes the girl's upbringing in the Catholic orphanage of Aubazine, where she was taken at the age of six following the death of her mother. Even this theory is impossible to prove conclusively, as there is no trace of Chanel in the orphanage's records.

Despite the uncertainty surrounding her origins, there is one thing about Coco Chanel's life that is unmistakably clear—she was a designer of unparalleled originality and genius. Hailed by *Vogue* magazine as a "revolutionist, a non-conformist, a lone rebel who let women out of the prison of the tight corset," she pioneered an entirely new concept in fashion. In an era dominated by elaborate and restrictive Victorian costumes, Coco broke with tradition to emphasize comfort and simple elegance over ornamentation. During the 1920s, her "New Look," with its reliance on jersey blouses, short narrow skirts, collarless cardigan jackets, and ropelike strands of pearls, became the trademark of the modern, well-dressed woman on both sides of the Atlantic.

The designer who altered the shape of women's fashion began her career in the summer of 1913, when she opened a tiny hat boutique in the affluent seaside village of Deauville. Gaudy net and feather hats were the prevailing millinery style of the day, and the practical Coco detested them. "How can the brain function under those things?" protested the young milliner, who defiantly proceeded to design less complicated hats with wide, wavering brims and almost no crown at all.

Chanel's first national exposure in France came during World War I, when the Germans threatened Paris. Wealthy socialites who had hastily fled the besieged capital with "only the clothes on their backs" innundated Deauville. Desperate, the women came to Chanel's millinery shop seeking not only hats but entire wardrobes, and Coco furnished them with simple straight ankle-length skirts and matching sailor blouses, a costume that she herself had been wearing for years. The outfit quickly became a favorite of affluent Frenchwomen, creating a rage for what was playfully called the "poor girl look."

Relocating in Paris in 1914, Chanel continued to turn out unconfining feminine apparel, free of what she called "ludicrous trimmings and fussy bits and pieces." Her designs struck a responsive chord with emancipated women of the postwar era, and her studio at 31 rue Cambon became a mecca for fashion-conscious Parisians. Wealthy women paid extravagant sums for her original creations, while others of more modest means bought the Chanel imitations made by American and European clothing manufacturers.

In 1922 Chanel capitalized on her growing fame by introducing a Chanel No. 5 perfume (so called because 5 was the designer's lucky number). Unlike other perfumes then on the market, No. 5 did not have a distinctively floral scent, and this undoubtedly increased its appeal to the "boyish" flappers of the Jazz Age. The revolutionary perfume contributed some $15 million to the personal fortune of its creator, who offered this explanation for its incredible success: "Women are not flowers. Why should they want to smell like flowers?"

Coco Chanel relished her role as the grand dame of fashion. She maintained a suite at the Ritz Hotel in Paris and an opulent home on the Faubourg St.-Honoré, where she threw lavish parties in the 1920s and 1930s for her international set of friends—a group that included Stravinsky, Picasso, the Grand Duke Dmitri, Dali, and Bérard.

A quick-witted woman, Coco spared neither friend nor foe her sharp tongue. "I prefer vitriol to honey," she once said, and some of her most caustic remarks were reserved for other designers. Typical of the Chanelian sarcasm: "Saint Laurent has excellent taste. The more he copies me, the better taste he displays."

The reign of Coco Chanel came to an abrupt end in the late 1930s, when women shifted their preference to the more elaborate designs of Elsa Schiaparelli, who celebrated her emergence as the new high priestess of

Coco Chanel strikes a classic Chanelian pose. Costume jewelry, one of the personal trademarks of the designer, elegantly drapes her neck. Colorful, sharp-tongued, and shrewd in her business dealings, Chanel was described by her friend Pablo Picasso as "the most sensible woman in Europe."

fashion by proclaiming, "Voilà . . . Feeneesh Chanel." For a time it seemed as if the Italian designer were right. Many observers of the fashion scene dismissed Chanel as a vestige of a bygone era. Disheartened, the creator of the post–World War I New Look retired in 1938, closing her couture and withdrawing from public view.

Coco Chanel, however, was far from "feeneeshed,"; fifteen years after her retirement, the designer, then seventy-one, achieved something miraculously rare in the fashion world—a comeback. On February 5, 1954, Chanel unveiled a new collection at her rue Cambon salon. The elegant but uncomplicated clothing that made up the collection was evocative of Coco's earlier designs. Despite its lukewarm reception from fashion critics who thought it too plain, Chanel's collection was a tremendous commercial success.

By 1960 the trim-fitting Chanel suit once again had become an essential wardrobe item for the sophisticated American female, including First Lady Jacqueline Kennedy (who was wearing a pink Chanel suit in Dallas when her husband was assassinated). Coco Chanel, exhibiting the energy of a woman half her age, continued to turn out new collections every year until her death at eighty-seven in 1971.

Although she never married, Chanel had many rich and famous lovers during her long life, including Hugh Richard Arthur Grosvenor, the 2d duke of Westminster. One of the wealthiest men in the world during the 1920s, the twice-married duke showered Coco with expensive jewelry, and speculation was rife that the designer was about to become the next duchess of Westminster. When asked by reporters if she planned to marry her aristocratic suitor, however, Chanel dismissed the idea: "There are a lot of duchesses, but only one Coco Chanel." Few who knew her would have argued with that.

The Lucky

C⎯⎯⎯⎯ 1851–1937
CHARLES E. HIRES

Hires Root Beer

Root beer may not be as romantic as champagne, but the man who introduced the frothy beverage to the world first tasted it on his honeymoon. Charles Hires, a prosperous twenty-four-year-old Philadelphia pharmacist, and his bride, Clara, journeyed to a rural New Jersey inn following their 1875 wedding. During their stay, the couple sampled a pitcher of herb tea, a uniquely delicious drink made by the innkeeper's wife. The beverage's excellent taste, said the woman, was the result of a family recipe that called for an assortment of sixteen wild roots and berries—including juniper, wintergreen, sarsaparilla, and hops.

Charles Hires listened to his hostess's explanation with more than polite interest. An enterprising businessman who had arrived in Philadelphia from his New Jersey home only eight years earlier as a scared teenager with 50¢ in his pocket, the young drugstore owner was quick to recognize the beverage's commercial possibilities.

Before returning home, Hires obtained the recipe for herb tea from the innkeeper's wife. Back at his drugstore, he solicited the help of two medical college professors, and together they developed a formula for making a solid concentrate of the beverage. When mixed with water, sugar, and yeast, the concentrate yielded a drink that tasted remarkably like the New Jersey woman's creation.

A devout Quaker, Hires intended to sell his "Hires Herb Tea" to hard-drinking Pennsylvania coal miners as a temperance alternative. The beverage soon acquired a more memorable name as a result of a suggestion made by a friend of the pharmacist, the Reverend Dr. Russell Conwell, founder of Temple University. Upon learning that Hires planned to market the new drink in the state's coal country, Dr. Conwell is said to have advised, "No, the miners would never drink it if it were called a tea. Let's call it a beer—root beer."

In 1876 Hires Root Beer made its debut at the Philadelphia Centennial Exposition, its creator promoting the beverage by giving free drinks to thirsty fairgoers. The public's enthusiastic response to the drink convinced Hires that his marketing effort should extend beyond Pennsylvania's coal-mining communities. He began advertising in newspapers the following year and later became the first advertiser to buy a color ad on the back cover of *Ladies Home Journal.* In most of the advertisements, Hires touted his beverage as a healing tonic and a wholesome alternative to beer of the alcoholic variety.

The advertising exposure paid off handsomely, making Hires an early leader in the soft drink industry. At a time when Coca-Cola, Dr. Pepper, and other soda pops were small regional beverages with limited followings, Hires's yellow 25¢ box of solid root beer extract (it made five gallons of the drink) was a familiar sight in homes and drugstore fountains throughout America. By 1890 Hires had added a three-ounce bottle of liquid extract to his line and formed the Charles E. Hires Co. on $300,000 capital to manufacture and sell his two root beer products. Five years later, the rapidly growing Hires company was recapitalized at a half million dollars, and it was bottling ready-to-drink root beer at local plants in different regions of the country.

Few who knew Charles Hires would have been surprised at how he had turned a chance encounter with a countrywoman's herb tea into a booming national business. Years before his honeymoon, Hires had converted another accidental discovery into a successful commercial venture. In December 1869 the eighteen-year-old business prodigy borrowed some $3,000 to start his own Philadelphia apothecary shop. A short time later he was walking by his Spruce Street store when he saw a work crew excavating a cellar. The astute teenager recognized the soil that the workmen were removing as potter's clay. Upon learning that no one wanted the "dirt," the youth had it dumped in the basement of his drugstore, where he cut it into circular cakes, wrapped it in tissue paper and sold it throughout the city as "Hires Potter's Clay." Hires earned over $6,000 selling his potter's clay (which was used to remove stains from woolen garments) and was more than able to repay his debts.

Even as a middle-aged millionaire soft drink executive, Hires was still eager to take advantage of new business opportunities. In 1896, twenty years after he had begun making root beer, he opened a plant to condense milk in Pennsylvania. Eventually he organized a half dozen milk condensing companies that operated twenty-one plants in four states and Canada. When Hires sold his dairy interests to the Nestlé Company in 1918, he received more than $1 million.

Hires remained active in his soft drink company during the entire time he was involved in the milk business. He served as president of the root beer firm until he retired in favor of his son Charles Hires, Jr., in 1923, and continued as chairman of the board until his death twelve years later.

Throughout his rise in the business world, Hires remained a dedicated member of the Society of Friends. He helped finance the reopening of the

Merion Meeting House where William Penn had worshiped. In 1917 the self-educated businessman (he had to leave school at twelve to work in a Bridgeton, New Jersey, drugstore) wrote a book commemorating the historic Quaker meetinghouse.

In addition to his activities with his church, Hires (whose mother was a descendent of Martha Washington) was involved in Republican politics and various trade associations. His chief hobby was deep-sea fishing, and it was while preparing to leave his Haverford, Pennsylvania, home for a fishing trip in July 1937 that the eighty-five-year-old soft drink maker suffered a fatal stroke. At the time of his death, Hires's namesake beverage was the top-selling root beer in the world.

W———— 1870–1957
WILLIAM COLEMAN

Coleman Camping Equipment

As a student at the University of Kansas Law School in 1899, William Coleman suffered from two troublesome afflictions: poor eyesight and an exhausted bank account. The visually impaired former schoolteacher overcame the first obstacle by having friends read to him from assigned law texts. His second problem, however, was not as easily solved. Even though he lived on a steady diet of canned tomatoes, brown sugar, and day-old bread for months on end, Coleman ran out of money during his final year of school.

Still wanting to become a lawyer, the ex-student took a job as a traveling typewriter salesman. His plan was to spend a year or so on the road to earn the money needed to complete his education. But with his twenty-ninth birthday already behind him, the financially strapped Kansan had good cause to wonder whether he would ever manage to earn his law degree.

One miserable rainy night late in 1899, Coleman found himself in the coal-mining town of Brockton, Alabama. As he sloshed through the muddy, unpaved streets of the little mining hamlet, he noticed an unbelievably bright light coming from a drugstore window. Entering the store, Coleman learned that the source of the light was a hanging lamp powered by gasoline. Unlike the inefficient wick-type oil lamps that were then commonplace, the gas model cast such a clear, white light that even the dim-visioned salesman could read in its glow.

So impressed was Coleman with his discovery that he decided to drop typewriters and sell the powerful lamp to store owners in rural areas where electricity was still unavailable. He took the money he had made from type-

William Coleman with one of his most famous products, the Coleman lantern. A struggling typewriter salesman, Coleman was walking past a Brockton, Alabama, pharmacy one rainy night in 1899, when he noticed the particularly brilliant light produced by the store's hanging gas lamp. He was so impressed with the lamp's illuminatory power that he dropped typewriters and began selling the lighting device, thus laying the groundwork for what would become the multimillion-dollar Coleman Co.

writers, bought a small supply of lamps from their Memphis, Tennessee, manufacturer, and headed west to peddle his merchandise.

Coleman's first stop was Kingfisher, a frontier trading town in the Oklahoma territory. As it turned out, he could hardly have picked a more horrendous spot to begin the new venture. A smooth-talking salesman had just breezed through Kingfisher and swindled the town's merchants, selling them gas lamps that became hopelessly clogged with carbon after a few days. Having been hoodwinked once, the leery store owners were not eager to buy the lamps offered by this second stranger.

After a week in Kingfisher, Coleman had sold only two of his $15 lamps. He was on the verge of admitting defeat and moving on to the next town, when he was struck with an idea for a new marketing plan. Instead of trying to sell the lamps, he would rent them to the merchants for $1 a week. If the lamps became clogged or malfunctioned in any way, the store owner wouldn't owe him a penny.

Even the suspicious Kingfisher businessmen had a hard time resisting this "no light, no pay" guarantee. Four days after launching his rental service, Coleman had signed up some one-hundred store owners. Within two years, he was supplying rental lamps to merchants in more than twenty towns across the West, including Wichita, Albuquerque, and Las Vegas. (Electricity was available in many of these cities, but Coleman's gas-fired lamp was twenty times more powerful than the carbon-filament electric bulb then in use.)

In 1903 Coleman purchased the rights to the gas lamp from his Tennessee supplier for $3,000 and began marketing it as the Coleman Arc Lamp. By the end of the decade, the lamp had established such a strong reputation for quality that the former law student was able to phase out his rental program and sell the product directly to the customer.

An astute promoter, Coleman drew attention to his lamps by providing lighting for major outdoor events such as G.A.R. reunions, lodge picnics, and county fairs, as well as one of the earliest college football games played in the evening, an October 6, 1905, contest in which Fairmount College (now Wichita State) beat Cooper College.

As his business grew, Coleman expanded his product line to include a gas table lamp for home use, an outdoor lantern, and a portable gas camping stove. The Coleman Arc Lamp still remained the backbone of the business, however, with sales ranging between 300,000 and 500,000 units throughout the 1920s.

Then in 1932 newly elected Franklin Roosevelt began a rural electrification program, which drastically reduced the demand for gas lamps. With its main product rapidly becoming obsolete, the Coleman Company seemed destined for bankruptcy, but its founder refused to surrender without a fight. Displaying the same resourcefulness that had served him so well back in Kingfisher more than thirty years earlier, Coleman began to look for ways to modernize his product selection. This time he was not alone; his sons, Sheldon and Clarence, had joined the company, and together the trio developed two new Coleman products—oil space heaters and inexpensive floor furnaces. The economical heating units caught on quickly in the depression market, and Coleman's annual volume rose from $3 million in 1932 to $49 million by the outbreak of World War II. During the conflict, the Coleman Company designed one of its most famous products, the GI pocket stove. Smaller than a quart milk bottle and weighing just three-and-a-half pounds, the stove could operate on any kind of fuel at temperatures ranging from 60 degrees below zero to 125 degrees above zero. Ernie Pyle wrote fifteen articles about the stove, rating it and the jeep as the two most important pieces of noncombat equipment to come out of the war.

After the war, Coleman went back to making space heaters and floor furnaces for the civilian market. In the late 1950s the spread of central heating cut into the demand for the company's principal products. Once again showing an uncanny ability to adapt to change, Sheldon and Clarence Coleman expanded their production of portable stoves and added a line of tents and insulated coolers to take advantage of the rising demand for camping equipment.

By the end of the 1960s, Coleman had become the largest manufacturer of camping equipment in the world, and helped by the growing outdoor leisure boom, the company's sales reached $134 million a year.

Although he never lived to see the phenomenal growth of his company's camping equipment business, William Coleman—who died of a heart attack in 1957—would undoubtedly have been very pleased by this development. Descended from hardy New England stock (his ancestors settled Nantucket Island in 1630), the tall, broad-shouldered executive was a skilled lake fisherman and canoeist despite his lifelong visual impairment.

W——— 1860–1951
ILL K. KELLOGG

Kellogg's Breakfast Cereals

Raised in an austere Seventh-Day Adventist home, Will K. Kellogg grew into a shy, dour young man with few friends, limited interests, and no discernible talents. At thirteen he was taken out of school, where he had been deemed a slow learner, and sent to work at his father's Battle Creek, Michigan, broom-making shop. He toiled as a traveling broom salesman for a few years before moving on to other, equally unpromising jobs. Even by the most ordinary standards, this was an unremarkable track record, but it seemed pitiable when compared to the singular success enjoyed by Will's brother, Dr. John Harvey Kellogg.

Older than Will by eight years, J. H. was an eminent surgeon and the superintendent of the nationally famous Battle Creek Sanitarium. He was also the author of several widely read books on "biologic living," a revolutionary theory on health and nutrition that advocated treating many ailments with a combination of exercises, hydrotherapy, and a strict vegetarian diet.

In 1880 Dr. Kellogg offered his younger brother a job at the sanitarium. Will, recently married and short on funds, accepted, and for the next twenty-five years he worked at the institution as a self-described "bookkeeper, cashier, packing and shipping clerk, errand boy and general utility man." Will Kellogg wasn't at the sanitarium long before he began to resent the high-handed treatment he received from his older brother. In his more bitter moments, he referred to himself as "J. H.'s flunky." Few who knew the Kelloggs would have been shocked by this hostility. Reportedly, one of Will's "jobs" at the sanitarium was to give his brother a shave and shoeshine. On spring and summer mornings, when Dr. John peddled his bicycle to work, Will would jog along next to him and receive instructions for the upcoming day.

An added thorn in the side of Will Kellogg was the excessive stinginess of his brother. Despite the fact that his sanitarium grossed as much as $4 million a year and that he himself lived in a beautiful home with grounds that covered more than an entire city block, Dr. Kellogg never paid his younger brother more than $87 a month. The situation once led Will to lament in his diary, "Am afraid that I will always be a poor man."

Indeed, Will Kellogg might have remained a "poor man," laboring in the shadow of his egotistical brother, had not fate intervened one day in 1894 in the form of a food experiment gone awry. At the time, Will was assisting his brother in developing a new kind of easily digestible wheat meal. Working in the sanitarium's kitchen, the two men would boil wheat dough for varying lengths of time before running it through rollers that pressed it into thin sheets. On one occasion, a batch of boiled dough was inadvertently left out overnight. When the exposed wheat was run through the rollers the next day, instead of forming the expected sheet, it broke up into small flakes.

By letting the dough stand, the Kelloggs had allowed moisture to be distributed evenly to each individual wheat berry. Thus, when the dough passed through the rollers, the berries formed separate flakes instead of binding together in a single sheet. This process is now known to makers of flaked cereals as "tempering."

Dr. Kellogg suggested grinding the accidentally made flakes into small pieces, but Will convinced him to toast them and serve them as they were to patients. The idea of a flaked cereal was unknown at the time, but the unusual food was an immediate success in the sanitarium dining room. Following their experiments with wheat flakes, the Kelloggs began cooking flaked cereals made of barley, oats, corn, and other grains. (Corn flakes became particularly popular after Will improved their flavor by substituting corn grits for the tougher and less tasty whole-corn kernel used in his original formula.)

Soon after they began serving cereal in the sanitarium dining room, the brothers were forced to set up a small mail-order business to satisfy the demands of former patients who wanted to enjoy the flaked food at home. This convinced Will that flaked cereal had tremendous potential as a consumer item, and for almost a decade, he tried to persuade his brother to sell their product to the retail grocery trade. Dr. John, however, believed that such a blatantly commercial venture would compromise his professional integrity, and he persistently vetoed the idea.

The doctor's stubborn opposition eventually proved too much even for his docile younger brother to endure. In 1906 the forty-six-year-old Will finally stepped out of the shadows, buying his brother's share of their cereal-making patents and forming his own cereal company.

Given the chance to be his own boss, Will Kellogg exhibited a business genius that few would have believed he possessed. His first product was corn flakes, and to promote its sale, he developed an advertising campaign that was decades ahead of its time. Kellogg became one of the first advertisers to make use of four-color magazine ads, test markets (new ideas were tried in Dayton, Ohio, before going national), and widespread sampling. In one novel 1907 ad, he proclaimed that "Wednesday is Wink Day in New York" and offered a free box of corn flakes to every woman who winked at her grocer on the appointed day. The ad was considered risqué by some, but it helped to boost Kellogg's New York City sales from two railroad carloads a month to a carload a day. As his volume grew, Kellogg poured more money into advertising, erecting electric billboards in big cities and commissioning famous artists like Norman Rockwell to design cereal box covers.

The profits generated by his cereal empire made Will Kellogg one of the nation's richest men. Despite his great wealth, however, he never earned the respect of his older brother. The two men remained almost totally estranged after their 1906 break. Finally, in 1943, ninety-one-year-old Dr. John wrote a conciliatory letter, acknowledging that he had wronged Will in many ways. Ironically, the letter's delivery was delayed, and by the time it reached Will, Dr. John was dead.

PARKER BROTHERS

James B. Beam Distilling Co.

Elizabeth Arden INC

Baldwin

Chris•Craft

MURRAY CHRIS-CRAFT CRUISERS, INC.
MURRAY CHRIS-CRAFT SPORTBOATS, INC.

MORTON SALT
DIVISION OF MORTON-NORWICH

English HEATH Toffee

L. S. HEATH & SONS, Inc.

Wally Amos, who "discovered" Simon and Garfunkel at a Manhattan club in the 1960s when he was a talent agent with the William Morris Agency. In 1975 Amos opened a chocolate chip cookie store in Los Angeles, which he transformed into a $5-million-a-year business by the end of the decade.

———— 1936–
WALLY AMOS

Famous Amos Cookies

There may indeed be no business like show business, but Wally Amos decided to forsake his career as a Los Angeles talent agent in 1975 to open a chocolate chip cookie store. Within five years, his business grew into a national cookie company, selling its products to exclusive department stores and chalking up $5 million in annual sales. A frequent talk show guest, Amos has used his Hollywood connection (stars like Bill Cosby and Helen Reddy have invested in his business) to create a celebrity aura for his cookie, leading *Time* to describe him as the man who "put the chic into chips." The cookie maker developed his promotional skills at the William Morris Agency, where he was the firm's first black talent agent. "I was the Jackie Robinson of the theatrical agency business," recalled Amos, who is credited with "discovering" Simon and Garfunkel at a Manhattan club. Amos acquired his taste for chocolate chip cookies growing up in Harlem, where his Aunt Della baked them for the family. Despite his success, Amos still gets involved in making cookies. "I talk to them while they're baking," he once said; "sort of give them words of encouragement."

E LIZABETH ARDEN
1891–1966

Elizabeth Arden Cosmetics

Elizabeth Arden started life as Florence Nightingale Graham, an ambitious girl from Toronto who, inspired by her famous namesake, wanted to become a nurse. Her energy was rechanneled into the beauty business after she moved to New York in 1908 and took a job with cosmetic specialist Eleanor Adair. Two years later, Florence launched her own beauty salon in a converted brownstone on Fifth Avenue. It was at this point that she adopted the more euphonious name Elizabeth Arden; the "Elizabeth" taken after an associate, Elizabeth Hubbard, and "Arden" from Tennyson's "Enoch Arden," a favorite poem. With the aid of New York chemist A. F. Swanson, Arden developed two beauty products in 1914 that were to make her a multimillionaire—Cream Amoretta (a face cream) and Ardena Skin Tonic. The transplanted Canadian went on to devise over three-hundred other cosmetic products, and her Fifth Avenue beauty salon grew to occupy eleven stories. After achieving success in the beauty field, Arden became interested in thoroughbred horse racing. She purchased the Maine Chance Farm in Lexington, Kentucky, and in 1947 one of her thoroughbreds, Jet Pilot, won the Kentucky Derby.

P HILIP D. ARMOUR
1832–1901

Armour Hot Dogs

Best known for giving us "the dogs kids love to bite," Philip Armour was himself bitten by the California gold bug when he was nineteen. Leaving his family's Stockbridge, New York, farm, the broad-shouldered redhead journeyed to San Francisco, making a good part of the trip on foot. Soon after arriving on the West Coast, Armour concluded that gold digging was too speculative for his tastes and got into the steadier business of selling mining equipment. Within five years, the shrewd upstate New Yorker had squirreled away $8,000—enough to buy a good-sized farm back in Stockbridge. On the way home, Armour stopped at Milwaukee and was so impressed with the growing Great Lakes city that he changed his plans and settled there, acquiring an interest in a produce and commission business. In 1863 Armour became a partner in a Milwaukee pork-packing firm. Four years later, he set up the Armour & Co. packinghouse in Chicago, which he built into one of the world's largest pork processors. As his business grew in the 1870s, Armour added branded consumer products to his line, most notably Armour Star Ham. The energetic packer remained the active president of his company until a year before his death.

T————— 1836–1908
HOMAS M. ARMSTRONG

Armstrong Floors and Ceilings

Nice guys don't always finish last. One of several businessmen contracted by the Sanitary Commission (a forerunner of the Red Cross) to make medical supplies for Union troops during the Civil War, Pittsburgh cork maker Thomas Armstrong was the only supplier who didn't pad profits by substituting inferior goods for the specified materials. Later, when the frauds came to light, Armstrong was singled out as the only honest man among a gang of perfidious profiteers. Orders for bottle and jar corks came pouring into Armstrong's factory as a result of the publicity surrounding the revelations, and the honest Pennsylvanian became a national leader in the cork industry. Armstrong probably would have continued to devote his full attention to cork making, were it not for the specter of Prohibition (some of the biggest cork customers were breweries). With an eye toward the day America would go dry, the cork maker and his son Charles decided to enter the linoleum business—a logical choice, since finely ground cork was a major ingredient in the floor covering. In 1908 the company opened a linoleum plant in Lancaster, Pennsylvania, paving the way for its expansion into its now famous tiles and ceilings.

R————— 1907–
. STANTON AVERY

Avery Self-Adhesive Labels

Back in 1935, virtually all labels sold in the United States were of the lick-and-stick water gum variety. Then R. Stanton Avery, a twenty-eight-year-old Oklahoman, began to manufacture and market the first self-adhesive price-marking labels. A graduate of Pomona College (class of '32), Avery launched his firm, the Kum-Kleen Adhesive Products Co., out of a small Los Angeles office with less than $100 in capital. Later, the name of the company was changed to Avery International, and under Stan Avery's leadership it pioneered many industry breakthroughs, including the first manual and automatic dispensers for self-adhesive labels. The greater convenience that Avery's product offered over gum-backed labels led to its immediate acceptance by businesses and consumers. By 1980 Avery International's annual sales were over $600 million, making the Pasadena, California, firm one of the nation's five-hundred largest corporations. Still involved in the company he founded, Stan Avery has also served as the chairman of the board of trustees of the California Institute of Technology.

DON FACUNDO BACARDI

Bacardi Rum

Don Facundo Bacardi was fourteen years old when he arrived in Cuba from Spain in 1830. Settling in Santiago, he found work with a local merchant and later opened his own wine shop. In his spare time, Bacardi experimented with different rum-making techniques, eventually developing a unique light rum that was smooth enough to be consumed straight. For years the wine merchant confined himself to making rum in the back of his shop for friends and good customers. Then, in 1862, he purchased a small local distillery for $3,500 and, at forty-six, started what would become the world's largest rum company. Bacardi was searching for a suitable trademark for the new product when his wife, Doña Amalia, inspired by the colony of bats that lived in the rafters of the distillery's tin roof, suggested the now famous black bat illustration. Twenty years later, the company's fortunes received a big boost when Jennings Cox, a mining engineer in the Cuban hamlet of Daiquiri, mixed light Bacardi Rum with lime juice to create the Daiquiri cocktail.

DWIGHT H. BALDWIN
1821–1899

Baldwin Pianos

A physically frail youth, Dwight Baldwin's dream was to become a Presbyterian minister, an ambition he pursued by enrolling in the Oberlin College divinity school in 1840. Poor health forced Baldwin to end his studies after just one year, and he moved to Cincinnati, where he became a music teacher. Baldwin left his teaching job in 1862, and at the age of forty-one, sank his $2,000 life savings in a piano store. In all likelihood, Baldwin's store never would have grown into a major national manufacturing firm had not he sold a one-sixth interest in the business to his bookkeeper Lucien Wulsin. Bright, ambitious, and twenty-four years Baldwin's junior, Wulsin got the company into manufacturing in the late 1880s after one of its suppliers (Steinway) suddenly dropped it as a dealership. As the aging Baldwin devoted more and more time to church activities, Wulsin and a group of several recently admitted partners developed large markets for the firm's Hamilton reed organ and Baldwin piano (introduced in 1891). When Dwight Baldwin died in 1899, his personal share in the business amounted to nearly half a million dollars. Looking back on Baldwin's career in 1953, Lucien Wulsin II (then company president) noted, "Mr. Baldwin was outstanding for his ability to surround himself with partners a lot abler than he was."

E̲DMUND BALL F̲RANK BALL
1855–1925   1857–1943

Ball Jars

Heeding their mother's advice to "always stick together," the five Ball brothers became partners in several businesses, including a container plant and a rug-cleaning establishment. All their early ventures ended in failure until Edmund and Frank Ball launched a Buffalo, New York, can company in 1880. A short time later, they were joined by brothers George, Lucius, and William, and together they devised a method of fastening cans that eliminated a previously required patent royalty, thereby increasing their profits. In 1886, the Balls branched out into glass fruit jars, and eight years later—after relocating to Muncie, Indiana—they were making 31 million jars annually. The family business became one of the world's leading producers of fruit jars, turning out 90 million jars in 1910. When home canning fell out of fashion in the ensuing decades, the brothers began producing bottles for post-Prohibition alcoholic beverage makers. In the mid-1950s, the brothers' successors continued to keep pace with change, forming an aerospace division to build satellites, antennas, and cameras. A Ball camera on the Skylab launched in 1973 took detailed photographs of the sun's surface.

H̲ENRY BASS
1843–1925

Bass Shoes

A cobbler from Wilton, Maine, Henry Bass took a pragmatic view of his product. "When I think of footwear," he once remarked, "I like to think of a foot doing things, not just shoes in a box." It was this kind of no-nonsense attitude that won Bass a large following among New England farmers soon after he began making shoes in 1876. His first product was a fourteen-inch high farmer's shoe. This was followed by other utilitarian shoes like the National Plow Shoe, Bass Guide Shoe, and Bass Best (a lumberjack's shoe). Henry's sons, John and Willard, joined the business in the early 1900s, when it was adding moccasins to its line. Years later, the Basses noted the popularity a Norwegian slipper moccasin was enjoying in Europe and developed a similar product (the Weejun) for the American market. Introduced in 1936, the leather Weejun featured a strap stitch over the instep. More than twenty years later, it became a fad on college campuses, forcing an expansion of company facilities to meet the demand for the shoe. In 1978, with the Weejun boom long over, Bass was acquired by Chesebrough-Ponds.

J—— 1866–1965
JOHN D. BASSETT

Bassett Furniture

After peddling the Appalachian oak lumber of his native Blue Ridge Mountains to furniture makers in Grand Rapids and other northern cities, John D. Bassett became convinced that he could build tables and chairs equal to those of his Yankee clients. Furthermore, Bassett was sure that he could make and sell furniture for less money because of his proximity to the source of raw material. In 1902 the Virginia salesman and three partners formed the Bassett Furniture Co. on $27,500 capital. From his earliest days in business, Bassett strove to keep his overhead down by paying his employees penurious wages. At a time when the average American worker was earning 22¢ an hour, the hourly wage at the Bassett plant was only a nickel. The price of Bassett furniture was also well below the national average; early company records list such bargains as beds for $1.50 and large dressers for $4.75. Seemingly indestructible, Bassett (who died at the age of ninety-eight in 1965) lived to see his company become the world's largest maker of wooden furniture, with annual sales in excess of $82 million.

E—— 1898–
EDDIE BAUER

Eddie Bauer Outdoor Gear

Keeping warm during winter visits to their favorite fishing holes was a major concern for Eddie Bauer and other sportsmen in the Pacific Northwest prior to 1936. In that year, Bauer, the thirty-eight-year-old owner of a Seattle sporting goods establishment, solved this problem by designing and patenting America's first quilted goose-down jacket. The warmth and light weight of Bauer's jacket made it an immediate favorite of hunters, fishers, mountain climbers (it was worn by the first American expedition to conquer Mt. Everest), and others who had to contend with frigid temperatures. Foom jackets, Bauer branched out into down sleeping bags and other outdoor products, including rain gear, woolens, hunting and fishing accessories, tents, and boots. Like L. L. Bean in Maine, the Washington sportsman merchandised his products through direct-mail catalogs as well as his retail stores. Although he has retired from business, the octogenarian Bauer, who lives in the Seattle area, is still an active fisherman. His $100-million-a-year company is now owned by General Mills.

J___ 1830–1925 H___ 1828–1908
JOHN BAUSCH HENRY LOMB

Bausch & Lomb Optical Products

A native of Burghaun, Germany, Henry Lomb immigrated to Rochester, New York, in 1849 and several years later invested his $60 savings in an eyeglass business recently started by John Bausch. Undoubtedly, local doomsayers predicted that Lomb would never see his money again. Bausch had already launched one optical company that failed, and it seemed likely that his newest venture would meet a similar fate, since many Americans were indifferent toward eye care. The young partners had trouble overcoming this obstacle at first (they had to repair windows to keep their company solvent), but gradually the public's attitude began to change. In 1866 Bausch and Lomb enjoyed considerable success making optical instruments from vulcanite. More than a decade later, their fortunes were aided by Dr. Oliver Wendell Holmes, who enthusiastically endorsed one of their microscopes. Bausch and Lomb received another big boost when fellow Rochester resident George Eastman used their lenses in the Kodak camera he patented in 1888. When Henry Lomb died in 1908, the business he had bought into for $60 was producing over 20 million lenses annually, making it the largest company of its kind in the world.

C___ 1864–1947
COL. JAMES B. BEAM

Jim Beam Bourbon

Although he was neither the first nor the only Beam involved in the family distillery, Kentucky Colonel James Beam was the one whose name wound up on the famous bourbon. This came about following the repeal of the Eighteenth Amendment, when Jim, who was then head of the D. M. Beam & Sons Distillery, celebrated the end of Prohibition by renaming the business after himself. Despite its new name, the distillery's bourbon remained virtually unchanged, being made with the same strain of jug yeast and limestone-spring-fed lake water that had been used before Prohibition. Jim Beam learned the secrets of bourbon making at sixteen, when he went to work at the distillery founded by his great-grandfather, Jacob Beam, in 1795. A distiller in Maryland and Virginia, Jacob Beam moved to north central Kentucky sometime around 1790, soon after a local minister, the Reverend Eliza Craig, produced the world's first true bourbon (a fermented grain mash of at least 51 percent corn and aged a minimum of two years in new charred oak barrels). After remaining active in the distillery for sixty-seven years, Jim Beam died on December 27, 1947, and was succeeded by his son, T. Jeremiah Beam.

L———— 1872–1967
LEON LEONWOOD BEAN

L. L. Bean Outdoor Products

"My life up to the age of 40 years was most uneventful," Leon "L. L." Bean once wrote. Indeed, few who knew the amiable Freeport, Maine, merchant in the early 1900s would have had him pegged as a future millionaire. L. L. was far more interested in hunting and fishing than in the fortunes of the small haberdashery shop he ran with his brother, Ervin. Then in 1912, the middle-aged sportsman found a way to combine business and pleasure when he designed a unique outdoor boot that featured a leather upper section and a rubber overshoe bottom. Calling his invention the Maine Hunting Shoe, Bean manufactured it in his store's basement and sold it through the mail. As the popularity of his boots grew, Bean began carrying other products for the outdoorsman, describing the merits of each item in a colorfully written, twice-yearly mail-order catalog. By 1937 Bean's annual catalog and retail store sales passed the $1 million mark. Still heading his company in 1951, the seventy-nine-year-old Bean instituted the policy of keeping his store open twenty-four hours a day. Following Bean's 1967 death, his grandson Leon Gorman became company president.

O——— 1903– W——— 1892–1950
OLIVE ANN BEECH   WALTER H. BEECH

Beechcraft Aircraft

Aviation pioneer Walter Beech did not always see eye to eye with his business associates. A World War I Army Air Corps veteran, Beech became general manager of the Swallow Airplane Co. in 1923. After helping to build the Wichita firm into the leader in the light aircraft field, Beech resigned in 1925 to pursue his own design ideas. He then joined with Clyde Cessna and Lloyd Stearman to form the Travel Air Manufacturing Co. Although Travel Air prospered, capturing over 25 percent of the aviation market at its peak, the partnership was marred by disputes over aircraft design. Again seeking greater creative freedom, Beech resigned in 1932 and formed his own company. This time, however, there was a built-in rapport between Beech and his closest associate, who was his twenty-nine-year-old wife, Olive Ann. With Olive as secretary-treasurer and Walter Beech as president, the firm introduced the famous Beechcraft biplane in 1934. Four years later, its sales exceeded $1 million, and the Beechcraft dominated the general aviation market in the 285-to-459-HP class. Following Walter's death in 1950, Olive Beech became president of the Wichita-based corporation.

D——— 1869–1934 A——— 1879–1951
DONALD J. BELL   ALBERT S. HOWELL

Bell & Howell Audiovisual Equipment

Donald Bell was a projectionist at a Chicago movie theater in 1905, when he met an engineer from a local machine shop named Albert Howell. The two men became friends, and in 1907 they formed the Bell & Howell Company to manufacture and service equipment for the new motion picture industry. With Bell handling the administrative end of the business as company president, and his younger partner running the engineering lab, the firm got off to a fast start; its annual sales jumped from $10,000 to $165,000 within a decade. Along the way, Albert Howell pioneered an impressive series of technological innovations, including an improved method of feeding film through a Kinedrome projector to prevent flickering and a continuous-contact 35-mm film printer that made high-speed printing possible. In recognition of these and other contributions, Bell & Howell became the first manufacturer to receive an Academy Award in 1954 (it subsequently won three more Oscars). In 1917 Bell sold his interest in the company to outside investors, but Howell remained active in the business for forty years. Today, the Chicago company produces a range of products, including business equipment and information systems.

DR. JULES BENGUÉ ◆ *Ben Gay Ointment*

On a trip to Europe in 1898, Thomas Leeming, Jr., the co-owner of a small New York pharmaceutical firm, paid a visit to noted French pharmacist Dr. Jules Bengué. Leeming left Bengué's office with the American rights to manufacture several of the Frenchman's preparations, including an analgesic pain reliever made of menthol, salicylate of methyl, and lanolin. At first, Leeming tried to market the treatment as Baume Bengué, before dividing the doctor's name into the catchier Ben Gay trademark. Touted as a remedy for gout, rheumatism, and neuralgia, the balm quickly became a fixture on drug store shelves, helping Leeming's company emerge as an industry leader.

E——— 1814–1879 ERASTUS B. BIGELOW

Bigelow Carpets

There is a measure of poetic justice in the fact that Erastus Bigelow was instrumental in the founding of the Massachusetts Institute of Technology in 1861. A bright youth whose family's financial plight deprived him of formal schooling, Bigelow educated himself and became a respected scholar, inventor, and economist. After leaving his West Boylston, Massachusetts, home at ten, Bigelow worked at a number of menial jobs until 1837, when he devised a power loom to produce lace. He followed this with other notable looms, including several designed to weave carpeting. In 1843 Bigelow and his brother established the Clinton Co. mill near Lancaster, giving rise to what is now Clinton, Massachusetts. (The mill later became the center of the giant Bigelow carpet works.) During his lifetime, the textile industry leader also became widely known as an authority on tariffs, writing several treatises on the subject between the early 1860s and the time of his death at his Boston home.

CLARENCE BIRDSEYE

Birds Eye Foods

It was while on a fur-trapping expedition to Labrador in 1915 that Clarence Birdseye made an observation that led to a revolutionary new method of freezing foods. The fish caught and frozen by the twenty-nine-year-old trapper's party tasted fresh and juicy when thawed weeks or even months later. In contrast, Birdseye knew that efforts to freeze meat and vegetables commercially in the United States had failed because the foods did not keep their flavor or texture. When he returned home to Gloucester, Massachusetts, in 1917, Birdseye was determined to discover why his Labrador catch had retained so much of its original taste after freezing. He learned that the speed with which the fish froze in the subzero Arctic temperatures prevented the formation of cell-damaging (and flavor-robbing) ice crystals. Deciding to put this knowledge to commercial use, Birdseye patented a "Quick Freeze Machine" and in 1925 went into the frozen food business. Despite the superiority of his quick-freezing process, Birdseye could not overcome consumers' negative image of frozen foods. Finally, in 1929, he sold the struggling business to the Postum Corporation. Drawing on its extensive financial resources, the cereal giant launched a massive promotional campaign to upgrade the image of frozen foods. As part of its marketing effort, Postum divided Birdseye's name in two, creating the famous Birds Eye trademark.

ANNA BISSELL 1846–1934   MELVILLE BISSELL 1843–1889

Bissell Carpet Sweepers

The Bissells were just another couple running a ma-and-pa store in the 1870s, when Mel developed an allergy to straw dust, a particularly worrisome affliction, since most of the merchandise sold at their Grand Rapids crockery shop was shipped in straw. Hoping to relieve his allergy and save his business, Mel designed a lightweight sweeper to pick up excess dust from the shop floor. His machine worked so well that customers who saw it in action began asking where they could buy one. In 1876 the couple formed the Bissell Carpet Sweeper Co., with Anna supervising the production of machines and her mustachioed husband handling sales. Flamboyant and outgoing, Mel would hook customer after customer with a sales pitch that began with him picking up a handful of dirt from the street, throwing it on the floor, and then dramatically whisking it up into the sweeper. When Mel died only twelve years after the business was founded, he was succeeded as president by Anna, who led Bissell to a position of undisputed leadership in the carpet sweeper industry.

S. DUNCAN BLACK 1883–1953   A. LONZO G. DECKER 1884–1956

Black & Decker Power Tools

Like Orville and Wilbur, Stanley and Livingstone, and Butch Cassidy and the Sundance Kid, the names Black and Decker will be forever linked in our collective consciousness. The famous partnership was born in the early 1900s in the Maryland office of the Rowland Telegraph Co., where two young men named S. Duncan Black and Alonzo G. Decker were employed as a superintendent and design engineer, respectively. In 1907 the two decided to go into business for themselves with plans to make such handy devices as a milk bottle capper, a postage stamp slitter, and a candy dipper. Only a lack of funds stood in their way, so to raise the needed capital Black sold his prized Maxwell-Briscoe Runabout for $600 to Charles Fox, Decker's father-in-law. Mr. Fox then lent Decker $600 to keep things even. Black and Decker produced the world's first electric drill in 1914, and by the end of the decade, their original $1,200 investment had mushroomed into a company with annual sales of over $1 million.

B. ILL BLASS 1922–

Bill Blass Fashions

Impeccably dressed, elegantly mannered, and widely traveled, Bill Blass was one of the first American couturiers to make the transition from high fashion to high society in the mid-1960s. The handsome bachelor has not only designed clothes for some of the most socially prominent women of the era, he has also escorted them to dinners on Fifth Avenue and parties at Southhampton. Blass's early life was in sharp contrast to the elite circles he would travel in later. Born in Ft. Wayne, Indiana, he and his sister were raised by their mother, following the suicide of their father who owned a hardware store at the beginning of the depression. After high school where he played football, Blass moved to New York and took a job as a sketch artist for a sportswear firm. He enlisted in the army during World War II and served in Europe. Upon his discharge, Corporal Blass returned to Manhattan and became a designer. In 1961 he was made vice-president of the prosperous Maurice Renter, Ltd., and shortly thereafter he formed Bill Blass, Inc., to license his signature on menswear and other products. By 1968 the gentlemanly designer was earning an estimated $250,000 a year.

W—— 1881–1956
WILLIAM E. BOEING

Boeing Aircraft

What is now one of the world's best-known aeronautical firms began in the early twentieth century as a wealthy timberman's hobby. An avid fisherman, William Boeing learned to fly seaplanes in 1915 because he wanted a fast means of transportation between his Seattle home and his favorite Canadian lakes. Boeing wasn't flying long before he decided to try his hand at building an aircraft. In 1916 he and a partner, naval officer G. C. Westervelt, constructed the B&W Seaplane, using piano wire, spruce lumber, and some strong linen fabric. One year later the new firm changed its name from Pacific Aero Products to Boeing Airplane Co., and it began providing training craft to the U.S. armed services during World War I. The company continued to grow throughout the 1920s, and by the end of the decade Boeing had organized United Aircraft & Transport Corporation, a conglomerate (headed by Boeing) that would eventually include Boeing Airplane, Pratt & Whitney, United Airlines, and other companies, before it was broken up by the government in September 1934. Two years before his death in 1956, William Boeing was the honored guest at ceremonies marking the introduction of his 707, America's first commercial jet aircraft.

The original Chef Boy-ar-dee, Italian immigrant Hector Boiardi, who started his food business in 1936 with the help of two brothers. Prior to launching his namesake company, Boiardi was a chef at several prominent New York hotels, including the Plaza, where his brother was the maitre d' of the famed Persian Room.

H—— 1897–
HECTOR BOIARDI

Chef Boy-ar-dee Foods

His name has the ring of a Madison Avenue brainstorming session, but "Chef Boy-ar-dee" is in fact a real person. Italian-born Hector Boiardi began his career as an apprentice chef when he was nine years old. After working in European hotel kitchens for a number of years, Boiardi moved to Manhattan and became a chef at the Plaza, where his brother Richard was a waiter. Hector left the Plaza in 1929 to start a Cleveland, Ohio, restaurant. His piquant sauce became so popular with customers that he began retailing his spaghetti dinners in bottles. In 1936, Hector, Richard, and another brother, Mario, formed a company to market the chef's specialties under the phonetic Chef Boy-ar-dee label. A short time later, the brothers got their big break when Richard, who was also the maitre d' at the Plaza's Persian Room, served Hector's spaghetti to John Hartford, a favored patron and cohead of the A&P chain. Hartford apparently enjoyed his meal, because Chef Boy-ar-dee dinners soon appeared on the shelves of A&P stores. The brothers sold their company to American Home Products in 1946 for a reported $6 million.

E—— 1859–1947
EMIL J. BRACH

Brach's Candies

German immigrant Emil Brach was forty-five years old in 1904 when he sank his $1,000 life savings into a small candy store–factory in Chicago. One year later, he brought his two teenage sons into the business to lend a hand. Realizing that the neighborhood trade would never be large enough to support the family venture, seventeen-year-old Edwin and fourteen-year-old Frank looked for ways to expand their dad's market. Edwin concentrated on building a mail-order business for Brach caramels, the family specialty, while Frank sold the candy wholesale to downtown department stores. A natural salesman, the younger Brach brother gave Saturday demonstrations at the city's big emporiums, often moving 1,000 pounds of candy in a day. As a result of his sons' efforts, Brach was able to expand his business steadily, and by 1921 he could afford to build a $4 million candy plant. Frank Brach (who outlived his father and brother) was the head of the family business in 1966 when it merged with American Home Products Corporation.

M—— 1836–1911
MILTON BRADLEY

Milton Bradley Games

When Abraham Lincoln first grew a beard during the 1860 presidential campaign, it almost spelled financial ruin for a young Massachusetts lithographer named Milton Bradley. The owner of a Springfield print shop, Bradley had been cashing in on the upcoming election by reproducing a portrait that showed the Republican candidate with a hairless chin. When Lincoln suddenly rendered the likeness obsolete, Bradley was forced to destroy several hundred thousand prints. This put the lithographer on the razor's edge of bankruptcy, until a friend suggested that he try inventing a board game, which he could then print with his idle press. Bradley followed his friend's advice and came up with the Checkered Game of Life, a contest in which players racked up points by landing on squares with words like *Truth* and *Honor*, while avoiding ones with *Ruin* and *Intemperance.* Peddling the game personally throughout New York and New England, Bradley sold 45,000 copies the first year. Shortly thereafter he became the top game manufacturer in the United States, a multimillionaire—and, undoubtedly, one of the biggest fans of Abe Lincoln's beard.

— 1877–1965
JOHN BRECK

Breck Shampoo

One day in the early 1900s, John Breck, the captain of the Willimansett, Massachusetts, Volunteer Fire Department, noticed that he was beginning to lose his hair. Distressed by the prospect of going bald while still in his twenties, the handsome firefighter visited several physicians in nearby Springfield. Every doctor consulted agreed that there was no cure for baldness, but Breck refused to accept this diagnosis. He spent hours in libraries pouring over medical texts before concluding that regular massages at the base of the neck could correct many hair and scalp problems. Brock developed his own massage preparations, and soon balding friends were dropping by his home for scalp treatments. In 1908 Breck opened a small "scalp treatment center" in Springfield, and a few years later, he was shipping his preparations to beauty salons throughout western Massachusetts. The scalp specialist gradually expanded his product line, introducing a shampoo for normal hair in 1930, and shampoos for oily and dry hair in 1933. By the end of the decade, Breck had achieved national distribution for his hair care products. At the time of his death, Breck's company was America's shampoo leader, with 15 percent of the market. Despite the success of his hair products, Breck remained partially bald.

In 1845 the Henry Brooks & Co. store occupied this site on the corner of Catharine and Cherry streets in Manhattan. Five years later, Henry's sons changed the name of the business to "Brooks Brothers," creating one of America's oldest and most prestigious ready-to-wear apparel labels.

H————— 1770?–1833
HENRY SANDS BROOKS

Brooks Brothers Apparel

Actually Henry Sands Brooks was not a Brooks brother; he was the father of Daniel, John, Elisha, Edward, and Henry, the brothers who are alluded to on the famous menswear label. It was the senior Brooks, however, who started the family business in 1817, opening a clothing store on Manhattan's Cherry Street, which, incidentally, makes the firm America's oldest clothier. A dapper Connecticut-born merchant, Brooks did a large trade with the sea captains who visited New York harbor. The impatient seafaring men often did not want to wait for custom-fitting garments, so Brooks became a pioneer in the making of ready-to-wear apparel. As an added inducement to its harbor customers, his store served complimentary drinks of Medford rum. Henry Brooks was succeeded by his sons, who changed the firm's name to Brooks Brothers in 1850. In the ensuing years, the Brooks Brothers' label became the cornerstone of the well-dressed gentleman's wardrobe. Abraham Lincoln was wearing Brooks Brothers clothing when he was assassinated. Teddy Roosevelt and Woodrow Wilson wore suits made by the firm to their inaugurations. Even glamorous women like Marlene Dietrich have worn menswear that bore the Brooks Brothers' legendary golden fleece trademark.

J———— 1855–1926
JOHN MOSES BROWNING

Browning Firearms

Raised in his father's Ogden, Utah, gunsmith shop, John Browning made his first rifle while he was still a child. In 1879 the twenty-four-year-old invented a metallic cartridge rifle, which was purchased by the Winchester company. Over the next four decades, Browning sold dozens of major firearm designs to Winchester, Colt, Remington, and other manufacturers. His most famous invention, the automatic machine gun, was patented in 1897. Although he earned millions of dollars in royalties, Browning did not allow his name to be put on a firearm until he developed a thirty-two-pound machine gun for the armed services during World War I. Capable of firing over 20,000 rounds in succession, the Browning gun was hailed by military experts as "the best machine gun made." The six-foot-three-inch tall Browning remained a man of simple tastes despite his great wealth, dividing his time between tinkering in his Ogden workshop, fishing in local trout streams, and playing the banjo in his plainly furnished living room.

J———— 1892–
JAMES E. BROYHILL

Broyhill Furniture

Vowing that he had "followed the mule long enough," twenty-one-year-old James Broyhill left his family's impoverished North Carolina farm in 1913 to enroll in a teachers' college. Broyhill raised money for his tuition by working as a barber and trapping rabbits in nearby hills. Then, shortly before graduation, his plan of becoming a teacher was cut short when he was drafted in the army during World War I. Following his discharge, the twenty-seven-year-old veteran felt too old to return to school, so he joined the small Lenoir, North Carolina, furniture factory owned by his brother Tom. In 1926, Broyhill borrowed $5,000 to launch his own furniture business, the Lenoir Chair Co. The onetime farm boy built his business steadily during the depression, buying bankrupt factories for pennies on the dollar and specializing in the production of inexpensive furniture. An industry pioneer in mass production techniques, Broyhill was among the first furniture manufacturers to make extensive use of the assembly line in his plant. Like another Appalachian furniture maker, J. D. Bassett, Broyhill prospered during the post–World War II housing boom, his company growing into the industry's second largest, outpaced only by its Virginia-based competitor.

J———— 1819–1890
OHN BRUNSWICK

Brunswick Bowling Equipment

Everybody has to have a dream, and John Brunswick's was to build a perfect billiard table. The Swiss-born cabinetmaker was seized by this ambition in the early 1840s, after he moved to Cincinnati, and became frustrated by the poor quality of the tables at local billiard establishments. By 1845 Brunswick had completed work on his flawless table, and it was quickly accepted by pool hall owners. Brunswick's billiard-table business continued to grow over the next two decades, and in the 1870s he merged with two competitors to form what would eventually become the Brunswick Corporation. When the taverns that had been major billiard-table customers began installing bowling lanes in the 1880s, Brunswick's son-in-law Moses Bensinger added pins and bowling balls to the company's line of products. As an outgrowth of its work with rubber in making billiard tables and bowling balls, Brunswick diversified into other rubber products—including the first hard-rubber toilet seat and automobile tires. The firm sold its tire business to B. F. Goodrich in 1922.

D———— 1855–1929
AVID DUNBAR BUICK

Buick Cars

Fortune was a fickle friend for David Dunbar Buick. At fifteen he left school to take a job with a Michigan plumbing supply company, where he worked his way up the ladder, eventually assuming control of the prosperous firm. At this point Buick should have left well enough alone, but in 1902 the automobile bug bit and the middle-aged plumbing supply man went into the business of making cars. The original Buick was a good little vehicle, but it failed miserably on the showroom floor. Faced with insurmountable financial problems, its maker approached General Motors founder Will Durant, who invested $1.5 million in the struggling firm. Despite the large influx of capital, only two cars were sold in 1905, and one year later Buick was forced out of the company he had founded. In the years that followed, the fortunes of David Buick and his namesake car traveled in opposite directions; the automobile emerged as one of GM's best-sellers, while its inventor became involved in ill-fated business ventures and sank ever deeper into poverty. Buick died in 1929, a poorly paid and forgotten clerk at a Detroit vocational school.

JOSEPH BULOVA

Bulova Watches

Despite his Old World background as a jeweler's apprentice in a small village in Austria-Hungary, Joseph Bulova was determined to keep up with the faster pace of his new land when he arrived in America in the early 1870s. The young immigrant settled in New York, and by 1875 he had saved enough money to start his own jewelry manufacturing business. An innovative designer—he patented the first signet ring with interchangeable initials—Bulova quickly established a prosperous jewelry trade. In the early 1900s he added watches to his line, and in the ensuing years the Eastern European pioneered many innovations in watchmaking, developing the first movement with interchangeable standardized parts. Bulova was no slouch when it came to promoting his products, either. He ran the country's first radio spot in 1926, when an announcer on Pittsburgh's KDKA gave the time, followed by "B-U-L-O-V-A, Bulova Watch Time." (In 1941 his company would again make history when it sponsored the first television commercial, a nine-dollar, twenty-second spot during a Dodgers baseball game.) For relaxation, Bulova enjoyed racing his Hispano-Suiza on Long Island's Vanderbilt Roadway. Joseph Bulova remained president of his firm until his death in 1935.

WILLIAM BURROUGHS

Burroughs Information Systems

As a bank teller, William Burroughs was well aware of how costly a simple human error could be when adding a long list of figures. This experience led the Auburn, New York, native to begin experimenting with a machine that could tabulate numbers automatically in 1884. Seven years later, after having spent $300,000 on failed prototypes, he completed a working model of the world's first practical adding and listing machine. Initially, Burroughs believed that his invention would sell only to banks, but soon all kinds of businesses were buying the adding machine, which was to the late-nineteenth-century office what the computer is to the office of the 1980s. Sickly for most of his adult life, Burroughs retired from his company in 1897 and died a year later. His successors changed the name of the firm in 1905 (the year it was moved from St. Louis to Detroit) from American Arithmometer to the Burroughs Adding Machine Co. in his honor.

J——— 1801–1889
J OHN CADBURY

Cadbury Chocolates

Although his name is now famous for chocolates, it was coffee and tea that most interested John Cadbury in 1824, when he opened a small shop on Bull Street in Birmingham, England. An enterprising young Quaker, Cadbury built a solid trade as a coffee and tea merchant, later adding roasted cocoa beans to his selection. By 1841 he was using a mortar and pestle to pound the beans into paste for his fifteen varieties of eating chocolates. Over the years, Cadbury was joined in the business by his brother, Benjamin, and his sons, Richard and George. Gradually the firm concentrated more and more on its confectioneries, building a sprawling chocolate factory at Bournville in 1879, which became one of Britain's most famous industrial plants. In its new location, the firm introduced many well-known chocolates, including Milk Tray (1914), the first boxed assortment to achieve national marketing success in the United Kingdom. Ninety years after the move to Bournville, Sir Adrian Cadbury, a great-grandson of the founder, merged the chocolate maker with the Schweppes beverage company, creating an international corporation that by 1980 had plants in over fifty countries.

J——— 1817–1900
J OSEPH CAMPBELL

Campbell Soup

Convinced that the future was bright for canned foods, Philadelphian Joseph Campbell quit his job as a purchasing agent for a produce wholesaler to enter the canning business in 1869. Campbell became a partner of Abram Anderson, a Camden, New Jersey, canner who specialized in jellies, mincemeat, and the "celebrated Beefsteak Tomato." Together, the partners created many excellent products; their preserves won a medal at the 1876 Centennial Exposition. The two men were often at odds philosophically, however, with Campbell advocating aggressive expansion and Anderson urging a more conservative course. Anderson sold his interest in the company around the time of the exposition, and Campbell was joined by a new partner, Arthur Dorrance. It was Dorrance's nephew John Dorrance who, more than twenty years later, developed the company's famous line of condensed soup. Introduced in 1898 in the now familiar red-and-white cans (colors inspired by Cornell football uniforms), Campbell soup was selling at the rate of 16 million cans annually within six years. Joseph Campbell was able to see the early success of his namesake soup, living until 1900, when he collapsed—and later died—on his way to the Camden factory.

J———— 1852–1921
JAMES W. CANNON

Cannon Towels

To paraphrase Gertrude Stein: a towel is a towel is a towel. The modest household item rarely carried a brand name in the late 1880s, when North Carolina general store owner James Cannon entered the textile business. Cannon broke with tradition in 1894 when he put his name on the flat-weave huck towels produced at his Concord, North Carolina, mill in the hope of creating an easily recognized identity for his product. Cannon's decision proved to be an astute one, as customers began to specify his towels by name. In 1907 the former merchant moved his growing business to a 1,600-acre cotton plantation, which he converted into a state-of-the-art production facility called *Kannapolis*, Greek for "city of looms." When James Cannon died, his youngest son, Charles A. Cannon, took over the textile business. Charles carried his father's branding strategy on step further in 1923, when he developed machinery to sew the Cannon name, along with the familiar cannon-and-balls trademark, on the corner of every towel.

P———— 1922–
PIERRE CARDIN

Pierre Cardin Fashions

Long before the word *unisex* entered the fashion lexicon, Pierre Cardin startled his fellow couturiers by becoming the first major women's designer to introduce a collection of men's clothing. The historic apparel made its debut in 1960, and despite sneers from some quarters, it proved to be so popular that within five years ready-to-wear versions of Cardin's men's lines were reportedly earning greater profits than his creations for women. Born in Venice, where his French parents were vacationing, the innovative couturier demonstrated a flair for fashion early in life, making a silk dress for a neighbor child's doll when he was only eight. Nearly twenty years later, he achieved international acclaim as one of the chief architects of Christian Dior's New Look. In 1979 the flamboyant Frenchman astonished Paris once again by purchasing Maxim's and proceeding to open branches of the fabled restaurant in cities around the world—including Peking.

W——— 1830–1918
WILLIAM CARTER

Carter's Infant Wear

As a youth, William Carter spent half of each weekday in a back-parlor school and the other half helping his grandfather make knitting machines. When the Derbyshire, England, native immigrated to the United States in 1857, he used the skills learned from his grandfather to secure a job with a New York stocking maker. By 1860 Carter had moved to Highlandville (later Needham Heights), Massachusetts, where he began to make and sell cardigan jackets out of his home. Demand for the jackets and other knit goods grew steadily, and soon a full-fledged mill was acquired. Carter began to manufacture his famous infant wear and a general line of knit underwear in 1878. Forty years later, when Carter died, he was succeeded as president of the company by his son, William H. Carter (1864–1955). A brilliant businessman and inventor, the younger Carter devised the latch-needle principle of knitting. Refusing to patent his invention, Carter made it available to the general industry, which quickly adopted it as a standard. William also distinguished himself in politics; a Republican, he served in the U.S. House of Representatives from 1915 to 1918.

O——— 1918–
OLEG CASSINI

Oleg Cassini Fashions

Oleg Cassini almost certainly would have followed his father into the czar's diplomatic corps, were it not for the Bolshevik Revolution. The son of a Russian count, Oleg was born in Paris and later moved to Florence, where he earned a degree in law. The artistic youth found illustration more to his liking than litigation, however, so he left Italy for the United States in 1938 to become a cartoonist at the *Washington Times Herald*. At the outbreak of World War II, Cassini joined the U.S. Army and served four years. After the war, he became a design consultant for Twentieth Century–Fox and later started his own fashion studio in New York. In the early 1960s, Oleg Cassini was named official couturier to Jacqueline Kennedy. The appointment made his name a household word and spurred a tremendous demand for his label in the lucrative retail license market.

CLYDE CESSNA

Cessna Aircraft

After witnessing his first air show in 1911, Clyde Cessna knew that he wanted to become an aviator. So, despite the fact that he had no training in his newly chosen field, the thirty-one-year-old Enid, Oklahoma, car salesman assembled his own monoplane. An impatient man, Cessna never bothered to take flying lessons, and he crashed fourteen times, collecting an assortment of broken bones, before completing his first flight. Nevertheless, the determined Cessna overcame this shaky start and became a success on the barnstorming circuit. In 1925 Cessna entered the aircraft manufacturing business, teaming up with Wichita aviation pioneers Walter Beech and Lloyd Stearman to form the Travel Air Manufacturing Co. Two years later, the ex-barnstormer left the firm after a dispute with his partners—they wanted to build biplanes, but he preferred monoplanes. Following his resignation, Cessna formed his own company, and in 1928 he introduced his famous A Series Comet, America's first full cantilever-wing light airplane. Upon Cessna's retirement in 1936, his nephew Dwane Wallace became president of the company. During his thirty-five-year tenure, Wallace built the Wichita firm into the nation's biggest maker of general avaiation craft.

WALTER CHRYSLER

Chrysler Cars

If Lee Iacocca could have traveled back in time in 1978 to seek advice on how to resurrect a dying auto company, he could not have found a more sagacious oracle than Walter Chrysler. Ironically, the man whose namesake company came close to going under before the arrival of Iacocca was himself skilled at saving troubled automakers. A thirty-six-year-old Kansas railroad man, Chrysler became manager of Buick's Flint, Michigan, plant in 1912. Within four years, he had increased the plant's output from forty-five to two-hundred cars a day and was made head of GM's Buick division. Chrysler resigned his $500,000-a-year job after a dispute with GM management, and he became a consultant to Maxwell Motors. Although many had predicted bankruptcy for Maxwell, Chrysler revived the company's fortunes in 1924, when he introduced a popular luxury car at the New York auto show. One year later, he acquired a controlling interest in Maxwell, and the company was renamed Chrysler Corporation. Under Chrysler's leadership, the firm continued to grow, acquiring the Dodge Motor Co. in 1928. Walter Chrysler retired as president of his firm in 1935, after having built it into the nation's second largest automaker.

G———— 1887–1956
GEORGE W. CHURCH

Church's Fried Chicken

At sixty-five, an age that is customarily associated with retirement, George Church entered a new and unproved industry. The bespectacled, white-haired Texan had already enjoyed a twenty-year career as a salesman of poultry incubators in 1952, when he opened "Church's Fried Chicken to Go" in downtown San Antonio. Fast food was still a novelty at the time, but the grandfatherly businessman was convinced that a restaurant that served only quickly prepared, carry-out orders would be in step with the needs of the more mobile American consumer. As an added attraction, Church positioned his fryers right by the window of his small, walk-up chicken stand, so customers could actually see their orders being cooked. When Church died in 1956, his company operated four restaurants in the San Antonio area. Under the leadership of Church's sons, Bob and George, Jr., the firm continued to grow. By 1968, the year it opened its first location outside the state of Texas, it had forty-four stores and annual sales of $7.2 million.

D———— 1864–1939
DAVID L. CLARK

Clark Bar

When the United States entered World War I in 1917, Pittsburgh candy maker David L. Clark contracted to supply confections to the U.S. Army. Doughboys overseas liked Clark's chocolate drops and various penny items just fine, but there was one problem—the candy's thirty-pound shipping cases were difficult for the post exchanges to distribute efficiently. Asked to come up with a package that would be easier to handle, Clark began to manufacture his best-selling candy in a more convenient bar size. Initially, the new bar was called Clark, but later its name was lengthened to the familiar Clark Bar. The five-cent Clark Bar became a huge commercial success after the war, and David Clark added other bars to his product line. An Irish immigrant and self-made millionaire, Clark launched his confection empire out of the back of a small north Pittsburgh house, when he was still a teenager. He remained the active president of his candy company and the Clark Brothers Chewing Gum Co. (makers of Clark's Teaberry Gum) until his death in 1939.

RUTH CLEVELAND ◆ *Baby Ruth Candy Bar*

It was not home-run slugger Babe Ruth, but "Baby Ruth" Cleveland, the popular eldest daughter of President Grover Cleveland (she was born between his two administrations), who inspired the naming of the famous candy bar. Chicago confectioner Otto Schnering, the man who created the nickel nut-roll bar in the teens, first called it "Kandy Kake." The candy was rechristened in 1921, after one of Schnering's employees suggested "Baby Ruth" in a contest.

W——— 1783–1857
WILLIAM COLGATE

Colgate Toothpaste

British-born William Colgate was brought to the United States as a boy by his pro–American Revolution parents. At age twenty he became an apprentice to a New York City candle and soapmaker, and three years later, having mastered the craft, he set up his own factory. Colgate's firm prospered from the start, partly because he was the only soapmaker in the city to offer a delivery service. His business received a big boost during the War of 1812, when imported soap from England was cut off from the U.S. market. As his soap sales increased, Colgate branched out into other products, building one of the largest starch plants in the United States near Jersey City, New Jersey, in 1820. A deeply religious man, Colgate gave one-tenth of his earnings to church charities and was instrumental in forming the American Bible Society, a group that dispensed free Bibles. (He did this after a valuable family heirloom Bible was stolen.) The soapmaker also was responsible for uniting two rival church schools into a major institution, named Colgate University in his honor.

S——— 1814–1862
SAMUEL COLT

Colt Revolver

Although his famous namesake revolver brings to mind images of the "wild West," Samuel Colt was a descendent of old New England stock. The grandson of Maj. John Caldwell (president of the first insurance company in Hartford, Connecticut), Colt left Amherst Academy in 1830 and hopped on a ship bound for Calcutta. During his journey, the adventurous teenager made a wooden model of the revolving-breech pistol that would later bear his name. Upon his return home to Ware, Massachusetts, Colt made two working models of his six-shooters, so called because they had automatically revolving sets of six chambers. In 1832 the inventor raised money to finance the development of his firearm by touring the country as "Dr. Coult" and demonstrating nitrous oxide (laughing gas). Four years later, Colt began manufacturing guns in a New Jersey factory. Despite some severe early setbacks (his company became insolvent in 1842), Colt eventually prospered, thanks largely to an 1847 order for one thousand $28 revolvers received from Gen. Zachary Taylor during the Mexican War. Colt, who tried unsuccessfully to interest the navy in an early torpedo, continued to head his company until his death.

M——————— 1861–1931
MARQUIS M. CONVERSE

Converse Basketball Sneakers

Although his namesake basketball sneakers are worn by many of America's finest athletes, Marquis Converse was himself sidelined by medical problems during much of his early adulthood. Born in Lyme, New Hampshire, and educated at the Thetford Academy in Vermont, Converse was a superintendent at Boston's Houghton & Dutton department store in the mid-1880s when an illness forced him to resign. He recovered in 1887 and cofounded a rubber shoe sales agency. The business prospered, but poor health plagued Converse again, and he had to spend three years convalescing at his Andover, Massachusetts, farm. Apparently farm life worked wonders on Converse's constitution, and with his health restored he became a successful salesman. In 1908 Converse launched his own manufacturing firm, the Converse Rubber Shoe Co., and within two years his Malden, Massachusetts, plant was producing 5,500 pairs of rubber shoes a day. Despite this early success, a declining demand for its product forced the firm into receivership in 1929, when Converse sold out to an investor. Two years later, he suffered a fatal heart attack while at the wheel of his car on Milk Street in Boston.

A—— 1847–1929
ADOLPH COORS

Coors Beer

Orphaned at fifteen, Adolph Coors became a brewer's apprentice in Germany before immigrating to America in 1868. Five years later, after he had labored at a succession of menial jobs in various states, he was able to start a small Golden, Colorado, brewery with a partner named Joseph Schueler. Coors bought out Schueler in 1880, and over the next ten years, he enjoyed a prosperous trade selling beer in the mining towns that cropped up along the Front Range. By the end of the century, however, the Prohibition movement was gaining strength in Colorado, where local-option laws allowed individual communities to vote themselves dry. In 1914 Coors's own town of Golden voted to ban the sale of all alcoholic beverages. Undaunted, the brewmaster responded to the threat of national Prohibition by branching out into other products, including cement, malted milk, and pottery. Adolph Coors never lived to see the repeal of Prohibition; he plunged to his death on June 5, 1929, in an accidental fall from the sixth floor of the Cavalier Hotel in Virginia Beach, Virginia.

O—— 1932–
OSCAR DE LA RENTA

Oscar de la Renta Fashions

Long recognized as a fashion trend setter, Oscar de la Renta has also blazed new paths for couturiers on the financial front. In 1969 de la Renta sold his high-fashion and boutique business to Richton International, a fashion conglomerate, thus becoming the first designer whose enterprise offered shares on the stock market. Born in the Dominican Republic, de la Renta was "discovered" in Spain by the wife of the American ambassador John Lodge, who commissioned him to design a gown for her daughter Beatrice's debut. When Beatrice Lodge appeared on the cover of *Life* magazine wearing the dress, de la Renta's work earned widespread praise, and he was hired by Balenciaga's Madrid couture house. The handsome designer moved to Manhattan in 1963 to work for Elizabeth Arden. Two years later, he joined Jane Derby, Inc., and soon he acquired a controlling interest in the firm, which became Oscar de la Renta, Ltd. Although best known for elegant evening clothes, de la Renta has been a driving force behind many daring fashions of the 1960s and 1970s, including see-through chiffons and bare-midriff dresses.

J__ 1806–1880
JOHN DEWAR

Dewar's Scotch

If Robert Burns or Sir Walter Scott wanted to imbibe at home, he would have been obliged to tote his own jar to a shop that sold whisky out of a barrel. No one thought of packaging Scotch in bottles until John Dewar came up with the idea in the mid-nineteenth century. Born on a small Perthshire, Scotland, farm, Dewar moved to the city of Perth when he was twenty-two to work in his uncle's wine cellar. In 1846 he set up his own wine and spirits shop in a small storefront at 111 High Street, and a short time later he began blending and bottling his own Scotch. Although his bottled spirits were of the finest quality, the cautious Scot was slow to expand his market. It wasn't until 1860 that he employed his first traveler to sell his product outside of Perth. Dewar's sons, John and Thomas, assumed control of the business following his death in 1880. Together they built it into one of the world's most successful distilleries, with annual output passing the one-million-gallon mark soon after the turn of the century.

C_____ 1905–1957
CHRISTIAN DIOR

Christian Dior Fashions

A superstitious sort, Christian Dior often consulted fortune-tellers before making important decisions. Unfortunately, the Normandy-born designer must have patronized the wrong clairvoyants most of his life, because prior to achieving international acclaim at the age of forty-two, he endured an unbroken series of adversities. In 1928 Dior and a friend started an art gallery, which folded three years later during the depression. Following the failure of his gallery, he traveled through France and Spain, weaving tapestries and doing fashion illustrations, but never scratching out more than a meager living. In 1938 the luckless, five-foot-five-inch tall Frenchman landed a job as a fashion designer, but his career was suddenly derailed the following year by World War II. Fortune finally smiled on Dior in 1946 when Marcel Boussac, a wealthy industrialist, backed him in a fashion design studio. One year later, Dior introduced the New Look, a collection of apparel with delicately rounded shoulders, tiny waists, and full skirts, which quickly swept the fashion world. Following the success of the New Look, the Dior name soon began appearing on a host of high-fashion items—including jewelry, furs, men's ties, and shoes.

J—— 1864–1920 H—— 1868–1920
JOHN DODGE HORACE DODGE

Dodge Cars

John and Horace Dodge began the 1890s as struggling bicycle makers, operating out of a small shed in Detroit. Before their deaths in 1920 (both from natural causes), the brothers had completed an incredible rags-to-riches saga, leaving behind a fortune of over $200 million. The Dodges amassed this wealth in the auto industry, beginning in the early 1900s when they supplied transmissions for the Oldsmobile Runabout. In 1902 they contracted to make parts for Henry Ford, each receiving a 5 percent interest in the Ford Motor Co. as part of the deal. Although the subsequent success of the Model T made them multimillionaires, the Dodges never got along with the autocratic Mr. Ford, and in 1914 the brothers left to start their own auto company. When announcing their decision to build cars, John observed caustically, "Think of all the Ford owners who will someday want an automobile." It didn't drive Ford under, but the efficient Dodge car was an immediate success, with sales totaling 6 million vehicles in the first six years.

J—— 1877–1958
JAMES DOLE

Dole Pineapples

After graduating from Harvard, James Dole moved to Hawaii in 1899, intending to make his fortune raising pineapples. The young Ivy Leaguer's plan evoked patronizing smiles from skeptical island farmers, who had long since discounted the pineapple as a cash crop because it spoiled too quickly to withstand the journey to markets on the mainland. Dole intended to overcome this problem by shipping the fruit as a canned product, rather than in its fresh form. Erecting a small cannery in the town of Wahiawa, Dole canned 1,893 cases of pineapple in 1903. The entire inventory was sold through a San Francisco food broker, and output rose to 32,000 cases within three years. Pineapple proved very popular with Americans, most of whom had never before tasted the succulent tropical fruit, and Dole's success encouraged other Hawaiian farmers to follow suit. The industry eventually became Hawaii's second largest, with Dole's Hawaiian Pineapple Co. accounting for 35 percent of all canned pineapple shipped from the islands. But problems arose in 1931, when the depression cut into the worldwide demand for the fruit, forcing Hawaiian Pineapple to undergo a major

James Dole surrounded by his favorite fruit. A transplanted Ivy Leaguer, Dole made the pineapple the center of his life after moving to Hawaii at the turn of the century. It was largely through his efforts that the tropical fruit was transformed from a minor local crop to a nationally distributed food product.

reorganization. In the process, founder Dole was squeezed out of the firm. Dejected, he left Hawaii for San Francisco, not returning to the islands until January 1958, five months before his death.

—— 1840–1921
JOHN B. DUNLOP

Dunlop Tires

It was an act of fatherly concern that got the modern tire industry rolling. John Dunlop, a veterinary surgeon from Scotland, was looking for a way to make his son's tricycle ride more smoothly in 1888, when he wrapped air-filled rubber tubes in Irish linen and taped them to the metal wheel rims. Prior to that time, cycle wheels were typically covered with belts of solid rubber, providing plenty of durability, but not much of a cushion against bumps. Although he took out a patent on his invention, Dr. Dunlop did not wish to abandon his prosperous practice for what seemed like a risky venture. He sold the rights to his tire for a small sum. By the turn of the century, Dunlop's pneumatic tire had begun to gain widespread acceptance from bicycle makers and motor car pioneers, after the development of clinchers made it possible to fasten the rubber securely to the rim.

1825–1902
Eugene R. Durkee

Durkee Spices and Famous Sauce

In 1857 Eugene R. Durkee, a New York City purveyor of herbs and spices, introduced what was probably the world's first commercially packaged salad dressing. Hailed as a delicious accompaniment to vegetables, beef, poultry, or seafood, the dressing achieved widespread fame as Durkee's Famous Sauce. Abraham Lincoln requested that the dressing be served at the White House, and almost a century later, Tennessee Williams referred to it by name in *The Glass Menagerie*. Durkee, who began his business in 1850 peddling spices door to door in Buffalo, New York, promoted his dressing by packaging it in decorative bottles. Beginning in the 1870s, the condiment maker embossed a gauntlet trademark on his bottles, reasoning that the medieval armored glove would evoke an image of product integrity. When Durkee retired in 1884, he was succeeded as president of the company by his son, Eugene W. Durkee. The firm was acquired by Glidden Paint in 1929, and almost forty years later Durkee and Glidden were merged into the SCM Corporation.

1877–1934
Ole Evinrude

Evinrude Outboard Motors

According to legend, the inspiration for the world's first practical outboard motor occurred on a hot summer day in 1904, when Milwaukeean Ole Evinrude took a neighbor girl named Bessie Cary out to a picnic on an island in Lake Michigan. After a while Bessie got a craving for a cool, refreshing dish of ice cream, and the gallant Ole offered to row the 2½ miles back to shore to fetch some. Unfortunately, the summer heat melted the ice cream into a globby mess by the time Ole completed his return trip. The embarrassing experience prompted the young mechanic to look for a more efficient means of propelling a small boat. In 1909 Evinrude patented his revolutionary outboard motor and formed the Evinrude Motor Co. to manufacture it. Before long, his firm was swamped with orders for the dependable little one-cylinder engine. Much of this success was the result of Ole's mechanical skills, but some of the credit must also to the business manager and advertising director of the company, Bessie Cary Evinrude. Obviously impressed by Ole's chivalry, she had married him soon after their fateful Lake Michigan picnic.

PETER CARL FABERGÉ ◆ *Faberge Cosmetics*

American Samuel Rubin wanted to give his newly formed cosmetics firm an image of Continental elegance in the 1930s, so he borrowed the name of Peter Carl Fabergé (1846–1920), the world's most celebrated goldsmith. Fabergé had become famous during the late nineteenth century for the lavishly jeweled Easter eggs and other ornate baubles he fashioned for the czar's court. Apparently Rubin's choice of names was a good one, since Fabergé has gone on to become one of the ten top-selling brands in the cosmetics and toiletry market.

JAMES FARAH — 1916?–1964 WILLIAM FARAH — 1919–

Farah Pants

It is doubtful that any brother-partners were ever as unalike and yet worked as well together as Jimmie and Willie Farah. Jimmie was easygoing with a natural flair for selling. Willie is a tough-minded man who is far more skilled at working with machines than with people. Together, the two built the small apparel factory they inherited from their father in 1937 into a leading maker of men's pants. In the early 1960s, the brothers capitalized on the boom in moderately priced brand-name apparel by introducing Farah slacks. Then in 1964, Jimmie died of a heart attack. Missing his brother's marketing skills, Willie Farah failed to keep pace with the fashion trends of the 1970s. Willie also missed his brother's tact in dealing with people; his pugnacious 1972 stand against the Amalgamated Clothing Workers of America resulted in a bitter two-year strike and a national boycott of Farah products, before the union was allowed in his plant. Not surprisingly, Farah's sales plummeted from $165 million in 1971 to $91 million by 1979. Willie Farah rebounded in the new decade, however, unveiling higher priced apparel lines that boosted his 1980 sales by 35 percent.

SIMON W. FARBER

Farberware Kitchenware

For Russian-Jewish immigrant Simon Farber, 1905 was a memorable year. It was in 1905 that the young tinsmith was able to move his growing five-year-old metalworking business from a cramped, gaslit basement in Manhattan's Lower East Side to a more modern and spacious location at Broadway and Grand streets. Also that year Simon met, and shortly thereafter married, Ella Sachs, a teacher at the Norwich Business College in Connecticut. An attractive, intelligent woman, Ella quickly became involved in her husband's business, and together they built it into one of the leading and most innovative companies in the housewares industry. The couple introduced the first line of Farberware, silver-and-nickel-plated serving accessories and giftware, in 1910. Other notable products made by their factory included clamp-on reading lamps, chrome-plated accessories, electric coffee percolators, and electric table broilers. Simon and Ella (who died in 1956) had two sons, Isidor and Milton, both of whom later assumed leadership of the company. In 1966 the housewares firm was acquired by Walter Kidde & Co., Inc.

BORROWED IMAGE

FANNIE MERRITT FARMER ◆ *Fanny Farmer Candy*

Hoping to expand the market for his confections, John Hayes, founder of Canada's Laura Secord candy store chain, opened a Rochester, New York, store in 1919. Hayes decided to call his American outlet by a different name, Fanny Farmer, after Fannie Merritt Farmer (1857–1915). A noted culinary expert, Fannie Farmer wrote *The Boston Cooking School Cookbook* in 1896, a work that is still published in revised form as *The Fannie Farmer Cookbook*. It was because of his admiration for Farmer's courage in overcoming a paralytic stroke she had suffered as a teenager that Hayes thought of her when naming his American store.

E——— 1898–
ENZO FERRARI

Ferrari Cars

Few automobiles of the 1950s and 1960s rivaled the Ferrari's achievements on the racing circuit. The blood-red car with the legendary prancing black horse trademark won the twenty-four-hour Le Mans race every year between 1960 and 1965. Its success in racing helped to make the company's commercial sports cars a favorite of the jet set. Interestingly, Enzo Ferrari, the man behind the statusy automobile, led a reclusive, almost monklike existence for much of his adult life. Born in Modena, Italy, to a foundry owner, Ferrari has had one overriding interest in life—fast automobiles. He began his career as a racing driver in 1919, becoming a member of Alfa Romeo's team a year later. In the early 1930s, Ferrari switched from driving to designing cars, first for Alfa Romeo and then, in 1947, under his own name. A tall, dour man, Ferrari has eschewed the glamour surrounding his car. During his middle years, he lived in an apartment over his warehouse, worked seven days a week without a vacation, and rarely ventured outside Italy. Enzo Ferrari even avoided attending auto races, because he couldn't bear to see his cars mishandled by drivers.

H——— 1868–1938
HARVEY FIRESTONE

Firestone Tires

By the time of Harvey Firestone's death, the tire company he had started on $20,000 had mushroomed into a $100-million-a-year business. Despite his success, however, the Ohio-born industrialist remained a small-town boy at heart. Reared on a farm in the hamlet of Columbiana, Firestone drifted through a series of business ventures as a young man, including a stint as a traveling medicine-extract salesman. It wasn't until he was thirty-one years old that Firestone launched his namesake tire company in Akron on August 3, 1900. The business started off slowly, but its big break came in 1906 when Ford ordered 2,000 sets of tires. One year later, the company sold 105,000 tires at a $538,177 profit. As his fortune grew, Firestone remained rooted in the country, spending much of his free time working on his farm in Columbiana. Influenced by this experience, he developed the first practical pneumatic tire for farm tractors in 1932. Firestone liked to escape the pressures of his business by going on extended camping trips to remote regions with a group of companions that included Henry Ford, Thomas Edison, and John Burroughs.

HERMAN G. FISHER ᴵRVING L. PRICE
1898–1975   1884–1976

Fisher-Price Toys

What is now the world's largest manufacturer of infant and preschool toys began in 1930 when three western New Yorkers converted an old frame-and-concrete-block house outside Buffalo into a small factory. Although short on start-up capital, the partners brought a wealth of experience to the new venture. One of them, Herman Fisher, was a veteran toy salesman; another, Irving Price, was a retired chain-store executive; and the third, Helen Schelle (who missed getting her name on the company logo), was the former operator of the Penny Walker Toy Shop in Binghamton. The first year they introduced a line of sixteen toddler toys, all made of rugged Ponderosa pine and enlivened with nontoxic lithographs and finishes. Despite the fact that most Americans were not in a toy-buying mood during the depression, the partners' whimsical creations like Granny Doodle and Snoopy Sniffer captured the imagination of preschool youngsters. By 1936 their business turned its first real profit, and one decade later, its annual net sales were a respectable $1.6 million.

CHARLES FLEISCHMANN
1834–1897

Fleischmann's Yeast and Margarine

When Austrian distiller Charles Fleischmann came to the United States in 1866 to attend his sister Josephine's wedding, he was struck by the poor quality of the bread served in this country. Fleischmann concluded that the sorry state of American bread was due to the inferior yeast used by the nation's bakers. In 1868, when he settled in Cincinnati and became a partner in a local distillery, Fleischmann, not surprisingly, persuaded his associates to add baker's yeast as a sideline. Unlike other yeasts then on the market, which were liquid, Fleischmann's was sold in compressed, foil-wrapped cakes, making it easier and more reliable to use in baking. The superiority of Fleischmann's product soon made his company America's leading yeast producer, and to capitalize on this success the firm diversified into vinegar, malt, feed, and later, margarine. Charles Fleischmann remained active both in his company and in Ohio politics until his death. He was twice elected to the state senate, served as a delegate to the Republican National Convention in 1880 and 1884, and was the fire commissioner of Cincinnati.

J——— 1835–1889
AMES A. FOLGER

Folger's Coffee

James Knox Polk is never ranked among America's great leaders, but our eleventh president did at least one memorable thing while in office. In a December 1848 speech, Polk described the vast gold deposits that could be found in the mountains of northern California, thus sparking the gold rush. Influenced by Polk's message, brothers Edward, Henry, and James Folger left Nantucket, Massachusetts, in 1849 for San Francisco. While the older men went off to the mountains soon after they arrived, fifteen-year-old James stayed behind and started a coffee business, eventually building a prosperous trade selling roasted and ground beans to miners. In 1859 Folger became a partner in a coffee and spice mill. Later, when the mill failed during the 1865 recession, he bought out his partner and convinced his creditors to allow him to continue operating the business. Within a decade, all the firm's debts were paid and its name was changed to J. A. Folger & Co. In addition to running his business, Folger was an Oakland city councilman and a captain in San Francisco's "vigilante army." His son, James II, succeeded him as head of the firm in 1889.

H— 1863–1947
ENRY FORD

Ford Cars

Success did not come quickly to the man who revolutionized mass production techniques and put America on wheels. Henry Ford was forty years old when he started his famous auto company. Prior to that time, the rail-thin mechanic held a number of jobs, including one as a $135-a-month engineer at the Detroit Edison Company. It was while at Edison that Ford began tinkering with motorcars in his home workshop, prompting guffaws from neighbors, who dubbed him "Mad Henry." He completed his first practical car, the Quadri-cycle, in 1896, and soon after he formed the Detroit Automobile Company. The new venture faltered, however, and Ford sold out to two businessmen who later revived the firm by introducing a car called Cadillac. In 1903 Ford launched the Ford Motor Co., using $28,000 raised from twelve investors. The lucky dozen made a monumentally smart decision; one backer, James Couzens, earned $30 million from his $2,500 investment in less than fifteen years. During his lifetime, Ford's unorthodox political views received almost as much publicity as his mass production genius. An ardent isolationist, he made unsuccessful bids for the Senate (1918) and the presidency (1924).

R̶OBERT T. FRENCH
1823–1893

French's Mustard

Most of Robert French's adult life was spent working as a salesman for a New York City wholesaler of coffee, tea, and spices. The Ithaca, New York, native didn't get around to forming his own business until 1880, when he was fifty-seven. A short time later French was joined by his sons, George and Francis, and in 1883 the firm was moved to Rochester, where it produced spices and other products including bird seed. It was French's sons who introduced the family's famous mustard in 1904. Prior to that time, American mustards were typically of the hotter-than-fire variety, but the French brothers believed that there was an untapped market for a lighter creamy condiment. As things turned out, their assumption proved to be an accurate one; French's Cream Salad Mustard was a success from the start. In 1912 the company built a new Rochester plant to keep up with the demand for its product. Ten years later, a second factory was erected, and national advertising was begun. When the R. T. French Company celebrated its centennial in 1980, the firm was selling 500,000 jars of mustard a day.

R̶OY HALSTON FROWICK
1932–

Halston Fashions

Born in Des Moines, Iowa, this famous couturier made a name for himself after discarding two of his given names—the first and last. Halston, born Roy Halston Frowick, got off to an early start in his chosen field selling women's hat designs while still at Indiana University. After moving to New York in 1957, he worked for Lilly Daché before joining Bergdorf Goodman. He was thrust into the limelight a few years later, when Jacqueline Kennedy wore his pillbox hat to her husband's inaugural. From hats, Halston branched out into dresses, sportswear, and gowns, his creations characterized by their simple classic shapes. In the late 1960s, he began designing ready-to-wear apparel, and in 1972 he formed Halston Originals, which was acquired the following year by Norton Simon Inc. Some fashion purists were irked in 1983 when Halston introduced an exclusive collection for J. C. Penney, but the arrangement has worked out well for the monomial designer as well as the department store chain.

A———— 1885–1973
ALFRED C. FULLER

Fuller Brushes

It seemed to those who knew him that Alf Fuller could do nothing right. The awkward Nova Scotian youth was fired from three successive jobs after moving to Massachusetts at eighteen. His first job as ticket taker for the Boston Elevated was lost after he took a motorcar on a joyride and crashed. A short time later, he was let go from his second job as a gardener-stablehand, because he neglected to care for a prized horse. Alf's own brother discharged him from his third job as a messenger, when he lost an important package. Fed up with being fired, Fuller decided to start his own business in 1905, selling brushes door to door. Surprisingly, the heavyset Canadian turned out to be a spectacular salesman, making enough money his first year on the road to invest $375 in his own brush-making shop. By 1910 Fuller was able to hire twenty-five salesmen to peddle his brushes throughout the Northeast. When Alf Fuller retired as president of his company in 1943, its annual sales were over $10 million, and his Fuller brush men had become a familiar part of the American scene.

E———— 1909?– J———— 1910?–
ERNEST GALLO JULIO GALLO

Gallo Wine

It is one of modern industry's most unusual stories that Ernest and Julio Gallo first learned about wine making at their local public library. In 1933 Ernest visited the Modesto, California, public library, where he came across a couple of two-page pamphlets, one on fermentation and the other on the care of wine. He and his brother then proceeded to follow the instructions prescribed in the booklets to start a winery out of a rented warehouse. For the Gallos, wine making represented an escape from the back-breaking toil of working the patch of land left to them by their late father, a struggling farmer who supplied grapes to sacramental wine makers during Prohibition. At first, the brothers sold bulk wine to regional bottlers throughout the United States, and then in 1940 they began to market wine under their own label. Astute forecasters of trends, the Gallos prospered during the 1960s by anticipating the pop wine explosion and coming out with such standards as Spañada and Ripple. When the American wine market began to mature in the 1970s, the brothers again led the way with mid-priced varietals. By 1976 the Gallos were reportedly selling over 100 million gallons of wine a year.

H————— 1927–
HUBERT DE GIVENCHY

Givenchy Fashions

At six feet, six inches, Hubert de Givenchy is one of the most physically imposing men in his field. As the head of a couture house that has enjoyed unbroken success since it opened in February 1952, Givenchy also stands tall among designers in longevity. Ironically, few would have wagered on the twenty-five-year-old Beauvais native's chances when he launched his venture in the midst of a haute couture recession that saw four established Paris houses fail in 1951. Commenting on Givenchy in its March 3, 1952, issue, *Life* magazine noted, "The time hardly seemed propitious for anyone to be opening a new house—least of all a youngster without too much money." Despite these obstacles, Givenchy, who only eight years earlier had been an apprentice designer, won the immediate approval of critics for capturing the "spirit of youth." Givenchy's stylish separates and open-neck blouses brought him a large American following during the 1950s. In the ensuing years, the prolific couturier attracted international attention with his elegant day and evening wear. Other interests in Givenchy's fashion empire include ready-to-wear apparel, perfume, costume jewelry, and an array of licensed items.

B————— 1841–1888
BENJAMIN F. GOODRICH

B. F. Goodrich Tires

As a small-town physician during the mid-nineteenth century, Benjamin Goodrich was accustomed to accepting payment other than cash for his medical services. In the 1860s, one of the doctor's Jamestown, New York, patients paid for treatment with some shares of stock in the Hudson River Rubber Co. Later, the doctor acquired more stock in the firm, and by 1869 he and a partner had become its full owners. Despite its new owners' best efforts, the little company's sales performance was unimpressive. Goodrich believed that relocating to the Midwest, where there were no competing rubber makers, would boost the firm's fortunes. In 1870 the doctor-entrepreneur formed the forerunner of today's B. F. Goodrich Co. in Akron. Just as Goodrich had predicted, the move west had a stimulating effect on the rubber business. Selling hoses, belts, and other rubber products, the company prospered, and when Goodrich died at forty-six in 1888, its annual sales volume exceeded a half million dollars. About ten years later, the doctor's successors found a new use for rubber, when they furnished Alexander Winton with tires for the first gasoline motorcar made for sale in America.

CHARLES GOODYEAR

Goodyear Tires

Charles Goodyear had but one major interest in life—to make rubber stronger. The Connecticut inventor's single-minded pursuit of this goal drove him into poverty, alienated him from his friends, and earned him the nickname "India rubber maniac." Rubber had been known for a century when Goodyear began working with the material, but its use had been severely limited by its tendency to melt in the summer and freeze stiff in the winter. After years of seeking a solution to this problem, Goodyear accidentally discovered the secret of vulcanization, when he dropped a piece of sulfur-cured rubber on a stove in 1839. The resultant material hardened and subsequently maintained its shape in severe heat and cold. Goodyear received some sixty patents on rubber-making processes and was awarded a medal at the 1851 London World's Fair. Despite the fact that his vulcanized rubber was used in five-hundred different products during his lifetime, Goodyear mismanaged his business ventures and died in debt. In 1898, thirty-eight years after his death, Goodyear was memorialized by Akron, Ohio, brothers Frank and Charles Seiberling, who named their new business the Goodyear Tire & Rubber Company.

SYLVESTER GRAHAM ◆ *Graham Cracker*

Derided by Ralph Waldo Emerson as a "poet of bran bread and pumpkins," the Reverend Sylvester Graham (1794–1851) believed that the way to a man's soul was through his stomach. Graham traveled about the East in the 1830s, preaching on the evils of meat, alcohol, and processed flour. His disciples, "Grahamites," often lived in "Graham boardinghouses," where, in accordance with his teachings, they followed a strict vegetarian diet, drank only water, and slept with the windows open, even in winter. In 1837 Graham published a treatise in which he urged the faithful to bake their own brown bread, instead of buying the highly processed products made at commercial bakeries. The book created ill feelings among bakers, who began to harass the reverend during his speaking tours. Once, Graham had to be barricaded inside a Boston hotel when a mob of bakers gathered outside. Eventually, the bakers adopted a more conciliatory attitude, and capitalizing on Graham's popularity, they applied his name to an array of whole wheat baked goods, including the graham cracker. Despite his advocacy of a healthy life-style, Sylvester Graham was a sickly man, who died when he was only fifty-seven.

G—— 1881–1953
GUCCIO GUCCI

Gucci Loafers

Few fashion accessories have attained the notoriety of the Gucci loafer. Novelists need only to put a pair of the famous heeled loafers on a character to convey an image of stylish success. Guccio Gucci, the man who lent his name to the statusy shoe, began his career in 1906 when he used his wife's dowry to open a saddle shop in Florence, Italy. In the ensuing years, Gucci diversified into other leather goods, including handbags and luggage, all of which bore his "GG" signature. When Mussolini's 1935 invasion of Ethiopia cut off Gucci's source of English leather, he developed his own cattle herds. (Gucci leather goods still are made from the hides of specially bred Val di Chiana cattle.) One year prior to Gucci's death in 1953, his sons, Aldo, Rodolfo, and Vasco, introduced the family's products to the United States, opening a Gucci shop in Manhattan. Early in the next decade, the Guccis brought their celebrated loafer to America. Under the direction of Aldo Gucci, the firm entered a new field in 1969, when it came out with apparel collections for men and women.

A——— 1725–1803
ARTHUR GUINNESS

Guinness Beer

After operating a leased brewery at Leixlip, Ireland, for three years, Arthur Guinness decided to start his own business in 1759. Initially, Guinness wanted to launch his enterprise in Wales, because British export restrictions and a heavy tariff limited the development of the Irish brewing industry. After being unable to find a ready-built brewery across the Irish Sea, however, he purchased a twenty-four-acre site in Dublin that included "a dwelling house, a brewhouse, two malt houses and stables." The brewery built up a prosperous trade over the ensuing years, while its strong-willed proprietor became embroiled in a series of disputes. Arthur Guinness engaged the Dublin Corporation in a continuing battle over water rights, which culminated in 1775 when the brewer used a pickax to scare away a corporation committee that was attempting to seal off his water supply. Eventually, he settled his disagreement with the Dublin Corporation and went on to serve in the city council. In 1778 Guinness began brewing a distinctive porter that became known as Guinness's black Protestant porter because of his opposition to the United Irishmen.

J——— 1892–
JOSEPH M. HAGGAR

Haggar Slacks

Born Maroun Hajjar in the Syrian village of Jazzin, the man who founded the Haggar Co. left his family's one-room home in 1905 when he was thirteen and immigrated to Mexico. Three years later he moved to the United States, where he toiled as a dishwasher, railroad worker, cotton grader, and thread salesman. Along the way, Hajjar changed his name to the Anglicized Joseph Haggar. He also put aside enough money to start his own Dallas, Texas, garment factory in 1925. Haggar's business grew quickly, and by the end of the decade, his plant employed five-hundred people. In 1938 his son Ed Haggar joined the business after graduating from Notre Dame. It was the junior Haggar who transformed the company into an industry giant by using national advertising to create a brand identity for the firm's apparel, an unorthodox strategy for a middle-level menswear maker at the time. A rugged, broad-shouldered man, Joseph Haggar was still showing up at his Dallas office in 1980, when his son Ed told *Forbes*, "Sure my dad is tough, but you can't be in business and be a pushover."

BARBARA HANDLER ◆ *Barbie Doll*

Prior to 1958, the only dolls that little girls played with were those of the cherub-faced infant variety. Then along came Barbie, a buxom eleven-and-a-half-inch "fashion model doll." The stylish plaything was the brainchild of toy makers Ruth and Elliot Handler, who named the doll after their daughter Barbie. Later, the couple capitalized on Barbie's popularity by giving her a boyfriend doll called "Ken" in honor of Ken Handler, their son.

PLEASANT H. HANES 1845–1925   JOHN WESLEY HANES 1850–1903

Hanes Hosiery and Underwear

The name on the famous hosiery and underwear may be the same, but the two Hanes products were christened after different people. Brothers Pleasant (underwear) and John (hosiery) Hanes were partners in a very successful plug tobacco firm in 1900 when they sold out to R. J. Reynolds for $200,000. Although the Winston, North Carolina, brothers got along well, each decided to strike out on his own after the sale. Pleasant, a genial Civil War veteran who served as a courier to Robert E. Lee, launched the P. H. Hanes Knitting Co. in 1902 to manufacture men's and boys' underwear. Meanwhile, husky John Hanes started what would become Hanes Hosiery Mills to produce men's and, later, women's stockings. Both Hanes enterprises continued to grow along their separate, but similar, intimate apparel paths over the next six decades under the direction of Pleasant's and John's descendents. Finally in 1965, family ties prevailed when the underwear and stocking companies merged to form the Hanes Corporation. In 1979 Hanes was acquired by Consolidated Foods Corporation of Chicago.

$$\text{W} \underline{} \text{1880–1943} \quad \text{W} \underline{} \text{1870–1937}$$

WILLIAM HARLEY WILLIAM DAVIDSON
1881–1950 1876–1942
ARTHUR DAVIDSON WALTER DAVIDSON

Harley-Davidson Motorcycles

There are no free rides in life; witness the story of Walter Davidson. In 1902 the Milwaukee machinist was in Kansas on a railroad job, when he got a letter from his brother, Arthur, inviting him to ride a "motorized bicycle" that Art and a friend, Bill Harley, had just designed. Later, Walt returned to Milwaukee expecting to take his brother up on the offer, but was told that before he could go for a ride, he would have to use his skill as a machinist to help Art and Harley (neither of whom had his training) build a prototype of their machine. Walt agreed, and soon another Davidson brother, William, was persuaded to join the venture. The foursome completed their first machine in 1903, and the Davidsons' father donated a backyard shed to serve as their factory. Only sixty-one machines were made by the partners from 1903 to 1907, but they steadily increased production, and by the mid-teens Harley-Davidson was America's third largest motorcycle maker. With the original partners at the helm, the business continued to grow in the ensuing decades. Following World War II, Harley-Davidson became the only American manufacturer to survive an influx of foreign motorcycles.

J —— 1806–1879
JOHN HARVEY

Harvey's Bristol Cream

His father and grandfather were legendary British sea captains, but John Harvey grew up with a distinct aversion to the nautical life. In fact, the youth's horror of the sea was so strong that he refused to board his father's ship for even the short journey from the family's Bristol home to Avonmouth. Since he obviously was not going to follow in his father's footsteps, John was apprenticed to his uncle's Bristol wine firm in 1822. John eventually became a partner and was later joined in the business by two of his sons. Like most wine merchants of their city, the Harveys specialized in blended wines, especially Bristol Milk, a blend of Oloroso sherries and other Iberian wines. They blended several varieties of Bristol Milk, but one pale sherry was a particular source of pride. One day in the 1880s, an aristocratic lady toured the wine cellar and was asked by John Harvey II to compare the family's standard Bristol Milk with the special blend. The woman, whose name is lost to history, is supposed to have sampled each and exclaimed, "If that be milk, then this is cream." Harvey adopted his visitor's declaration to create the famous Bristol Cream name.

H——— 1914–
HOWARD HEAD

Head Skiing Equipment

Bored and restless with his job, Baltimore engineer Howard Head decided that he needed a vacation in the spring of 1947, so he went to Stowe, Vermont, to do a little late-season skiing. Head performed terribly on the slopes, a situation that he attributed to the inherent inefficiency of his equipment. Determined to find an alternative to the hickory skis that dominated the market at the time, the tall, lanky engineer began to experiment with designs for lighter, more flexible aluminum skis. After two years of research, Head finally developed a workable prototype of his invention, and by the early 1960s it was the best-selling ski in America. Never comfortable in the role of corporate executive, the free-spirited Head sold his company to AMF for $16 million in 1969 and retired with some $4.5 million in cash. Less than a decade later, Head was back, forming a successful business to manufacture the Prince, an oversized aluminum tennis racket he had invented.

L——— 1869–1956
LAWRENCE S. HEATH

Heath Bar

After twenty-one years as a schoolteacher and principal, Lawrence "L. S." Heath was familiar with children's fondness for candy. This, no doubt, influenced the forty-five-year-old educator's decision to open a small confectionery on the west side of the public square in Robinson, Illinois. Heath was joined in the business by two of his four sons, and together they sold fountain drinks, ice cream, and homemade candy, most notably a distinctive English toffee that was cooked up in the shop's back-room kitchen. The store's confections soon were attracting a large following, and the Heaths started selling candy to merchants in neighboring cities. In 1931 the ex-teacher and his sons moved to a larger building, where they began manufacturing a five-cent Heath Toffee Candy Bar (later shortened to Heath Bar). Within a decade, the candy-making family was forced to mechanize its facility to keep up with the demand for the one-ounce toffee bar. Although he was fond of his namesake confection, L. S. Heath never suffered the caloric consequences of candy eating. A small, spry man, he sometimes weighed less than 105 pounds.

R———— 1876?--1971
RICHARD HELLMANN

Hellmann's Mayonnaise

Although it had been a part of European kitchens since the mid-eighteenth century, mayonnaise did not become popular in America until more than a hundred years later, when it was introduced to our shores by the French chefs of East Coast millionaires. Word of the delicately blended sauce's versatility quickly spread to other economic classes, and it wasn't long before ordinary homemakers were busily mixing their own mayonnaise. Mayonnaise making is an exacting process, however, and many do-it-yourself efforts ended in failure. By the early 1900s, Americans were ripe for a good, premixed mayonnaise, and Richard Hellmann was the man who gave it to them. The German-born owner of a Manhattan delicatessen, Hellmann began selling mayonnaise packaged in one-pound wooden "boats" in 1912. One year later, he put the product in glass jars and delivered it to other stores in the city by pushcart. Eventually the cart was replaced by a truck, and Hellmann opened a small plant. In 1927 the Postum Co. acquired Hellmann's business, but he continued to serve on its board following the sale. Today Hellmann is owned by Best Foods, a division of CPC International, Inc.

R———— 1720–1800
RICHARD HENNESSY

Hennessy Cognac Brandy

It isn't unusual for a soldier in a foreign land to send souvenirs to friends and family back home. Rarely, however, does this practice have such far-reaching consequences as it had for Richard Hennessy of County Cork, Ireland. Hennessy was fighting in France as a member of the Irish Brigade in the mid-eighteenth century, when he discovered the distinctive charm of the brandy produced in the Cognac region. He was so impressed with the brandy that he shipped a few casks to friends in Ireland. Apparently they shared his enthusiasm, because Hennessy was soon besieged with requests for additional casks. Recognizing an opportunity, the soldier set up a part-time business exporting brandy. Then in 1765, after a battle wound had put an end to his military career, Hennessy settled in Cognac and established the distillery that produces his famous namesake brandy.

M‾‾‾‾‾‾‾‾ 1857–1945
MILTON S. HERSHEY

Hershey Chocolates

Milton Hershey's first million dollars in the candy business did not come from Hershey Bars, Kisses, or any of the other famous chocolates that bear his name. Long before he mixed his first batch of creamy milk chocolate, Hershey established a successful Lancaster, Pennsylvania, caramel factory, which made him a millionaire when he sold the business in 1900. Although he could have retired in comfort at this point, the candy maker reentered the confection industry three years later, building a chocolate factory in the town of Derry Church. His marketing plan was to mass produce an inexpensive, but fine quality, milk chocolate bar called the Hershey Bar. The idea proved to be a good one; by 1911 Hershey's annual sales were $5 million. Drawing from the fortune he made in the candy business, Milton Hershey donated generously to Derry Church (renamed Hershey in 1906), building homes, schools, and recreational facilities. The childless millionaire's favorite cause, however, was the Milton Hershey School, an orphanage. Thanks to various trusts established by Hershey and his wife, Kitty, the school is the largest shareholder in Hershey Foods, owning 56 percent of the corporation.

W‾‾‾‾‾‾‾ 1913– D‾‾‾‾‾‾‾ 1912–
WILLIAM HEWLETT DAVID PACKARD

Hewlett-Packard Information Systems

Electronic harmonica tuners and weight-reducing machines ordinarily are not considered high-technology products, but it was by making these and similar devices that two young Stanford graduates launched what is now one of the nation's foremost computer firms. William Hewlett and David Packard began their enterprise in 1939 with capital of $538, which they used to buy a secondhand Sears press and set up a small workshop in the garage of Packard's Palo Alto home. The partners' first sale was to Walt Disney, who purchased eight of their audio-oscillators, at $71.50 each, for the sound track of *Fantasia*. With the studious Hewlett furnishing the engineering genius and the imposing, six-foot, five-inch Packard the management expertise, the firm quickly became a leader in the high-tech field, developing an array of innovative electronic measuring devices and information systems. In 1969 Packard, who supported Nelson Rockefeller's bid for the Republican presidential nomination, became deputy secretary of defense in the Nixon administration. Two years later, the high-tech billionaire left government and returned to Hewlett-Packard. Both he and Hewlett have since remained active in the management of the company.

A——— 1851–1933 R——— 1856–1934
AUSTIN H. HILLS REUBEN W. HILLS

Hills Brothers Coffee

Vacuum-packed coffee in cans was first introduced in 1900 by San Francisco food merchants Austin and Reuben Hills. Born in Maine, the Hillses moved to California with their parents in 1873. They got their start in the food business selling eggs and butter from a stall in San Francisco's Bay City Market. With the profits made from their stall, the brothers purchased the Arabian Coffee and Spice Mills in 1878 and roasted coffee, tea, spices, and other products. The brothers first learned of the vacuum-packing method of canning foods when they were looking for a safe, efficient way of packaging butter for export. Successful in this venture, they began to vacuum pack coffee. Prior to this time, coffee was packaged in paper bags and nonhermetic tins. Sparked by their innovative package, which preserved the freshness and aroma of their product, the brothers' coffee business grew quickly. By 1923 the Hills brothers had dropped all other products to concentrate on coffee.

BORROWED IMAGE

DUNCAN HINES ◆ *Duncan Hines Cake Mix*

Author of *Adventures in Good Eating,* a widely read restaurant guide for travelers, Duncan Hines (1880–1959) came to symbolize quality food for millions of Americans in the 1940s. Hines capitalized on his reputation in his later years by lending his name to hundreds of food products, ranging from chili and pickles to orange juice and ice cream. All that survives of the licensed products are the Duncan Hines cake mixes, which are manufactured by Procter & Gamble.

B—— 1909–1946
BERTA HUMMEL

Hummel Figurines

Hummel figurines, the brightly colored porcelain cherubs collected by millions around the world, were inspired by the drawings of a Bavarian nun named Berta Hummel. Born in the village of Massing, Berta's artistic training began when she enrolled in the Munich Academy of Fine Arts as a girl. After she earned her degree in 1931, her professors urged her to remain for graduate work, but Berta heeded the call of her religious convictions and entered the convent of Siessen. She continued to develop her artistic skills as Sister Maria Innocentia, her sketches of bright-eyed children at play becoming a popular subject of German postcards. In 1933 the sister's work came to the attention of porcelain manufacturer Franz Goebel, who wanted to reproduce the whimsical illustrations in a series of figurines. The first Hummel figurines were introduced by Goebel at the Leipzig Fair in March 1935 and were immediately accepted by European collectors. Although Sister Maria Innocentia died of tuberculosis in 1946 at the age of thirty-seven, she left behind a wealth of sketches. Much of her work is still being converted into porcelain figurines today by the Goebel company.

C—— 1883–1939
CARL JANTZEN

Jantzen Swimwear

If Carl Jantzen had had his way, he would not be listed among the individual who have lent their names to famous products. A shy man from Aarhus, Denmark, Jantzen was a partner in a small Portland, Oregon, knitting mill in 1913, when he invented a rib-stitch method of making bathing suits. He and his partners were so impressed with the lightweight suits that resulted from the rib-stitch process that they decided to market their product nationally. Before this could be done, however, they agreed that the company would need a snappier trade name than the "PK" it had been using since its 1910 founding. The three partners began their search with their own names. Two of them were brothers, John and Roy Zehntbauer, who—for obvious reasons—argued that their name lacked the necessary marketing appeal. This left Carl Jantzen. Despite the pleas of his partners, Jantzen refused to lend his name to the product. Finally, in 1916, John Zehntbauer secretly arranged to have his reticent partner's name printed on the firm's stationery, thus presenting Jantzen with a fait accompli. Accepting the inevitable, Jantzen helped to build his namesake product into a national and, by 1925, international line of swimwear.

M———— 1889–1929 K— 1844–1929
MERCEDES JELLINEK KARL BENZ

Mercedes-Benz Cars

Little Mercedes Jellinek was only eleven years old in 1900 when her namesake car made its debut. No child prodigy, Mercedes was the daughter of Emil Jellinek, an Austrian automobile wholesaler, who helped Germany's Daimler Engine Corporation develop the car that was named in her honor. Unlike other automobiles, which had their engines mounted behind or under the driver, the Mercedes's engine was positioned in front of the vehicle. The car set off a revolution in automotive design and catapulted the Daimler firm to industry leadership. Daimler's success with the Mercedes dealt a damaging blow to a rival company headed by automaking pioneer Karl Benz. Prior to the advent of the Mercedes, Benz was Germany's automobile leader, producing 575 cars in 1899. The conservative Benz refused to adopt the new front-engine Mercedes design, however, despite the advice of his investors, and in 1903 he resigned from his troubled company under pressure. Karl Benz later returned to the firm as an adviser, and he lived to see it merge with its old Daimler nemesis in 1926 to produce the car that is now prized as the Mercedes-Benz.

A———— 1852–1929
ANDREW JERGENS

Jergens Lotion

Prodigious Andrew Jergens had already made a tidy sum of money in the lumber business when he met Cincinnati soapmaker Charles Geilfus in 1880. Jergens, a twenty-eight-year-old Dutch immigrant, was looking for an investment opportunity; Geilfus was in search of a financial backer, and so a partnership was struck to manufacture fancy toilet soap. Initially, the firm was called the Western Soap Company, but in 1882 its name was changed to the Andrew Jergens Company. A hardworking man, Jergens—who was born in the Duchy of Holstein and came to the United States at the age of seven—remained at the helm of his company until his death in January 1929. Jergens was succeeded as president of the firm by his son, Andrew Jergens, Jr. (1881–1969), who soon started a major radio advertising campaign centered around the sponsorship (for sixteen years) of Walter Winchell's Sunday night broadcasts.

Samuel C. Johnson

Johnson's Wax

It was a common practice among business owners of the late nineteenth century to give their customers small gifts as premiums. Usually such gifts were insignificant items intended only as a simple token of goodwill. But for carpenter Samuel Johnson, the premium proved to be so popular that it became his main product. Johnson was selling parquet floors in the 1880s when he decided to give away free floor wax with every sale. Soon, customers who had purchased floors were returning to Johnson's shop wanting to buy his polish. Faced with this unexpected demand, the fifty-three-year-old carpenter entered the floor polish business in 1886, establishing the S. C. Johnson Co. in Racine, Wisconsin. When Johnson died in 1919, his firm was a major wax manufacturer. It was his grandson, Herbert Johnson, however, who built the business into a diversified giant, developing nonwax products like Raid insecticide (1956) and Glade air freshener (1961). A generation later, Herbert Johnson's son Samuel diversified the company further by introducing Agree hair care products. Following the example set by his premium-minded great-grandfather, Samuel Johnson gave away 30 million samples of the company's Agree hair conditioner as part of its 1977 debut.

Alexander H. Kerr

Kerr Jars

Perhaps it was the proximity of his fortieth birthday or simply a desire to add new meaning to his life, but for whatever reason grocery wholesaler Alexander Kerr resolved in 1902 to give 10 percent of whatever he earned during his remaining years to church charities. As things turned out, 1902 also marked the occurrence of an event that would have a profound impact on the size of Kerr's tithe. In that year, the Portland, Oregon, businessman purchased, for a very small sum, a fruit jar patent and formed the Kerr Glass Manufacturing Company. By 1914 the venture had grown into one of the most successful businesses of its kind in the country, producing millions of jars, lids, and caps a year. True to his word, the jar maker gave a tenth of his fortune to missions, churches, homes, hospitals, and similar institutions, even turning over his Portland mansion for use as a nursery home for underprivileged children. Kerr, whose name still appears on the popular canning jar, wrote two pamphlets on tithing, including a 1916 tract, "God's Loving Money Rule for Your Financial Prosperity."

WILLIAM WALLACE KIMBALL

Kimball Pianos and Organs

Like Prof. Harold Hill of *Music Man* fame, William Wallace Kimball was a slick-talking salesman whose wheeling and dealing landed him in the piano business in 1857. Prior to that time, the Rumford, Maine, native earned his living selling real estate and insurance in the Midwest. It was while living in Chicago that Kimball chanced to meet a musical instrument salesman and proceeded to trade the man four lots in Decorah, Iowa, for four pianos. Although not much is known about Decorah property values in the mid-nineteenth century, it is safe to assume that Kimball ultimately got the better end of the deal. He sold all four pianos, bought more with the profits, and soon opened a retail music store on Chicago's Lake Street. His company began making its own pianos and organs in the 1880s, and by the end of the early twentieth century it was the largest manufacturer of keyboard instruments in the world. The firm remained in the hands of Kimball and his descendents until 1959, when it was purchased by the Jasper Corporation of Jasper, Indiana.

1803–1866
JOHN K. LABATT

Labatt's Beer

Labatt's, one of Canada's most successful breweries, might never have gotten started were it not for the high cost of living in England during the 1840s. John Labatt, a farmer from London, Upper Canada (now Ontario), traveled to England in 1846 to visit his father-in-law and check on some family investments. Apparently the investments were not very lucrative, because although he liked England and considered moving his family there, Labatt found the day-to-day living expenses too high, so he returned to Canada. Once home, he sold his farm and, in 1847, invested in the brewery operated by his friend Samuel Eccles. Soon, the partners were producing three brands of beer, unimaginatively called XXX, XX, and X. In 1854 Eccles retired and Labatt acquired control of the brewery. During the remaining twelve years of his life, John Labatt guided the brewery through a period of steady growth, opening new markets in Toronto, Montreal, and other cities. The brewery remained under the control of the Labatt family until 1964. Today, Labatt's is a diversified firm with interests in brewing, food products, chemicals, and the Toronto Blue Jays baseball club.

René Lacoste

Lacoste Apparel

On tour with the French Davis Cup team, René Lacoste paused one day in 1923 to do some window shopping in Boston. The teenage tennis star was so taken with an alligator suitcase he saw at one store that he told his trainer he wanted the luggage as a reward if he won his upcoming match. Lacoste lost the match—and his chance to acquire the bag—but his request earned him the tag *le crocodile* from his teammates. A decade later, when he began manufacturing tennis shirts, Lacoste drew upon his nickname to patent a "crocodile" (actually an alligator) trademark for his apparel. Since that time, the 1¼-inch scaly status symbol has appeared on shirts, slacks, and other garments sold in more than eight nations (marketed in the United States by Izod). All this has, of course, made the former USTA Men's Singles champion a multimillionaire. Lacoste refused to rest on his laurels, however. In 1965 he designed Wilson's first metal tennis racket, the T-2000, and over ten years later he helped invent a racket that supposedly prevents tennis elbow. It was Lacoste's oldest son, Bernard, who engineered the company's rapid growth during the 1970s.

René Lalique

Lalique Glassware

For René Lalique, the world indeed was "made of glass." During his long and highly acclaimed career, the French artisan worked with glass to fashion a wide range of objects, from automobile radiator caps to crucifixes to the dining hall decorations for the ocean liner *Normandie*. Born in the province of Champagne, Lalique was a jeweler's apprentice as a youth, becoming a free-lance designer in 1890. A decade later, his modernistic creations, which made unprecedented use of materials such as enamels, ivory, and horn, caused a sensation at the Paris Exposition. Lalique began experimenting with glass in the early 1900s and again demonstrated his flair for original designs by introducing a dazzling array of shapes and colors in his products. In 1933 the French government invited him to display his glassware at the Louvre. This was followed two years later by a Lalique exhibit at Altman's in New York. As the popularity of his designs grew, Lalique established a factory in Wingen, Alsace. Prior to World War II, the Lalique factory was the town's only industry.

J— 1857–1930 E— 1891–1973
JOHN LANE EDWARD LANE

Lane Furniture

For forty years after its founding in 1912, the Lane Co. manufactured only one product—cedar chests. The sole exception was during World War I, when it made ammunition chests for the army. This concentration on a single product was in sharp contrast to the divergent interests of the senior founder of the firm, John Lane. A talented administrator, Lane was a successful engineering contractor, cotton mill operator, farmer, and horse breeder before he turned his attention to furniture. His contracting firm had built many major civil projects, including a section of the New York State Barge Canal, and one of his horses won the 1906 Clabaugh Memorial Cup at Pimlico. Although not as versatile as his father, Edward Lane also was a capable businessman. It was Edward who added tables, chairs, and other wood furniture products to the company's internationally famous Lane cedar chests in the 1950s. Edward, who was an avid steeplechase rider as a youth, was a generous supporter of the athletic program at his alma mater, Virginia Polytechnic Institute. In 1965 the school named its new stadium in his honor.

R— 1939–
RALPH LAUREN

Ralph Lauren Apparel

Little in Ralph Lauren's background indicated that he would one day emerge as a high priest of haute couture. Born Ralph Lifshitz in the Bronx (his family legally changed their name to Lauren in the mid-1950s), the man whose Polo label would become synonymous with the word *preppy* attended the public DeWitt Clinton High School and worked part time at Alexander's discount department store. After graduation, Lauren enlisted in the army and upon his return home became an assistant buyer for Allied Stores. He applied for a job as a designer with Brooks Brothers and other menswear makers, but was turned down because he had no portfolio. Finally, in 1967 he was hired by Beau Brummell Ties, and within months he designed a trend-setting wide tie. Lauren left Beau Brummell in 1968 to form his own tie company, which he called Polo, for its upper-drawer image. From wide ties, Lauren diversified into large-collar shirts, wide-lapel jackets, coats, shoes, and in 1971, women's wear (he created Diane Keaton's look in *Annie Hall*). In 1978 Lauren became the first American couturier to both manufacture and license his designs, when he purchased Lanham Clothing. The designer broke new ground once again in 1983, introducing four complete home-furnishings packages, each built around a separate decorating theme (Log Cabin, Thoroughbred, New England, and Jamaica) and featuring products ranging from bed and bath linens to tableware, wallcoverings and rugs.

H—— 1909–1982
HERMAN W. LAY

Lay's Potato Chips

A familiar sight to Nashville, Tennessee, grocers, Herman Lay began peddling potato chips out of the trunk of his touring car in 1932. Two years later, the twenty-five-year-old distributor had six sales routes, and he expanded his business steadily, until his Atlanta supplier ran into financial difficulties in 1938, threatening his source of product. Acting quickly, Lay purchased the troubled company and soon transformed it into a thriving operation. Near the end of World War II, he signed a contract to become a regional manufacturer and distributor of corn chips for the Dallas-based Frito Company, beginning what would grow into the nation's most ubiquitous snack food partnership. The Frito Company and H. W. Lay & Co. merged in 1961, and within three years the firm had a network of forty-five plants scattered throughout the country, thus enabling Lay's to become the first successfully marketed national potato chip brand. Lay's meteoric career reached new heights in 1965, when the Frito-Lay Co. merged with Pepsi to form PepsiCo. Chairman of the board of the new corporate giant and its largest single stockholder was the onetime Tennessee salesman, Herman Lay.

H—— 1849–1928
HENRY D. LEE

Lee Jeans

His jeans are most commonly thought of as a youthful fashion item, but Henry D. Lee already was in his sixties when he began to manufacture his famous pants in 1911. Born in Vermont, Lee left home as a young man and started a successful kerosene distributing business in Galion, Ohio. In 1888 he sold out to John Rockefeller's Standard Oil Co. and moved to Salina, Kansas, where he formed a wholesale grocery house. From food, the versatile businessman gradually branched out to distribute hardware, stationery, and work clothes. Lee might have been content to remain a wholesaler had not his eastern apparel supplier been persistently late in making deliveries. Tired of waiting for his orders to be filled, Lee established a small Salina plant to produce overalls, jackets, and dungarees. His rugged apparel caught on quickly in the western market, and by 1916 he was operating four garment plants. Henry Lee continued to head the clothing firm until his death in 1928. One year earlier his company had achieved the distinction of selling the first cowboy pants with a zipper fly.

W——— 1859–1920
WALTER S. LENOX

Lenox China

When Nancy Reagan wanted new White House china in 1981, she placed a $209,508 order with Lenox, Inc., for a 4,372-piece dinnerware service. Although many recession-weary taxpayers took issue with her expensive taste, Mrs. Reagan could argue that she was merely continuing a china policy begun more than sixty years earlier when Woodrow Wilson bought a 1,700-piece dinnerware service from the New Jersey company. Politics notwithstanding, Walter Lenox is usually credited with launching America's fine china industry. Prior to 1894, when the Trenton-born craftsman started his company, all the better dinnerware sold here came from Europe. The part owner of a small ceramics house at the time, Lenox acquired his partner's interest and began making porcelain dinnerware modeled after that produced by Belleek Pottery in Ireland. His fledgling venture received its first big break in the early 1900s when it sold a large china order to Tiffany's. Ironically, Lenox never saw many of his aesthetic dinnerware designs, having lost his vision as a result of illness in the 1890s. Despite this affliction, Lenox remained active in his company until his death.

A——— 1831–1899 C——— 1838–1895
ARTHUR LIBBY CHARLES LIBBY

Libby Foods

Meat packer Arthur Libby was a firm believer in the "early to bed, early to rise" school of thought. In 1868 Libby, his brother Charles, and fellow Chicagoan Archibald McNeill (1836–1904) pooled $3,000 to start a business producing corned beef in barrels. Convinced that he could obtain better livestock for his new firm by arriving at the stockyards before his established competitors, Arthur left home at three every morning for the South Water Street Market. With the quality of its raw material thus ensured, the business got off to a good start, utilizing 1,210 cattle and realizing almost $60,000 in sales the first year. The company's fortunes took a sharp turn upward in 1875, when the partners began packing corned beef and other compressed meats in tapered tin cans. As one of the earliest producers of canned compressed meats, the firm flourished—the number of cattle slaughtered jumping from 100,000 to 200,000 between 1877 and 1879. By the time the twentieth century arrived, the original partners were either deceased or retired. It was their successors who branched out into other canned foods, introducing sauerkraut in 1904, salmon in 1912, and tomato juice in 1923.

BORROWED IMAGES

DR. JOSEPH LISTER ◆ *Listerine Mouthwash*

Eminent British surgeon Joseph Lister became widely known in the 1870s for his theory that invisible airborne germs were a major cause of operating room infections. Through his public speaking tours and tireless efforts, Dr. Lister pioneered the acceptance of antiseptic surgical procedures in Europe and America. When the Lambert Pharmaceutical Co. of St. Louis introduced a germ-killing mouthwash in 1880, its management gave the product an appropriately antiseptic image by calling it Listerine in honor of the Englishman.

SARA LEE LUBIN ◆ *Sara Lee Cakes*

Yes, Virginia, there really was a Sara Lee. She was the teenage daughter of Charles Lubin, a retail baker in Chicago whose ambition was to mass produce cakes that "not even grandma's grandma could bake." In 1951 Lubin formed the Kitchens of Sara Lee to turn out premium-priced cheesecake, coffee cake, and pound cake in volume. Five years later, the business was acquired by Consolidated Foods Corporation.

W———— 1859–1949
WILLIAM H. LUDEN

Luden's Cough Drops

Reading, Pennsylvania, native William Luden started out making candy in his mother's five-by-six-foot kitchen in 1881. His first product was moshie, a Pennsylvania Dutch treat made primarily out of corn syrup and brown sugar. A few years later, the young confectioner added cough drops to his line. Luden's menthol-flavored drops were colored amber to distinguish them from the many red lozenges on the market at the time. As an added innovation, he lined his cough drop packages with waxed paper to preserve the product's freshness and flavor. Luden promoted his cough drops with national magazine ads that, in addition to touting their cough-suppressing abilities, claimed that they were effective in "sweetening the breath and clearing the head." Still located in Reading, Luden's namesake company now occupies an eight-acre facility and ranks among the top ten candy makers in the country.

M———— 1902–1971   R———— 1909?–
MAURICE MCDONALD   RICHARD MCDONALD

McDonald's Hamburgers

Brothers Maurice and Richard McDonald left their New Hampshire village of Bedford for Hollywood in 1928 with dreams of becoming actors. It wasn't on theater marquees, however, but under the golden arches of a San Bernardino hamburger restaurant that the two would later see their name in lights. After failing to make it as actors, the McDonalds ran several businesses, including a movie theater, before opening their hamburger stand in 1948. Unlike similar restaurants that prepared food to order, the McDonalds' stand served precooked ready-to-go hamburgers for 15¢. In 1954 their business caught the attention of Ray Kroc (1902–1984), a former big band pianist who was then working as a sales agent for a milkshake mixer firm. Kroc convinced the brothers to allow him to sell the McDonalds' name and concept to other restaurant operators. There were some three-hundred McDonald's franchises by 1961, when Kroc bought out the brothers (who then retired) for $2.7 million. Although this sum would seem small compared to the company's eventual success, the brothers remained philosophical. "We didn't know if this was just a fad that would peter out," Richard McDonald recalled in 1983, "but I have no regrets."

J ___ 1864?–1924
JOHN M. MACK

Mack Trucks

Back around the turn of the century, when Ford, Olds, the Duryea brothers, and others were pioneering the development of the motorcar, Brooklyn wagon maker John Mack was blazing new paths for bigger vehicles. Mack and his brothers, William and Augustus, built one of the world's first gasoline-powered buses in 1900, an eighteen-passenger vehicle, which they sold to the operator of a New York sightseeing service. Five years later, the trio moved to Allentown, Pennsylvania, where they formed the Mack Brothers Motor Car Co. with John Mack as president. Soon after their arrival in Allentown, the Macks (who were joined by two more brothers, Joseph and Charles) began to build gasoline-powered trucks. The truck business grew slowly but steadily, and seeking capital for further expansion, the Macks turned to the banking house of J. P. Morgan. As so often happened when engineering innovators hooked up with big bankers, the bankers quickly took over. In October 1911 the Morgan bank merged Mack Brothers into the International Motor Co., a truck-making holding company. Following the merger, all the Macks except William left the firm, having nothing more to do with their Mack trucks.

R ___ 1857–1914
RABBI DOV BER MANISCHEWITZ

Manischewitz Matzo and Wine

When Rabbi Dov Ber Manischewitz arrived in Cincinnati in the mid-1880s, he was troubled by the scarcity of kosher foods in the city. Deciding that something had to be done to improve the situation, he started a small matzo bakery in the spring of 1888. Unlike other matzo bakers, who used antiquated black-iron coal stoves, the rabbi installed new gas-fired ovens in his plant, thereby gaining better control over the baking process. Initially, Manischewitz sold his matzos to other Cincinnati rabbis and members of his congregation, but as his reputation as a baker grew, he began supplying Jewish communities in other cities. The rabbi was succeeded at his namesake company by three generations of the Manischewitz family—beginning with his son Hirsch (1891–1943)—who steadily branched out into other products over the years, including the popular Manischewitz wines.

F————— 1904–
FORREST MARS, SR.

Mars Bar

Described by *Business Week* as the "Howard Hughes of the candy industry," Forrest Mars, Sr., possesses a passion for privacy. Over the course of his career, the secretive confectioner has rarely talked to the press, or anyone else save a close circle of family and associates. Despite his reclusiveness, Mars has a remarkable ability to read America's candy market. Throughout the 1970s he produced at least half of the nation's ten top-selling candy bars, including Snickers, the perennial number one. Mars began his career after graduating from Yale by going to work for his father, Frank Mars, who invented the Milky Way bar in 1923. The father and son had a stormy relationship, however, and in the early 1930s Frank reportedly gave Forrest some money and ordered him to start his own business overseas. Forrest moved to England, where he not only became a major confectioner, but also, eventually, Britain's leading pet food maker. During World War II, Mars returned to America and introduced M&Ms as well as the non-confectionery Uncle Ben's Rice. In 1964 he merged his business with the company founded by his father. Now headed by Forrest's sons, the Mars firm is the world's largest candy maker.

E————— 1898?–1975
ERNESTO MASERATI

Maserati Cars

No European-made car had ever won the Indianapolis 500 when a Maserati captured the event twice in a row, in 1939 and 1940. The consecutive victories were just one example of the success the Italian automaker enjoyed in pre–World War II racing circles. Ernesto Maserati, the man whose family name appears on the powerful racing machine, began driving and building cars as a teenager. It wasn't until 1922, however, that a Maserati won its first race at the Mugello Autodrome near Florence. Working with his brothers, Alfieri, Bindo, and Ettore, the Bologna automaker built a long line of distinguished racing cars during the 1920s and 1930s (a 16-cylinder Maserati swept most of the Grand Prix events in 1930). On the eve of World War II the Maseratis sold their business to a group of Italian investors. The new owners, who appointed Ernesto Maserati director of the company, immediately began to develop the luxury sports car that has since become associated with the name Maserati.

PAUL MASSON

Paul Masson Wine

When bon vivant Paul Masson threw a party, it was more than a simple beer and potato chips affair. The lavish entertainments at his California mountain vineyard, La Cresta, attracted the most glittering names from the society and theater pages of the early 1900s and shocked the sensibilities of middle-class America. (At one 1917 soirée, Masson supposedly gave singer Anna Held her legendary bath in a tub of champagne.) Born in Burgundy, Masson's road to fame and merrymaking began in 1878 when he immigrated to California, where he found work with wine maker Charles Lefranc. A decade later, he married Lefranc's daughter, Louise, and was soon made a partner in the winery. Masson acquired complete control of the business in 1892, changing its name to the Paul Masson Champagne Company. The flamboyant Frenchman built an international reputation for his champagne, which won an honorable mention at the 1900 Paris Exposition. During Prohibition, Masson continued to prosper, since he held the first government permit to make "medicinal champagne," a product purchased by prescription. Although he sold his vineyard in 1933, Masson continued to make champagne in a San Jose cellar until his retirement three years later.

PRINCE GEORGES MATCHABELLI

Prince Matchabelli Perfume

As a student at the Royal Academy at Berlin, handsome Georges Matchabelli charmed the girls by blending exotic perfumes to match their personalities. The oldest son of a noble Russian family, Matchabelli returned home after graduation to become a mining engineer. Following the Russian Revolution, the prince (who was a close friend of Czar Nicholas) fled his homeland, coming to New York in 1923, where he opened an antique shop at 545 Madison Avenue. It was at this shop that the Russian émigré began making perfumes for his favored customers. Word of his talent spread, and Matchabelli was soon forced to drop antiques to keep up with the demand for his perfume. A skilled marketer, Matchabelli packaged his perfumes in crown-shaped porcelain bottles and named them after royal women such as the duchess of York and Catherine the Great. Prince Matchabelli headed his internationally known perfume firm until his death from pneumonia at the age of fifty in 1935.

After fourteen years of manufacturing farm equipment, Iowan Fred Maytag diversified his business by introducing the "Pastime" washer in 1907. Made of cypress wood, the hand-operated machine had a grooved tub interior to duplicate the function of a conventional washboard. By 1909 Maytag had come out with his first mechanically powered washer, the "Hired Girl," and was well on his way to making his name a true household word.

F—— 1857–1937
FRED MAYTAG

Maytag Washers

"Dirty clothes know no season"; it was with this realization in mind that Fred Maytag entered the washing machine business in 1907. More than a decade earlier, the Newton, Iowa, native and three associates had begun manufacturing farm machinery. The seasonal fluctuations of the agricultural industry eventually forced the partners to look for products that could be added to boost sales during off periods. As part of its diversification, the company introduced the hand-operated Pastime washer. The washer at first was one of several sidelines for the firm, which even tried to market a Maytag automobile (1909) without much success. By the time Fred Maytag resigned in 1920, however, washers had clearly become the firm's dominant product (one year earlier the manufacturer had developed the world's first aluminum washer tub). In 1923 the company dropped all other products to concentrate on producing its recently developed "gyrafoam washer." Unlike other machines that simply pulled clothes through the water, the Maytag used blades to force water through the clothes, resulting in cleaner laundry. Riding the popularity of its "gyrafoam," Maytag's sales shot from $1.25 million in 1921 to $28.7 million in 1925, making it the world's biggest washing machine maker. The Newton, Iowa, firm held its leadership position until it was usurped by Whirlpool in 1950.

F——— 1824–1888
FREDERIC MILLER

Miller Beer

Handsome, prosperous, and highly regarded in his native country as a brewmaster to the royal court at the Hohenzollern Castle, Frederic Miller was a far cry from the typical needy immigrant when he arrived in New Orleans in 1854. The thirty-year-old German (who wanted to escape the political turmoil of his homeland) spent a year touring the United States, looking for a site where he could establish a brewery. His prerequisites were a good harbor and abundant supplies of grain, water, and skilled labor—all of which could be found in Milwaukee. In 1855 Miller bought a brewery in the city for $8,000, and by the end of the year he had produced three-hundred barrels of beer. Miller's business grew steadily, and he began bottling beer in 1883, shipping it to nine states. When Frederick Miller died five years later, the brewery's annual output was eighty-thousand barrels. Miller beer sales didn't reach gigantic proportions until the 1970s, however, after the company purchased the "Lite" trademark from Chicago's failing Meister Brau Brewery. Introduced in 1973 Lite beer became an immediate success, vaulting Miller from seventh to second place in the brewing industry by the end of the decade.

H——— 1905–
HOWARD MILLER

Howard Miller Clocks

Located in western Michigan, Zeeland (pop. 4,700) looks like the sort of small midwestern town that hasn't changed in fifty years. Despite its bypassed appearance, Zeeland has kept pace with the times as the home of three clock companies. Largest of the town's clock makers and largest in America is Howard Miller, a firm that sold twice as many clocks as its nearest competitor in 1982. Howard Miller, the man who lent his name to the company, came to Zeeland as a boy after his father, Herman, became manager of a local clock factory. In 1925 the senior Miller started his own business, the Herman Miller Furniture Co. One year later, he branched out into clocks and, with his son, founded the Herman Miller Clock Co. It soon became obvious that the similar names created too much confusion, even in a small town, so the clock business was rechristened the Howard Miller Clock Co. Initially, the firm made only wall and mantel clocks, but in 1948 Howard developed its popular grandfather clocks. The original Howard Miller still runs the business as board chairman, with assistance from sons Jack (president) and Phil (vice-president).

J —— 1764–1836
JOHN MOLSON

Molson Beer

Molson, the famous Canadian beer, has a history that is older than that of the nation of Canada itself. In 1782 John Molson, an eighteen-year-old orphan from Lincolnshire, England, immigrated to Montreal, where he quickly became rich, trading in meats and other foodstuffs. A short time later, Molson and a partner started a small brewery. He acquired complete control of the business in 1785 and built it into a successful brewery by the end of the century. As his beer business grew, Molson turned his attention to other interests, including politics (he served in Canada's colonial legislature), banking (he was president of the Bank of Montreal), and shipping. On August 19, 1809, he launched the *Accommodation*, the first steamship to ply the St. Lawrence between Montreal and Quebec. Later, Molson was joined in business by his sons, John, Jr., Thomas, and William. Inheriting their father's diverse talents, the Molson brothers expanded the family empire in all directions, pioneering Canadian railroad development and forming the Molson Bank in addition to nurturing the brewery.

J —— 1855–1934
JOY MORTON

Morton Salt

It isn't always easy to emerge from the shadow of a father like J. Sterling Morton, a famous conservationist who served as secretary of agriculture in Grover Cleveland's second administration and who is recognized by historians as the founder of Arbor Day. As imposing as J. Sterling's achievements were, however, they did not intimidate his son, Joy Morton. Raised on the family's homestead at Arbor Lodge, Nebraska, Joy demonstrated an independent spirit as a youth when he and his brothers would periodically hop freight cars for visits to neighboring Plains territories. At sixteen, he left school for good and took a job as an errand boy at a Nebraska City bank, eventually working his way up to teller. In 1880 Morton used his savings to purchase a small interest in a Chicago salt company. Five years later, the tall, mustachioed Nebraskan acquired complete control of the firm, changed its name to Joy Morton & Co., and built it into the nation's largest salt supplier by engineering a series of transportation and production innovations. Millionaire Joy Morton paid tribute to his father in 1922, dedicating the highly regarded Morton Arboretum at Lisle, Illinois.

CHRISTIAN F. MUELLER

Mueller Noodles

What began as a part-time business in the kitchen of Christian Mueller's Newark, New Jersey, home in 1867 would, by the turn of the century, become one of the country's leading noodle companies. An immigrant baker from Wurttemberg, Germany, Mueller supplemented his income from noodles in the early years by selling eggs and cheese. Gradually, the popularity of Mueller's noodles spread beyond his neighborhood, and in 1885 the bearded, bespectacled German was able to open a small factory in Newark. At first, Mueller made only egg noodles, but in 1894 he purchased a macaroni press, and soon he was turning out five-hundred pounds of macaroni a day. In 1905 the growing business was incorporated as the C. F. Mueller Co., with Christian Mueller as president, a post he held until his retirement a decade later. That Mueller became a wealthy man from his noodle company was fortunate, because he had a large family to support, having been married four times (his first three wives died) and siring ten children.

HENRI NESTLÉ

Nestlé's Chocolates

Swiss businessman Henri Nestlé could look back on his life with a justifiable sense of pride in 1875, when he sold his Vevey food company to three investors for a million francs. The sixty-one-year-old Nestlé had come to Vevey from Germany in 1843 and had struck it rich by first inventing an acclaimed baby food formula and then developing a popular brand of condensed milk. Even Nestlé, however, would have been shocked by the colossal proportions his namesake company would later attain. Beginning in the early twentieth century, Nestlé's successors engineered a series of mergers and acquisitions that transformed the Swiss firm into the world's largest food processing company. By the end of the 1970s, Nestlé and its subsidiaries were marketing over 650 major brands of food products (including Taster's Choice, Nestea, and Stouffer's frozen dinners) to rack up more than $11 billion in sales. Ironically, Nestlé's famous chocolate dates back to the year Henri Nestlé sold his business. Vevey chocolatier Daniel Peter mixed condensed milk purchased from Nestlé with a batch of chocolate in 1875 to create the world's first milk chocolate. Riding the popularity of its milk chocolate, Peter's firm grew into a major confectionary house, and in 1904 it merged with a rival business to form the Swiss General Chocolate Company. The Nestlé Company contracted to market the new firm's products outside Switzerland. In return, Swiss General (which was purchased by Nestlé in 1929) agreed to produce a line of milk chocolate under the Nestlé name.

R—— 1864–1950
RANSOM E. OLDS

Oldsmobile Cars

When the Model T was still only an idea in Henry Ford's head, the Oldsmobile Runabout became the world's first mass produced automobile. In 1902 the sturdy little vehicle with the curved dashboard and $650 price tag accounted for roughly a third of the estimated nine-thousand cars sold in America. A short time later, the Runabout was made the subject of a song, "In My Merry Oldsmobile," giving it the distinction of being the first automobile to be immortalized in music. The man behind this car was a Lansing, Michigan, machine shop owner, who began experimenting with gasoline-powered vehicles in the mid-1890s. Convinced that he could mass produce cars, Ransom E. Olds built America's first true auto factory in Detroit in 1899. Olds did not have much time to savor the success of his company, being forced out of the business in 1904 following a dispute with his investors, who wanted to replace the Runabout with a bigger, more profitable touring model. After leaving his namesake firm, Olds formed the Reo Motor Car Co., a successful maker of cars and trucks during the early years of the American auto industry.

C—— 1868–1943
CAMILLO OLIVETTI

Olivetti Typewriters

When he moved his growing electrical tool business from Ivrea to Milan in 1902, Italian engineer Camillo Olivetti had to find a new use for the building that had served as his original factory. The red brick structure on the outskirts of Ivrea stood idle for several years until Olivetti reequipped it for the production of typewriters in 1908. A Turin Polytechnic graduate and former lecturer at Stanford University, Olivetti studied under electrical-energy pioneer Galileo Ferraris. It didn't take the brilliant engineer long to develop a high-precision typewriter, the MI, which was introduced at the 1911 Turin Exhibition. Within the next two decades, the Olivetti typewriter had become an internationally marketed product, and the small Ivrea factory had grown into a sprawling industrial complex with its own iron found-

A graduate of Turin Polytechnic, Italian Camillo Olivetti came to the United States in 1893 and spent a year at Stanford, where he was an assistant lecturer of electrical engineering. Upon his return to Italy, Olivetti founded a factory on the outskirts of Ivera to manufacture electrical measuring tools. In 1908 he added his namesake typewriters, which later became one of the best-selling brands in Europe and the United States.

ry. Olivetti was joined in the business by his son, Adriano, in 1926, and together they guided the company to further growth, employing 2,300 workers by the outbreak of World War II. Aged Camillo Olivetti left Ivrea in 1943 when it was occupied by Nazi troops. He died on December 4 of that year in a Biella, Italy, hospital.

G———— 1863–1937 EORGE SAFFORD PARKER

Parker Pens

Hoping to augment his meager salary as a teacher by selling pens to students, George Parker made a deal with an Ohio fountain pen company in 1888 to distribute their products. The Janesville, Wisconsin, telegraphy instructor got more trouble than he bargained for, however, when the poorly made pens flunked out in the classroom. Parker, who felt obliged to service what he sold, wound up spending more time repairing leaky pens than preparing his daily lessons. Vowing that he could build a better product, the teacher designed his own fountain pen in 1889, and two years later he formed the Parker Pen Co. The firm prospered quickly, thanks to the many technical innovations pioneered by its founder, most notably the Lucky Curve (1894), a rubber feed bar that prevented ink leakage. By 1918 Parker's annual sales were $1 million, and plans were drawn for a five-story Janesville factory. A likable man, George Parker toured Europe, Asia, and Australia during the early 1920s to create an international network of distributors for his products, which were among the world's best-selling pens by the end of the decade.

G———————— 1866–1952
GEORGE SWINNERTON PARKER

Parker Brothers Games

Medford, Massachusetts, native George Parker invented his first board game—a borrowing-lending contest called Banking—when he was only sixteen. Receiving a three-week leave of absence from high school, the teenager managed to produce and sell five-hundred copies of his game for Christmas distribution. Despite this prodigious achievement, Parker's parents remained unimpressed and steered their son away from the uncertainties of game making toward the more secure world of journalism. After graduating from Medford High, George signed on as a cub reporter with Boston's *Commercial Bulletin*. In 1886 a respiratory ailment forced him to seek a less strenuous line of work, and to the surprise of no one, the erstwhile newspaperman fell back on his first love—game making. Two years later, he and his brother Charles formed Parker Brothers game company (a third brother, Edward, joined the business in 1898). Together, the trio built the firm into an industry leader, which has produced such classics as Monopoly, Clue, and Risk.

J———————— 1918–
JENO FRANCISCO PAULUCCI

Jeno's Frozen Pizza

It would be hard to imagine the zany Italian chef of the Jeno's commercials serving up anything but pizza, but Jeno Paulucci, who plays himself in the television spots, made his fortune in ethnic foods of an entirely different flavor. In 1954 the Minnesota-born businessman founded ChunKing, the canned and frozen Chinese food company. Paulucci's switch from egg rolls to pizza rolls came following his 1967 sale of ChunKing to R. J. Reynolds Industries, when he formed Jeno's Inc. For a time, Jeno rode on top of America's billion-dollar-a-year frozen pizza market, but his Duluth-based company slipped to number two in the late 1970s, after Pillsbury developed a new frying process to improve the crust of its Totino brand. Rebounding from the setback, Jeno's came out with its own fried pizza crust, and by 1980 its annual sales were in the $200 million neighborhood. A tireless worker, Paulucci arrives at the plant every morning at 6:30 to search for wasted food, even though he has relinquished formal control of his namesake company to his three children.

C———— 1820?–1882
CHARLES PHILLIPS

Phillips' Milk of Magnesia

English-born pharmacist Charles Phillips was the owner of an Elizabeth, New Jersey, drugstore in 1849, when he tired of retailing and decided to become a manufacturer. Phillips moved to Glenbrook, Connecticut, where he established a small laboratory to make beeswax. The business prospered for a while, but then candle makers began to choose the more efficient paraffin over beeswax. With the market for his main product disappearing, Phillips set to work on finding a replacement. He came up with one in 1873, when he patented a method of converting powdered antacid-laxative magnesia into a safer, more convenient liquid form. Calling his creation Phillips' Milk of Magnesia, the pharmacist-manufacturer continued to develop a market for the product until his death in 1882. Three years later, his Glenbrook laboratory was incorporated as the Charles H. Phillips Chemical Co. under the management of his four sons. In 1923 the nation's largest milk of magnesia producer was acquired by Sterling Products—later Sterling Drug Inc.

C———— 1842–1899
CHARLES PILLSBURY

Pillsbury Cake Mixes

Nothing in his Dartmouth education had prepared Charles Pillsbury for a career as a miller. Yet, when the twenty-seven-year-old New Englander traveled to Minnesota to visit his uncle, John Pillsbury, in 1869, he became interested in buying a one-third share in a struggling Minneapolis mill. The persuasive Ivy Leaguer managed to convince his uncle John (a man who would later become governor of the state) to lend him part of the $10,000 he needed to buy into the milling business. Despite his lack of experience, Pillsbury demonstrated a natural talent for his new industry. He made several changes in the mill's production techniques that allowed the business not only to stop losing money but to actually turn a profit in 1870. One year later, Pillsbury acquired complete control of the business, which he renamed the C. A. Pillsbury Co. and gradually built into the world's largest milling enterprise, with daily production reaching ten-thousand barrels of flour by 1889. As a result of his successful milling empire, Pillsbury became one of Minnesota's most prominent citizens, and following the example of his uncle John, he entered politics, serving five terms in the state senate.

W——— 1881–1970
WILLIAM T. PIPER

Piper Aircraft

Often called "the Henry Ford of aviation" because he pioneered the mass production of cheap, dependable aircraft, William Piper did not learn how to fly until he was fifty years old. Piper was a millionaire construction engineer from Bradford, Pennsylvania, in 1928, when members of the local chamber of commerce asked him to represent them on the board of a small aircraft company that had just located in town. Reluctantly Piper agreed, but soon he was so taken with aviation that he learned how to fly and eventually acquired control of the company. Convinced that a market existed for a durable, but affordable aircraft, the Harvard-educated engineer (class of 1903) introduced the Piper Cub in the 1930s. The lightweight, inexpensive Cub became to general aviation what the Model T was to automobiles. By the time of his death, Piper had built more airplanes than anyone else in the world, according to the *New York Times*. Crucial to the success of all Piper aircraft was Bill Piper's insistence on keeping the controls simple. "I'm a poor pilot myself," he once said, "but any fool can fly a Piper. I planned it that way."

A——— 1871?–1933   W——— 1882?–1957
ARTHUR PITNEY   WALTER BOWES

Pitney Bowes Postage Meters

It is common to hear complaints about the slow pace of mail deliveries, but few people have ever been as frustrated with the U.S. Postal Service as Arthur Pitney. A clerk at a Chicago wallpaper firm, Pitney patented a machine in 1902 that was capable of stamping envelopes mechanically. The invention offered time-saving advantages to businesses and other heavy mail users because it eliminated the need to lick and stick adhesive stamps. It also promised to save the postal service money by allowing it to print stamps in smaller quantities. Despite the obvious benefits of his machine, however, Pitney spent over sixteen years trying to interest the postal service in his invention without success. In 1919 the frustrated inventor became partners with Walter Bowes, a Connecticut businessman. With the personable Bowes leading the lobbying effort, the men won official authorization for their postage meters in 1920. Nine years later, Pitney Bowes had a gross income of roughly $1.5 million from the postage meter. Ironically, Arthur Pitney never fully profited from this success, having disassociated himself from the firm in 1924 after a policy dispute with Bowes.

FERDINAND PORSCHE

Porsche Cars

As a teenager, Ferdinand Porsche amazed his parents by installing an electric light system in the family's Maffersdorf, Austria, home. At twenty-five the youth codesigned an electric car with a twenty-three-mile-per-hour top speed that was the talk of the 1900 Paris Auto Show. In the ensuing years, Porsche moved to Germany, where he continued to demonstrate remarkable inventive skills, designing airplane engines, diesel trucks, motorcycles, and a legendary series of Mercedes sports cars. Unfortunately, the automaker's wisdom in political matters did not match his mechanical genius. Porsche was awarded Germany's "national culture prize" in 1938 as the designer of the Volkswagen, the "people's car" promised by Hitler. The Nazi dictator again honored Porsche as one of three new "pioneers of labor" in May 1942. Following World War II, Porsche was arrested by the French government, which released him after his son paid a one-million-franc bond. Porsche returned to automaking in 1949, introducing his namesake sports car. A perfectionist, Porsche continued to make refinements in the design of his superlative car throughout the remaining two years of his life.

BORROWED IMAGE

DR. ALBERT RALSTON ◆ *Ralston Purina Pet Foods and Cereal*

Born Albert W. Edgerly, it was as Dr. Ralston that this early health foods advocate became famous as an author and nutrition expert in the late 1800s. Around the turn of the century, Dr. Ralston was persuaded to endorse the Purina whole wheat cereal manufactured by St. Louis Miller William Danforth. The doctor's name became so strongly associated with the wholesome breakfast product that Danforth renamed the firm the Ralston Purina Company in 1902.

$\underline{\qquad\qquad}$ 1907–
ORVILLE REDENBACHER

Orville Redenbacher's Gourmet Popping Corn

There may not be a grocer named George Whipple or a waitress named Rosie, but the Orville Redenbacher who began hawking his "gourmet popping corn" on television in the mid-1970s is the genuine article—as down-home as the Brazil, Indiana, cornfields from which he sprang. Redenbacher's interest in the snack food dates back to his days at Purdue, where he studied popping-corn hybridization. Following graduate work in agronomy and plant breeding, he was employed as an agriculture teacher, a Terre Haute County farm agent, and manager of an Indiana corn farm. In 1952 Redenbacher and a college chum, Charles Bowman, teamed up to develop a new hybrid yellow popping corn that popped open more widely than ordinary varieties. Established popcorn companies, which were geared toward selling their products on the basis of price, turned down the partners' hybrid because it was too expensive. Undaunted, Redenbacher began packaging his corn and selling it to retail groceries. Despite its high price, the product caught on with popcorn customers. In 1976 Redenbacher's growing business was acquired by Hunt-Wesson Foods, which retained him as a spokesperson and goodwill ambassador. Since the acquisition, the Redenbacher brand has become America's best-selling popcorn.

$\underline{\qquad\qquad}$ 1879–1956
HARRY B. REESE

Reese's Peanut Butter Cup

After toiling at a number of menial jobs for most of his first thirty-eight years, Harry "H. B." Reese moved to Hershey, Pennsylvania, to manage one of the dairy farms owned by the town's most famous citizen, confectioner Milton Hershey. H. B. wasn't at his new job long before his neighbor's success inspired him to launch his own candy company. He relocated to nearby Hummelstown (and later Palmyra) and began making Lizzie Bars, a caramellike molasses and coconut treat that met with limited success. Reese returned to the town of Hershey, and in 1923 he acquired a plant on Chocolate Avenue where he turned out a new candy, suggested by a customer, that consisted of specially processed peanut butter covered with milk chocolate. Calling his product a peanut butter cup, the farmer-confectioner initially sold it in five-pound boxes for use in candy assortments. In the mid-1930s, H. B. introduced individual penny sizes of the candy, and by the following decade his factory had dropped all other products to concentrate on the amazingly popular Reese's Peanut Butter Cup.

The Hershey and Reese paths crossed again in 1963, when the giant candy company purchased its Chocolate Avenue neighbor from H. B.'s descendents.

ADOLPH REMPP

Adolph's Meat Tenderizer

Diners would wait in line for hours during the 1940s at Adolph Rempp's Los Angeles and Santa Barbara steak houses, where a juicy steak dinner could be bought at hamburger prices. The secret behind the bargain entrées was Rempp's own papaya extract tenderizer, which transformed inexpensive, tough cuts like chuck into soft-as-butter slabs that could almost pass for filet mignon. One day in 1947, two struggling World War II veterans, Larry Deutsch and Lloyd Rigler, visited Rempp's Los Angeles eatery, attracted by the idea of saving money on a steak dinner. As it turned out, the meal had a far greater impact on their finances than either man could have imagined. Deutsch and Rigler were so impressed with their steaks that they bought the rights to sell Rempp's tenderizer to the retail grocery market. Billed as Adolph's Meat Tenderizer, the product was introduced at the 1949 Los Angeles Home Show. Its sales soared—$125,000 in 1950, $250,000 in 1951, and $500,000 in 1952—making Deutsch and Rigler wealthy. Adolph Rempp, meanwhile, remained in the restaurant business. Today, he and his son Dolph own the Sailing Ship restaurant in San Francisco.

1877–1944
LOUIS RENAULT

Renault Cars

The twenty-year-old son of a wealthy Parisian button manufacturer, Louis Renault began building a small number of motor cars as a diversion in 1897. Two years later, Louis was taking automaking more seriously, and he formed the Société Renault Frères with his brother Marcel. The Renaults promoted their new company by becoming competitive drivers, each of them winning several prestigious racing trophies. Then tragedy struck in 1903, when Marcel Renault was killed in a crash during the Paris-to-Madrid race. Louis, who was leading the event at the time, was told of his brother's accident after he had completed the first leg of the race at Bordeaux. News of Marcel's death so depressed Louis that he immediately disbanded the entire Renault racing team. Later, the grief-stricken Louis was planning to drop out of the auto industry completely, until a third brother, Fernand Renault, encouraged him to continue by leaving the family button business and joining the car company.

RICHARD S. REYNOLDS
1881–1955

Reynolds Wrap

Richard S. Reynolds, the man who created Reynolds Wrap, was one of two members of his family with the same first and last names who developed famous products. The other Richard Reynolds, his uncle, was the head of the R. J. Reynolds Tobacco Co. In 1903 R. S. went to work at R. J.'s business, and together the two introduced many new tobacco blends as well as the Prince Albert tobacco tin. Reynolds left his uncle's firm in 1912, and seven years later, after a few unsuccessful ventures, he formed the U.S. Foil Co. in Louisville to manufacture a lead-and-tin cigarette wrapping. When a relatively new and unproven metal called aluminum appeared on the scene in the mid-1920s, Reynolds became the first in the cigarette foil industry to switch to the material. As aluminum technology advanced, so too did Reynolds's fortunes, and in 1935 he opened new packaging markets by pioneering a method of rotogravure printing on the shiny metal. Reynolds Metals entered the lucrative kitchen-wrap market when it introduced the now familiar 0.0007-inch thick foil, Reynolds Wrap, in 1947. The following year, Richard Reynolds retired as president of his company to become its board chairman.

WILLARD F. ROCKWELL
1888–1978

Rockwell Tools and Electronics

Long before the term became a part of America's vernacular, Willard Rockwell was traveling in the "fast lane." A graduate of MIT, Rockwell was a consulting engineer in 1915, when the Torbensen Axle Company asked him to manage its Cleveland plant. Within three years, he helped to transform the firm into the nation's biggest truck axle manufacturer. The strong-willed engineer left his $25,000-a-year job in 1919, however, after the company's executives refused to modernize its axle designs. Rockwell then moved to Wisconsin to form his own axle business, which became Rockwell-Standard, an industry leader. Meanwhile, as he was building his axle firm, the hardworking executive was putting together a separate company (later called Rockwell Manufacturing) in an abandoned Pittsburgh auto plant to make gas meters, parking meters, and taxi cab meters. Eventually, Rockwell-Standard branched out into automotive parts, aircraft, and materials-handling equipment, while Rockwell Manufacturing added power tools and railroad parts to its product line. A tireless worker who once hired a racing driver as his chauffeur to cut down on commuting time, Willard Rockwell remained active in both companies until he was in his eighties.

H ELENA RUBINSTEIN

Helena Rubinstein Cosmetics

The three intruders who entered Helena Rubinstein's Manhattan apartment in 1964 were not prepared for the resistance they encountered. After binding and gagging her staff, the armed trio turned to Rubinstein and demanded that she hand over her jewelry collection. In a calm, steady voice, the ninety-three-year-old cosmetics executive said that the thugs could shoot her if they wished, but she would not cooperate. Unnerved by the sight of a resistant nonagenarian, the would-be robbers left empty-handed. It was this kind of determination that propelled the daughter of a middle-class Polish-Jewish merchant from Krakow into one of the world's wealthiest businesswomen. At eighteen Rubinstein left home for Australia, where she opened a Melbourne beauty salon. A short time later, she used the profits from this venture to launch a European business. Rubinstein had salons in Europe and the United States by 1918, when she began selling her cosmetics in department stores. The beauty expert continued to expand her business, distributing 160 different products to three-thousand retailers by World War II. A tireless worker, Rubinstein was at her office just two days before she died at the age of ninety-four.

Y VES ST. LAURENT

1936–

Yves St. Laurent Fashions

One day in 1953, Yves St. Laurent, a gangly seventeen-year-old, showed sketches of his dress designs to Michel de Brunhof, a Paris executive with French *Vogue*. The fashion veteran stared pop-eyed at the illustrations, unable to believe how much they resembled the dresses that were then being completed at the House of Dior. Convinced that the teenager was not a fraud, de Brunhof took St. Laurent to meet France's premier designer. Apparently Dior also liked what he saw; after a fifteen-minute conference, he hired St. Laurent as his assistant. Over the next four years, the famous couturier came to regard St. Laurent as his protégé, referring to the youth as "my prince." When Dior died in 1957, leadership of Paris's famous couture house passed into the twenty-one-year-old hands of St. Laurent. Despite his youth, St. Laurent showed several successful collections. Then in 1960, he was drafted into the army and after his induction was replaced as head of Dior. St. Laurent suffered a nervous disorder in the army, and after his discharge he was admitted to a private clinic near Paris for his convalescence. The Algeria-born couturier returned to the fashion world in 1962, when he introduced his first independent collection and quickly established himself as a major designer in his own right.

J ___ 1877–1937
JACOB SCHICK

Schick Razors

During a 1911–14 mining expedition to British Columbia, U.S. Army veteran Jacob Schick became annoyed at having to heat a pot of water every morning so that he could shave in the subzero temperatures. To dispense with this nuisance, the impatient American designed a manual razor that could be used without soap and water. After successfully employing the device for the remainder of his trip, the inventor sent prototypes of his "dry razor" to several manufacturers when he returned home, only to have it rejected by all of them. Nevertheless, Schick remained determined to market a shaver that could be used without water, and after a second stint in the army during World War I, he began working on plans for an electrically powered razor. Over a decade elapsed (during which time he mortgaged his home for $10,000) before Schick introduced his electric razor in 1931. Although it was heralded as a technological breakthrough, sales of the razor were slow at first, largely because its $25 price tag seemed steep. Shick soon lowered the price to $15, and by the time of his death in 1937, more than 1.8 million of the razors had been sold.

J ___ 1831–1875
JOSEPH SCHLITZ

Schlitz Beer

In 1849 brewmaster August Krug founded the Krug Brewery in a former Milwaukee restaurant. Having no son of his own, but wanting the business to remain in family hands, Krug intended to groom his young nephew, August Uihlein, as his successor. But Krug died prematurely in 1856, and with the Uihlein lad not yet in his teens, the brewery's twenty-five-year-old bookkeeper Joseph Schlitz took over the management of the business. Schlitz also courted Krug's widow, eventually marrying her and renaming the brewery after himself. Fate works in strange ways, however—in 1875 Schlitz and his wife died on a vacation voyage to Germany when the steamer *Schiller* went down in the Irish Sea. Thus, in the end, Krug's wishes were fulfilled. Control of the brewery passed to his nephew following the death of Joseph Schlitz. Under the leadership of August Uihlein and later his descendents, the brewery grew steadily, briefly occupying the number one spot in the nation's beer industry during the 1950s.

J——— 1740–1821
JACOB SCHWEPPE

Schweppes Soda Water

What is now one of the world's most famous brands of tonic, ginger ale, and other mixers began as a father-daughter business in 1792. Jacob Schweppe, a middle-aged bottler of mineral waters from Geneva, Switzerland, immigrated to Bristol, England, where he and his daughter Colette pioneered a method of carbonating still water into soda water. the Schweppes established a prosperous trade selling their effervescent beverage in distinctive round-end bottles. They eventually grew homesick, however, and returned to Switzerland, after revealing "The Whole Art, Mystery, and Process of Making and Composing Artificial Mineral Waters" to three investors from Jersey. Under its new ownership, the soda company grew to national prominence in Britain, being granted a Royal Warrant in 1836 by the duchess of Kent, Queen Victoria's mother. In 1969 Schweppes merged with the chocolate maker Cadbury to form Cadbury-Schweppes Ltd.

I——— 1860–1948
IGNAZ SCHWINN

Schwinn Bicycles

Bicycle pioneer Ignaz Schwinn spent most of his early years as an itinerant machinist in northern Germany. In the 1880s, Schwinn was working at a Frankfurt machine shop that supplied parts to bicycle maker Heinrich Kleyer. The two men became friends, and Kleyer eventually hired Schwinn as his designer and works manager. At the Kleyer factory, Schwinn built some of the earliest "safety bicycles" to appear in Germany. Deciding to start his own business in America, the thirty-one-year-old bike maker moved to Chicago in 1891. Four years later, he joined with Adolph Arnold, president of a local meat-packing house, to form Arnold, Schwinn & Company. With Schwinn providing the technical know-how and Arnold the management skills, the new company was an immediate success, selling twenty-five-thousand bicycles the first year. Ignaz Schwinn bought out his partner in 1908 and remained the active head of the firm for the rest of his long life. By 1974 output at the Chicago company, which was then headed by Frank Schwinn, a grandson of the founder, passed 1.5 million bicycles a year.

J ─── 1841–1919
OSEPH SEAGRAM

Seagram Whiskey

Following his 1869 marriage to Stephanie Urbs, Stratford, Ontario, native Joseph Seagram went to work at the distillery run by his bride's uncle, William Hespeler. Although he was a miller by trade, Seagram showed an immediate aptitude for his new business, and he soon purchased an interest in the firm. In 1883 he acquired complete control of the Waterloo, Ontario, distillery, and under his leadership, it soon enjoyed a sharp upturn in sales, thanks to the introduction of its popular Seagram 83 and Seagram V.O. brands. The Canadian distiller used the money he made from his business to further his two main interests—politics and racehorses. He served in several government posts and was one of the founders of the Canadian Racing Association. Nine years after his death, Seagram's sons merged his company with the Distillers Corporation, a concern run by the legendary Sam Bronfman. It was the mercurial Bronfman who built Seagram into the world's largest liquor company.

BORROWED IMAGE

GEORGE SEALY ◆ *Sealy Mattress*

The Sealy mattress would today be called the Haynes mattress if it had been left to Daniel Haynes. In 1884 Haynes launched his mattress business in Sealy, Texas, a railroad town named after Galveston banker George Sealy. The manufacturer called his product the Haynes mattress, but customers soon began to refer to it as "the mattress from Sealy" and, finally, "the Sealy mattress." When Haynes sold out to a group of investors in 1906, the name of the firm was officially changed to the Sealy Mattress Company.

SAMUELE SEBASTIANI

Sebastiani Wines

Italian immigrant Samuele Sebastiani arrived in San Francisco in 1895 to tend artichoke and cabbage fields. With an eye toward getting started in the wine business, he later moved to nearby Sonoma County, supporting himself by hauling cobblestones from area quarries to San Francisco, where they were being used to pave the city's streets. By 1904 the thirty-year-old Tuscan had saved enough money to purchase a 501-gallon redwood vat, a rudimentary press, and a supply of Zinfandel grapes. The following year, he bought a portion of northern California's oldest vineyards, which were originally planted in 1825 by the Franciscan fathers. Sebastiani established a prosperous trade selling bulk wine to bottlers throughout the United States, and he became one of Sonoma's leading citizens, building a community theater, skating rink, and bowling alley. It was Samuele's son, August Sebastiani, who modernized the winery following World War II and introduced the company's well-known bottled varietal wines.

WALTER A. SHEAFFER

Sheaffer Pens

His father owned a jewelry store, but Walter Sheaffer was determined to strike out on his own before he followed the path that led to the family business. At twelve the Bloomfield, Iowa, youth went to work as a printer's devil for a dollar a week. Later, he worked as a grocery clerk and an outdoor peanut vendor before returning home in 1888 to become a partner in his father's store. Walter Sheaffer still was running a jewelry store twenty years later, when he patented a lever-operated, self-filling fountain pen. Initially, Sheaffer regarded his invention as a sideline, assembling pens in a room behind his shop. The growing demand for his writing instruments, however, forced him to start a separate pen company in 1912. Sheaffer stepped down as president of the pen firm in 1938 to devote more time to other interests, including politics—he was a delegate and alternate at two Republican conventions. The pen maker was succeeded by his son, Craig Sheaffer. Unlike his father, the younger Sheaffer did not wait to join the family business. He entered the pen company after graduating from Dartmouth and remained there throughout his career.

H——— 1842–1916 E——— 1843–1903
HENRY ALDEN SHERWIN EDWARD PORTER WILLIAMS

Sherwin-Williams Paint

Before the 1870s, when you needed a bucket of paint, you had to buy the ingredients separately, measure them out, and mix them yourself. Ready-mixed paint was unheard of—until two convenience-minded Ohioans named Henry Alden Sherwin and Edward Porter Williams began manufacturing it in 1873. Sherwin and Williams, whose names were to become as intermingled as the ingredients in their revolutionary product, first met when their separate companies began doing business with each other. Sherwin was a partner in a Cleveland firm that manufactured paint of the old variety, and Williams owned a share in a Kent, Ohio, glass factory. Both in their twenties and restless, they shared an ambition to do something bigger; so when Sherwin spoke of his desire to develop a ready-mixed paint process, Williams agreed to back him with $2,000. Sherwin soon came up with a formula for a durable premixed paint, which Williams, whose strength lay in marketing, promoted with a then-unheard-of money-back guarantee. In 1905 the firm adopted its now-famous "Cover the Earth" trademark, even though it did little exporting of its product at the time.

Z——— 1828–1910
ZALMON G. SIMMONS

Simmons Bedding Products

President of both the Rock Island Railroad and the Northwest Telegraph Co., as well as owner of a prosperous Kenosha, Wisconsin, general store, Zalmon G. Simmons could afford to be generous with a hard-pressed inventor who owed him money in the 1860s. Instead of insisting on cash, Simmons agreed to accept the inventor's patent for a woven-wire bedspring as payment for the debt, even though the man cautioned that the spring was too costly to ever be mass produced profitably. Disregarding this warning, Simmons showed a prototype of the invention to a friend, who figured out how to reduce production costs from $5 to less than $1 per unit. In 1870 Simmons (who was also mayor of Kenosha) began to manufacture the bedspring. A short time later, he capitalized on its growing popularity by adding a complementary line of brass bedsteads. This was followed over the years by the introduction of other bedding products, including the famous Beautyrest mattress, which was introduced in 1925 by the founder's son, Zalmon G. Simmons, Jr.

I‾‾‾‾‾‾‾‾ 1811–1875
ISAAC MERRITT SINGER

Singer Sewing Machine

Would-be actor Isaac Singer found himself stranded in Fredericksburg, Ohio, in the late 1840s, after his traveling theatrical troupe was suddenly disbanded. Short on funds, the Pittstown, New York, native took a job at a printer's type factory in the Ohio town. While at the factory, Singer invented a type carver, and hoping to sell it to publishers, he traveled to New York and Boston in 1850. Not one publisher was interested in the device, but Singer's journey wasn't wasted. It was in the Boston workshop of Orson Phelps at 19 Harvard Place that Singer encountered his first sewing machine. He was immediately curious about the machine and suggested several improvements in its design. With financial backing from Phelps and a man named George Zieber, Singer built a sewing machine that incorporated all his ideas, and in 1851 he formed a company to manufacture the product. Five years later, the courts ruled that Singer's needle and lockstitch violated Elias Howe's patents, and he had to pay the Massachusetts inventor a $25-per-machine royalty. Despite this, Singer's firm grew into the world's largest sewing machine maker by 1863, when he retired to England.

A‾‾‾‾‾‾‾‾ 1860–1947
AMANDA W. SMITH

Mrs. Smith's Pies

Amanda W. Smith was a hardworking, bespectacled widow from Pottstown, Pennsylvania, who started baking commercially in 1919 when she supplied pies to the YMCA lunch counter operated by her seventeen-year-old son, Robert. Three years later, Robert Smith, who was then enrolled at Penn State, dropped out of college to devote his full attention to selling his mother's fruit pies and Pennsylvania Dutch specialties. Removing the rumble seat from his Dodge coupe, he fitted the car with a custom-made pie rack and solicited business from local grocery stores and restaurants. Initially, the pies were made at the Smith home on South Street, but in 1923 Robert acquired a five-tray professional oven and moved the baking operation to a small storefront. Despite the rapid commercialization of the business that followed the relocation, Amanda Smith continued to have a hand in baking pies until her semiretirement in 1925—the same year the bakery was incorporated under the name Mrs. Smith's Delicious Homemade Pies, Inc.

CHRISTOPHER COLUMBUS SMITH

Chris-Craft Boats

Most people in Algonac, Michigan, expected him to follow in his father's footsteps and become a blacksmith, but with a name like Christopher Columbus Smith the lure of the sea was just too strong. As a boy, Chris spent countless hours whittling wooden boats on the steps of his father's shop. In 1881 he began building rowboats and duck boats for Lake St. Clair hunters, and later he turned his attention to gasoline-powered inboard motorboats. The superior design of his crafts attracted the attention of promoter-financier John J. Ryan, who agreed to back Smith in a speedboat-building venture. Their company achieved notoriety for its Baby Reliance boats, single-step hydroplanes that broke virtually every speed record in the early 1900s. Ryan left the firm in 1913, and Smith was then joined by four sons and a daughter. Beginning in the 1920s, the Smiths introduced a series of production innovations that streamlined the boat-building process and eventually enabled them to turn out over one-thousand power crafts a year. When Chris Smith retired in 1930, his company had annual sales of $6 million, and its Chris-Craft boats were distributed worldwide by 250 dealers.

1850–1910   1852–1937
LYMAN SMITH   WILBERT SMITH

Smith-Corona Typewriters

If the pen is mightier than the sword, then the typewriter must be more powerful than the shotgun. That's the conclusion that can be drawn from the story of Lyman and Wilbert Smith, Syracuse, New York, firearms makers. In the mid-1880s the Smiths hired Alexander Brown, an inventor-engineer, to make improvements in one of their shotgun models. After completing the project, Brown asked the brothers if they would like to make a typewriter he had designed. Typewriters had only recently arrived on the scene, and firearms were a more proven product, but the Smiths took Brown up on his offer. Their faith in the engineer was quickly rewarded; Brown's double keyboard machine was completed in 1886, and it proved to be such a success that by the end of the decade the brothers had dropped gunmaking to specialize in typewriters. Lyman and Wilbert Smith joined with six other manufacturers to form the Union Typewriter Co. in 1893, but they pulled out of this firm ten years later, and together with two other brothers (Hurlbut and Monroe Smith) started a new typewriter company in Syracuse. In 1926 the Smith company merged with another New York concern, the Corona Typewriter Co. The "Smith" and "Corona" names have been linked above the keyboard ever since.

Jerome Smucker

Smucker's Jelly

Looking for something to do with his Orville, Ohio, mill when the apple cider season was over, thirty-nine-year-old Jerome Smucker resurrected an old family recipe for apple butter and began churning out the spread in 1897. At first Smucker made apple butter only for local farmers who provided their own apples, but soon city dwellers were asking for his product, too. Expanding his original mill, he began packing apple butter in gallon and half-gallon crocks for the grocery trade around the turn of the century. In 1915 the Orville mill produced $59,000 worth of apple butter, and eight years later its owner added a line of jellies and jams. As Smucker's business grew, so too did his family; he sired four children—Willard, Welker, Wilma, and Winna. It was the Smucker boys, Willard and Welker, who later took over the reins of the company, which was producing enough apple butter annually to cover some 480 million slices of bread by the time of its founder's death in 1948. Although the J. M. Smucker co. still makes apple butter, its best-selling product is now strawberry preserves, with grape jelly a close second.

Edward R. Squibb

Squibb Vitamins

Sailors traditionally gripe about the food served on board navy ships, but Edward Squibb's biggest complaint concerned not the galley but the sick bay. A ship's surgeon in the late 1840s, Dr. Squibb was convinced that the poor quality of the pharmaceuticals used by the U.S. Navy often caused more harm than good to ailing sailors. The Delaware physician managed to persuade his superiors to establish a drug-manufacturing laboratory at the Brooklyn, New York, Navy Hospital in 1852. One year later, Squibb was named director of the facility, and under his stewardship it not only provided the navy with a safe, reliable supply of drugs, it also pioneered several pharmaceutical innovations—including the first steam-produced ether. Squibb resigned from the navy in 1857 and was planning to launch his own pharmaceutical plant the following year, when he was severely burned in a fire caused by an ether explosion. In 1859 Squibb, having recovered from his injuries, finally started his drug company. The former naval officer headed the firm for most of the remainder of the century, building it into an early leader of the pharmaceutical industry.

J———— 1830–1906
JOHN BATTERSON STETSON

Stetson Hats

Although his name has become synonymous with the ten-gallon hats worn by cowboys, John Batterson Stetson was hardly the type to be at home on the range. Born in East Orange, New Jersey, Stetson was sent to the West as a young man to convalesce from an illness. The transplanted easterner was so impressed by the wide-brimmed hats worn by cowboys that he decided to go into the business of making them when he returned home in 1865. At first, he made hats by hand and sold them to local retailers, but his styles caught the public's fancy, and he soon had to open a full-fledged factory to keep pace with the demand. By the time of his death in 1906, Stetson's Philadelphia plant was employing 3,500 workers who produced 2 million hats a year. The successful milliner was a generous supporter of a small Baptist academy at DeLand, Florida, which was later renamed Stetson University in his honor.

A———— 1852–1916
ANNA STOKELY

J———— 1875–1922   J———— 1876–1919
JAMES STOKELY   JOHN STOKELY

Stokely Foods

Widowed at thirty-eight and with nine children to support, Anna Stokely was determined to keep her family's French Broad, Tennessee, farm going. She also intended to see each of her five sons get a college education. The strong-willed southerner took a step toward achieving both goals in 1891 by devising her own work-study program. Anna made her oldest son, William, manage the farm for a year, before sending him to Wake Forest in 1892. Following William's departure, her second son, James, ran the farm, and when he left for school, the homestead was managed by the next son, John. By the time the youngest Stokely, George, was ready for school, Wiliam had graduated and returned to work the farm. With this much education behind them, the Stokelys were quick to see the market potential in canning what they grew. In 1898 Anna, James, and John established a small cannery, and in only six years they were selling fifty-thousand cases of canned produce annually. The family-run firm (all the Stokelys eventually were associated with the business) had become a major national food packer by 1933, when it acquired the Van Camp company.

V———— 1901–1974
VERNON B. STOUFFER

Stouffer's Frozen Foods

After graduating from the Wharton School of Business, Vernon Stouffer set out to make his fortune in transportation, first establishing a bus company and then a trucking firm. Both ventures ended in failure, however, and in 1924 the discouraged twenty-three-year-old went to work at the luncheonette that his parents ran in downtown Cleveland. Although the quality of the food served at his family's eatery was excellent, Stouffer realized that operating only one location limited their business potential, so he proceeded to open a chain of restaurants, forming the Stouffer Corporation in 1929. The ambitious restaurateur continued to expand his business in the ensuing years, and in 1954 he introduced frozen versions of his most popular entrées and side dishes for the retail grocery market. Having ushered at the Cleveland Indians baseball park as a youth, the food millionaire purchased a 75 percent share of the team in 1966, when the Indians were rumored to be leaving Cleveland, to ensure that the club remained in the city. In 1967 Stouffer merged his business with Litton Industries. Six years later, the Stouffer Corporation was acquired from Litton by the giant Swiss firm Nestlé S.A.

R———— 1888–1954
RUSSELL STOVER

Russell Stover Candies

Unlike most husbands in the little town of Hume, Saskatchewan, Canada, who occasionally brought home a box of candy, Russell Stover surprised his wife, Clara, with a candy business. The Stovers were married for a little over a year in 1912, when Russell came home with some secondhand equipment and announced that they would make and sell confections. Despite the fact that neither of them had any experience, the couple's chocolates developed a local following. In 1919 World War I rationing made sugar scarce in Canada, and the Stovers moved to Chicago, where they established another candy enterprise. Their Chicago business proved to be a struggle from the start, and the couple closed shop in 1920 so Russell could take a candy job with a Des Moines confectioner. One year later, Russell helped develop the Eskimo Pie, the world's first patented chocolate-covered ice-cream bar. Russell sold his interest in Eskimo Pie for $30,000, and in 1923 the Stovers moved to Denver and launched the company that is now Russell Stover Candies, Inc. Clara Stover succeeded her husband as president of the firm following his death in 1954. When she sold the business seven years later, it was producing 22 million pounds of candy annually.

L<small>EVI</small> S<small>TRAUSS</small>
—— 1829?–1902

Levi Jeans

Like many ambitious merchants of 1850, Levi Strauss journeyed to San Francisco to furnish supplies to gold-rush prospectors. After trying to sell tenting canvas with no success, the German-born peddler used the material to fashion sturdy pants suitable for the rigors of mining. The garments caught on quickly with miners, and before long Strauss had completely exhausted his supply of canvas and was forced to write to his brothers in New York for more material. Unable to obtain the canvas, the merchant's family sent him a heavy cotton called serge de Nimes, so named because it came from Nimes, France. Later, the material's name would be shortened to de Nimes and, finally denim. The French cotton proved to be a much better material than the canvas, and soon Strauss's Levi pants had acquired a large following throughout northern California. As his business grew, Strauss made only two changes in his namesake garment—he dyed the denim a distinctive indigo to give his jeans a unique appearance and he added copper rivets to the corners of the pockets to prevent them from tearing under the weight of miner's tools. Following Strauss's death in 1902, his company was willed to two nephews.

B<small>ERNHARD</small> S<small>TROH</small>
—— 1822–1882

Stroh's Beer

Many beer drinkers first heard the name "Stroh's" in April 1982, when the Detroit brewery (then the nation's seventh largest) acquired the third largest beer producer, Schlitz. The move summarily increased the Stroh Brewery Co.'s share of the U.S. beer market from 5 to 13 percent, paving the way for the transformation of Stroh's from a regional (basically Midwest) brand to a nationally distributed product. Bernhard Stroh, the man who had founded this expansion-minded brewery was a German brewmaster who escaped the political turmoil of his native land in 1848 by immigrating to the New World. After a brief stop in South America, Stroh moved to Detroit, where he used his $150 savings to establish a small brewery in 1850. Unlike most local brewers who produced heavy ales and porters, Stroh made a lighter lager beer in copper kettles. Later, he introduced an extremely popular Bohemian-style beer that was brewed over a direct fire. When Stroh died in 1882 and was succeeded by his eldest son, Bernhard Stroh, Jr., the brewery was the largest in Michigan. Still a family business, Stroh's has been headed since 1968 by Peter Stroh, a great-grandson of the founder.

Introduced by Omaha brothers Gilbert and Clarke Swanson in 1953, the "TV Dinner" was one of our earliest convenience foods. Like this beef-and-gravy dinner, all of the Swansons' products offered Americans the chance to enjoy a complete entree-and-side-dish meal simply by sticking an aluminum tray in the oven for a prescribed period.

1876–1949

CARL A. SWANSON

Swanson TV Dinners

In 1896 Carl Swanson arrived in America, a nearly penniless seventeen-year-old with a sign around his neck that read, "Carl Swanson, Swedish. Send me to Omaha. I speak no English." Three years later, the friendly youth had not only learned the language of his new land but had saved enough money to buy a share in a food wholesaling company. Swanson eventually acquired his partners' interests in the firm, and in the late 1920s, he transformed the wholesale house into a food processor. Swanson at first concentrated on processing three main products: butter, eggs (frozen and dehydrated), and turkey (frozen and packaged). By the early 1940s, he had built up a $33-million-a-year food business, and the roughly 1.5 million turkeys he processed annually led *Fortune* magazine to dub him "the U.S. Turkey King." Following Swanson's death, control of the business passed to his sons, Gilbert and Clarke. Anticipating the trend toward convenience foods, the brothers introduced their first TV dinner in 1953 (turkey, mashed potatoes, and gravy). The Swansons sold their Omaha business to the Campbell Soup Co. in 1955, receiving 641,000 shares of Campbell stock.

G——— 1839–1903
GUSTAVUS F. SWIFT

Swift Meat Products

A partner in a Boston meat business, Gustavus Swift moved to Chicago in 1875 to establish a cattle-buying office for his firm. The thirty-six-year-old butcher wasn't in the city long before he became convinced that the newly developed refrigerated railroad car would bring major changes to the beef industry. From the time of their establishment, the midwestern meat markets had shipped live cattle to the big eastern cities, where the animals were slaughtered at local stockyards. With the advent of the refrigerated car in the 1870s, however, cattle could be killed and dressed in Chicago and shipped east without spoiling. This method of shipping would lower freight costs considerably, reasoned Swift, since only the edible parts of the animal would be carried by the railroad. In 1877 Swift sold his interest in the Boston business to form a new firm that pioneered the practice of rail-shipping dressed Chicago beef. Despite the often hostile opposition of eastern stockyards (which feared the loss of business) and the railroads (which feared the reduction in freight rates), Swift's business prospered, growing into a $160-million-a-year giant by the time of his death in 1903.

W——— 1860–1937
WILLIAM J. TAPPAN

Tappan Microwave Oven

It isn't every day that one captures a solar eclipse on film; so when Tom Tappan journeyed to Siberia in the 1880s to photograph a comet as it blocked out the sun, the folks back in Mansfield, Ohio, were buzzing with excitement. Tom's son William was so proud of his father's achievement that he changed the name of his business from the Ohio Valley Foundry to the Eclipse Stove Co. Will Tappan had gotten started in the business of selling coal and wood-burning stoves in 1881, peddling his products by wagon through the hills of eastern Ohio and often accepting livestock as payment from cashless farmers. The small business grew quickly, and by the time of the name change, its owner had already become one of Mansfield's leading citizens. In 1920 Tappan's expanding concern ran into an Illinois company that also was called the Eclipse Stove Co. Realizing that there wasn't room for two "Eclipses" under the sun, the competitors agreed to rechristen themselves, using their family names. As the Tappan Co., the Ohio firm continued to grow during the ensuing decades, diversifying into other products, including the familiar Tappan microwave ovens.

No longer able to produce its principal product, the Taylor winery began turning out grape juice in bottles and kegs during Prohibition. The company boosted the sale of its new product by furnishing customers with detailed booklets on "How not to turn the juice into wine."

1858–1934
WALTER TAYLOR

Taylor Wine

In 1829 an Episcopal minister named William Bostwick discovered that the soil around New York's Finger Lakes was ideal for cultivating grapes. The Reverend Bostwick's revelation sparked the development of a local vineyard industry that was still going strong some fifty years later when Walter Taylor moved to the region from nearby Tioga County, New York. A carpenter, Taylor supplied barrels to local wine makers for a year, before establishing his own seven-acre vineyard, where, in addition to growing Catawba grapes, he produced table wines and dessert ports. As his vineyards grew to cover seventy acres, Taylor was joined in the business by his three sons. When the Eighteenth Amendment went into effect, the Taylors continued to prosper by selling sparkling white grape juice in bottles and kegs along with explicit instructions on "how not to turn the juice into wine." The beverage was a big hit with the bars and consumers who purchased it, but not with the Federal Bureau of Internal Revenue, which ordered it off the market. In 1977, when Taylor's last surviving son had died, the winery was purchased by the Coca-Cola Company.

Melinda Lou ◆ *Wendy's Hamburgers*
"WENDY" THOMAS

When Melinda Lou Thomas was growing up in Columbus, Ohio, her younger siblings had a hard time pronouncing her name, so she became Wendy. In 1969 her father, R. David Thomas, a former Kentucky Fried Chicken franchisee, used her nickname on his new hamburger restaurant. Thomas also decided to decorate his store sign with an illustration of his freckle-faced, pig-tailed daughter, then eight years old. That illustration today appears on more than two-thousand Wendy's restaurants worldwide.

1855–1919
Samuel Bath Thomas

Thomas's English Muffins

Quiet and unassuming, Samuel Thomas was too shy to put his name on the New York City bakery he opened in 1880. But the people who walked by his little Ninth Avenue shop every morning didn't need an overhead sign to know the nature of Thomas's business; the aroma of gluten bread, raisin bread, and English muffins made it deliciously clear that he was a baker. Thomas learned his trade as a youth in his native Plymouth, England. After immigrating to the United States at the age of twenty-one, he worked at menial jobs before saving enough money to start his own business. New Yorkers quickly developed a taste for the specialties the baker had brought over from his homeland, particularly English muffins. Soon Thomas began selling English muffins to restaurants, and overcoming his modesty, he built glass-domed display cases with "S. B. Thomas" stenciled on them in gold. From restaurants, the businessman branched out into retail food stores, and by the time of his death, Thomas's bakery was selling English muffins throughout the New York area. In 1970 the S. B. Thomas Co., then run by Samuel's descendents, became a subsidiary of Best Foods.

S —— 1785–1859
SETH THOMAS

Seth Thomas Clocks

A carpenter by trade, twenty-two-year-old Seth Thomas was hired by Connecticut clock maker Eli Terry to assist in the construction of four-thousand wooden tall-clock movements in 1807. The young carpenter soon developed an affinity for timepieces, and six years later he used his $1,500 savings to launch his own clock company in the town of Plymouth Hollow, Connecticut. Thomas's business grew quickly, his inexpensive wood-movement clocks capturing a large share of the American market. In the 1840s he began to produce superior, and more costly, brass clocks, which by the middle of the century were being exported to Europe and Asia. With the money he made in clocks, Thomas invested in other successful ventures, including a cotton mill and wire mill. By the time of his death in 1859, Thomas was one of the wealthiest men in Connecticut and the leading citizen of Plymouth Hollow, which was renamed Thomaston in 1865 in his honor.

C —— 1812–1902
CHARLES LEWIS TIFFANY

Tiffany Jewelry

Plainfield, Connecticut, is a long way from Fifth Avenue, but the man behind one of Manhattan's most fashionable nameplates began his career there, operating a general store with his father. In 1837 Charles Tiffany moved to New York, where he and a friend opened a fancy goods shop. Sales the first three days totaled only $4.98, but the partners went on to establish a lucrative trade, acquiring a reputation for their exquisite jewelry imported from England and Italy. When European revolutions depressed diamond prices in 1848, the partners began to manufacture their own jewelry. Their line quickly attracted attention because of its aesthetic designs, including the Tiffany setting, a raised ring mounting with prongs used to hold the stone in place. The business was incorporated in 1868 as Tiffany & Co., and by the time of Tiffany's death, the firm was America's largest jewelry company. Charles Tiffany was not the only member of his family to create beautiful objects. His son, artist Louis Comfort Tiffany (1848–1933), pioneered the technique of coloring glass while it was still in a molten state. Louis Tiffany fashioned many objects with his iridescent glass, including vases, jewelry, and the famous lamps that bear his name.

The 1936 Toyota AA pictured here was the Japanese automaker's first production model. Although this and subsequent models were a success in their native land, it would be almost thirty years before the company was able to gain a foothold in the U.S. market with the popular Toyota Corona.

1894–1952
KIICHIRO TOYODA

Toyota Cars

In 1929 a Japanese textile mill owner named Sakichi Toyoda (1867–1930) sold the rights to manufacture his patented automatic loom in Britain for 100,000 pounds. Toyoda used this money to back his son, Kiichiro, in a car-making venture. Working in a section of the family mill, Kiichiro Toyoda introduced his first production-model car in 1936. The auto company grew steadily over the next five years, but Japan's World War II defeat almost destroyed it. Kiichiro Toyoda then made a monumental decision; instead of competing with GM and other makers of large cars, he would manufacture compact vehicles. The decision reaped immediate dividends in the Japanese market, and in 1956 Toyoda's successors decided to export cars to the United States. Their first import (the Toyopet Crown) failed, but in 1965 they introduced the successful Toyota Corona. One decade later, Toyota became the U.S. import leader, selling 328,918 vehicles here in 1975. About the name change from *Toyoda* to *Toyota*—a numerologist suggested it in 1937, because *Toyoda* requires ten pen strokes when written in Japanese, whereas *Toyota* requires eight. It was said that the number 8 would bring luck to the Toyoda family. In light of the automaker's success, who's to argue?

A self-described "ham inventor and yankee trader," Earl Tupper tried to sell his Tupperware containers through drug and department stores in the late 1940s. The results were disappointing, and in 1951 Tupper decided to sell his product directly to the consumer through in-home Tupperware parties such as this one, which took place in Sarasota, Florida, at the end of the decade.

E——1907–1983
EARL TUPPER

Tupperware Food Containers

Although he invented a revolutionary line of temperature-resistant food storage containers, Earl Tupper's greatest talent was not in creating goods but in selling them. Born on a Harvard, Massachusetts, farm, Tupper demonstrated strong Yankee trader instincts early in life by building a thriving business selling his neighbors' produce while still in his teens. After engaging in a variety of businesses with mixed results, Tupper developed one of the first airtight plastic containers in 1945. Calling his product Tupperware, he initially distributed it to retail stores, but sales did not live up to his expectations. Then, in 1950, the inventor came up with a plan to market the containers through in-home sales parties. By 1954 Tupper had some nine-thousand dealers holding parties in the homes of women who agreed to act as hostesses in exchange for a small gift. The firm's sales volume that year was roughly $25 million. Tupper sold his business to Rexall Drugs in 1958 and quietly faded from public view. In 1973 he moved to Costa Rica and became a citizen of that country. He died in San Jose, Costa Rica, in October 1983.

T———— 1675–1741
THOMAS TWINING

Twinings Tea

Tea, the most English of all drinks, was relatively new to Britain in 1706, when Thomas Twining started Tom's Coffee House at Devereux Court, London. It had been less than a half century since tea was introduced to England from the Continent where it was then popular, and many Britons still regarded the beverage as an exotic luxury. Twining served tea as a novelty drink at his shop, along with coffee, chocolate, brandy, and punch. Tom's became a favorite meeting place for barristers, solicitors, and the like, and by 1714 its proprietor had established two additional coffee shops. An astute merchant, Twining responded to his countrymen's growing taste for tea in 1717 by opening the Golden Lion, Britain's first teahouse. Unlike coffeehouses, which catered to men only, the Golden Lion welcomed both sexes. One observer recalled, "Great ladies flocked to Twining's house . . . to sip the enlivening beverage in small cups." By 1735 Twining was selling twice as much tea as coffee and chocolate combined. The Twining firm continued to grow during the nineteenth and twentieth centuries, often under the management of Tom Twining's descendents. It is best known in America for its specialty teas.

W———— 1787–1864
WILLIAM UNDERWOOD

Underwood Deviled Ham

A man of considerable tenacity—he walked from New Orleans to Boston as a youth—William Underwood was determined to build a successful business when he opened his Massachusetts cannery in 1821. But the British-born tinsmith faced stiff resistance from American consumers, most of whom viewed domestically canned foods as inferior versions of the more established English products. Underwood got around this obstacle by printing the word *England* on his labels, thereby giving his products a pseudoimported image. With customer confidence no longer a problem, the William Underwood Co. was able to expand quickly, branching out from broiled lobster—its first product—to turkey, mackerel, baked beans, jam, soup, cranberries, and other foods. William Underwood remained at the head of the cannery until his death in 1864, after which the company was controlled by successive Underwood descendents through the 1950s. It was the founder's grandson, Henry Oliver Underwood, who decided to trim the product line and concentrate only on the items that were most profitable—notably deviled ham. Henry also began a national advertising campaign that utilized the company's famous "red devil," a trademark that had been appearing on Underwood cans since 1867.

GILBERT VAN CAMP

1817–1901

Van Camp's Baked Beans

The idea of baking beans in tomato sauce came to the world in a flash of inspiration in 1890, when Gilbert Van Camp's son, Frank, was eating his lunch in the warehouse of the family's Indianapolis cannery. A fire had recently caused considerable damage to the warehouse, and the younger Van Camp was preoccupied with plans to rebuild it when he plucked a tomato from his lunchbox and absently set it down on a can of pork and beans. Upon noticing this juxtaposition, the young man was struck by a notion— why not mix the beans with the tomato? He did, and the result was so tasty that Frank had no trouble convincing his father to market the lunchtime discovery. Promoted with national magazine ads, the Van Camps' new product became such a success that eventually almost every manufacturer started baking its beans in tomato sauce. Following Gilbert Van Camp's death in 1901, Frank Van Camp assumed the presidency of the company, which is currently the largest producer of pork and beans in the United States.

GLORIA VANDERBILT

1924–

Gloria Vanderbilt Jeans

Heiress to one of America's most famous family fortunes, Gloria Vanderbilt was a household word long before her name appeared on a best-selling pair of jeans. The great-great-granddaughter of Commodore Cornelius Vanderbilt, Gloria's birth was heralded by a *New York Times* headline. In 1925 her father, sportsman Reginald Vanderbilt, died, and nine years later Gloria became the object of a front-page custody fight between her mother and paternal aunt (who won). At seventeen, the attractive heiress left school to marry a Hollywood agent, from whom she was divorced three years later. Vanderbilt tried her hand at a number of occupations over the next twenty-five years, including acting, painting, and writing poetry, before becoming active in fashion design in the 1970s. Although some in the industry dismissed her as yet another socialite dabbling in design, her tireless effort in promoting her namesake denims won over the cynics. Introduced by Murjani in 1977, 6 million pairs of the jeans were sold the first year. Gloria Vanderbilt's success prompted fellow fashion mogul Halston to acknowledge: "She's become a professional in the most difficult, cutthroat business there is, and I say, 'good show.'"

J OHN VAN HEUSEN

1869–1931

Van Heusen Shirts

Well-dressed men of the early 1900s were compelled to endure the discomfort of neckband shirts with separate white collars. Heavily starched, and affording all the roominess of a straitjacket, the collars caused plenty of rashes and stiff necks, but at least they held their shape without forming undignified wrinkles. It wasn't until 1919 that men were able to have both comfort and style, when John Van Heusen perfected a novel semisoft collar that was strong enough to maintain its shape without starch. Van Heusen, who together with his associate John Bolton had patented the collar design six years earlier, sold the rights to the invention to the Phillips-Jones shirt company. Royalties from the collar brought millions to the New York native, who turned his inventive talents to developing other devices such as a nonslip shoulder strap for women's lingerie. At first, Phillips-Jones used "Van Heusen" to describe only its semisoft collars, but later when one-piece dress shirts dominated the market, the name "Van Heusen" was applied to the entire garment.

JOSHUA VICK ◆ *Vick's Vaporub*

Wanting to come up with a catchier name for his Richardson's Croup and Pneumonia Cure Salve, North Carolina pharmacist Lunsford Richardson borrowed the surname of his brother-in-law Joshua Vick. Although a pharmacist himself, Vick had nothing to do with the development of the salve, which was first marketed by Richardson in 1905. Vick nevertheless agreed to lend his name to the product, and by 1919 it had achieved international distribution as Vick's Vaporub.

J——— 1904–
JOSEPH VLASIC

Vlasic Pickles

In 1937 the owner of a small pickle plant approached Joseph Vlasic and asked the Detroit food wholesaler to handle a new home-style pickle he had developed. The man had good cause to believe in Vlasic's skill at marketing food products. Only fifteen years earlier, Vlasic had acquired a small night-time milk run in Detroit as a teenager and already had built it into Michigan's largest wholesale milk company. Vlasic agreed to distribute his visitor's pickles, but only if he could label them under his own name. An astute salesman who recognized the importance of targeting his product toward a specific segment of the market, Vlasic directed his pickles at Detroit's large Polish community, even printing his first labels entirely in Polish. When Joseph Vlasic stepped down from active management of the company in the 1960s, he was succeeded by his son Robert. Like his father, Robert Vlasic was a talented marketer. Under his direction, the company embarked on a national television advertising campaign that featured a bow-tied stork with a Groucho Marx voice. This marketing effort propelled the small, privately owned company past its giant corporate rivals Heinz and Del Monte for leadership of the pickle industry. In 1978, the year it merged with the Campbell Soup Company, Vlasic had sales of over $350 million (compared to under $13 million a decade earlier) to give it a 27 percent share of the pickle market, far ahead of the 10 percent share claimed by its closest competitor, Heinz.

W—— 1880–1946
WILLIAM VOIT

Voit Balls

After working as a salesman for several rubber companies in California, William Voit formed his own business, the W. J. Voit Rubber Co., in 1924. His earliest product was camelback, a material used in recapping automobile tires. Hoping to expand his business, he developed a multicolored inflatable rubber beach ball in 1927. The new product became an immediate favorite of California beachgoers, and within two years Voit's Los Angeles plant employed four-hundred people and did a million dollars in annual sales. Then the stock market crash, plus an influx of cheaper Japanese products, burst Voit's beach-ball bubble, almost driving him out of business. The fifty-two-year-old manufacturer began a slow but steady comeback in 1932, when he introduced a rubber athletic ball, followed shortly thereafter by rubber basketballs and footballs. Voit's products proved superior to the leather balls that then dominated the market, and he expanded his line to include rubber soccer balls and volleyballs. By the time of his death in 1946, his company was providing balls and other rubber athletic goods to some 100,000 schools, colleges, and public playgrounds in America.

1946–
DIANE VON FÜRSTENBERG

Diane von Fürstenberg Fashions

Even by the standards of Seventh Avenue, where the fortunes of designers rise and fall as quickly as hemlines, Diane von Fürstenberg's emergence as a major couturier must be regarded as an overnight phenomenon. Arriving in New York in late 1969 with three shirtwaist dresses she had designed, the Belgian-born wife of Prince Eduard Egon von Fürstenberg tried to interest several major manufacturers in her "collection." All of the clothing makers turned her down, but the twenty-three-year-old brunette remained confident in her designs, and in April 1970 she sponsored her own show at the Gotham Hotel. Although she had no training as a designer, von Fürstenberg's midi-length dresses won immediate acceptance following the show. By 1976 she was selling twenty thousand dresses a week and grossing $64 million annually. She then increased her business by producing a line of cosmetics and licensing her signature to a range of fashion accessories. Despite her meteoric rise, von Fürstenberg maintained a sense of modesty, once responding to a critic who questioned her ability, "I never pretended I was a fabulous designer. I am a woman who makes clothes."

1920–
AN WANG

Wang Information Systems

In an era and an industry dominated by corporate giants, the rise of high-tech genius An Wang is reminiscent of the lone entrepreneur of an earlier day. The son of a Shanghai English teacher, Wang came to America in 1945 to earn a Ph.D. in physics at Harvard. Three years later, he revolutionized computer technology by inventing the magnetic memory core, a doughnut-shaped device that remained essential to the industry for the next two decades. Wang launched his own company in a room above an electrical supply store on Boston's Columbus Avenue in 1951. Total sales the first year were $15,000, but his volume grew at a 40 percent or higher annual rate during the next three decades, as a result of his technological innovations. In 1972 Wang began making word processors, and shortly thereafter he introduced a video display screen that became the standard for all such machines. A naturalized U.S. citizen, Wang has retained personal control over his company. He and his family own 40 percent of Wang Laboratories, worth roughly $1.6 billion in 1983, which, according to *Forbes*, makes Wang one of America's five wealthiest individuals.

D—— 1861–1934
DAVID WESSON

Wesson Oil

Scholarly pursuits don't often lead to commercial success, but David Wesson, a brilliant American chemist, became an exception to this rule when his lab experiments resulted in the discovery of a new refining process for cottonseed oil in 1899. Until that time, oil from the cottonseed was considered unfit for human consumption because of its rancid taste and foul odor. With his new method of refining impurities from the oil, the MIT graduate eliminated these objectionable traits, creating a pure, light liquid suitable for cooking. Southern Oil Co., a Georgia food manufacturer, quickly stepped in to buy the rights to the process, and in 1900 it began marketing the oil under the trade name Wesson Oil. Despite generous royalties from his invention and his position as manager of the company's technical department, Wesson remained a quiet, scholarly man who routinely eschewed displays of wealth.

S———————— 1823–1888
STEPHEN F. WHITMAN

Whitman's Candies

Market Street was one of Philadelphia's main commercial thoroughfares in 1842, when Stephen Whitman opened a small candy shop at number 426. The young Quaker's store attracted a varied mix of customers, including wealthy matrons from nearby residential neighborhoods and sailors who wandered up Market Street from the city's wharves. It was the sailors who sold Whitman exotic nuts and fruits acquired during their ocean journeys, which the confectioner used in his chocolates. In the early days, Whitman displayed his selection of candies on open tables and "sold" customers empty boxes of different sizes. After purchasing a box, customers were free to fill it with any assortment of confections they chose. As the popularity of his candy spread, Whitman began to market it in elaborately decorated prepacked boxes with names like "The Fussy Package for Fastidious Folks." The famous Whitman's Sampler first appeared in 1912, after Walter Sharp, who was then president of the firm, came across an embroidered sampler made by his grandmother and recognized its potential as a candy box. Except for some minor changes over the years, the original sampler design has been reproduced on the Whitman's package ever since.

OLIVER F. WINCHESTER

Winchester Rifles

Fashion and firearms might not have much in common, but both played key roles in Oliver Winchester's rise from a poor Boston orphan to a wealthy industrialist and prominent politician. Winchester was the owner of a Baltimore clothing store in 1847, when he sold the business and moved to New York, where he patented an improved shirtmaking method. With the money he made from his invention, the ambitious clothier bought a New Haven rifle company and built it into a major manufacturing concern by acquiring the patents of Hotchkiss, Browning, and other famous firearms makers. In 1860 Winchester's company introduced the Henry repeating rifle, which was widely hailed as the best military rifle during the Civil War. When an advanced side-loading magazine was incorporated into the Henry firearm in 1866, it was renamed the Winchester rifle and became a legend in the West. Aided by the notoriety of his rifle company, Oliver Winchester embarked on a successful career in politics. He was a presidential elector at large for Lincoln in 1864 and two years later was elected lieutenant governor of Connecticut.

LINUS YALE, JR.

Yale Locks

Like many fathers, locksmith Linus Yale, Sr., hoped his son would follow him into the family business, but the artistic Linn, Jr., had other plans. In the early 1840s, the young Newport, New York, native set out to become a portrait painter. By the end of the decade, however, Linn had dropped art and, upholding the family tradition, became a locksmith, opening a shop in Shelburne Falls, Massachusetts. Yale's earliest products were key-operated bank locks, but a demonstration at the 1851 London World's Fair convinced him that any key lock could be picked by someone possessing the necessary skill. At this point, he shifted his attention to combination locks, designing the first double-dial bank lock in 1863. Already famous for combination locks, Yale formed a partnership with John Towne in 1868 to manufacture a patented key lock that incorporated pin tumblers in its design. The tumbler lock Yale invented made it possible to use smaller keys and served as the foundation of the modern lock industry. Linus Yale died soon after starting the new venture. Many years later, in 1903, Towne began stamping the name Yale on the company's products.

Bibliography

Personality, Product, Marketing, Fortune

ASH, MARY KAY   For a thorough, well-researched account of Mary Kay's early life and subsequent rise in the business world, see P. Rosenfield, "The Beautiful Make-Up of Mary Kay," *Saturday Evening Post*, October 1981, pp. 58–63. Mary Kay's sales strategy is discussed in H. Rudnitsky, "The Flight of the Bumblebee," *Forbes*, 22 June 1981, pp. 104–6; and Robert L. Shook, *The Entrepreneurs* (New York: Harper & Row, 1980), pp. 103–14. Also see Mary Kay Ash, *Mary Kay* (New York: Harper & Row, 1981); and R. Tunley, "Mary Kay's Sweet Smell of Success," *Reader's Digest*, November 1978, pp. 17-. Information used in the preparation of this biography was also obtained from Mary Kay Cosmetics Inc., Dallas, Texas.

BASKIN, BURT, AND ROBBINS, IRV   Much of the information in this entry was obtained through two telephone interviews with Irvine Robbins, Rancho Mirage, California, in September 1983. An account of the Baskin-Robbins company's early growth can be found in "Happiness Is . . . 40 Times Earnings," *Forbes*, 15 December 1973, p. 63. For material on Irvine Robbins and the stories behind some of the company's noted ice-cream flavors, see L. B. Francke, "Chip Chip Hooray!" *Newsweek*, 16 February 1976, p. 71; N. Hazelton, "Creme Chantilly or Lunar Cheesecake," *National Review*, 6 February 1976, p. 99; and J. Klemesrud, "The Man Who Vetoed the Idea of Nudie Frutti Ice Cream," *New York Times*, 12 October 1973, p. 50. A brief description of Burt Baskin's early career is included in Paul Dickson, *The Great American Ice Cream Book* (New York: Atheneum, 1978), p. 48.

BICH, MARCEL   An informative overview of Marcel Bich's life and business is provided by P. Dewhurst, "Bich-Bic," *Made in France International*, Spring 1981, pp. 38–39-. A thorough analysis of Bich's marketing strategy can be found in "Gillette after the Diversification That Failed," *Business Week*, 28 February 1977, pp. 58-. For added information on the Bic-Gillette competition, see N. C. Nash, "How Bic Lost the Edge to Gillette," *New York Times*, 11 April 1983, sec. III, p. 7. The story of Bich's early penetration of the U.S. pen market is told in "King of the Ballpoints," *Newsweek*, 14 July 1969, pp. 77–78; and "Going Bananas over Bic," *Time*, 18 December 1972, p. 93. (The quote used in the Bich entry is taken from this article.) Also see C. H. Farnsworth, "Cheap Bic Pen Made Baron Bich Wealthy," *New York Times*, 29 December 1972, pp. 39–40; and for an account of Bich's activities as a yachtsman, see "The Challenger from France," *Business Week*, 15 August 1970, pp. 36–37.

BORDEN, GAIL   For a comprehensive account of Borden's life, see Joe B. Frantz, *Gail Borden: Dairyman to a Nation* (Norman: University of Oklahoma Press, 1951). A more concise, but informative account is provided by the Editors of News Front Year, *The 50 Great Pioneers of American Industry* (Maplewood: C. S. Hammond & Co.; New York: Year Inc., 1964), pp. 45–47. A description of some of Borden's inventions is offered by Milton Moskowitz et al., eds., *Everybody's Business* (San Francisco: Harper & Row, 1980), p. 7. Also see *McGraw-Hill Encyclopedia of World Biography*, s.v. "Gail Borden"; *Websters American Biographies*, s.v. "Gail Borden"; *The National Cyclopedia of American Biography*, vol. 7, p. 306; Reay Tannahill, *Food in History* (New York: Scarborough Books/Stein & Day, 1973), p. 373; Hannah Campbell, *Why*

Did They Name It? (New York: Fleet Publishing Co., 1964), pp. 55–62; and Laurence A. Johnson, *Over the Counter and on the Shelf* (Rutland, Vt.: Charles E. Tuttle Co., 1961), pp. 87–88. Information was also obtained from Borden Inc., Columbus, Ohio.

BRYANT, LANE   A lively, informative biography of Lane Bryant is provided by Tom Mahoney, *The Great Merchants* (New York: Harper & Bros. 1955), pp. 240–54. For a more formal account, see *The National Cyclopedia of American Biography*, vol. 47, p. 60. A good deal of information on the merchant and her company can be found in the Lane Bryant obituary, *New York Times*, 27 September 1951, p. 31. Also see Lois Decker O'Neill et al., eds., *The Women's Book of World Records and Achievements* (Garden City: Anchor Press, 1979), pp. 259–60; and the Lane Bryant obituary, *Time*, 8 October 1951, p. 97.

BURPEE, W. A.   A thoroughly researched history of W. A. Burpee and the Burpee company is Ken Kraft, *Garden to Order* (Garden City: Doubleday & Co., 1963). Also see Jeannette Lowe, "Burpee Celebrates Its Centennial," *Flower and Garden*, March 1976, pp. 26–29-; *The National Cyclopedia of American Biography*, vol. 16, p. 286; *Webster's Biographical Dictionary*, s.v. "W. Atlee Burpee"; and *Who Was Who in America*, vol. 1, s.v. "W. Atlee Burpee." Information was also obtained from the W. A. Burpee Co., Doylestown, Pennsylvania.

BUSCH, ADOLPHUS   For a detailed view of the Anheuser-Busch business following the repeal of Prohibition and one of the more accurate accounts of Adolphus Busch's career written prior to World War II, see "King of Bottled Beer," *Fortune*, July 1935, pp. 42–49-. Another well-researched and more recently written account is in *Dictionary of American Biography*, sup. 1, s.v. "Adolphus Busch." The St. Louis brewer's genius in sales and marketing is examined in James D. Robertson, *The Great American Beer Book* (Ottawa, Ill.: Caroline House Publishers, 1978), pp. 43–45; and in David P. Cleary, *Great American Brands* (New York: Fairchild Publications, 1981), pp. 24–35. A biographical sketch written during Busch's lifetime (published 1904) is in *The National Cyclopedia of American Biography*, vol. 12, p. 23. Also see Michael A. Weiner, *The Taster's Guide to Beer* (New York: Collier Books/Macmillan, 1977), pp. 187–88; the Adolphus Busch obituary, *New York Times*, 11 October 1913, p. 15. Information used in this entry also was obtained from Anheuser-Busch Companies Inc., St. Louis, Missouri.

CARRIER, WILLIS   A biography of the inventor that offers a long and detailed description of his work in devising a mathematical formula for air conditioning is Margaret Ingels, *Father of Air Conditioning* (Garden City: Country Life Press, 1951). Other biographies that offer insights into Carrier's personal life and his career as a businessman include *The National Cyclopedia of American Biography*, vol. E, p. 24; *Dictionary of American Biography*, sup. 4, s.v. "Willis Carrier"; and the Editors of New Front Year, *The 50 Great Pioneers of American Industry* (Maplewood: C. S. Hammond & Co.; New York: Year Inc., 1964), pp. 134–37. Also see *Who Was Who in America*, vol. 3, s.v. "Willis Carrier"; and Sterling G. Slappey, comp., *Pioneers of American Business* (New York: Grossett & Dunlap, 1970), pp. 28–33.

CHANEL, GABRIELLE   Much of the material on Chanel's life is unreliable, since the designer often invented romantic tales concerning her past. The most accurate and informative biography is Edmonde Charles-Roux, *Chanel* (New York: Alfred A. Knopf, 1975). Also informative is E. Nemy, "Fashion Was Her Pulpit," *New York Times*, 11 January 1971, 35-. For accounts of Chanel's post-World-War II comeback see E. O. Hauser, "Mlle. Chanel Comes Back," *Saturday Evening Post*, 13 June 1959, 34–35-; "What Chanel Storm Is About," *Life*, 1 March 1954, 48-; and "Feeneesh?" *Time*, 15 February 1954, 28. Also see the Gabrielle Chanel obituary, *New York Times*, 11 January 1971, 1-; and *Current Biography—1954*, s.v. "Gabrielle Chanel."

CHEVROLET, LOUIS   Informative biographies of Louis and Arthur Chevrolet are included in Ken Purdy, *Ken Purdy's Wonderful World of the Automobile* (New York: Thomas Y. Crowell Co., 1960), pp. 96–102; and Robert Cutter and Bob Fendell, *Encyclopedia of Auto Racing Greats* (Englewood Cliffs: Prentice-Hall, 1973), pp. 127–30. Also see Karl Ludvigsen, David B. Wise, et al., *The Encyclopedia of the American Automobile*, rev. ed. (Secaucus: Chartwell Books, 1979), pp. 36–38; Hannah Campbell, *Why Did They Name It?* (New York: Fleet Publishing Co., 1964), p. 175; the Louis Chevrolet obituary, *New York Times*, 7 June 1941, p. 17; and Marco Matteucci, *History of the Motor Car* (New York: Crown Publishers, 1970), pp. 267–68, 330.

COLEMAN, WILLIAM   A comprehensive account of Coleman's early career, his lantern, and his famous GI stove is offered in R. Jarman, "The Company That Should Have Gone Broke," *Saturday Evening Post*, 24 September 1949, pp. 26–27-. Similar material is covered in the William Coleman obituary, *New York Times*, 3 November 1957, p. 89. For a sympathetic, but useful account of Coleman and his namesake company given by the manufacturer's son and a Coleman Co. executive, see Sheldon Coleman and Lawrence M. Jones, *The Coleman Story: The Ability to Cope with Change* (New York: the Newcomen Society in North America, 1976). A biography written during Coleman's lifetime (published 1952) is available in *The National Cyclopedia of American Biography*, vol. H, p. 55. Information used in the preparation of this biography was also obtained from the Coleman Co., Inc., Wichita, Kansas.

COWEN, JOSHUA LIONEL   A great deal of material is available on the life of Joshua Lionel Cowen. The most rewarding biography is Ron Hollander, *All Aboard: the Story of Lionel* (New York: Workman Publishing, 1981). Also recommended, particularly for those interested in the development of the Lionel train-collecting hobby, is Tom McComas and James Tuohy, *Lionel: A Collector's Guide and History to Lionel Trains*, 2 vols. (Wilmette, Ill.: TM Productions, 1975, 1976). A concise and entertaining account of Cowen's activities as an inventor can be found in Marvin Kaye, *A Toy Is Born* (Briarcliff Manor: Stein & Day, 1973), pp. 27–33. Additional information can be found in the *Dictionary of American Biography*, sup. 7, s.v. "Joshua Lionel Cowen;" and *Who Was Who in America*, vol. 4, s.v. "Joshua Lionel Cowen."

CULLIGAN, EMMETT   Much of the information used in the preparation of this biography was obtained through correspondence with Donald M. Hintz, vice-president of Culligan International Co., who is preparing a history of the company for publication in 1986 to mark its fiftieth anniversary. Mr. Hintz has been with the firm since soon after its founding and was hired by Emmett Culligan himself. Of the already published material, one that outlines Culligan's marketing strategy during the early 1960s is "How to Get Salesmen through the Doorway," *Business Week*, 4 June 1966, pp. 84–86. For an account of Culligan's plan to use his product to sell his services, see "Softeners Rented," *Business Week*, 28 December 1946, p. 21. A detailed and highly positive account of Culligan's start in business is provided by G. Hamilton, "Hey Zeolite Man!" *Northbrook* (Ill.) *Star*, 26 February 1976, pp. 30–31. Also see Business Roundup, *Fortune*, May 1950, p. 30; and the Emmett Culligan obituary, *Chicago Tribune*, 4 June 1970.

DANIEL, JACK   A comprehensive account of Jack Daniel's life and his unusual career as a distiller is offered by Ben A. Green, *Jack Daniel's Legacy*, a 210-page self-published book copyrighted in 1967 (Shelbyville, Tenn.). Also see Sterling G. Slappey, comp., *Pioneers of American Business* (New York: Grossett & Dunlap, 1970), pp. 134–39. Information used in the preparation of this biography also was obtained from Jack Daniel Distillery, Nashville, Tennessee.

DEERE, JOHN   John Deere's contribution to the evolution of farm implements, particularly the development of the self-scouring plow, is covered in the following works: Marvin McKinley, *Wheels of Farm Progress* (St. Joseph, Mich.: American Society of Agricultural Engineers, 1980), pp. 6–11; John T. Schlebecker, *Whereby We Thrive: A History of American Farming—1607–1972* (Ames: Iowa State University Press, 1975), pp. 80–81, 102–3, 174–75; Michael Partridge, *Farm Tools Through the Ages* (Boston: New York Graphic Books/Promontory Press, 1973), p. 54; and Percy W. Blandford, *Old Farm Tools and Machinery* (Ft. Lauderdale: Gale Research Co., 1976), p. 60. An account of the marketing strategies employed by Deere to sell plows is furnished by Penrose Scull, *From Peddlers to Merchant Princes* (Chicago: Follett Publishing Co., 1967), pp. 66–67, 141. Information about Deere's personal life can be found in *Dictionary of American Biography*, vol. 3, pt. 1, s.v. "John Deere"; and *Webster's American Biographies*, s.v. "John Deere." Information used in the preparation of this biography was also obtained from Deere & Co., Moline, Illinois.

DIESEL, RUDOLPH   An informative biography, rich in details concerning Diesel's private life as well as in descriptions of his scientific work, is provided by Morton Grosser, *Diesel: The Man and the Engine* (New York: Atheneum, 1978). A good, concise biographical sketch of the inventor is offered by Marco Matteucci, *History of the Motor Car* (New York: Crown Publishers, 1970), p. 119. Also see Ernest V. Heyn, *Fire of Genius* (Garden City: Anchor Press/Doubleday, 1976), pp. 279–83; J. O. Thorne and T. C. Collocott, eds., *Chambers Biographical Dictionary* (Edinburgh: W. & R. Chambers Ltd., 1974), s.v. "Rudolph Diesel"; and John Day, *The Bosch Book of the Motor Car* (New York: St. Martin's Press, 1976), pp. 80–81.

FACTOR, MAX   The development of Max Factor Cosmetics from a small Los Angeles store to an international company is discussed in "Glamour for Sale," *Time*, 23 August 1954, pp. 69–70. A detailed description of the opening of Factor's new cosmetics factory and information about the cosmetician's early life are provided in "Make-Up Man," *Time*, 9 December 1935, p. 68-. Highlights of Factor's career are recounted in a very positive fashion by Sterling G. Slappey, comp., *Pioneers of American Business* (New York: Grossett & Dunlap, 1970), pp. 162–67. A more impartial overview of the makeup innovator's life is given in the Max Factory obituary, *New York Times*, 31 August 1938, p. 15. For details of Norton Simon's acquisition of the Max Factor firm, see "The Max Factor in Mahoney's Life," *Business Week*, 18 November 1972, pp. 22–23. Also see "Playing It Cozy," *Forbes*, 1 June 1968, p. 49; and Roger Manvell et al., eds., *The International Encyclopedia of Film* (New York: Crown Publishers, 1972), p. 191. Information used in the preparation of this biography was also obtained from Max Factor & Co., Hollywood, California.

GERBER, DANIEL   Daniel Gerber and his father (Daniel) Frank Gerber are the subjects of a concise biographical sketch in *Dictionary of American Biography*, sup. 5, s.v. "(Daniel) Frank and Daniel (Frank) Gerber." Also see *The National Cyclopedia of American Biography*, vol. 41, p. 242. Dan Gerber's account of the family's decision to begin manufacturing baby food is provided in "Babies Are Our Business," in *Business Decisions That Changed Our Lives*, ed. Sidney Furst and Milton Sherman (New York: Random House, 1964). The story of the Gerber baby trademark is told by Arnold B. Barach, *Famous American Trademarks* (Washington: Public Affairs Press, 1971), pp. 69–70. Further information is available in the Daniel Gerber obituary, *New York Times*, 18 March 1974, p. 32. Information in preparing this biography also was obtained from Gerber Products Co., Fremont, Michigan.

GILLETTE, KING C.   There is a wealth of published material on King Gillette. Among the most comprehensive and researched is Russell B. Adams, Jr., *King C. Gillette: The Man and His Wonderful Shaving Device* (Boston: Little, Brown & Co., 1978).

For a concise account of Gillette's career in the safety razor industry, see the Editors of News Front Year, *The 50 Great Pioneers of American Industry* (Maplewood: C. S. Hammond & Co.; New York: Year Inc., 1964), pp. 160–62; Ernest V. Heyn, *Fire of Genius* (Garden City: Anchor Press/Doubleday, 1976), pp. 37–38; Arnold B. Barach, *Famous American Trademarks* (Washington: Public Affairs Press, 1971), pp. 71–72; the King C. Gillette obituary, *New York Times*, 11 July 1932, p. 13; Hannah Campbell, *Why Did They Name It?* (New York: Fleet Publishing Co., 1964), pp. 156–59; and Meredith Hooper, *Everyday Inventions* (New York: Taplinger Publishing Co., 1976), pp. 37–39.

HALL, JOYCE   An excellent account of Joyce Hall's youth and early career is presented in *Current Biography—1953*, s.v. "Joyce C. Hall." Other good accounts of Hall's career and marketing genius are offered by David P. Cleary, *Great American Brands* (New York: Fairchild Publications, 1981), pp. 149–57; Milton Moskowitz et al., eds., *Everybody's Business* (San Francisco: Harper & Row, 1980), p. 864; and Sterling G. Slappey, comp., *Pioneers of American Business* (New York: Grossett & Dunlap, 1970), pp. 103–8. A richly illustrated profile of some of Hall's notable greeting card designs is presented by J. Howard, "Close Up: Joyce Hall, Greeting Card King," *Life*, 6 December 1968, pp. 53–56. Hall's activities as a sponsor of quality television programming are discussed in "The Sponsor Who Cares," *Newsweek*, 1 November 1965. Also see "Merry X-Mas—3 Billion Times," *Business Week*, 16 December 1950, pp. 89–90; "Card Shark," *Time*, 13 February 1950, p. 78; the J. C. Hall obituary, *New York Times*, 30 October 1982, p. 35; and Janet Podell, ed., *The Annual Obituary—1982* (New York: St. Martin's Press, 1983), pp. 521–22.

HEINZ, HENRY   A great deal of material has been published on the life and career of Henry Heinz, including the very extensive Robert C. Alberts, *The Good Provider: H.J. Heinz and His 57 Varieties* (Boston: Houghton Mifflin Co., 1973). Well-researched and concise accounts of Heinz's career are provided in *The National Cyclopedia of American Biography*, vol. 26, p. 294; and *Dictionary of American Biography*, vol. 4, pt. 2, s.v. "Henry Heinz." The story of the Heinz 57 trademark is told by Arnold B. Barach, *Famous American Trademarks* (Washington: Public Affairs Press, 1971), pp. 87–88. Also see Milton Moskowitz et al., eds., *Everybody's Business* (San Francisco: Harper & Row, 1980), pp. 39–40; the Henry Heinz obituary, *New York Times*, 15 May 1919, p. 17; Richard O. Cummings, *The American and His Food* (New York: Arno Press, 1970), p. 107; and Hannah Campbell, *Why Did They Name It?* (New York: Fleet Publishing Co., 1964), pp. 48–51.

HIRES, CHARLES   For a clear, comprehensive account of Hires's beginnings and his rise in the business world, see the Editors of News Front Year, *The 50 Great Pioneers of American Industry* (Maplewood, N.J.: C. S. Hammond & Co.; New York: Year Inc., 1964), pp. 81–83. A detailed analysis of Hires's advanced advertising program is provided in "The Advertising of Hires Root Beer," *Printers' Ink*, 21 September 1898, pp. 1-. The early years of the Hires business are covered in "From Nature's Heart," *Harpers Magazine Advertiser*, August 1893, 25–28. Also see *Webster's American Biographies*, s.v. "Charles Hires"; *Dictionary of American Biography*, sup. 2, s.v. "Charles Hires"; *Who Was Who in America*, vol. 4, s.v. "Charles Hires"; and the Charles Hires obituary, *New York Times*, 1 August 1937, sec. III, p. 7. Information used in preparing this biography was also obtained from Procter & Gamble Co., Cincinnati, Ohio.

HONDA, SOICHIRO   For a solidly researched account of Honda's youth, private life, and career, see Sol Sanders, *Honda: The Man and His Machine* (Boston: Little, Brown & Co., 1975). Honda's early career and his entry into the U.S. market are well covered by Joe Scalzo, *The Motorcycle Book* (Englewood Cliffs: Prentice-Hall, 1974), pp. 11–14. A good account of Honda's beginnings in the motorcycle industry is provided by Graham Forsdyke, *Motorcycles* (Secaucus: Chartwell Books, 1977), pp. 27–28. Also see A. H. Malcom, "Honda—One Man's Drive," *New York Times Biographical Service*, vol. 8, February 1977, p. 249; and "Youth Will Be Served," *Time*, 17 December 1973, p. 100. Information used in the preparation of this biography was also obtained from American Honda Motor Co. Inc., Gardena, California.

HOOVER, WILLIAM   Much of the material used in preparing this biography was obtained from the Hoover Co., North Canton, Ohio. Of particular interest are "The Story Begins on a Front Porch," *Hoover News*, special 75th anniversary edition, 1983, p. 1; and "Hard Work, Play Highlighted Sales Conventions at Hoover Camp," *Hoover News*, 16 September 1983, pp. 6–7. An account of J. Murray Spangler's invention and William Hoover's sales strategy is provided by Earl Lifshey, *The Housewares Story* (Chicago: National Housewares Manufacturers Association, 1973), pp. 297–98. Also see *The National Cyclopedia of American Biography*, vol. 27, p. 266; *Webster's Biographical Dictionary*, s.v. "William Hoover"; Penrose Scull, *From Peddlers to Merchant Princes* (Chicago: Follett Publishing Co., 1967), p. 268; Milton Moskowitz et al., eds., *Everybody's Business* (San Francisco: Harper & Row, 1980), p. 184; and Sterling G. Slappey, comp., *Pioneers of American Business* (New York: Grossett & Dunlap, 1970), pp. 128–33.

HORMEL, GEORGE   The most complete account of Hormel's life, although written in the overly sympathetic style that characterizes most company-published biographies, is Richard Dougherty, *In Quest of Quality* (Austin, Minn.: Geo. A. Hormel & Co., 1966). A more objective portrayal of the meat packer and his company is "The Name Is HOR-mel," *Fortune*, October 1937, pp. 127–32-. Hormel's rise from poor childhood to successful businessman is outlined in *The National Cyclopedia of American Biography*, vol. E, p. 84; and *Dictionary of American Biography*, sup. 4, s.v. "George Hormel." For information on Jay Hormel, see *Current Biography—1946*, s.v. "Jay C. Hormel"; and F. Levison, "Hormel: The Spam Man," *Life*, 11 March 1946, pp. 63–66-. Also see George A. Hormel obituary, *New York Times*, 6 June 1946.

JACUZZI, CANDIDO   The published material dealing with the Jacuzzi family is scarce, and much of the material used in the preparation of this biography was obtained as a result of an interview the authors conducted through the mail during August 1983 with Roy Jacuzzi, grandson of Joseph Jacuzzi (one of the seven "original" brothers) and president of Jacuzzi Whirlpool Bath, Walnut Creek, California. One of the most complete accounts of the growth of the Jacuzzi whirlpool, along with a description of Candido Jacuzzi's problem with the IRS, is presented by J. Kirshenbaum, "Jumping into the Wonderful World of Sports," *Sports Illustrated*, 18 August 1975, pp. 40-. The origins of the Jacuzzi firm are described by F. Johnson, "1920's Aircraft Disaster Led to Present Jacuzzi Business," United Press International story in *Arkansas Gazette*, 21 February 1982, sec. F, pp. 1–2. Added material on Candido Jacuzzi's problem with the IRS can be found in "IRS Seeks Jacuzzi," *New York Times*, 3 August 1969, p. 51. For an account of the acquisition of the Jacuzzi firm by Kidde & Co., see *Forbes*, 29 October 1979, p. 153. Also see "The Bath to Success," Associated Press story in *Dallas Morning News*, 14 November 1982, Leisure Section, p. 1. Information used in the preparation of this biography was also obtained from Jacuzzi Inc., Jacuzzi Bros. Division, Little Rock, Arkansas.

JOHNSON, EDWARD, JAMES, AND ROBERT   For a concise but complete account of Robert Johnson's career and his efforts in promoting Listerism, see *The National Cyclopedia of American Biography*, vol. 35, p. 318. Edward Mead Johnson's life and career, particularly the founding of Mead Johnson & Co., are meticulously detailed in "E. Mead Johnson's Mission: Feeding Babies Better," *Medical Times*, November 1958, pp. 1460–68. An account of the Johnson & Johnson firm's beginnings is provided in "The 88 Ventures of Johnson & Johnson," *Forbes*, 1 June 1972, pp. 24–26. A less objective, but more comprehensive account is provided in a company publication, L. G. Foster, "Johnson & Johnson—The Early Years," *Johnson & Johnson World Wide*, October 1980, pp. 9–13. Also see Tom Mahoney, *The Merchants of Life* (New York: Harper & Bros., 1959), p. 153; Milton Moskowitz et al., eds., *Everybody's Business* (San Francisco: Harper & Row, 1980), p. 224; and the Robert Wood Johnson obituary, *New York Times*, 31 January 1968, p. 36. Information used in the preparation of this biography was also obtained from Johnson & Johnson, New Brunswick, New Jersey.

JOHNSON, HOWARD   A warm account of the ice-cream maker's life, containing many of his most memorable quotes, is the Howard Johnson obituary, *New York Times*, 21 June 1972, p. 46. A history of Johnson's early career and an account of how the banning of *Strange Interlude* in Boston affected his restaurant is included in a biography of his son, Howard B. Johnson, in *Current Biography—1966*, s.v. "Howard B. Johnson." The story of Howard Johnson's trademark is told by Arnold B. Barach, *Famous American Trademarks* (Washington: Public Affairs Press, 1971), pp. 95–96. For an overview of Johnson's rise as an ice-cream maker/restaurateur, see J. R. Sprague, "He Had an Idea: Howard Johnson's Roadside Restaurants," *Saturday Evening Post*, 19 July 1958, pp. 16–17-; and Paul Dickson, *The Great American Ice Cream Book* (New York: Atheneum, 1978), pp. 118, 171. Also see *Webster's American Biographies*, s.v. "Howard Johnson." Information used in the preparation of this biography was also obtained from the Howard Johnson Co., Braintree, Massachusetts.

KELLOGG, WILL   Will Kellogg's life and career are treated in a deferential, but informative, fashion by Horace B. Powell, *The Original Has This Signature—W. K. Kellogg* (Englewood Cliffs: Prentice-Hall, 1956). The cereal maker's advertising genius is treated in a frank and thorough fashion by Frank Rowsome, Jr., *They Laughed When I Sat Down* (New York: McGraw-Hill, 1959), pp. 60, 62, 65–67. Good overviews of Kellogg's career are provided by Milton Moskowitz et al., eds., *Everybody's Business* (San Francisco: Harper & Row, 1980), pp. 49–50; *Dictionary of American Biography*, sup. 5, s.v. "Will K. Kellogg"; Meredith Hooper, *Everyday Inventions* (New York: Taplinger Publishing Co., 1976), pp. 101–6; the Editors of News Front Year, *The 50 Great Pioneers of American Industry* (Maplewood: C. S. Hammond & Co.; New York: Year Inc., 1964), pp. 166–68. Also see *Webster's American Biographies*, s.v. "Will K. Kellogg"; and *Who Was Who in America*, vol. 3, s.v. "Will K. Kellogg." Information used in the preparation of this biography was also obtained from Kellogg Co., Battle Creek, Michigan.

KINNEY, GEORGE   The most complete source on Kinney is a sympathetic, but candid, biography by Edward Holloway, *Kinney Shoes: The First 60 Years—1894–1955* (New York: G. R. Kinney Co., n.d.). Another source of information about Kinney's youth and business success is "The Making of the Billion-Dollar Kinney Shoe Corporation," *Kinney World*, November/December 1980, pp. 4–11. Added information on Kinney, his longtime associate Edwin Krom, and the early years of the Kinney company can be found in the E. H. Krom obituary, *New York Times*, 23 June 1945, p. 13. William Goodyear was a Kinney executive who became associated with the firm in 1917, and information on the company's development is included in an entry on him in *The National Cyclopedia of American Biography*, vol. 35, p. 350. Information used in the preparation of the biography was also obtained from the Kinney Shoe Corporation, New York.

KLEIN, CALVIN   Newspapers and magazines ran an abundant number of stories on
Klein during the late 1970s and early 1980s. Two of the most informative are by S. C.
Cowley, "Calvin Klein's Soft Sexy Look," *Newsweek*, 8 May 1978, pp. 80-; and A.
Chambers, "Calvin Klein's Romantic Season," *New York Times Magazine*, 30 January
1977, pp. 46–48. For a profile of the designer, see Barbara Walz and Bernadine
Morris, *Fashion Makers* (New York: Random House, 1978), pp. 140–45; and *Current
Biography—1978*, s.v. "Calvin (Richard) Klein." An authoritative account of Klein's
partnership with Barry Schwartz is provided by W. McQuade, "The Bruising
Businessman behind Calvin Klein," *Fortune*, 17 November 1980, pp. 106–9-. Also
see D. Dorfman, "Calvin Klein Makes Puritan Stock Sizzle," *Chicago Tribune*, 14 June
1981, pp. 1-, sec. 5; Anne Stegemeyer, *Who's Who in Fashion* (New York: Fairchild
Publications, 1980), pp. 132–33; E. Peer, "Stylish Calvinism," *Newsweek*, 3
November 1975, p. 48; and *Who's Who in America—1980–81*, s.v. "Calvin Klein."

KRAFT, JAMES   A great deal of material on Kraft's early life and career is provided by
Arthur W. Baum, "Man with a Horse and Wagon," *Saturday Evening Post*, 17
February 1945, pp. 14–15-. The growth of the Kraft company is covered by Milton
Moskowitz et al., eds., *Everybody's Business* (San Francisco: Harper & Row, 1980).
For a detailed account of Kraft's activities as an amateur lapidarist, see Wayne
Whittaker, "They Make Jewels at Home," *Popular Mechanics*, September 1951, pp.
89–93-. Also see the James L. Kraft obituary, *New York Times*, 17 February 1953, p.
34, and Richard O. Cummings, *The American and His Food* (New York: Arno Press,
1970), p. 107.

LEAR, WILLIAM   A highly sympathetic account of Lear's life is offered by Victor
Boesen, *They Said It Couldn't Be Done: The Incredible Story of Bill Lear* (Garden
City: Doubleday & Co., 1971). More objective accounts are provided in *Current
Biography—1966*, s.v. "William P. Lear"; and the William P. Lear obituary, *New York
Times*, 15 May 1978, sec. D, p. 12. For a comprehensive overview of Lear's career
as an aviation engineer and inventor, see G. C. Larson, "Living Legends: William P.
Lear," *Flying*, December 1976, pp. 53–57. An account of Lear's career with
Motorola, from the company's point of view, is presented by Harry M. Petrakis, *The
Founder's Touch: The Life of Paul Galvin of Motorola* (New York: McGraw-Hill Book
Co., 1965), pp. 68–69. Also see "King Lear?" *Forbes*, 1 March 1977, p. 74; P.
Garrison, "Lear," *Flying*, September 1977; and *Who Was Who in America*, vol. 7,
s.v. "William Lear."

LIPTON, THOMAS   For a detailed account of Lipton's career, his childhood, and his
activities as a yachtsman, see Alec Waugh, *The Lipton Story: A Centennial Biography*
(Garden City: Doubleday, 1950). Lipton's rise in the industry is discussed by James
N. Pratt, *The Tea Lover's Treasury* (San Francisco: 101 Productions, 1982), pp. 92–
93; and William H. Ukers, *All about Tea*, 2 vols. (New York: Tea and Coffee Trade
Journal Co., 1935). A good overview of Lipton's life can be found in L. G. Wickham
Legg, ed., *The Dictionary of National Biography, 1931–40* (London: Oxford
University Press, 1949), s.v. "Thomas Lipton." Also see the Thomas Lipton obituary,
New York Times, 3 October 1931, p. 1; *Chambers Biographical Dictionary*, s.v.
"Thomas Lipton"; and Laurence A. Johnson, *Over the Counter and on the Shelf*
(Rutland, Vt.: Charles E. Tuttle Co., 1961), p. 126.

MAYER, OSCAR   Material furnished by the Oscar Mayer Co., Madison, Wisconsin, was
used in the preparation of much of this biography. Of particular usefulness was a
special eightieth anniversary issue of the company publication *Link*, September/
October 1963. Also used was the company-published booklet "Links with the Past,"
1979. For added information on Mayer, see *The National Cyclopedia of American
Biography*, vol. 45, p. 74; *Who Was Who in America*, vol. 3, s.v. "Oscar F. Mayer";

and the Oscar F. Mayer obituary, *New York Times*, 12 March 1955, p. 19. A history of the Mayer business from its days as a Chicago butcher shop to a nationally known company is included in "How a Small Packer Does Better," *Business Week*, 22 November 1958, pp. 140–42-. For information on Mayer's son, Oscar G. Mayer, see *Dictionary of American Biography*, sup. 7, s.v. "Oscar G. Mayer"; and the Oscar G. Mayer obituary, *New York Times*, 6 March 1965, p. 25.

MENNEN, GERHARD   Although it tends to be overly reverent in parts, the most complete account of Gerhard Mennen and his company is Alfred Lief, *The Mennen Story* (New York: McGraw-Hill, 1954). Another account of the Mennen family and company is "American Male Likes to Smell Nice Too," *Business Week*, 9 May 1953, pp. 148-. A biography of Mennen written by a contemporary (published 1907) can be found in *The National Cyclopedia of American Biography*, vol. 5, p. 554. For information on Mennen's son and successor, William G. Mennen, see the William G. Mennen obituary, *New York Times*, 19 February 1968, p. 39; the William G. Mennen obituary, *Time*, 1 March 1968, p. 82; and *Who Was Who in America*, vol. 4, s.v. "William Mennen." Information used in the preparation of this biography was also obtained from the Mennen Co., Morristown, New Jersey.

OTIS, ELISHA   Material provided by United Technologies, Farmington, Connecticut, was extremely helpful in the preparation of this biography. Of particular value was an account of the inventor's life and work written by his son, Charles R. Otis, in 1911. A description of the world's first safety elevator is offered by Meredith Hooper, *Everyday Inventions* (New York: Taplinger Publishing Co., 1976), pp. 57–58. An account of Otis's demonstration at Crystal Palace in 1854 is furnished by Ralph A. Weller, "A World's Fair Stunt That Lifted Skylines," *Nation's Business*, January 1971, pp. 82–83. A brief analysis of the contribution to the development of the modern skyscraper made by Otis's elevator is included in *The Smithsonian Book of Invention* (Washington: Smithsonian Exposition Books, 1978). For a good overview of Otis and his sons, Charles and Norton, see *The National Cyclopedia of American Biography*, vol. 11, p. 119; and the Editors of News Front Year, *The 50 Great Pioneers of American Industry* (Maplewood: C. S. Hammond & Co.; New York: Year Inc., 1964), pp. 48–52.

PABST, FREDERICK   Frederick Pabst's role in transforming a small family brewery into an industry giant is detailed by Michael A. Weiner, *The Taster's Guide to Beer* (New York: Collier Books, 1972), pp. 202–5. For an idea of how Pabst's contemporaries viewed him, see *The National Cyclopedia of American Biography*, vol. 3, p. 342; and the Captain Frederick Pabst obituary, *New York Times*, 2 January 1904, p. 1. Pabst's career is also recounted by James D. Robertson, *The Great American Beer Book* (Ottawa, Ill.: Caroline House Publishers, 1978), pp. 89–90. For information on Pabst's son, Fred Pabst, see the Fred Pabst obituary, *New York Times*, 22 February 1958, p. 17. Also see "The Brotherly Brewers," *Fortune*, April 1950, pp. 103-; "Barrel of Fun," *Time*, 26 May 1958, pp. 53–54; and *Who Was Who in America*, vol. 1, s.v. "Frederick Pabst."

POST, CHARLES   A colorful figure, Post often created romanticized versions of his youth and career, so early accounts of his life should be read with caution. A good analysis of his brilliant advertising and marketing campaign is provided by Frank Rowsome, Jr., *They Laughed When I Sat Down* (New York: McGraw-Hill Book Co., 1959), pp. 60–63. Reliable overviews of Post's life can be found in *Dictionary of American Biography*, vol. 8, pt. 1, s.v. "Charles Post"; and *Webster's American Biographies*, s.v. "Charles Post." A comprehensive, though extremely worshipful, biography of Post was authored by Nettie L. Major, *C. W. Post: The Hour and the Man* (Washington: privately published, 1963). Also see James Trager, *The Food Book*

(New York: Avon Books, by arrangement with Grossman Publishers, 1970), pp. 384, 461; *Who Was Who in America*, vol. 1, s.v. "Charles Post"; Hannah Campbell, *Why Did They Name It?* (New York: Fleet Publishing Co., 1964), pp. 3–4; and Laurence A. Johnson, *Over the Counter and on the Shelf* (Rutland, Vt.: Charles E. Tuttle Co., 1961), pp. 79–80.

ROLLS, CHARLES, AND ROYCE, HENRY   A good general biography of Charles Rolls is offered by Sir Sidney Lee, ed., *The Dictionary of National Biography*, 1901–11 ed., s.v. "Charles Rolls"; and a similar account of Henry Royce's life is presented by L. G. Wickham Legg, *The Dictionary of National Biography*, 1931–40 ed., s.v. "Henry Royce." Useful descriptions of the Rolls-Royce automobile and insights into its creators' partnership can be found in Marco Matteucci, *The History of the Motor Car* (New York: Crown Publishers, 1970), pp. 149–50, 260; and Ralph Stein, *The Treasury of the Automobile* (New York: Ridge Press and Golden Press, 1961), pp. 114–22. Also see *Chambers Biographical Dictionary*, rev. ed., s.v. "Charles Rolls" and "Henry Royce." Information used in preparing this biography was also obtained from Rolls-Royce Ltd., Derby, England.

SCHOLL, WILLIAM   There is a limited amount of published material available on Scholl. One of the most complete accounts of his life is presented in *The National Cyclopedia of American Biography*, vol. 1, p. 298. Other thorough biographies are included in the William Scholl obituary, *New York Times*, 30 March 1968, p. 33; and the William Scholl obituary, *Chicago Tribune*, 30 March 1968. An account of Scholl's selling and marketing techniques is included in Hannah Campbell, *Why Did They Name It?* (New York: Fleet Publishing Co., 1964), pp. 125–30. Also see Bruce Felton and Mark Fowler, *Famous Americans You Never Knew Existed* (Briarcliff Manor: Stein & Day, 1979), pp. 160–61; the William Scholl obituary, *Time*, 5 April 1968, p. 102; and a profile of Scholl's brother and business associate, Frank Scholl, in *The National Cyclopedia of American Biography*, vol. 54, p. 96.

SCOTT, E. IRVIN AND CLARENCE   Relatively little has been published on the Scott brothers, and much helpful information has been provided to the authors by the Scott Paper Co., Philadelphia, Pennsylvania. A biography of the Scotts, together with a brief account of their pioneering efforts in marketing toilet tissue, is included in "Tissue Issue," *Time*, 22 August 1938, p. 52; and in "Scott Expands," *Business Week*, 9 June 1945, pp. 19–20. For a candid, concise history of the company, see Milton Moskowitz et al., eds., *Everybody's Business* (San Francisco: Harper & Row, 1980), p. 584. Also a history of the company is included in a biography of E. Irvin Scott's son, Arthur Hoyt Scott, in *The National Cyclopedia of American Biography*, vol. 40, p. 370.

SMITH, ANDREW AND WILLIAM   A lively, informative account of the Smith brothers is provided by J. Bainbridge, "The Boys," *New Yorker*, 6 September 1947, pp. 32–36-. For material on the famous Smith Brothers trademark, see Hannah Campbell, *Why Did They Name It?* (New York: Fleet Publishing Co., 1964), pp. 119–20; and Arnold B. Barach, *Famous American Trademarks* (Washington: Public Affairs Press, 1971), pp. 161–62.

SPALDING, ALBERT G.   A great deal of material has been published on Spalding. Good general biographies are included in *The National Cyclopedia of American Biography*, vol. 3, p. 394; and *Webster's American Biographies*, s.v. "Albert Goodwill Spalding." For an analysis of the marketing strategies employed by Spalding and his successors, see David P. Cleary, *Great American Brands* (New York: Fairchild Publications, 1981), pp. 280–86. Also see the Albert G. Spalding obituary, *New York Times*, 10 September 1915, p. 11; *Who Was Who in America*, vol. 1, s.v. "Albert G. Spalding"; and *The Baseball Encyclopedia*, s.v. "Albert G. Spalding." Spalding's brilliant baseball career is covered by Lee Allen and Tom Meany, *Kings of the Diamond* (New York: G. P. Putnam's Sons, 1965), pp. 20–22; and Jeanne McClow et al., eds., *A Baseball Century* (New York: Macmillan Publishing Co., 1976), pp. 26–27. Information used in the preparation of this manuscript was also obtained from Spalding Sports Worldwide, Chicopee, Massachusetts.

STEINWAY, HENRY   The story of Henry Steinway, his sons, and their piano company is extensively detailed in "Here Are the Steinways and How They Grew," *Fortune*, December 1934, pp. 99-. A more contemporary view of the Steinway company is provided by E. Rothstein, "At Steinway It's All Craft," *New York Times*, 22 February 1981, sec. E, p. 8; and S. Lohr, "The Steinway Tradition," *New York Times*, 24 August 1980, sec. III, p. 1. For an account of the Steinways' promotional activities and their relationship with Anton Rubinstein, see M. Goldin, "The Great Rubinstein Road Show," *High Fidelity*, September 1966, pp. 60–62. Interesting accounts of Steinway by his contemporaries are included in the Henry Steinway obituary, *New York Times*, 8 February 1871, p. 5; and "Opening of Steinway & Sons New Pianoforte Manufactory," *Frank Leslie's Illustrated Newspaper* (New York), 22 September 1860, p. 282. Also see R. Kammerer, "The Steinway Dynasty," *Musical America*, June 1961, pp. 7–8-; *The National Cyclopedia of American Biography*, vol. 2, p. 513. Information used in the preparation of this biography was also obtained from John H. Steinway, Steinway & Sons, Long Island City, New York.

STIFFEL, THEODOPHOLOUS   Most of the material used in the preparation of this biography was obtained from five interviews the authors conducted during August and September 1983 with Jules Stiffel (Chicago), the son of Theodopholous Stiffel and a former executive with the lighting firm. Additional information was obtained from Brenda McCauley, president of Brenda McCauley Associates, New York, public relations firm for the Stiffel Co., Chicago. Also see George Lazarus column, *Chicago Tribune*, 22 August 1973, sec. III, p. 8.

WEDGWOOD, JOSIAH   For a complete account of Josiah Wedgwood's life, see Anthony Burton, *Josiah Wedgwood* (Briarcliff Manor: Stein & Day, 1976). A detailed account also is provided by Sir Leslie Stephen and Sir Sidney Lee, eds., *The Dictionary of National Biography*, vol. 20 (London: Oxford University Press, 1917), s.v. "Josiah Wedgwood." Also see the *McGraw-Hill Encyclopedia of World Biography*, s.v. "Josiah Wedgwood." Good biographical sketches of Wedgwood in magazines include L. O. Thornton, "Story of Josiah Wedgwood," *Hobbies*, April 1949, pp. 112-; and L. A. Buskey, "Josiah Wedgwood: Artist and Industrialist," *Hobbies*, September 1950, pp. 94–96-.

WELCH, THOMAS   The most authoritative account of Thomas Welch and the development of grape juice is offered by William Chazanof, *Welch's Grape Juice: From Corporation to Co-operative* (Syracuse: Syracuse University Press, 1977). A bemused account of Welch's Prohibitionist activities is presented by Leon D. Adams, *The Wines of America* (Boston: Houghton Mifflin Co., 1973), pp. 66–67, 70, 116–17. For added information on Charles Welch, see *Who Was Who in America*, vol. 1, s.v. "Charles Welch."

WESTINGHOUSE, GEORGE   A great deal of helpful material was provided to the authors by Westinghouse Electric Corp., Pittsburgh. Especially useful was the booklet "George Westinghouse," company published, 1946. For a view of Westinghouse by his contemporaries, see the comprehensive George Westinghouse obituary, *New York Times*, 13 March 1914; and *The National Cyclopedia of American Biography*, vol. 15, p. 41. Good overviews of Westinghouse's career are provided by the Editors of News Front Year, *The 50 Great Pioneers of American Industry* (Maplewood: C. S. Hammond & Co.; New York: Year Inc., 1964), pp. 123–26; the

McGraw-Hill Encyclopedia of World Biography, s.v. "George Westinghouse";
Dictionary of American Biography, vol. 10, pt. 2, s.v. "George Westinghouse"; and
Webster's American Biographies, s.v. "George Westinghouse." An account of
Westinghouse's efforts to advance the development of alternating-current electricity
is furnished by G. L. Wilcox, "Mighty Transformation in Electricity," *Nation's
Business*, January 1971, pp. 92–93. Also see *Who Was Who in America*, vol. 1, s.v.
"George Westinghouse."

WRIGLEY, WILLIAM, JR.   The Wm. Wrigley, Jr., Co. furnished the authors with much
of the material used in preparing this biography. Also helpful was the comprehensive
account of the chewing gum executive's career given in the Wiliam Wrigley, Jr.,
obituary, *New York Times*, 27 January 1932, p. 21. Another comprehensive account
of Wrigley's career is provided by M. Crowell, "The Wonder Story of Wrigley,"
American Magazine, March 1920. For a good analysis of Wrigley's use of premiums
as a selling tool, see Laurence A. Johnson, *Over the Counter and on the Shelf*
(Rutland, Vt.: Charles E. Tuttle Co., 1961), pp. 102–3. Wrigley's career in the
chewing gum industry is discussed by Robert Hendrickson, *The Great American
Chewing Gum Book* (Radnor, Pa.: Chilton Book Co., 1976), pp. 36–38. Information
on Wrigley's marketing strategy can be obtained from David P. Cleary, *Great
American Brands* (New York: Fairchild Publications, 1981), pp. 287–94. Also see *The
National Cyclopedia of American Biography*, vol. B, p. 498; Milton Moskowitz et al.,
eds., *Everybody's Business* (San Francisco: Harper & Row, 1980), pp. 871–72; and
Meredith Hooper, *Everyday Inventions* (New York: Taplinger Publishing Co., 1976),
p. 36.

WURLITZER, RUDOLPH   Rudolph Wurlitzer's story appears in many books dealing
with the history of musical instruments. An excellent account of how Rudolph
Wurlitzer launched his business by eliminating the network of middlemen between
musical instrument factory and consumer is provided by Harvey N. Roehl, *Player
Piano Treasury* (Vestal, N.Y.: Vestal Press, 1961), pp. 97–105. The Wurlitzer
company receives a great deal of attention in John Krivine, *Jukebox Saturday Night*
(Secaucus: Chartwell Books, 1977). Also see the Diagram Group, *Musical
Instruments of the World* (New York: Paddington Press, 1976); *The National
Cyclopedia of American Biography*, vol. 16, p. 423, "Rudolph Wurlitzer", and vol. 57,
p. 746 "Farny Wurlitzer"; the Rudolph Wurlitzer obituary, *New York Times*, 17
January 1914, p. 9; Orpha Ochse, *The History of the Organ in the United States*
(Bloomington: Indiana University Press, 1975), p. 334. Information used in the
preparation of this biography was also obtained from John L. Yousling, The Wurlitzer
Co., Dekalb, Illinois.

Cameos

AMOS, WALLY   R. Harris, "For Famous Amos the Cookie Crumbles Just Right," *Ebony*,
1 September 1979, pp. 52-; "The Hot New Rich," *Time*, 13 June 1977, p. 76; J. G.
King, "King of Cookie Mountain," *Black Enterprise*, January 1981, pp. 34-; and
correspondence with Famous Amos Chocolate Chip Cookie Co., Hollywood,
California.

ARDEN, ELIZABETH   Alfred A. Lewis and Constance Woodworth, *Miss Elizabeth
Arden: An Unretouched Portrait* (New York: Coward McCann & Geoghegan, 1972);
Current Biography—1966, s.v. "Elizabeth Arden"; Alden Whitman, *Come to Judgment*
(New York: Viking Press, 1980), pp. 14–20; and correspondence with Elizabeth
Arden, Inc., New York.

ARMOUR, PHILIP   "Armour Centennial: 1867–1967," *Armour Magazine*, February 1967, pp. 22–25; *Dictionary of American Biography*, vol. 1, pt. 1, s.v. "Philip Armour"; and Wheeler Preston, *American Biographies* (New York: Harper & Bros., 1940), s.v. "Philip Armour."

ARMSTRONG, THOMAS   David P. Cleary, *Great American Brands* (New York: Fairchild Publications, 1981), pp. 1–6; Sterling G. Slappey, comp., *Pioneers of American Business* (New York: Grossett & Dunlap, 1970), pp. 6–10; and correspondence with Armstrong World Industries, Inc., Lancaster, Pennsylvania.

AVERY, R. S.   *Who's Who in Finance and Industry—1980–81*, s.v. "R. Stanton Avery"; and correspondence with Avery International Corp., Pasadena, California.

BACARDI, DON F.   Alexis Lichine, William Fifield, et al., *Alexis Lichine's Encyclopedia of Wines & Spirits* (New York: Alfred A. Knopf, 1967), p. 117; correspondence with Bacardi Imports, Inc., Miami; and correspondence with Compton Advertising, Inc., New York, public relations firm for Bacardi.

BALDWIN, DWIGHT H.   Lucien Wulsin, *Dwight Hamilton Baldwin and the Baldwin Piano* (New York: The Newcomen Society in North America, 1953); Morley P. Thompson, "D. H. Baldwin: The Multibank Music Company" (New York: The Newcomen Society in North America, 1974); and Penrose Scull, *From Peddlers To Merchant Princes* (Chicago: Follett Publishing Co., 1967), p. 54.

BALL, FRANK AND GEORGE   Frederic A. Birmingham, *Ball Corporation: The First Century* (Indianapolis: Curtis Publishing Co., 1980); and *Dictionary of American Biography*, sup. 3, s.v. "Frank Ball," and sup. 5, s.v. "George Ball."

BASS, HENRY   Streeter Bass, "G. H. Bass Company—1876–1976," company-published history, 1976; and "Innovation, Success Highlight Bass History," *Chesebrough-Ponds World*, December 1978, pp. 2-.

BASSETT, JOHN   Ozzie Osborn, "Family Owned Firm Has Had Many Years of Good Business," *Roanoke* (Va.) *Times & World-News*, 31 July 1983; the J. D. Bassett obituary, *Richmond* (Va.) *Times-Dispatch*, 28 February 1965; and correspondence with Bassett Furniture Industries, Inc., Bassett, Virginia.

BAUER, EDDIE   S. Netherby, "The Old Man and the Boy," *Field and Stream*, September 1982, pp. 99–100-.

BAUSCH, JOHN, AND LOMB, HENRY   The John Jacob Bausch obituary, *New York Times*, 15 February 1926, p. 19; *The National Cyclopedia of American Biography*, vol. 23, p. 343 (Henry Lomb); and *Dictionary of American Biography*. sup. 3, s.v. "Edward Bausch."

BEAM, JIM   Telephone interview with Booker Noe, Bardstown, Ky., master distiller of Beam Distilling Co. and grandson of Jim Beam, December 1983; and correspondence with James A. Beam Distilling Co., executive offices, Chicago.

BEAN, L. L.   Tom Mahoney, *The Great Merchants* (New York: Harper & Bros., 1955), pp. 294–304; and L. A. Gorman, *L. L. Bean Inc.: Outdoor Specialties by Mail from Maine* (New York: The Newcomen Society in North America, 1981).

BEECH, WALTER AND OLIVE   C. R. Roseberry, *The Challenging Skies* (Garden City: Doubleday & Co., 1966), pp. 412–14; *The National Cyclopedia of American Biography*, vol. G, p. 484, Walter Beech; and *Current Biography—1956*, s.v. "Olive Beech."

BELL, DONALD, AND HOWELL, ALBERT   E. W. Beals, "Bell & Howell Celebrates 75th Year," *Lincolnwood* (Ill.) *Life*, 6 May 1982, p. 12; Bell & Howell Annual Report—1981, 75th Anniversary; the Albert S. Howell obituary, *New York Times*, 4 January 1951, p. 29; the Albert S. Howell obituary, *Time*, 15 January 1951, p. 77; and correspondence with Bell & Howell Co., Chicago.

BENGUÉ, JULES   Correspondence with Pfizer Inc., New York.

BIGELOW, ERASTUS *Dictionary of American Biography*, vol. 1, pt. 2, s.v. "Erastus Bigelow"; *Webster's American Biographies*, s.v. "Erastus Bigelow"; *Who Was Who in America*, vol. H, s.v. "Erastus Bigelow."

BIRDSEYE, CLARENCE *Dictionary of American Biography*, sup. 6, s.v. "Clarence Birdseye"; Milton Moskowitz et al., eds., *Everybody's Business* (San Francisco: Harper & Row, 1980), p. 30; Bruce Felton and Mark Fowler, *Famous Americans You Never Knew Existed* (Briarcliff Manor: Stein & Day, 1979), pp. 67–69; Hannah Campbell, *Why Did They Name It?* (New York: Fleet Publishing Co., 1964), pp. 5–9; Meredith Hooper, *Everyday Inventions* (New York: Taplinger Publishing Co., 1976), p. 88; Edwin Wildman, *Famous Leaders of Industry* (Boston: Page Co., 1920), pp. 19–29; Arnold B. Barach, *Famous American Trademarks* (Washington: Public Affairs Press, 1971), pp. 19–20; obituary, *New York Times*, 9 October 1956, p. 35; and David P. Cleary, *Great American Brands* (New York: Fairchild Publications, 1981), pp. 7–12.

BISSELL, ANNA AND MELVILLE Earl Lifshey, *The Housewares Story* (Chicago: National Housewares Manufacturers Association, 1973), pp. 290–92; David P. Cleary, *Great American Brands* (New York: Fairchild Publications, 1981), pp. 13–18; and correspondence with Bissell Inc., Grand Rapids, Michigan.

BLACK, S. DUNCAN, AND DECKER, ALONZO David P. Cleary, *Great American Brands* (New York: Fairchild Publications, 1981), pp. 19–23; *The National Cyclopedia of American Biography*, vol. 46, p. 156, "Decker"; Milton Moskowitz et al., eds., *Everybody's Business* (San Francisco: Harper & Row, 1980), pp. 174–75; and David X. Manners, *The Great Tool Emporium* (New York: E. P. Dutton, 1979).

BLASS, BILL Nora Ephron, "The Man in the Bill Blass Suit," *New York Times Magazine*, 8 December 1968, pp. 52-; Barbara Walz and Bernadine Morris, *Fashion Makers* (New York: Random House, 1978), pp. 42–49; *Current Biography—1966*, s.v. "Bill Blass"; Anne Stegemeyer, *Who's Who in Fashion* (New York: Fairchild Publications, 1980), pp. 107–8; and O. E. Schoeffler and William Gale, *Esquire's Encyclopedia of 20th Century Men's Fashions* (New York: McGraw-Hill Book Co., 1973), pp. 605–6.

BOEING, WILLIAM The Editors of News Front Year, *The 50 Great Pioneers of American Industry* (Maplewood: C. S. Hammond & Co.; New York: Year Inc., 1964), pp. 186–88, 192–95; Milton Moskowitz, et al., eds., *Everybody's Business* (San Francisco: Harper & Row, 1960), pp. 685–86; *Dictionary of American Biography*, sup. 6, s.v. "William Boeing"; and C. R. Roseberry, *The Challenging Skies* (Garden City: Doubleday & Co., 1966), pp. 387–88.

BOIARDI, HECTOR The Richard Boiardi obituary, *New York Times*, 29 December 1969, p. 29; and correspondence with American Home Products, New York.

BRACH, EMIL *Who Was Who in America*, vol. 2, s.v. "Emil Brach," vol. 4, s.v. "Edwin Brach" and vol. 5, s.v. "Frank Brach"; the Emil Brach obituary, *New York Times*, 1 November 1947, p. 15; and correspondence with E. J. Brach & Sons, Chicago.

BRADLEY, MILTON James J. Shea, *It's All in the Game* (New York: G. P. Putnam's Sons, 1960); *Dictionary of American Biography*, vol. 1, pt. 2, s.v. "Milton Bradley"; *The National Cyclopedia of American Biography*, vol. 11, p. 472; and correspondence with Milton Bradley Co., East Longmeadow, Massachusetts.

BRECK, JOHN *The National Cyclopedia of American Biography*, vol. 52, p. 599; the John Breck obituary, *New York Times*, 18 February 1965, p. 33; and correspondence with Daniel J. Eldman, Inc., New York, public relations firm for Breck shampoo.

BROOKS, HENRY Tom Mahoney, *The Great Merchants* (New York: Harper & Bros., 1955), pp. 33–46; and correspondence with Brooks Brothers, New York.

BROWNING, JOHN   A. Merwyn Carey, *American Firearms Makers* (New York: Thomas Y. Corwell, 1953), pp. 13–14; Edwin Wildman, *Famous Leaders of Industry*, vol. 1 (Boston: Page Co., 1920), pp. 51–64; *Dictionary of American Biography*, vol. 2, pt. 1, s.v. "John Browning"; *The National Cyclopedia of American Biography*, vol. 20, p. 8; and *Webster's American Biographies*, s.v. "John Browning."

BROYHILL, JAMES   "From a Humble Beginning to Triumph in Business," *Nation's Business*, January 1977, pp. 45–46-; and *Who's Who in America—1974–75*, s.v. "James E. Broyhill."

BRUNSWICK, JOHN   Correspondence with Brunswick Corp., Skokie, Illinois.

BUICK, DAVID   *Buick's First Half Century* (Detroit: General Motors Corp., 1952); Karl Ludvigsen, David B. Wise, et al., *The Complete Encyclopedia of the American Automobile*, rev. ed. (Secaucus: Chartwell Books, 1979), pp. 17–19; Marco Matteucci, *History of the Motor Car* (New York: Crown Publishers, 1970), pp. 170–71; and *Webster's Biographical Dictionary*, s.v. "David Buick."

BULOVA, JOSEPH   Correspondence with Harry B. Henshel, grandson of Joseph Bulova; Hana Umlauf Lane, ed., *The World Almanac Book of Who* (Englewood Cliffs: Prentice-Hall, 1980); Dennis Sanders, *The First of Everything* (New York: Delacorte Press, 1981; Dell Publishing Co., 1982), p. 306; and correspondence with Bulova Watch Co., Inc., Flushing, New York.

BURROUGHS, WILLIAM   *The National Cyclopedia of American Biography*, vol. 27, p. 383; *Dictionary of American Biography*, sup. 1, s.v. "William Burroughs"; and *Who Was Who in America*, vol. H, s.v. "William Burroughs."

CADBURY, JOHN   *Chambers Biographical Dictionary*, s.v. "John Cadbury"; Carol Ann Rinzler, *The Book of Chocolate* (New York: St. Martin's Press, 1977), p. 32; and correspondence with Cadbury Schweppes USA, Stamford, Connecticut.

CAMPBELL, JOSEPH   R. Hambleton, "For Him Success Was in the Can," *Marketing*, 22 August 1983; Milton Moskowitz et al., eds., *Everybody's Business* (San Francisco: Harper & Row, 1980), p. 9; David P. Cleary, *Great American Brands* (New York: Fairchild Publications, 1981), pp. 53–59; Arnold B. Barach, *Famous American Trademarks* (Washington: Public Affairs Press, 1971), pp. 29–30; and Richard O. Cummings, *The American and His Food* (New York: Arno Press, 1970), p. 107.

CANNON, JAMES   C. G. Burck, "Reveille at Cannon Mills," *Fortune*. 26 January 1981, pp. 68-; Arnold B. Barach, *Famous American Trademarks* (Washington: Public Affairs Press, 1971), pp. 33–34; and correspondence with Cannon Mills Co., Kannapolis, North Carolina.

CARDIN, PIERRE   O. E. Schoeffler and William Gale, *Esquire's Encyclopedia of 20th Century Men's Fashions* (New York: McGraw-Hill Book Co., 1973), p. 608; *Current Biography—1965*, s.v. "Pierre Cardin"; P. Andriotakis, "Already a Household Name, Pierre Cardin Looks to Maxim-ize His Reputation," *People Weekly*, 8 August 1983, pp. 83–84-; and Anne Stegemeyer, *Who's Who in Fashion* (New York: Fairchild Publications, 1980), pp. 65–66.

CARTER, WILLIAM   *The National Cyclopedia of American Biography*, vol. 31, p. 124, "Wm. Carter", and vol. 46, p. 448, "Wm. H. Carter"; and the William H. Carter obituary, *New York Times*, 24 April 1955, p. 86.

CASSINI, OLEG   O. E. Schoeffler and William Gale, *Esquire's Encyclopedia of 20th Century Men's Fashions* (New York: McGraw-Hill Book Co., 1973), p. 609; and Anne Stegemeyer, *Who's Who in Fashion* (New York: Fairchild Publications, 1980), pp. 111–12.

CESSNA, CLYDE   Gerald Deneau, *An Eye to the Sky* (Wichita: Cessna Aircraft Co., 1962); C. R. Roseberry, *The Challenging Skies* (Garden City: Doubleday & Co., 1966), p. 412; and correspondence with Cessna Aircraft Co., Wichita.

CHRYSLER, WALTER   Walter P. Chrysler, *Life of an American Workman* (New York: Dodd, Mead & Co., 1937); *Dictionary of American Biography*, sup. 2, s.v. "Walter Chrysler"; Milton Moskowitz et al., eds., *Everybody's Business* (San Francisco: Harper & Row, 1980), pp. 262–63; Karl Ludvigsen, David B. Wise, et al., *The Complete Encyclopedia of the American Automobile*, rev. ed., (Secaucus: Chartwell Books, 1972), pp. 45–48; and Marco Matteucci, *History of the Motor Car* (New York: Crown Publishers, 1970), pp. 284–85, 334.

CHURCH, GEORGE   Brett C. Clapsaddle, "Church's Fried Chicken, Inc.: A Business History" (MBA thesis, University of Texas, 1978); and Annual Report—1971, Church's Fried Chicken, Inc., San Antonio.

CLARK, DAVID   Correspondence with D. L. Clark Co., division of Beatrice Foods, Pittsburgh, Pennsylvania.

CLEVELAND, RUTH   Arnold B. Barach, *Famous American Trademarks* (Washington: Public Affairs Press, 1971), pp. 11–12; and Dennis Sanders, *The First of Everything* (New York: Delacorte Press, 1981; Dell Publishing Co., 1982), p. 21.

COLGATE, WILLIAM   *Webster's American Biographies*, s.v. "William Colgate"; Milton Moskowitz et al., eds., *Everybody's Business* (San Francisco: Harper & Row, 1980), pp. 201–3; Laurence A. Johnson, *Over the Counter and on the Shelf* (Rutland, Vt.: Charles E. Tuttle Co., 1961), p. 63; and correspondence with Colgate-Palmolive Co., New York.

COLT, SAMUEL   A. Merwyn Carey, *American Firearms Makers* (New York: Thomas Y. Crowell, 1953), pp. 20–22; *Webster's American Biographies*, s.v. "Samuel Colt"; and *Dictionary of American Biography*, vol. 2, s.v. "Samuel Colt."

CONVERSE, MARQUIS   *Who Was Who in America*, vol. 1, s.v. "Marquis Converse"; and correspondence with Converse Inc., Wilmington, Massachusetts.

COORS, ADOLPH   Stanley Baron, *Brewed in America* (Boston: Little, Brown & Co., 1962), pp. 249–50; R. M. Ancell, "The Golden Boys," *Colorado/Business*, January 1980, pp. 14-; James D. Robertson, *The Great American Beer Book* (Ottawa, Ill.: Caroline House Publishers, 1978), pp. 54–55; and Michael A. Weiner, *The Taster's Guide to Beer* (New York: Collier Books/Macmillan Publishing Co., 1977), pp. 188–90.

DE LA RENTA, OSCAR   Barbara Walz and Bernadine Morris, *Fashion Makers* (New York: Random House, 1978), pp. 180–87; *Current Biography—1970*, s.v. "Oscar de la Renta"; Anne Stegemeyer, *Who's Who in Fashion* (New York: Fairchild Publications, 1980), p. 114; "American Chic in Fashion," *Time*, 22 March 1976, p. 68; and O. E. Schoeffler and William Gale, *Esquire's Encyclopedia of 20th Century Men's Fashions* (New York: McGraw-Hill Book Co., 1973), pp. 612–13.

DEWAR, JOHN   David Daiches, *Scotch Whisky: Its Past and Present* (London: Macmillan & Co., 1970), pp. 85–89; R. J. S. McDowall, *The Whiskies of Scotland* (London: Abelard Schuman, 1967), pp. 59–61; and correspondence with the Distillers Corporation, London.

DIOR, CHRISTIAN   *Current Biography—1948*, s.v. "Christian Dior"; and Anne Stegemeyer, *Who's Who in Fashion* (New York: Fairchild Publications, 1980), pp. 22–23.

DODGE, JOHN AND HORACE   Jean M. Pitrone and Joan P. Elwart, *The Dodges Auto Family Fortune and Misfortune* (South Bend, Ind.: Icarus Press, 1982); *The National Cyclopedia of American Biography*, vol. 20, p. 266, "Horace Dodge" and p. 267, "John Dodge"; Karl Ludvigsen, David B. Wise, et al., *The Complete Encyclopedia of the American Automobile*, rev. ed. (Secaucus: Chartwell Books, 1979), pp. 56–60; and Marco Matteucci, *History of the Motor Car* (New York: Crown Publishers, 1970), p. 288.

DOLE, JAMES   Frank J. Taylor, Earl M. Welty, and David W. Eyre, *From Land and Sea: the Story of Castle & Cook of Hawaii* (San Francisco: Chronicle Publishing Co., 1976), pp. 161–71; Henry A. White, *James D. Dole: Industrial Pioneer of the Pacific* (New York: The Newcomen Society in North America, 1957); "No Roads Went by Dole's Birthplace 75 Years Ago," *Castle & Cook Report*, 22 December 1976, pp. 2–3; obituary, *Honolulu Advertiser*, 15 May 1958, p. 1-; obituary, *Honolulu Star-Bulletin*, 15 May 1958, p. 1-; and F. J. Taylor, "Billion Dollar Rainbow," *Reader's Digest*, December 1954, condensed from *Advertising Agency*, September 1954.

DUNLOP, JOHN   H. W. C. David and J. R. H. Weaver, eds., *The Dictionary of National Biography*, 1912–21 ed. (London: Oxford University Press, 1927), s.v. "John Dunlop"; *Chambers Biographical Dictionary*, rev. ed., s.v. "John Dunlop"; John Day, *The Bosch Book of the Motor Car* (New York: St. Martin's Press, 1976), p. 1979; Meredith Hooper, *Everyday Inventions* (New York: Taplinger Publishing Co., 1976), p. 34; and Marco Matteucci, *History of the Motor Car* (New York: Crown Publishers, 1970), p. 18.

DURKEE, EUGENE   *The National Cyclopedia of American Biography*, vol. 20, p. 460; and correspondence with SCM Corp., New York.

EVINRUDE, OLE   Ernest V. Heyn, *Fire of Genius* (Garden City: Anchor Press/ Doubleday, 1976), pp. 283–85; the Editors of News Front Year, *The 50 Great Pioneers of American Industry* (Maplewood: C. S. Hammond & Co.; New York: Year Inc., 1964), pp. 172–74; and David P. Cleary, *Great American Brands* (New York: Fairchild Publications, 1981), pp. 80–86.

FABERGÉ, PETER CARL   Henry C. Bainbridge, *Peter Carl Fabergé* (London: B. T. Batsford, 1949); and correspondence with Prestwick Darlington and Beeston, Ltd., New York, public relations firm for Fabergé.

FARAH, JAMES AND WILLIAM   T. Mack, "A Painful Lesson," *Forbes*, 19 January 1981, pp. 51-; P. D. Ortego, "Farah Slacks and Pants: Chicanos Extend the Boycott," *Nation*, 20 November 1972, p. 497; and "A Bishop v. Farah," *Time*, 26 March 1973, p. 88.

FARBER, SIMON   Earl Lifshey, *The Housewares Story* (Chicago: National Housewares Manufacturers Association, 1973), pp. 278–80; and the Simon Farber obituary, *New York Times*, 5 April 1947, p. 19.

FARMER, FANNIE   The editors of *Fortune, 100 Stories of Business Success* (New York: Simon & Schuster, 1954), pp. 40–41; Carol Ann Rinzler, *The Book of Chocolate* (New York: St. Martin's Press, 1977), pp. 109–10; and *Webster's American Biographies*, s.v. "Fannie Farmer."

FERRARI, ENZO   *Current Biography—1967*, s.v. "Enzo Ferrari"; Ralph Stein, *The Treasury of the Automobile* (New York: Ridge Press and Golden Press, 1961), pp. 144–45; and Richard Hough, *A History of the World's Sports Cars* (New York: Harper & Bros., 1961), pp. 178–80.

FIRESTONE, HARVEY   Alfred Lief, *Harvey Firestone: Free Man of Enterprise* (New York: McGraw-Hill Book Co., 1951); Milton Moskowitz et al., eds., *Everybody's Business* (San Francisco: Harper & Row, 1980), pp. 285–86; and correspondence with Firestone Tire & Rubber Co., Akron, Ohio.

FISHER, HERMAN, AND PRICE, IRVING   Correspondence with Fisher-Price Toys, East Aurora, New York.

FLEISCHMANN, CHARLES   H. Weigl, "Getting to the Bakery on Time," *Nation's Business*, January 1971, pp. 90–91; and *The National Cyclopedia of American Biography*, vol. 22, p. 88.

FOLGER, JAMES   Ruth Waldo Newhall, *The Folger Way* (San Francisco: J. A. Folger Co., n.d.); William H. Ukers, *All about Coffee* (New York: Tea & Coffee Trade

Journal Co., 1935); and correspondence with the Procter & Gamble Co., Cincinnati, Ohio.

FORD, HENRY   David L. Lewis, *The Public Image of Henry Ford: An American Hero and His Company* (Detroit: Wayne State University Press, 1976); James Brough, *The Ford Dynasty: An American Story* (Garden City: Doubleday, 1977); and Ralph Stein, *The Treasury of the Automobile* (New York: Ridge Press and Golden Press, 1961), pp. 165–67.

FRENCH, R. T.   Correspondence with the R. T. French Co., Rochester, New York.

FROWICK, ROY HALSTON   Barbara Walz and Bernadine Morris, *Fashion Makers* (New York: Random House, 1978), pp. 90–97; Anne Stegemeyer, *Who's Who in Fashion* (New York: Fairchild Publications, 1980), pp. 122–23; and "American Chic in Fashion," *Time*, 22 March 1976, p. 63.

FULLER, ALFRED   *Current Biography—1950*, s.v. "Alfred C. Fuller"; J. Bainbridge, "May I Just Step Inside," *New Yorker*, 13 November 1948, pp. 36–38-; and "Fuller's Fillies," *Time*, 12 July 1948, p. 77.

GALLO, ERNEST AND JULIO   Bob Thompson and Hugh Johnson, *The California Wine Book* (New York: William Morrow & Co., 1976), pp. 126–29; Milton Moskowitz et al., eds., *Everybody's Business* (San Francisco: Harper & Row, 1980), pp. 806–7; and correspondence with E. & J. Gallo Winery, Modesto, California.

DE GIVENCHY, HUBERT   *Current Biography—1955*, s.v. "Hubert de Givenchy"; and Anne Stegemeyer, *Who's Who in Fashion* (New York: Fairchild Publications, 1980), pp. 72–73.

GOODRICH, B. F.   Milton Moskowitz et al., eds., *Everybody's Business* (San Francisco: Harper & Row, 1980), pp. 291–93; Sterling G. Slappey, *Pioneers of American Business* (New York: Grossett & Dunlap, 1970), pp. 91–96; and correspondence with the B. F. Goodrich Co., Akron, Ohio.

GOODYEAR, CHARLES   The Editors of News Front Year, *The 50 Great Pioneers of American Industry* (Maplewood: C. S. Hammond & Co.; New York: Year Inc., 1964), pp. 27–29; Meredith Hooper, *Everyday Inventions* (New York: Taplinger Publishing Co., 1972), pp. 29–34; and David P. Cleary, *Great American Brands* (New York: Fairchild Publications, 1981), pp. 128–29.

GRAHAM, SYLVESTER   E. B. Goodman, "Bran Bread Poet, "*Life and Health*, October 1977, pp. 21-; *McGraw-Hill Encyclopedia of World Biography*, s.v. "Sylvester Graham"; *Webster's American Biographies*, s.v. "Sylvester Graham"; and James Trager, *The Food Book* (New York: Avon Books by arrangement with Grossman Publishers, 1970), pp. 459–61.

GUCCI, GUCCIO   E. Victoria, "Move over Dallas: Behind the Glittering Facade a Family Feud Rocks the Hosue of Gucci," *People Weekly*, 6 September 1982, pp. 36–37-; Charlotte Calsibetta, *Fairchild's Dictionary of Fashion* (New York: Fairchild Publications, 1975), pp. 455, 579–80; A. Taylor, ". . . But at Gucci You'd Think People Had Money to Burn," *New York Times*, 21 December 1974, p. 12; and correspondence with Gucci shops, New York.

GUINNESS, ARTHUR   Henry Boylan, ed., *A Dictionary of Irish Biography* (Dublin: Gill & MacMillan, 1978), s.v. "Arthur Guinness"; James D. Robertson, *The Great American Beer Book* (Ottawa, Ill.: Caroline House Publishers, 1978), p. 160; and Michael A. Weiner, *The Taster's Guide to Beer* (New York: Collier Books/Macmillan Publishing Co., 1977), pp. 168–70.

HAGGAR, JOSEPH   *The National Cyclopedia of American Biography*, vol. G, p. 432; and "Building on a Rock," *Forbes*, 1 September 1980, p. 40.

HANDLER, BARBARA   Sibyle De Wein and Joan Ashabraner, *The Collector's Encyclopedia of Barbie Dolls and Collectables* (New York: Collector Books, 1977); and

Marvin Kay, *The Story of Monopoly, Silly Putty, Bingo, Twister, Frisbee, Scrabble Et Cetera* (Briarcliff Manor: Stein & Day, 1973), pp. 83–84.

HANES, PLEASANT AND JOHN   *The National Cyclopedia of American Biography*, vol. 22, p. 106, "Pleasant Hanes"; "Consolidated Foods Hungers for Hanes," *Business Week*, 25 September 1978, pp. 54-; and correspondence with Hanes Corp., Winston-Salem, North Carolina.

HARLEY, WILLIAM, AND DAVIDSON, ARTHUR   Joe Scalzo, *The Motorcycle Book* (Englewood Cliffs: Prentice-Hall, 1974), pp. 8–11; Graham Forsdyke, *Motorcyles* (Secaucus: Chartwell Books, 1977), pp. 16, 24; and correspondence with Harley-Davidson Motor Co., Inc., Milwaukee, Wisconsin.

HARVEY, JOHN   Julian Jeffs, *Sherry* (London: Farber & Farber, 1961), pp. 123–27; Adrian Ball & Associates Ltd., *Alphabet of Bristol Cream* (Bristol: John Harvey & Sons, 1970); and correspondence with John Harvey & Sons Ltd., Bristol, England.

HEAD, HOWARD   J. Dodge, "All the Ski World Loves a Cheater," *Sports Illustrated*, 18 December 1961, p. 48; and "Howard Head Strikes Again," *Forbes*, 1 June 1977, p. 76.

HEATH, LAWRENCE   The Lawrence Heath obituary, *New York Times*, 26 March 1956, p. 29; and correspondence with L. S. Heath & Sons, Inc., Robinson, Illinois.

HELLMANN, RICHARD   The Richard Hellmann obituary, *New York Times*, 4 February 1971, p. 38; and correspondence with CPC International, Englewood Cliffs, New Jersey.

HENNESSY, RICHARD   Henry Boylan, ed., *A Dictionary of Irish Biography* (Dublin: Gill & MacMillan, 1978), s.v. "Richard Hennessy"; Peter Kobotti and Frances Kobotti, *Key to Gracious Living Wine and Spirits* (Englewood Cliffs: Prentice-Hall, 1972), p. 29; and Hurst Hannum and Robert S. Blumberg, *Brandies and Liqueurs of the World* (Garden City: Doubleday, 1976), pp. 45–46.

HERSHEY, MILTON   David P. Cleary, *Great American Brands* (New York: Fairchild Publications, 1981), pp. 166–71; Milton Moskowitz et al., eds., *Everybody's Business* (San Francisco: Harper & Row, 1980), pp. 41–44; Arnold B. Barach, *Famous American Trademarks* (Washington: Public Affairs Press, 1971), pp. 91–92; *Webster's American Biographies*, s.v. "Milton Hershey"; and correspondence with Hershey Foods Corp., Hershey, Pennsylvania.

HEWLETT, WILLIAM, AND PACKARD, DAVID   *Current Biography—1969*, s.v. "David Packard"; Milton Moskowitz et al., eds., *Everybody's Business* (San Francisco: Harper & Row, 1980), pp. 431–34; *Who's Who in America—1980–81*, s.v. "David Packard" and "William Hewlett"; and "The Forbes Four Hundred," *Forbes*, Fall 1983, pp. 73-.

HILLS, AUSTIN AND REUBEN   William H. Ukers, *All about Coffee* (New York: Tea & Coffee Trade Journal Co., 1935); Ruth Waldo Newhall, *The Folger Way* (San Francisco: J. A. Folger Co., n.d.), p. 50; and correspondence with Hills Brothers Coffee Inc., San Francisco, California.

HINES, DUNCAN   Milton Moskowitz et al., eds., *Everybody's Business* (San Francisco: Harper & Row, 1980), pp. 357–59; and *Webster's American Biographies*, s.v. "Duncan Hines."

HUMMEL, BERTA (MARIA INNOCENTIA)   M. Stoddard, "The Beloved 'Children' of M. I. Hummel," *Saturday Evening Post*, January/February 1982, pp. 78–79-; and Eric Ehrmann, *Hummel: The Complete Collector's Guide and Illustrated Reference* (Huntington, N.Y.: Portfolio Press, 1976).

JANTZEN, CARL   Ingeborg Nielsen MacHaffie, *Danish in Portland: Past and Present* (Tigard, Oreg.: Skribent Press, 1982), pp. 39–47; and David P. Cleary, *Great American Brands* (New York: Fairchild Publications, 1981), pp. 182–91.

JELLINCK, MERCEDES, AND BENZ, KARL   Victor Boesen and Wendy Grad, *The Mercedes Benz Book* (Garden City: Doubleday & Co., 1981); Marco Matteucci, *History of the Motor Car* (New York: Crown Publishers, 1970), p. 103; Ernest V. Heyn, *Fire of Genius* (Garden City: Anchor Press/Doubleday, 1976), pp. 275–76; and David Scott-Moncrieff, *The Veteran Motor Car* (New York: Charles Scribner's Sons, 1956), pp. 192–93.

JERGENS, ANDREW   *Who Was Who in America*, vol. 4, s.v. "Andrew Jergens, Jr."; and correspondence with the Andrew Jergens Co., Cincinnati, Ohio.

JOHNSON, SAMUEL   Milton Moskowitz et al., eds., *Everybody's Business* (San Francisco: Harper & Row, 1980), pp. 865–68; the Herbert Johnson obituary, *New York Times*, 14 December 1978, sec. b, p. 23; the Herbert Johnson obituary, *Time*, 25 December 1978, p. 44; and correspondence with S. C. Johnson Co., Racine, Wisconsin.

KERR, ALEXANDER   *The National Cyclopedia of American Biography*, vol. 30, p. 570; and *Who Was Who in America*, vol. 1, s.v. "Alexander Kerr."

KIMBALL, WILLIAM   Orpha Ochse, *The History of the Organ in the United States* (Bloomington: Indiana University Press, 1975), pp. 302–4; *Who's Who in America— 1899–1900*, s.v. "William Kimball"; and correspondence with Kimball International, Jasper, Indiana.

LABATT, JOHN   Mary McD. Maude, *Dictionary of Canadian Biography*, vol. 9 (Toronto: University of Toronto Press, 1976), s.v. "John Labatt"; and James D. Robertson, *The Great American Beer Book* (Ottawa, Il.: Caroline House Publishers, 1978), pp. 141–45.

LACOSTE, RENÉ   Larry Lorimer, *Tennis Book* (New York: Random House, 1980), pp. 90–91; and P. Andriotakis, "See You Later Alligator?" *People Weekly*, 15 October 1979, pp. 131-.

LALIQUE, RENÉ   P. Garner, "Jeweler Who Loved Glass," *Country Life*, 6 June 1974, pp. 1438-; the René Lalique obituary, *New York Times*, 10 May 1945, p. 23; and *Chambers Biographical Dictionary*, s.v. "René Lalique."

LANE, JOHN AND EDWARD   *The National Cyclopedia of American Biography*, vol. 45, p. 552, "John Lane"; and vol. 58, p. 708, "Edward Lane"; and David P. Cleary, *Great American Brands* (New York: Fairchild Publications, 1981), pp. 202–10.

LAUREN, RALPH   *Current Biography—1980*, s.v. "Ralph Lauren"; Barbara Walz and Bernadine Morris, *Fashion Makers* (New York: Random House, 1978), pp. 148–53; Anne Stegemeyer, *Who's Who in Fashion* (New York: Fairchild Publications, 1980), pp. 136–37; O. E. Schoeffler and William Gale, *Esquire's Encyclopedia of 20th Century Men's Fashion* (New York: McGraw-Hill Book Co., 1973), pp. 622–23; Fred Ferretti, "The Business of Being Ralph Lauren," *New York Times Magazine*, 18 September 1983, pp. 112–14 +.

LAY, HERMAN   J. C. Louis and Harvey Yazijian, *The Cola Wars* (New York: Everest House Publishers, 1980), pp. 118, 133–34, 146; correspondence with Frito-Lay, Inc., Dallas, Texas; and correspondence with Estate of Herman W. Lay, Dallas, Texas.

LEE, HENRY   *The National Cyclopedia of American Biography*, vol. 40, p. 413 "Roland Caywood"; and correspondence with Lee Co., Shawnee Mission, Kansas.

LENOX, WALTER   Eric Ehrmann, "The Lenox Heritage," *Collector Edition*, Winter 1980, pp. 33–36; *The National Cyclopedia of American Biography*, vol. 40,, p. 515, "Frank Holmes"; and correspondence with Ruder Finn & Rotman, Inc., New York, public relations firm for Lenox Inc., Lawrenceville, New Jersey.

LIBBY, ARTHUR AND CHARLES   Louisa Libby Burrows, "Arthur Albion Libby— Pioneer in the Refrigeration and Canning of Meats," privately published 15-page pamphlet, n.d.; Milton Moskowitz et al., eds., *Everybody's Business* (San Francisco:

Harper & Row, 1980), pp. 53–54; and correspondence with UM Communications Inc., New York, public relations firm for Libby, McNeill & Libby, Inc., Chicago.

LISTER, JOSEPH   H. W. C. Davis and J. R. H. Weaver, eds., *The Dictionary of National Biography*, 1912–21 ed. (London: Oxford University Press, 1927), s.v. "Joseph Lister"; and Dennis Sanders, *The First of Everything* (New York: Delacorte Press, 1981; Dell Publishing Co., 1982), pp. 14, 379.

LUBIN, SARA LEE   "Let 'em Eat 79-Cent Cake," *Fortune*, November 1955, p. 239; and correspondence with Kitchens of Sara Lee, Deerfield, Illinois.

LUDEN, WILLIAM   The William Luden obituary, *New York Times*, 9 May 1949, p. 25; the William Luden obituary, *Time*, 16 May 1949, p. 100; and correspondence with Luden's, Inc., Reading, Pennsylvania.

MCDONALD, MAURICE AND RICHARD   Max Boas and Steve Chain, *Big Mac: The Unauthorized Story of McDonald's* (New York: E. P. Dutton, 1976); Ray Kroc and Robert Anderson, *Grinding It Out: The Making of McDonald's* (New York: Berkley Publishing, 1978); "McDonald Who?" *Forbes*, Fall 1983, pp. 251–52; and the Maurice J. McDonald obituary, *New York Times*, 14 December 1971, p. 48.

MACK, JOHN   G. N. Georgano, *The Complete Encyclopedia of Commercial Vehicles* (Iola, Wi.: Krause Publications, 1979), pp. 398–99; and *The National Cyclopedia of American Biography*, vol. 31, p. 502 (Augustus Mack), and vol. 40, p. 429, "Joseph Mack".

MANISCHEWITZ, RABBI DOV BER   Leon D. Adams, *The Wines of America* (Boston: Houghton Mifflin Co., 1973), pp. 350–51; and correspondence with the B. Manischewitz Co., Jersey City, New Jersey.

MARS, FORREST   "Mars: Behind Its Chocolate Curtain Is a Sweet Performer," *Business Week*, 14 August 1978, pp. 52-; H. B. Meyers, "Sweet Secret World of Forrest Mars," *Fortune*, May 1967, pp. 154-; and Milton Moskowitz et al., eds., *Everybody's Business* (San Francisco: Harper & Row, 1980), p. 869.

MASERATI, ERNESTO   Richard Hough, *A History of the World's Sports Cars* (New York: Harper & Brothers, 1961), pp. 67–68, 191; the Ernesto Maserati obituary, *New York Times*, 2 December 1975, p. 42; and the Ernesto Maserati obituary, *Time*, 15 December 1975, p. 64.

MASSON, PAUL   Robert L. Balzer, *This Uncommon Heritage: The Paul Masson Story* (Los Angeles: Ward Ritchie Press, 1970); and Leon D. Adams, *The Wines of America* (Boston: Houghton Mifflin Co., 1973), pp. 363–64.

MATCHABELLI, GEORGES   Hannah Campbell, *Why Did They Name It?* (New York: Fleet Publishing Co., 1964), pp. 146–49; and the Georges Matchabelli obituary, *New York Times*, 1 April 1935, p. 19.

MAYTAG, FRED   A. B. Funk, *Fred Maytag: A Biography* (Cedar Rapids, Ia.: privately published, 1936); *Dictionary of American Biography*, sup. 2., s.v. "Fred Maytag"; "Maytag Fights to Retake Lead," *Business Week*, 9 October 1954, pp. 108-; and the Fred L. Maytag obituary, *New York Times*, 27 March 1937, p. 15.

MILLER, FREDERIC   James D. Robertson, *The Great American Beer Book* (Ottawa, Ill.: Caroline House Publishers, 1978), pp. 83–84; and "The Miller Legacy," Milwaukee Miller Brewing Co., 1980.

MILLER, HOWARD   Correspondence with Howard Miller Co., Zeeland, Mich.; and S. Fucini, "Clockmaking in Western Michigan," *Watch & Clock Review*, April 1983, pp. 15–19.

MOLSON, JOHN   Mary McD. Maude, ed., *Dictionary of Canadian Biography*, vol. 9 (Toronto: University of Toronto, 1976), s.v. "Thomas Molson"; Michael A. Weiner, *The Taster's Guide to Beer* (New York: Macmillan Publishing Co., 1977), pp. 119–21; James D. Robertson, *The Great American Beer Book* (Ottawa, Ill.: Caroline House

Publishers, 1978), pp. 146–50; and W. Stewart Wallace, ed., and W. A. McKay, 4th ed., *The Macmillan Dictionary of Canadian Biography*, 4th ed. (Toronto: Macmillan of Canada, 1978), s.v. "John Molson."

MORTON, JOY   *The National Cyclopedia of American Biography*, vol. 17, p. 168; *Webster's Biographical Dictionary*, 1st ed., s.v. "Joy Morton"; Hannah Campbell, *Why Did They Name It?* (New York: Fleet Publishing Co., 1964), pp. 42–48; and *Who Was Who in America*, vol. 1, s.v. "Joy Morton."

MUELLER, CHRISTIAN   *The National Cyclopedia of American Biography*, vol. 34, p. 503; and Milton Moskowitz et al., eds., *Everybody's Business* (San Francisco: Harper & Row, 1980), pp. 815–16.

NESTLÉ, HENRI   Milton Moskowitz et al., eds., *Everybody's Business* (San Francisco: Harper & Row, 1980), pp. 59–60; Carol Ann Rinzler, *The Book of Chocolate* (New York: St. Martin's Press, 1977), pp. 83–84; Marjorie Stiling, *Famous Brand Names, Emblems and Trademarks* (New Abbot, Devon: David & Charles, 1980), p. 37; and correspondence with the Nestlé Co., White Plains, New York.

OLDS, RANSOM   Marco Matteucci, *History of the Motor Car* (New York: Crown Publlishers, 1970), pp. 76–79; Karl Ludvigsen, David B. Wise, et al., *The Complete Encyclopedia of the American Automobile*, rev. ed. (Secaucus: Chartwell Books, 1979), pp. 129–33; and Ralph Stein, *The Treasury of the Automobile* (New York: Ridge Press and Golden Press, 1961), pp. 56–59.

OLIVETTI, CAMILLO   *Current Biography—1959*, s.v. "Adriano Olivetti"; and correspondence with Ing. C. Olivetti & c., S.p.A., Ivrea, Italy.

PARKER, GEORGE SAFFORD   David P. Cleary, *Great American Brands* (New York: Fairchild Publications, 1981), pp. 223–31; George Safford Parker obituary, *New York Times*, 20 July 1937, p. 23; and correspondence with the Parker Pen Co., Janesville, Wisconsin.

PARKER, GEORGE SWINNERTON   *The National Cyclopedia of American Biography*, vol. 40, p. 62; the George Swinnerton Parker obituary, *New York Times*, 27 September 1952, p. 17; *Who Was Who in America*, vol. 3, s.v. "George Swinnerton Parker"; and correspondence with Parker Brothers, Beverly, Massachusetts.

PAULUCCI, JENO   "Pizza Peddler," *Fourtune*, 26 January 1981, pp. 15–16; *Who's Who in America—1980–81*, s.v. "Jeno Paulucci"; and "The Forbes Four Hundred," *Forbes*, Fall 1983, pp. 73-.

PHILLIPS, CHARLES   "Glenbrook—100 Years of Phillips Milk of Magnesia, 50 Years with Sterling," company-published booklet, 1973; Dr. Forde Morgan, "Charles Phillips and the Charles H. Phillips Chemical Company: Their Origin and Progress," Paper prepared for Chas. H. Phillips Co., Glenbrook, Conn., 31 March 1934, p. 2; and Dr. Forde Morgan, "Magnesia—Its Distinctive and Comparative Value," Paper prepared for Chas. H. Phillips Co., Glenbrook, Conn., 18 May 1934. p. 2.

PILLSBURY, CHARLES   John Storck and Walter D. Teague, *Flour for Man's Bread* (St. Paul: University of Minnesota and North Central Press, 1952), pp. 211, 235, 253–54; *Dictionary of American Biography*, vol. 7, s.v. "Charles Pillsbury"; Milton Moskowitz et al., eds., *Everybody's Business* (San Francisco: Harper & Row, 1980), p. 68; and B. Glancy, "Pillsbury Celebrates 100th Year," *Pillsbury Reporter*, September 1969, pp. 1–2-.

PIPER, WILLIAM   C. R. Roseberry, *The Challenging Skies* (Garden City: Doubleday & Co., 1966), pp. 418–19; David P. Cleary, *Great American Brands* (New York: Fairchild Publications, 1981), pp. 232–38; and the William Piper obituary, *New York Times*, 17 January 1970, p. 31.

PITNEY, ARTHUR, AND BOWES, WALTER   William Cahn, *The Story of Pitney-Bowes* (New York: Harper & Bros., 1961); and Sterling G. Slappey, comp., *Pioneers of*

American Business (New York: Grossett & Dunlap, 1970), pp. 221–26.

PORSCHE, FERDINAND   Jules Weitman, *Porsche Story*, trans. Charles Meisl (New York: Arco Publishing Co., 1967); Ken Purdy, *Ken Purdy's Book of Automobiles* (Chicago: Playboy Press, 1972), pp. 335–39; and the Ferdinand Porsche obituary, *New York Times*, 31 January 1951, p. 25.

RALSTON, DR. ALBERT   David P. Cleary, *Great American Brands* (New York: Fairchild Publications, 1981), pp. 239–45; and Milton Moskowitz et al., eds., *Everybody's Business* (San Francisco: Harper & Row, 1980), pp. 72–76.

REDENBACHER, ORVILLE   G. Breu, "To the Top," *People Weekly*, 13 November 1978, pp. 77-; "The Growth of Orville and His Dream," *Hunt-Wesson's World*, May/June 1980, pp. 2–5; and Orville Redenbacher, *The Popping Corn Book* (Fullerton, Calif.: Hunt-Wesson Foods, 1975), 32 pages.

REESE, H. B.   Correspondence with Hershey Foods Corp., Hershey, Pennsylvania.

REMPP, ADOLPH   Adolph Rempp, San Francisco, telephone interview with authors, December 1983; L. M. Miller, "They Make Tough Meat Tender," *Reader's Digest*, February 1953, pp. 66-; and correspondence with Chesebrough-Pond's Inc., Greenwich, Connecticut.

RENAULT, LOUIS   Marco Matteucci, *History of the Motor Car* (New York: Crown Publishers, 1970), pp. 138–41; John Day, *The Bosch Book of the Motor Car* (New York: St. Martin's Press, 1976), pp. 96, 161; and David Scott-Moncrieff, *The Veteran Motor Car* (New York: Charles Scribner's Sons, 1956), pp. 198–201.

REYNOLDS, RICHARD   Milton Moskowitz et al., eds., *Everybody's Business* (San Francisco: Harper & Row, 1980), pp. 566–68; Sterling G. Slappey, *Pioneers of American Business* (New York: Grossett & Dunlap, 1970), pp. 240–46; *Current Biography—1967*, s.v. "Richard Reynolds, Jr."; and correspondence with Reynolds Metals Co., Richmond, Virginia.

ROCKWELL, WILLARD   "Making Know-How Pay," *Nation's Business*, November 1967, pp. 88-; and "How Willard Rockwell Piles Success on Top of Success," *Nation's Business*, July 1975, pp. 45-.

RUBINSTEIN, HELENA   Helena Rubinstein, *My Life for Beauty* (New York: Simon & Schuster, 1964); *Current Biography—1943*; and correspondence with Helena Rubinstein, Secaucus, New Jersey.

ST. LAURENT, YVES   A. Burgess, "All about Yves," *New York Times Magazine*, 11 September 1977, pp. 118-; Anne Stegemeyer, *Who's Who in Fashion* (New York: Fairchild Publications, 1980), pp. 90–93; and *Current Biography—1964*, s.v. "Yves St. Laurent."

SCHICK, JACOB   Ernest V. Heyn, *Fire of Genius* (Garden City: Anchor Press/Doubleday, 1976), pp. 38–39; Earl Lifshey, *The Housewares Story* (Chicago: National Housewares Manufacturers Association, 1973), pp. 352–53; *The National Cyclopedia of American Biography*, vol. 30, p. 306; and Meredith Hooper, *Everyday Inventions* (New York: Taplinger Publishing Co., 1976), p. 39.

SCHILITZ, JOSEPH   Will Anderson, *The Beer Book* (Princeton: Pyne Press, 1973), pp. 153–55; James D. Robertson, *The Great American Beer Book* (Ottawa, Ill.: Caroline House Publishers, 1978), pp. 113–14; Sterling G. Slappey, comp., *Pioneers of American Business* (New York: Grossett & Dunlap, 1970), pp. 253–57; and "The Brotherly Brewers," *Fortune*, April 1950, pp. 101-.

SCHWEPPE, JACOB   Correspondence with Cadbury Schweppes USA, Stamford, Connecticut.

SCHWINN, IGNAZ   Michael J. Kolin and Denise de la Rosa, *The Custom Bicycle* (Emmaus, Penn.: Rodale Press, 1974), pp. 143–45; and correspondence with Schwinn Sales Inc., Chicago.

SEAGRAM, JOSEPH   Peter C. Newman, *King of the Castle* (New York: Atheneum, 1979); W. Stewart Wallace, ed., and W. A. McKay, 4th ed. ed., *The Macmillan Dictionary of Canadian Biography*, 4th ed., (Toronto: Macmillan of Canada, 1978), s.v. "Joseph Seagram"; and correspondence with Joseph E. Seagram & Sons, Inc., New York.

SEALY, GEORGE   Jane Pinckard, "Biography of George Sealy, Founder of This City," *Sealy* (Texas) *News*, 28 June 1979, p. 61; I. B. Singer, "Sealy's Birth and Early Growth Are Linked with Railroad," *Sealy News*, 28 June 1979, p. 27; and correspondence with Sealy, Inc., Chicago.

SEBASTIANI, SAMUELE   Sylvia Sebastiani, Sonoma, California, telephone interview by authors, September 1983; Nathan Chorman, *The Treasury of American Wines* (New York: Rutledge-Crown Publishers, 1973), p. 147; and Bob Thompson and Hugh Johnson, *The California Wine Book* (New York: William Morrow & Co., 1976), pp. 89–90.

SHEAFFER, WALTER   The Walter Sheaffer obituary, *New York Times*, 20 June 1946, p. 23; *Who Was Who in America*, vol. 2, "Walter Sheaffer," and vol. 4, "Craig R. Sheaffer"; and Ernest V. Heyn, *Fire of Genius* (Garden City: Anchor Press/Doubleday, 1976), pp. 28–29.

SHERWIN, HENRY, AND WILLIAMS, EDWARD   David P. Cleary, *Great American Brands* (New York: Fairchild Publications, 1981), pp. 256–60; *The National Cyclopedia of American Biography*, vol. 21, p. 422, "Sherwin," and p. 175, "Williams"; Arnold B. Barach, *Famous American Trademarks* (Washington: Public Affairs Press, 1971), pp. 157–58; and correspondence with Sherwin-Williams Co., Cleveland, Ohio.

SIMMONS, ZALMON   *The National Cyclopedia of American Biography*, vol. 15, p. 136; and David P. Cleary, *Great American Brands* (New York: Fairchild Publications, 1981), pp. 261–68.

SINGER, ISAAC MERRITT   Ruth Brandon, *A Capitalist Romance: Singer and the Sewing Machine* (Philadelphia: J. B. Lippincott Co., 1977); the Editors of News Front Year, *The 50 Great Pioneers of American Industry* (Maplewood: C. S. Hammond & Co; New York: Year Inc., 1964), pp. 34–36; Meredith Hooper, *Everyday Inventions* (New York: Taplinger Publishing Co., 1976), pp. 109–11; and *Webster's American Biographies*, s.v. "Isaac Singer."

SMITH, AMANDA   "Integrity Builds a Business," company-published 32-page history, 1968; "Yes, Mr. Rooney, There Really Was a Mrs. Smith!" *Kellogg News*, October 1980, pp. 1–2; and correspondence with R. L. Nichols, president and chief executive officer, Mrs. Smith's Frozen Foods Co., Pottstown, Pennsylvania.

SMITH, CHRISTOPHER C.   *The National Cyclopedia of American Biography*, vol. 27, p. 208; and correspondence with Murray Chris Craft Cruisers, Inc., Bradenton, Florida.

SMITH, LYMAN AND WILBERT   *The National Cyclopedia of American Biography*, vol. 35, p. 324, "Lyman," and vol. 33, p. 430, "Wilbert"; E. Moshier and J. Gaska, "A Brief History—The Typewriter and Smith-Corona," company-published 16-page booklet, 1976; and correspondence with SCM Consumer Products, Dewitt, New York.

SMUCKER, JEROME   The Jerome Smucker obituary, *New York Times*, 22 March 1948, p. 23; James Trager, *The Food Book* (New York: Avon Books, 1970), p. 98; *The National Cyclopedia of American Biography*, vol. 56, p. 452, "Willard Smucker"; and correspondence with J. M. Smucker Co., Orrville, Ohio.

SQUIBB, EDWARD   The Editors of News Front Year, *The 50 Great Pioneers of American Industry* (Maplewood: C. S. Hammond & Co.; New York: Year Inc., 1964), pp. 38–41; Milton Moskowitz et al., eds., *Everybody's Business* (San Francisco: Harper & Row, 1980), pp. 244–46; Arnold B. Barach, *Famous American Trademarks*

(Washington: Public Affairs Press, 1971), pp. 163–64; and *Dictionary of American Biography*, vol. 9, s.v. "Edward Squibb."

STETSON, JOHN *Dictionary of American Biography*, vol. 9, pt. 1, s.v. "John Stetson"; *Webster's American Biographies*, s.v. "John Stetson"; and Wheeler Preston, *American Biographies* (New York: Harper & Bros., 1940), s.v. "John Stetson."

STOKELY, ANNA William Stewart, "Yesterday, Today and Tomorrow . . . This Is Stokely-VanCamp," company-published 32-page history, 1981; and *The National Cyclopedia of American Biography*, vol. 35, p. 524, vol. 37, p. 350, vol. H, p. 138, and vol. K, p. 616 (biographies of various members of the Stokely family).

STOUFFER, VERNON The Vernon Stouffer obituary, *New York Times*, 27 July 1974, p. 32; and *Who Was Who in America*, vol. 6, s.v. "Vernon Stouffer."

STOVER, RUSSELL *The National Cyclopedia of American Biography*, vol. 43, p. 530, "Russell Stover," and vol. 50, p. 600, "Clara Stover"; the Russell Stover obituary, *New York Times*, 12 May 1954, p. 31; and Carol Ann Rinzler, *The Book of Chocolate* (New York: St. Martin's Press, 1977), p. 121.

STRAUSS, LEVI Harry Golden, *Forgotten Pioneer* (Cleveland: World Publishing Co., 1963), pp. 121–53; Eric Sevareid, *Enterprise* (New York: McGraw-Hill Book Co., 1983), pp. 79–81; David P. Cleary, *Great American Brands* (New York: Fairchild Publications, 1981), pp. 211–16; and *Webster's American Biographies*, s.v. "Levi Strauss."

STROH, BERNHARD K. McKinsey, "Stroh's Strategy: Go Big to Survive," *Detroit Free Press*, 18 April 1982, pp. 1-, sec. G; James D. Robertson, *The Great American Beer Book* (Ottawa, Ill.: Caroline House Publishers, 1978), pp. 119–20; Will Anderson, *The Beer Book* (Princeton: Pyne Press, 1973), p. 162; and correspondence with the Stroh Brewery Co., Detroit.

SWANSON, CARL "Big Butter-and-Egg Man—The Saga of Carl A. Swanson," *Fortune*, October 1943, pp. 122–25-; "Help in the Kitchen," *Time*, 20 December 1954, p. 64; and correspondence with Campbell Soup Co., Camden, New Jersey.

SWIFT, GUSTAVUS The Editors of News Front Year, *The 50 Great Pioneers of American Industry* (Maplewood: C. S. Hammond & Co.; New York: Year Inc., 1964), pp. 91–94; Sterling G. Slappey, comp., *Pioneers of American Industry* (New York: Grossett & Dunlap, 1970), pp. 277–81; and correspondence with Esmark, Inc., Chicago.

TAPPAN, WILLIAM Correspondence with the Tappan Co., Mansfield, Ohio.

TAYLOR, WALTER Leon D. Adams, *The Wines of America* (Boston: Houghton Mifflin Co., 1973), pp. 96–99; William E. Massee, *McCall's Guide to Wines of America* (New York: McCall Publishing Co., 1970), pp. 143–44; and correspondence with Michael J. Doyle, president, the Taylor Wine Co., Inc., Hammondsports, New York.

THOMAS, MELINDA LOU "WENDY," S. Berry, "256 Ways to Fortune," *Columbus* (Ohio) *Dispatch Sunday Magazine*, 30 January 1983; and correspondence with Wendy's International, Inc., Dublin, Ohio.

THOMAS, SAMUEL Milton Moskowitz et al., eds., *Everybody's Business* (San Francisco: Harper & Row, 1980), p. 93 (CPC); and correspondence with Michael W. Hogarty, president and chief executive officer, S. B. Thomas, Inc., Totowa, New Jersey.

THOMAS, SETH Chris A. Bailey, curator, American Clock & Watch Museum, "Seth Thomas—The Conservative Clockmaking Yankee," in *Catalogue of Seth Thomas Clock Co.* (Bristol, Conn.: American Clock & Watch Museum, 1973), pp. 62–66; *The National Cyclopedia of American Biography*, vol. 3, p. 118; *Webster's American Biographies*, s.v. "Seth Thomas"; and *Seth Thomas Catalogue—1981*, p. 40.

TIFFANY, CHARLES *Dictionary of American Biography*, vol. 9, pt. 2, s.v. "Charles

Tiffany"; *Who Was Who in America*, vol. 1, s.v. "Charles Tiffany"; and *The National Cyclopedia of American Biography*, vol. 2, p. 57, "Charles Tiffany," and vol. 36, p. 167, "Louis Tiffany."

TOYODA, KIICHIRO   W. S. Rukeyser, "World's Fastest Growing Auto Company—Toyota," *Fortune*, December 1969, pp. 76-; "Creativity, Challenge and Courage," company-published 36-page history, 1983; "1983 Fact Book," 12-page booklet published by Toyota Motor Sales USA Inc.; Albert L. Lewis and Walter A. Musciano, *Automobiles of the World* (New York: Simon & Schuster, 1977); and correspondence with Toyota Motor Corp., Toyota City, Japan.

TUPPER, EARL   "Tupperware," *Time*, 8 September 1947, p. 90; "Selling a Party Line," *Business Week*, 16 January 1954, pp. 130-; R. Schiller, "Help Yourself to Happiness," *Women's Home Circle*, August 1954, pp. 34–35-; and "How Brownie Wise Whoops Up Sales," *Business Week*, 17 April 1954, pp. 54–58-.

TWINING, THOMAS   William Ukers, *All about Tea* (New York: Tea and Coffee Trade Journal, 1935), vol. 1, p. 46, and vol. 2, pp. 156–58; Nancy H. Woodward, *Teas of the World* (New York: Macmillan Publishing Co., 1980), pp. 62–65; and Sir Leslie Stephen and Sir Sidney Lee, eds., *The Dictionary of National Biography*, vol. 19 (London: Oxford University Press, 1917), s.v. "Richard Twining."

UNDERWOOD, WILLIAM   *The National Cyclopedia of American Biography*, vol. 25, p. 437; Laurence A. Johnson, *Over the Counter and on the Shelf* (Rutland, Vt.: Charles E. Tuttle Co., 1961), p. 86; and Meredith Hooper, *Everyday Inventions* (New York: Taplinger Publishing Co., 1976), p. 79.

VAN CAMP, GILBERT   Laurence A. Johnson, *Over the Counter and on the Shelf* (Rutland, Vt.: Charles E. Tuttle Co., 1961), p. 93; William Stewart, "Yesterday, Today and Tomorrow . . . This Is Stokely-Van Camp," company-published 32-page history, 1981; and Stokely-Van Camp Inc. 1980 Annual Report, p. 6.

VANDERBILT, GLORIA   S. Francesca, "The Marketing of Gloria Vanderbilt," *New York Times Magazine*, 14 October 1979, pp. 29-; and *Current Biography—1972*, s.v. "Gloria Vanderbilt."

VAN HEUSEN, JOHN   *The National Cyclopedia of American Biography*, vol. 14, p. 209; the John Van Heusen obituary, *New York Times*, 19 December 1931, p. 19; and correspondence with the Van Heusen Co., New Brunswick, New Jersey.

VICK, JOSHUA   Hannah Campbell, *Why Did They Name It?* (New York: Fleet Publishing Co., 1964), pp. 130–32; and Marjorie Stiling, *Famous Brand Names, Emblems and Trademarks* (New Abbot, Devon: David & Charles, 1980), p. 57.

VALSIC, JOSEPH   Harvard Business School Case History on Vlasic Foods Inc., no. 4-371-307 BP, 1005, 1971; J. Thomas, "Who's Got Heinz in a Pickle?" *Forbes*, 15 August 1977, pp. 63–64; "Vlasic Foods: Sales Keep Barrelling Along," *Sales and Marketing Management*, January 1978, pp. 16–17; and Eric Sevareid, *Enterprise* (New York: McGraw-Hill Book Co., 1983), p. 100.

VOIT, WILLIAM   Editors of Fortune, *100 Stories of Business Success* (New York: Simon & Schuster, 1954), pp. 126–28; and *The National Cyclopedia of American Biography*, vol. 35, p. 145.

VON FÜRSTENBERG, DIANE   *Current Biography—1976*, s.v. "Diane Von Fürstenberg"; L. B. Francke, "Princess of Fashion," *Newsweek*, 22 March 1976, pp. 52-; Barbara Walz and Bernadine Morris, *Fashion Makers* (New York: Random House, 1978), pp. 212–17; and Anne Stegemeyer, *Who's Who in Fashion* (New York: Fairchild Publications, 1980), pp. 162–63.

WANG, AN   "The Guru of Gizmos," *Time*, 17 November 1980, p. 81; "The Forbes Four Hundred," *Forbes*, Fall 1983, pp. 173-; "Off for Ireland," *Fortune*, 14 January 1980, p. 18; and *Who's Who in America—1980–81*, s.v. "An Wang."

WESSON, DAVID *The National Cyclopedia of American Biography*, vol. 27, p. 79; *Who Was Who in America*, vol. 1, s.v. "David Wesson"; "And the Rest Is History," *Hunt-Wesson's World*, July/August 1980, pp. 2–5; and correspondence with Hunt-Wesson Foods, Inc., Fullerton, California.

WHITMAN, STEPHEN Carol Ann Rinzler, *The Book of Chocolate* (New York: St. Martin's Pres, 1977), pp. 126–27; and correspondence with Whitman's Chocolates, Philadelphia, Pennsylvania.

WINCHESTER, OLIVER *Dictionary of American Biography*, vol. 10, pt. 2, s.v. "Oliver Winchester"; *Webster's American Biographies*, s.v. "Oliver Winchester"; Laurence A. Johnson, *Over the Counter and on the Shelf* (Rutland, Vt.: Charles E. Tuttle Co., 1961), p. 119; and A. Merwn Carey, *American Firearms Makers* (New York: Thomas Y. Crowell, 1953), p. 134.

YALE, LINUS Edwin Wildman, *Famous Leaders of Industry*, vol. 1 (Boston: Page Co., 1920), pp. 341–49; Meredith Hooper, *Everyday Inventions* (New York: Taplinger Publishing Co., 1976), pp. 12–13; and *Dictionary of American Biography*, vol. 10, pt. 2, s.v. "Linus Yale."

Selective Bibliography

Adams, Leon D. *The Wines of America*. Boston: Houghton Mifflin Co., 1976.

Anderson, Will. *The Beer Book*. Princeton, N.J.: Pyne Press, 1973.

Barach, Arnold B. *Famous American Trademarks*. Washington: Public Affairs Press, 1971.

Baron, Stanley. *Brewed in America*. Boston: Little, Brown & Co., 1962.

Bird, Caroline. *Enterprising Women*. New York: W. W. Norton Co., 1976.

Calasibetta, Charlotte. *Fairchild's Dictionary of Fashion*. New York: Fairchild Publications, 1975.

Campbell, Hannah. *Why Did They Name It?* New York: Fleet Publishing Co., 1964.

Carey, A. Merwyn. *American Firearms Makers*. New York: Thomas Y. Crowell, 1953.

Chorman, Nathan. *The Treasury of American Wines*. New York: Rutledge-Crown Publishers, 1973.

Cleary, David P. *Great American Brands*. New York: Fairchild Publications, 1981.

Cummings, Richard O. *The American and His Food*. New York: Arno Press, 1970.

Current Biography. 44 vols. New York: H. W. Wilson Co., 1940–83.

Dictionary of American Biography. 10 vols., 7 sups. New York: Charles Scribner's Sons, 1927–81.

Eggenberger, David I., et al., eds. *The McGraw-Hill Encyclopedia of World Biography*. New York: McGraw-Hill Book Co., 1973.

Georgano, G. N. *The Complete Encyclopedia of Commercial Vehicles*. Iola, Wis.: Krause Publications, 1979.

Heyn, Ernest V. *Fire of Genius*. Garden City: Anchor Press/Doubleday, 1976.

Hooper, Meredith. *Everyday Inventions*. New York: Taplinger Publishing Co., 1976.

Hough, Richard. *A History of the World's Sports Cars*. New York: Harper & Bros., 1961.

Johnson, Laurence A. *Over the Counter and on the Shelf*. Rutland, Vt.: Charles E. Tuttle Co., 1961.

Lifshey, Earl. *The Housewares Story*. Chicago: National Housewares Manufacturers Association, 1973.

Mahoney, Tom. *The Great Merchants*. New York: Harper & Bros., 1955.

Massee, William E. *McCall's Guide to Wines of America*. New York: McCall Publishing Co., 1970.

Matteucci, Marco. *History of the Motor Car*. New York: Crown Publishers, 1970.

Moskowitz, Milton, et al., eds. *Everybody's Business*. San Francisco: Harper & Row, 1980.

Neilson, William Allan, et al., eds. *Webster's Biographical Dictionary*. 1st ed. Springfield, Mass.: G. & C. Merriam Co., 1964.

News Front Year, editors of. *The 50 Great Pioneers of American Industry*. Maplewood, N.J.: C. S. Hammond & Co.; New York: Year Inc., 1964.

Preston, Wheeler. *American Biographies*. New York: Harper & Brothers, 1940.

Purdy, Ken. *Ken Purdy's Book of Automobiles*. Chicago: Playboy Press, 1972.

Rinzler, Carol A. *The Book of Chocolate*. New York: St. Martin's Press, 1977.

Robertson, James D. *The Great American Beer Book*. Ottawa, Ill.: Caroline House Publishers, 1978.

Roseberry, C. R. *The Challenging Skies*. Garden City: Doubleday & Co., 1966.

Rowsome, Frank, Jr. *They Laughed When I Sat Down*. New York: McGraw-Hill Book Co,., 1959.

Schoeffler, O. E., and William Gale. *Esquire's Encyclopedia of 20th Century Men's Fashions*. New York: McGraw-Hill Book Co., 1973.

Scull, Penrose, *From Peddlers to Merchant Princes*. Chicago: Follett Publishing Co., 1967.

Slappey, Sterling G., comp. *Pioneers of American Business*. New York: Grossett & Dunlap, 1970.

Stegemeyer, Anne. *Who's Who in Fashion*. New York: Fairchild Publications, 1980.

Stein, Ralph. *The Treasury of the Automobile*. New York: Ridge Press & Golden Press, 1961.

Stiling, Marjorie. *Famous Brand Names, Emblems and Trademarks*. New Abbot, Devon: David & Charles, 1980.

Tannahill, Reay. *Food in History*. Briarcliff Manor, N.Y.: Stein & Day, 1973.

The National Cyclopedia of American Biography. 74 vols. Clifton, N.J.: James T. White Co., 1891–1982.

Thorne, J. O., and T. C. Collocott. *Chambers Biographical Dictionary*. Rev. ed. Edinburgh: W. & R. Chambers, 1978.

Ukers, William H. *All about Tea*. 2 vols. New York: Tea and Coffee Trade Journal Co., 1935.

Van Doren, Charles, ed. *Webster's American Biographies*. Springfield, Mass.: G. & C. Merriam Co., 1974.

Walz, Barbara, and Bernadine Morris. *Fashion Makers*. New York: Random House, 1978.

Weiner, Michael A. *The Taster's Guide to Beer*. New York: Collier Books, 1972.

Who Was Who in America. 8 vols. Chicago: A. N. Marquis Co., 1942–81.

Wildman, Edwin. *Famous Leaders of Industry*. 2 vols. Boston: Page Co., 1920.

Index